Bonapartists in the Borderlands

Bonapartists in the Borderlands

French Exiles and Refugees on the Gulf Coast,
1815–1835

Rafe Blaufarb

THE UNIVERSITY OF ALABAMA PRESS
Tuscaloosa

The University of Alabama Press
Tuscaloosa, Alabama 35487-0380
uapress.ua.edu

Hardcover edition published 2005.
Paperback edition published 2016.
eBook edition published 2009.

Inquiries about reproducing material from this work should be addressed to the University of Alabama Press.

Typeface: Adobe Garamond

Manufactured in the United States of America
Cover image: *Vue d'Aigleville, Colonie du Texas ou Champ d'Asile*, color aquatint by and after Yerenrag, published in Paris by Basset (c. 1816); courtesy of Anne S. K. Brown Military Collection, Brown University Library
Cover design: Erin Bradley Danger / Danger Design

∞

The paper on which this book is printed meets the minimum requirements of American National Standard for Information Science–Permanence of Paper for Printed Library Materials, ANSI Z39.48-1984.

Paperback ISBN: 978-0-8173-5880-8
eBook ISBN: 978-0-8173-8261-2

A previous edition of this book has been catalogued by the Library of Congress as follows:
Library of Congress Cataloging-in-Publication Data
Blaufarb, Rafe.
Bonapartists in the borderlands : French exiles and refugees on the Gulf Coast, 1815–1835 / Rafe Blaufarb.
p. cm.
Includes bibliographical references and index.
ISBN-13: 978-0-8173-1487-3 (cloth : alk. paper)
ISBN-10: 0-8173-1487-3
1. Vine and Olive Colony. 2. French Americans—Alabama—History—19th century. 3. French Americans—Land tenure—Alabama—History—19th century. 4. Agricultural colonies—Alabama—History—19th century. 5. Alabama—History—19th century. I. Title.
F335.F8B58 2006
976.1'05—dc22
2005015331

Contents

Preface

This project has taken me down historical pathways I never expected to tread. Trained as a historian of early modern and revolutionary France, I had always assumed my research would focus on the metropole. And it surely would have had I not accepted a position at Auburn University and met Wayne Flint, then the department's preeminent historian of Alabama. Wayne told me about the Vine and Olive colony, the short-lived French settlement founded in western Alabama in 1817, and suggested that the University of Alabama Press might be interested in publishing a book on the subject. In following his advice, I found that the story of Vine and Olive was more than just a colorful episode in Alabama history. It was enmeshed in the broader process of the reordering of Atlantic geopolitics in the aftermath of Waterloo.

Tracking down the French who came to the Gulf Coast after 1815 was not an easy task. Many were Bonapartists, political opponents of the Bourbon regime, who continued to plot (or at least fulminate) against it. Since they were being shadowed by the agents of France and Spain, the expatriates tried to leave as few traces as possible. There is thus no central archive containing their records. Indeed, I found myself obliged to use sources from more than twenty repositories in five countries to reconstruct, however imperfectly, their activities. These were the National Archives and Records Administration, Library of Congress, Archives Nationales, Archives des Affaires Etrangères, Archives de la Guerre, Bibliothèque Nationale, Centre des Archives Diplomatiques, Public Record Office, Archivo Histórico Nacional, Archivo General de la Nacion, Alabama Department of Archives and History, Birmingham Public Library, Demopolis Public Library, University of North Carolina Southern Historical Collection, Tulane University Howard-Tilton Memorial Library Manuscript Department, Louisiana State University Hill Memorial Library Special Collections, University of Texas Center for American History, Firestone Library of Princeton University (especially the tireless interlibrary loan department),

American Philosophical Society, Huntington Library, Anne S. K. Brown Military Collection at Brown University, Filson Historical Society, Missouri Historical Society, Massachusetts Historical Society, and Virginia Historical Society. Wherever I went, I received gracious and expert assistance. Of all the many archivists and librarians who aided me, I especially thank three people. The first of these is Samuel Gibiat of the Archives de la Guerre (Service Historique de l'Armée de Terre), a colleague in eighteenth-century French military history whom I met when we were both doing dissertation research at the Château de Vincennes. He helped me track down the personnel dossiers of several prominent Vine and Olive members. The second is Peter Harrington of the Anne S. K. Brown Military Collection who generously (and expeditiously) found and furnished the cover illustration. The third is Norwood Kerr of the Alabama Department of Archives and History whose assistance was always just a phone call, or an e-mail, away.

At different points along the way, I have benefited from the feedback of colleagues, experts in Gulf or southern history, the Domingan diaspora, the Atlantic world, and diplomatic history. Their patient advice helped me to find my way through a rich field of scholarship I did not know. Jeff Jakeman and Steve Murray of the *Alabama Review* read drafts of an article I published in that journal and answered numerous queries about Alabama history. Their expert editing and tolerance of my frequent visits to their offices dramatically eased my foray into this field. Anthony Carey, Robin Fabel, Gene Smith, and Mills Thornton III also graciously agreed to comment on various parts of my manuscript and offer their suggestions on how it could be improved. Jeremy Adelman, Jean-François Berdah, James Boyden, Suzanne Desan, Laurent Dubois, Daniel Feller, David Geggus, Evan Haefeli, G. Ward Hubbs, James Lewis, Victor Macias-Gonzalez, Darrell Meadows, David Messenger, Bradford Perkins, Robert Smith, and Leona Stemple all offered useful feedback along the way. My colleague Marie Francois and her husband, Juan Rodriguez, helped me with translating some difficult Spanish diplomatic dispatches. The allotment maps are courtesy of Michelle Messner of the Auburn University Department of Geography. Finally, I owe a debt of gratitude to Kent Gardien who gave me access to his unpublished genealogical and historical research notes on the members of the Vine and Olive colony.

The support of the Auburn University history department and the College of Liberal Arts has also been invaluable. Their generous financial contributions, as well as their permission to spend the spring semester of 2002 on leave at Princeton University, allowed me to complete my research and writing in a timely fashion. I also thank the Princeton history department for appointing me a visiting fellow during that time, as well as the Friends of the Firestone Library for awarding me a Rare Books and Special Collections research grant.

The field of Alabama history owes much to the tireless efforts of those Alabamians who love their state's past and work to keep it before the public eye. I thank two of its staunchest supporters, Gwen Turner of Marengo County and Nick Cobbs of Hale County, who each took me on fascinating trips around the lands that constituted the old French grant and introduced me to the beautiful country of western Alabama. My appreciation also goes to Leah Atkins, the Auburn history department's first Ph.D. and another champion of Alabama history.

I thank numerous friends and family for their input and help along the way. In particular, I acknowledge Nira Kaplan, Xavier Marechaux, Hugh Lane, Carol Harrison, Hines Hall and his late wife, Joy, Rachel and Rick Potter, Iqbal Siddiqui, Sarah and Humayun Ansari, Phyllis and Joe Felser, Nigel Hamilton, Beatrice Mienville and Serge Aberdam, and Chris Schmidt-Nowara. I especially thank my father, Herbert Blaufarb, for reading the entire manuscript, offering valuable suggestions, and giving me unstinting support.

The people at the University of Alabama Press have constantly supported my project since its inception four years ago. I also thank the anonymous readers who gave the manuscript their careful attention and whose suggestions I have incorporated to make it a better book.

My wife, Claudia Liebeskind, has lived with this project since its inception. From the scrawled first draft of the proposal, which she deciphered one sunny morning on our West Drake Street porch, to the final printout of the completed manuscript, Claudia has read every word I have written on the French expatriates. I came to rely on her keen editorial eye and, more importantly, her penetrating (sometimes infuriatingly so, to this impatient author) queries about organization and content. She has put up with Lallemand, Galabert, and company for more than three years, yet has never seemed to tire of their antics. It is to my wife, Claudia, that I dedicate this book.

Introduction

In 1817 the Congress of the United States granted four townships—144 square miles of recently conquered Indian lands near the confluence of the Tombigbee and Black Warrior rivers—to a group of several hundred French expatriates based primarily in Philadelphia. In return, the group was to plant the grant with grape vines and olive trees, thereby forming (it was hoped) the nucleus of a domestic American wine industry. The story of this settlement, best known as the Vine and Olive colony, provides one of the most colorful chapters in the history of antebellum Alabama and, indeed, of the entire Old South. Although the majority of the colonists were actually middle-class refugees from the slave revolt of Saint-Domingue (Haiti), some of whom eventually established successful cotton plantations on the grant, popular accounts of the colony tell a very different tale. Composed of aristocratic Napoleonic officers and their elegant ladies, the story goes, Vine and Olive shone briefly as a center of sophistication and grace. But dash, wit, and refinement alone could not tame the wilderness. More at home on a battlefield or the parquet of a palace ballroom, the French exiles made little headway in their agricultural endeavors. Lacking the experience of their Anglo-American neighbors, these aristocratic pioneers soon gave up in frustration. A tourist brochure in Demopolis, the city originally founded by the colonists, relates the story succinctly. "Romance, adventure, and politics first put Demopolis on the map. Napoleonic refugees came here in 1817 with land grants to establish a 'Vine and Olive Colony.' These French officers and their ladies were ill-suited to the cultivation of grapes and olives, as were the soil and the climate. The colonists left, but they are remembered."[1]

What requires explanation is not why the Vine and Olive colony has been remembered but rather why it has been remembered in this particular way. Why has its story centered on the failure of exiled Napoleonic aristocrats to introduce viticulture to the Deep South instead of the successful efforts of refugee merchants from Saint-Domingue to become cotton planters? While there is a grain of truth in the popular account—a number of senior Napoleonic officers (and even one marshal) did receive land shares in the colony—it is but a grain. Only one of these distinguished military men ever settled on the grant, and he stayed a mere two years. It is true that a number of these generals bore titles of nobility, but these had been minted only a few years earlier by Napoleon in his attempt to build a hereditary elite attached to his dynasty. Although they may have been called knight, baron, or count, the exiled generals—with just one exception—had been born in modest, even plebeian circumstances and risen to high rank thanks only to the French Revolution's abolition of noble privilege, its seemingly endless wars, and their almost feral courage. Even if all the generals had come to Alabama, it would still be a stretch to style such battle-hardened soldiers aristocrats.

My intention here is not to denounce the popular account of the Vine and Olive colony as a fabrication. Instead, it is to recognize the tale of exiled French aristocrats for what it was, a myth that—like all myths—works to create meaning. Specifically, the Vine and Olive story belongs to the broader process of southern mythmaking that transformed planters into genteel aristocrats.[2] The story, however, has a distinctive twist that may reflect white southerners' unvoiced anxieties about their social status, their repugnance for the authoritarian political culture of the French exiles, their distaste for Catholicism, or even all these concerns together. Even as it highlights the exiles' illustrious standing, the popular account of the Vine and Olive colony brings them back to earth by emphasizing their inability to master the Alabama wilderness. That the French ultimately failed where the Anglo-Americans—the storytellers—eventually succeeded allows them to reclaim for themselves a sense of superiority, one based on a certain inner fortitude and true nobility of character lacking in the decadent scions of Old Europe. In addition to the ambiguous appeal of aristocracy so evident in the popular account, another factor tends to magnify the role of the Napoleonic officers while diminishing that of the Domingans who actually formed the backbone of the colony. Given that the Domingans came to the United States as refugees from a successful slave rebellion, it is perhaps understandable that white southern storytellers would—until recently—have been reluctant to focus on their experience.

The popular account of the Vine and Olive colony had already acquired its basic outlines a decade before the Civil War. The very first published description, a chapter devoted to the colony by Albert James Pickett in his general history of Alabama, detailed the failed attempts of aristocratic Napoleonic officers and their ladies to plant vine and olive in Alabama. Pickett's pioneering effort was seconded during the later decades of the nineteenth century by a handful of brief, highly romanticized, and frequently repetitive accounts that were part of the larger post-Reconstruction cultural project of refurbishing southern identity by articulating a new sense of what the South had been before the war.[3] Only in the first years of the twentieth century did the story of the colony receive scholarly treatment—by Gaius Whitfield Jr. in a paper delivered to the Alabama Historical Society—but for many years no further attempts were made to reflect critically on the episode.[4] In the years immediately following the First World War, in fact, the well-worn popular account enjoyed a renaissance of sorts as local newspapers and historical societies began churning out pieces on the aristocratic French settlers. These articles and papers did little more than reiterate Pickett's version of the story, thereby reinforcing the existing popular account.[5] The reasons for this sudden burst of interest are speculative. In 1915 D. W. Griffith's film *Birth of a Nation* put the Old South on a movie screen for the first time, helping to spur renewed interest in Alabama's distinctive variant on the moonlight-and-magnolias theme. The Vine and Olive story held added allure in these years, moreover, because Americans were still full of admiration for the valiant French, who had just helped save civilization from the Kaiser's hordes. Another factor was the 1919 centennial of Alabama's statehood, which provided the occasion for local historical societies to celebrate one of the most alluring episodes in the state's past. And finally, the appointment in 1920 of Marie Bankhead Owen to replace her husband, Thomas M. Owen, as director of the state archives, probably also played a role in fostering the Vine and Olive myth. Viewing her principal role as that of encouraging state pride through history, she emphasized commemoration over critical analysis, setting a tone that influenced the elaboration of the Vine and Olive myth.

In the 1930s the story of Vine and Olive briefly entered the national consciousness. One might assume that it was the runaway success of *Gone with the Wind* (1939) that stimulated interest in the aristocratic Old South generally and in Alabama's French variant on the myth in particular. But national interest in the Vine and Olive story apparently predated both Margaret Mitchell's bestseller and the movie it spawned. Emma Gelder Sterne's *Some Plant Olive Trees,* a fictional account of Vine and Olive that, while not quite a bodice-ripper, was heavily larded with amorous encounters was published in 1937. Another, even earlier example can be found in Carl Carmer's *Stars Fell on Alabama* (1934). Based heavily on Pickett's chapter, Carmer's concise rendition brought together all the salient inaccuracies that make the popular account such a potent myth-making tool. Introduced as "Bonapartists," "aristocrats," and "the most influential in France," the exiles are depicted carrying out the rudest tasks of the frontier. "Dressed in rich uniforms, they cleared wooded land, ditched it, plowed it. Their wives, delicate women still in Paris gowns, milked the cows, carried water to the men in the field, cooked meals over coals in the fireplace." Their opulent vestments (emphasized in most renditions of the popular account) served to remind that, despite their rude labors, the French settlers were people of breeding and refinement. The fact that they sought to acquire as many slaves as they could to labor for them goes curiously unmentioned in this—and most other—accounts. These literary efforts were followed several years later by an appalling John Wayne film, *The Fighting Kentuckian* (1949), a blatant attempt to cash in on the cinematic trend unleashed by *Gone With the Wind*. In this odd tale, American populism (as incarnated by Wayne's Kentucky rifleman returning home from the Battle of New Orleans) rides to the rescue of the French and helps the uniformed Napoleonic officers fight off an attack by unscrupulous American land speculators. *The Fighting Kentuckian* represented the peak of American interest—as well as the nadir of historical accuracy—in the story.

The role played by the Vine and Olive story in constructing planter identity would be well worth examining in depth. But, trained as a historian of France, I can only recommend this subject to a scholar more particularly concerned with (and better equipped to treat) the history of the American South. The emphasis of this book lies elsewhere. First, it seeks to offer an archivally based account of the Vine and Olive colony that is both accurate and analytical. This was not an easy task because few local sources remain. Nor is there a single repository in which Vine and Olive materials have been concentrated. To piece together its history has therefore required gleaning bits of information in dozens of collections not only in the United States but also in Europe and Latin America. Second and more importantly, this book aims to elucidate the broader historical significance of the episode by exploring its connections with the world beyond Alabama and, indeed, the United States. Situating Vine and Olive in an international context will not only transform our understanding of the colony but also throw into relief certain critical developments in the Atlantic world during the age of revolution.

One of the connections between the colony and the broader history of the revolutionary Atlantic was the flight of tens of thousands of people, not all of them white, from the massive uprising of slaves on the French sugar island of

Saint-Domingue. Although Gaius Whitfield Jr. was probably the first scholar to realize that an important group of Domingan refugees had been part of the Vine and Olive colony, popular accounts continued to downplay or totally ignore their presence even after the publication of his article. But in the years leading up to the sesquicentennial of the foundation of the colony, local historians in western Alabama began to take a new, more scholarly look at its history and rediscovered the Domingans. Exemplary among the various reappraisals published at this time was Winston Smith's *Days of Exile* (1967). A former English professor at the University of Alabama and a lifelong citizen of Demopolis, Smith probably deserves credit for bringing the Domingans back to the center of the Vine and Olive stage. Offering a series of biographical sketches on some of the leading Domingan families on the grant, Smith recognized that their influence was decisive, especially during the later years of the colony. Yet despite this realization, he did not go so far as to abandon the popular account of Napoleonic aristocrats. Instead, Smith tried to reconcile the two versions of the story by distinguishing distinct phases in the history of Vine and Olive. Bonapartist officers dominated the colony until 1820, Smith asserted, when "a large group of new settlers arrived, . . . French refugees from the West Indies."[6] In subsequent years, however, the findings of another scholar, Kent Gardien, have made Smith's compromise solution untenable. Through years of painstaking genealogical research, Gardien discovered that, from the outset, the colony was a Domingan affair and that most of the Napoleonic officers granted allotments never came to Alabama.[7] Offering to the researcher a ready-made sample of the Domingan diaspora in the United States, the Vine and Olive colony allows a glimpse into the experience of these refugees as they sought to make new lives for themselves in the Deep South.

Although Smith, Gardien, and others have traced the pathway leading from Alabama back to Saint-Domingue, the links between the Vine and Olive colony and the concurrent phenomenon that was shaking the entire Atlantic world—the struggle for Latin American independence—have gone unrecognized. Many of the soldiers associated, however loosely, with the Vine and Olive colony participated in the conflict between Spain and its colonies during their period of American exile. Like veterans demobilized from the other European armies that had fought in the wars of Napoleon and the French Revolution, they had known only the life of the sword and sensed in the troubled affairs of Spanish America an opportunity for action. Some sought commissions from representatives of the insurgency in the United States, which served throughout the 1810s as a safe haven and arms dealer for the rebels.

Others tried to join one or another of the quasi-piratical sorties launched from American territory against Spanish shipping and colonies. And in one of the last filibustering episodes of the age, French military men inscribed as shareholders in the Vine and Olive colony undertook an independent, armed expedition into Spanish territory. The troubles of Spanish America not only provided the backdrop against which the Vine and Olive colony was founded but also represented a competing pole of attraction that diverted many of its military members from Alabama.

Recognizing that the French military expatriates were deeply involved in the affairs of Latin America alters our understanding of the Vine and Olive colony. More importantly, it reveals the insurrection of Spain's colonies in a new, international light. At stake in the struggle was not merely independence for this or that country in the Americas but also a fundamental reordering of international power relations in the Atlantic world. The revolt of the colonies provoked a geopolitical revolution, as the various Western powers (England, France, the United States, Portugal, and even Russia) scrambled to appropriate Spain's former empire or prevent their rivals from doing so. Like the crumbling of the Ottoman Empire, which raised similar concerns in subsequent decades, the upheaval in Spanish America posed a question of its own, a Western question—who would profit from the collapse of Spanish power in America?—that became the focus of intense international diplomacy and intrigue in the early nineteenth century. Although just a small episode in this vast drama, the Vine and Olive colony serves as a vantage point from which to view this previously overlooked panorama.

Historians of Latin America have not sufficiently emphasized the broader international significance of the struggle of Spain's colonies for independence. In part this is a symptom of the national segmentation of the field (Mexican history, Peruvian history, Argentinian history, etc.), but it also reflects nationalistic biases that crop up from time to time in histories of national independence. It is understandable that a nation might want to remember its struggle for independence as the exclusive work of its own citizens (one need only think of how France's contribution to American independence is often neglected in popular accounts of that revolution), but such patriotic omission can distort historical reality. In the case of Latin American independence, its effect is to obscure not only the vital role played by foreigners—whether adventurers, mercenaries, pirates, or diplomats—in the struggle, but, more significantly, its profound geopolitical repercussions.[8]

Most U.S. scholars of Latin American independence are not prone to these nationalistic biases. Nonetheless, they, too, often overlook the international import of the breakup of Spain's colonial empire. Since the 1960s historians in this field have embraced social and cultural approaches—history from below—to the near exclusion of more traditional methods of analysis such as diplomatic history. While the resulting scholarship has provided sensitive and sophisticated pictures of the lives, experiences, and beliefs of ordinary people, it tends to narrow the focus of research to small units like provinces, cities, villages, or even single families. In their determination to make visible the obscure and give voice to the voiceless, practitioners of history from below have unwittingly introduced a parochial flavor to their subject.[9] This has not only obscured the role played in Latin American independence by the extraordinary international community of revolutionaries, adventurers, and scoundrels (whose doings, in fact, offer ample material for what could be termed "diplomatic history from below") but also hidden the wider Atlantic and even global significance of the collapse of Spanish dominion in the Americas.

By the middle of the twentieth century, diplomatic historians had already gone far toward elucidating the most important elements of the Western question but had not assembled them into a coherent whole. Dorothy Goebel, R. A. Humphreys, William Kaufman, W. Alison Philips, and C. K. Webster exhaustively treated the all-important question of the foreign and mercantile policies of England, by 1815 the hegemonic power in the Atlantic world.[10] That of the United States toward Latin American independence has received even more attention from distinguished historians such as Samuel Flagg Bemis, Isaac Joslin Cox, Worthington Chauncey Ford, Hubert Bruce Fuller, Charles Carroll Griffin, Dexter Perkins, and Arthur Preston Whitaker.[11] Others have focused on relations between the two English-speaking powers: Fred Rippy, Edward Howland Tatum Jr., R. A. Humphreys, and (a bit later than the others) Bradford Perkins with his superlative study of Castlereagh and Adams.[12] Although most of the scholarship has focused on Great Britain and the United States, the other European powers that sought, albeit with less effect, to play a role in the affairs of Latin America have not been ignored. William Spence Robertson has examined French policy; Russell Bartley, that of Russia; and Timothy E. Anna and Michael P. Costeloe, that of the most neglected protagonist of all, Spain itself.[13] But, like the blind men who mistook the elephant's leg for a tree trunk, its trunk for a snake, and its flank for a wall, the diplomatic historians have failed to perceive that their particular nationally based accounts were components of a broader phenomenon: the struggle to pick up the pieces of Spain's crumbling empire and, in so doing, create a new Atlantic order. Although the chapters of the Western question were written long ago, no one has ever assembled them into a single narrative, nor even recognized that they fit together as parts of a coherent historical dynamic.

The Vine and Olive episode is certainly not the whole story, nor even an entire chapter. Yet it highlights a unique aspect of the Western question: the struggle between the United States and Spain over their land border in North America. Unlike the European powers, which (with the exception of Portuguese Brazil) did not abut the Spanish colonies, the United States found itself in the almost unique position of being able to profit directly from Spain's troubles by annexing its insurrection-wracked provinces of Florida, Texas, and (some hoped) Mexico itself. Blurring the line between American westward expansionism and the insurgency in the Spanish colonies, the possibility of direct military intervention by the United States lent the Western question in the borderlands a distinctive character. Intended to be peopled with Napoleonic veterans, situated on a strategic waterway connecting the contested port of Mobile with the interior of the United States, located within marching distance of Florida, and just a short sea voyage from Texas, the Vine and Olive colony was no mere agricultural experiment, but a move in a treacherous diplomatic chess game: the struggle between Spain and the United States over their contested borderland. Recognized as such by the European powers, the history of the colony places in the context of the Western question the interrelated problems of American public land policy, western expansionism, and the Latin American independence movement.

While this book addresses these issues and highlights previously unrecognized connections between them, it is fundamentally a narrative. It begins by introducing the two main groups of French expatriates in America—recently arrived Bonapartist exiles and refugees from the slave rebellion of Saint-Domingue who had fled to America in the 1790s—and providing short biographical sketches of some of the most prominent protagonists in the story. The second chapter relates the genesis of the colonial project within this composite group and the initial efforts to realize it in practice. It explores the first attempts to organize a Society for the Cultivation of the Vine and Olive among the expatriates, their efforts to secure congressional support for the idea, and the hidden strategic considerations that induced Congress to back this unorthodox venture.

Chapter 3 shifts away from the activities of the expatriates as they prepared to move south to focus more broadly on the international context in which the Vine and Olive colony was taking shape. Dominated by the insurrection of the colonies of Spanish America and the general reordering of power relations in the Atlantic world after the defeat of Napoleon, this context created innumerable opportunities for adventurism, espionage, and profiteering. The European diplomatic corps scrutinized the French expatriates' every move for indications of how their activities might fit into the shadowy puzzle of the Western question. The diplomats' suspicions were not groundless. Even before the Society the Cultivation of the Vine and Olive had dispatched the first boatload of settlers to Alabama, some of its members were already hatching a plot to tap the resources of the Society to fund an armed expedition to the Spanish colonies. Chapter 4 discusses the elaboration, execution, and outcome of this tragicomic enterprise—which resulted in the establishment of a short-lived establishment known as the Champ d'Asile (the Field of Asylum)—and seeks to discern its true aim.

The penultimate chapter analyzes the development of the original Vine and Olive colony in the absence of the adventurers. While most of the shareholders never went personally to Alabama, a tight-knit group dominated by refugees from Saint-Domingue did establish themselves there. Quickly abandoning the impossible cultivation of grape vines and olive trees for the more familiar southern combination of slavery and cotton, they soon began to prosper in their new home. Joined by increasing numbers of Anglo-American settlers, they came to form a Franco-American elite linked by ties of marriage, a common lifestyle, and shared economic interests. By the time of the Civil War, little remained of the colony's distinctive identity. The final chapter treats the fate of the former grantees after the end of their colonial experiences.

I use the term "colony" at many points to refer to something broader than the physical settlement in Alabama founded by the Society for the Cultivation of the Vine and Olive. Throughout this book the term "colony" also includes the approximately four hundred individuals whose names appeared at one time or another on the society's list of shareholders. Seen in the light of this broader definition, the history of the Vine and Olive colony ranged beyond the boundaries of Alabama to encompass its most famous offshoot, the Champ d'Asile, as well as the international context of geopolitical revolution in which the French expatriates maneuvered. This broader perspective not only renders more comprehensible the history of the Vine and Olive colony in Alabama but also points toward a truly Atlantic approach to the history of the early nineteenth century, one capable of bringing together previously isolated strands of U.S., Latin American, and diplomatic history.

Bonapartists in the Borderlands

I

The New Atlantic France

The news spread quickly across New York City that August morning in 1815: the distinguished Frenchman who had just disembarked from the *Commerce* after a monthlong Atlantic crossing was Lazare Carnot.[1] The military engineer who, as a member of the Committee of Public Safety, had saved revolutionary France from the monarchical armies of Europe was a hero to republicans the world over. But as admiring Americans flocked to the boardinghouse where the illustrious arrival had taken rooms, it became clear that a mistake had been made. The traveler was not Carnot, but rather a figure who, while less impressive for his own accomplishments, was more relevant to the political realities of the day: Joseph Bonaparte, elder brother of Napoleon and former king of Spain from 1807 to 1814 when that country had been occupied by French arms.

Joseph was not the only member of his family to consider fleeing to America after Waterloo.[2] Within days of Napoleon's defeat, four of the five Bonaparte brothers met outside Paris and decided to seek refuge in the United States, one of the few republics in the world. Lucien, Napoleon's independent-minded younger brother, initially set out for the Channel port of Boulogne, but abruptly doubled back and headed south toward Italy. Arrested and imprisoned in Turin, he was released only at the request of the pope who allowed him to live comfortably (albeit under Vatican surveillance) in Rome. Jerome, former king of Westphalia, first made for an Atlantic port but, on being recognized, returned to Paris where he hid in the house of a Corsican shoemaker. Once discovered, he was allowed to escape to Switzerland by a Bourbon government eager to avoid the tumult of a public trial. From there he continued to Wurtemburg to join his wife, Catherine, daughter of the local duke, but was imprisoned by his father-in-law in a crude attempt to pressure the couple into a divorce. Napoleon himself reached the port of Rochefort where, after much hesitation, he rejected his retainers' pleas that he sneak past the British blockade and sail for America. Instead, he decided to throw himself on the mercy of England and its much-vaunted legal protections. This proved a mistake for, once he was on board the English warship *Bellerophon*, the cabinet of Saint-James decided to incarcerate him on the remote island of Saint Helena.[3] He died there in 1821.

Of all the Bonapartes, only Joseph made it to America. With evident relief the former king set aside his public political role to embrace the simpler life of a country gentleman. Facilitating his transformation was the large fortune he had brought with him into exile, as well as the good offices of Stephen Girard, the merchant and banker reputed to be the wealthiest man in the United States.[4] With Girard's help, Joseph transferred his assets into real estate and government bonds and constructed a magnificent country seat for himself near Bordentown, New Jersey.[5] Here Joseph lived a "markedly reserved life"—so reserved, in fact, that all the French consul in New York City could report in early 1816 was that he occasionally "gives small dinner parties."[6] Known to some as the Count de Survilliers (after one of his estates in France), to others as "that peaceable gentleman," and to others still as simply "Mr. Bonaparte," Joseph deserved the title bestowed on him by a recent biographer, "the gentle Bonaparte."[7]

Although he was the only Bonaparte to make it to the United States, other French refugees—Bonapartists and revolutionaries, military officers hounded from the army for their political views or discouraged by the prospect of stagnation in peacetime, young men with a taste for adventure born a few years too late, and poor emigrants in search of economic opportunity—soon joined Joseph in America.[8] Upon their arrival, these voluntary and involuntary exiles encountered a large community of fellow expatriates, composed overwhelmingly of refugees from the slave revolt of the former French colony of Saint-Domingue, that had preceded them and established themselves in Philadelphia, New Orleans, and other cities. The two groups gravitated toward one another, forming what the French ambassador to the United States Jean-Guillaume Hyde de Neuville (a noble who had himself escaped the Revolution by fleeing to America) dubbed the "New Atlantic France."[9]

Bourbon Restoration and Reaction

The first Bonapartist emigrants to follow Joseph to America were political exiles. During the First Restoration (April 1814–February 1815), the Bourbons had extended a remarkable degree of clemency to the Bonapartist establishment, allowing most administrative and military officials to keep their positions. Their generosity was repaid with betrayal when Napoleon returned to France from his Elban exile, and the Bonapartists greeted him with open arms. Thus, after Waterloo and Napoleon's final abdication, the Bourbons were understandably less forgiving. They were particularly implacable toward those who had directly aided Napoleon's return or had accepted positions in his hundred-day regime. An ordinance of proscription issued on 24 July 1815 targeted some of Napoleon's most devoted military and political servants. Drafted by Joseph Fouché, the slippery Napoleonic minister of police who had jumped the Bonapartist ship just in time to receive a position in the Bourbon government, the lengthy initial list was pared down as powerful royalist figures sought to remove the names of their compromised protégés. In the end, the definitive ordinance named only fifty-seven individuals.[10] A law passed six months later, on 12 January 1816, by the first elected legislative assembly of the restored monarchy completed the legal framework of Bourbon retribution. It swelled the ranks of exiles by banishing the regicides (deputies to the National Convention who had voted for the execution of Louis XVI in 1793), those individuals who had already been sentenced to internal exile by the first ordinance of proscription, and all members of the Bonaparte family.[11] These official exiles, essentially military men and politicians, would furnish the most famous names associated with the Vine and Olive colony.

Whether these measures were too strict or too lax is (and was at the time) a matter of debate.[12] What is clear is that the repression would have been harsher had the government—led by the relatively moderate prime minister Armand-Emmanuel du Plessis, Duke de Richelieu—not tempered the vengeful zeal of the legislature, which wanted to add entire categories of people to the proscription lists. One advocate of retribution, the Count de la Bourdonnaye, urged his fellow legislators to "use irons, executioners, and torture" against the revolutionaries and Bonapartists. "Death, and only death," he thundered, "can frighten their accomplices and put an end to their plots. . . . We must be ready to spill a few drops of blood in order to avoid having it run in torrents."[13]

La Bourdonnaye's fear that the people of France would take matters into their own hands if they did not see the government meting out justice were not groundless. In the months preceding the convocation of the legislature in early October 1815, large parts of the country—especially in the south—had been gripped by a wave of violent popular reaction known as the White Terror. The trouble began in Marseille when the sudden withdrawal of the Bonapartist commander on the night of 24 June 1815 sparked two days of royalist score-settling in which about 250 people were killed or wounded and 200 arbitrarily imprisoned. From there, local royalists marched on nearby Toulon, which they similarly "liberated": more than 800 people were imprisoned and at least as many fled the city.[14] In the département of the Gard, home to one of the greatest concentrations of Calvinists in France, the collapse of Napoleon's hundred-day regime reawakened longstanding Catholic hostility toward their Protestant neighbors, hostility that was expressed in months of lynching, arbitrary imprisonment, destruction of property, and mass flight.[15] Equally violent (although nonsectarian) disturbances shook the other major cities of the South: Lyon, Avignon, and Toulouse.[16] In the last-named city, a crowd publicly murdered the king's local military commander, a moderate but sincere royalist, for attempting to restrain the ultraroyalist militia. By revealing the popular violence of the White Terror as a threat to not only former revolutionaries and Bonapartists but also the government's authority, this episode helped pave the way for a more systematic approach to punishing the supposed crimes of the revolutionary past.[17]

To rein in popular violence, the legislature passed a series of laws—allowing arrest without trial, prohibiting seditious speech, and reestablishing the quasi-military provost courts—that were collectively intended to form the armature of a second (this time legal) White Terror.[18] Between July 1815 and June 1816, approximately six thousand people were convicted of political crimes.[19] Even more far-reaching were the purges that took place at all levels of the central and local administration. Mindful of the disastrous consequences of having left intact the imperial bureaucracy after Napoleon's first abdication in 1814, the Bourbons were in no mood to repeat the experience. Although no exact figures are available, it has been estimated that between fifty thousand and eighty thousand government employees were removed from their positions.[20] These men—together with those whose names were included in the proscription lists, those who feared popular vengeance, and others repelled by the prospect of life under monarchy—swelled the ranks of potential emigrants and exiles.

Of the many state institutions subjected to royalist scrutiny during the first years of the Restoration, none received greater attention than the army. It was widely believed in royalist circles that Napoleon's return to power in 1815 was the result of a military conspiracy.[21] Indeed, certain generals—including three who would later join the Vine and Olive colony (the brothers Henri and Charles Lallemand and Charles Lefebvre-Desnouettes)—had concocted plans to lead their troops in rebellion if Napoleon attempted to recover his throne. Upon learning of his return, they set these plans in motion.[22] But the plot failed miserably. In the end, it was not the conspiracy but rather the devotion the former emperor still inspired in the troops sent to arrest him that brought him to power once again.[23]

After Waterloo restored his throne, Louis XVIII took immediate steps to ensure the loyalty of the army. The war ministry wasted no time in ordering a purge of its leadership. In October 1815 a military commission was convened to examine the political tendencies of the entire officer corps and, with help from reliable local officials, classify each one according to his political sentiment. While of unprecedented scope and rigor, the purge of politically suspect officers was just one facet of the Restoration's new military policy. The other measures adopted—including the canceling of advancement and decorations bestowed during the Hundred Days, the drastic downsizing of the army, and the replacement of veteran imperial officers with royalist favorites—probably did even more damage to the army's morale. Approximately twenty thousand officers were removed from active service and placed on half-pay between September 1815 and December 1816.[24] The literary image of the *demi-soldes* (half-pay officers) as a restless crowd of grumblers, barely disguised Bonapartists, and outright plotters greatly exaggerates the degree of their opposition to the Bourbon regime (most were perfectly willing to become royalists in order to get their jobs back); nonetheless they provided a solid cadre of malcontents. Another group augmented the pool of potential plotters and adventurers: young men whose boyhood dreams of playing an active part in the Napoleonic legend were dashed with Waterloo. These were the men described by one of their number, Alfred de Vigny, as "that generation born with the century and suckled on the dispatches of the Emperor, who saw a naked blade ever present before their eyes—but became ready to grasp it only at the very moment when France returned it to the scabbard of the Bourbons."[25]

For men like these—soldiers of the empire whose careers had been prematurely ended by the Restoration and young men disappointed in their dreams of martial glory—the prospect of service in foreign lands held great attraction.[26] For despite the end of the Napoleonic Wars in Europe (and their American offshoot, the War of 1812), the world of 1815 was by no means a peaceful place. Opportunities abounded for French soldiers in places like Persia and Egypt, countries eager to recast their armies along Western lines. Others preferred to pursue their profession in the cause of revolution. In 1820, for example, many lent their services to the new constitutionalist government of Spain. When Bourbon France invaded three years later to restore the absolutism of Ferdinand VII, its troops were opposed by other Frenchmen, organized in units with telling names like the "Liberal Foreign Legion" and the "Lancers of Napoleon II." The Greek insurrection, too, would attract its share of French veterans and adventurers. But by far the greatest opportunities after 1815 were to be found in the Western Hemisphere, in the maelstrom of the civil war between Spain and her colonies.[27] French exiles and adventurers discerned especially promising possibilities in a distinctive theater of this multifaceted struggle, in the contested borderlands of North America, where local independence movements intersected with the territorial disputes of the United States and Spain to produce a "great game" no less intricate than its Central Asian equivalent.[28]

The Coriolani of France

The first refugees to join Joseph in America were members of the Napoleonic political and military elite designated by the proscription ordinance of 24 July 1815.[29] With few exceptions, they were insiders whose proximity to the regime and efforts to reestablish it after Napoleon's first abdication in 1814 marked them for retribution. Of the fifty-seven on the list, eleven would take part in the Vine and Olive venture. They included one marshal (Emmanuel de Grouchy), six generals (the Lallemand brothers, Lefebvre-Desnouettes, Bertrand Clausel, Dominique-Joseph-René Vandamme, and Antoine Rigau), two government officials (Pierre-François Réal and Jacques Garnier des Saintes), and two minor Bonapartists (the journalist Louis-Marie Dirat and Col. J. Jerome Cluis). After the passage of the law of 12 January 1816, they were joined by several former deputies to the National Convention, including two who would take part in Vine and Olive: Joseph Lakanal and Jean-Augustin Pénières-Delors.[30]

Of all who were proscribed, the military men were the most desperate to leave France. The ordinance of 24 July 1815 had ordered their trial before military courts on the charge of having "betrayed the King," "attacked France and the government with arms in hand," and "seized power."[31] Given the capital charges they faced and the nature of the tribunals designated to try them, the officers were afraid that if they delayed leaving France their lives would end before a firing squad. Anxious to avoid potentially embarrassing trials and executions of celebrated Napoleonic war heroes, the royal government did all it could to speed them on their way. The example of Marshal Ney, whose stubborn refusal to flee forced the reluctant Bourbons to put him to death, not only confirmed the worst fears of the proscribed officers but also induced others to leave France before any new measures of repression were enacted.

Another sentiment fueled the hostility of the officers to the Bourbon regime. With hardly an exception, they owed their elevated professional and social status to the meritocratic changes made by the Revolution and confirmed by Napoleon. Before 1789 all but fourth-generation nobles were essentially excluded from the officer corps. Aspirants who could not provide the required parchment proofs had to begin their military careers in the ranks. The Revolution changed all that. By abolishing the genealogical requirements that had previously kept the officer corps an aristocratic preserve, the National Assembly opened military careers to talent. This fundamental transformation—together with the opportunities for advancement generated by the emigration of thousands of noble officers, national military mobilization, and nearly twenty-five years of unrelenting warfare—allowed many young men of non-noble lineage to rise to the top of the military profession. With the consolidation of Napoleon's regime, their newly won professional standing received social reinforcement in the form of titles, offices, and land. Owing everything they had to the Revolution and Napoleon, they had everything to lose by the return of the Bourbons and their vengeful noble supporters, some of whom wanted to turn back the clock to the days of aristocratic predominance.[32]

An exception was Marshal Grouchy. From an ancient and well-connected family of the Norman nobility, Grouchy, unlike his fellow exiles, had been destined by birth for a brilliant military career.[33] Officer by the age of fourteen and colonel of his own regiment at twenty-five, his already-rapid advancement was accelerated by his decision not to emigrate, as had most noble officers, but rather serve the Revolution. He received the rank of general just before turning twenty-six and an independent army command only four years later. Although he initially protested against Napoleon's seizure of power, Grouchy soon made his peace with the new regime and was rewarded with important commands that placed him in close contact with the imperial family. In early 1808 he helped install Joseph Bonaparte on the throne of Spain and, as governor of Madrid, put down a revolt that threatened Joseph's new crown. After his Spanish service, Grouchy held commands in Italy and central Europe, before being tapped to lead a corps in the ill-fated invasion of Russia. During the disastrous winter retreat, he command the Sacred Squadron, the select bodyguard of officers formed to escort Napoleon to safety. During the early stages of Napoleon's return from Elba, Grouchy—who had been kept on active service by the Bourbons—defeated a royalist force marching to intercept Napoleon. For this crucial intervention, he received the rank of marshal from Napoleon, but only enmity and eventual proscription from the Bourbons. Having left Europe on 1 October 1815, Grouchy was probably the first of the proscribed military men to arrive in the United States.[34] There he became embroiled in bitter polemics (which continue to this day) over his supposedly decisive negligence at the Battle of Waterloo.[35]

Despite the royalist wrath he had incurred by facilitating Napoleon's return, Grouchy—by virtue of his high birth, family connections, and fortune—had everything to gain by conducting himself with circumspection during his American exile. As a member of the aristocracy, Grouchy stood a better chance than his lower-born comrades of winning a royal pardon. The situation was less promising for his fellow exile Gen. Henri-Dominique Lallemand.[36] Son of a wigmaker, Henri had known only the military life. Trained as an artillery officer as a teenager, he won his spurs in the Egyptian expedition. After Bonaparte's seizure of power, Henri transferred to the artillery of the Consular (later Imperial) Guard in which he served throughout his career. Veteran of the Prussian, Spanish, and Russian campaigns, he finally achieved the rank of general in 1814. For his role in the ill-fated military coup in 1815, he was appointed by Napoleon to command the artillery of the guard, in which capacity he was wounded at Waterloo. After the fall of the empire, Henri fled France, where he would surely have been condemned to death by a military court for his participation in the abortive uprising. He arrived in Philadelphia in May 1816.[37] His brother Charles joined him the following year.

Like his fellow conspirators, the Lallemand brothers, Charles Lefebvre-Desnouettes was a born soldier.[38] Before the age of sixteen, he had already run away three times from school to enlist in an infantry regiment. Each time his father, a Parisian cloth merchant, had to purchase his impetuous son's discharge. The Revolution shattered what little parental control remained and gave free rein to the young man's military inclinations. Napoleon's aide-de-camp at the Battle of Marengo and a general by his early thirties, Lefebvre-Desnouettes was considered one of the most dashing cavaliers of the empire.[39] Like the Lallemands, he served in Napoleon's major campaigns, including the invasion of Spain and the brutal guerilla war that followed. For attempting to lead his troops in rebellion against the Bourbons in 1815, Napoleon rewarded Lefebvre-Desnouettes with command of the light cavalry of the guard, at whose head he charged valiantly (but unsuccessfully) at the Battle of Waterloo. Named in the ordinance of 24 July 1815, he evaded a nationwide manhunt and fled via the Low Countries to the United States, leaving behind a wealthy wife whose fervent Bonapartism made her salon a natural meeting place for disgruntled officers and other opponents of the regime.[40] He arrived in New York City in early 1816.

In America, Lefebvre-Desnouettes developed a close relationship with another exiled general, Bertrand Clausel.[41] Like Lefebvre-Desnouettes, Clausel was the son of a merchant. But in Clausel's case, his family supported his precocious military inclinations. When the Revolution opened the officer corps to non-nobles, the Clausels mobilized their provincial connections—including an uncle who had been elected to the National Assembly, the local bishop, and ultimately the entire delegations of the Ariège, Haute-Garonne, Aude, and Pyrénnées Orientales—to get Bertrand an officer's commission. Combined with his personal merit, this potent support ensured rapid advancement for the young man, often in advantageous staff positions and diplomatic missions under powerful patrons like Generals Perignon, Grouchy, and Bonaparte. Promoted to general himself at age twenty-six, Clausel served in the Italian, Haitian, and Iberian campaigns, as well as with the Grand Army in Central Europe and Russia. Retained as a corps commander by the Bourbons during the First Restoration, he expelled the royalists from Bordeaux when he learned of Napoleon's return. This earned him a place alongside the Lallemands and Lefebvre-Desnouettes in the proscription ordinance. With the aid of the American consul at Bordeaux, William Lee, Clausel fled to the United States in early 1816, thus avoiding the death sentence pronounced against him later that year.[42]

Another proscribed general who came to America and took part in the Vine and Olive colony was Dominique-Joseph-René Vandamme.[43] As a young man, Vandamme joined the colonial troops just before the Revolution and was stationed briefly in Martinique. After deserting in 1790, he returned to France where he raised and commanded his own irregular cavalry unit. He climbed rapidly through the ranks, becoming a general in 1793 at the age of twenty-two. A born fighter, Vandamme was not the most scrupulous administrator. Indeed, he had the reputation of being one of the army's most shameless pillagers. Repeatedly accused of lining his own pockets with illegal contributions levied on the population of conquered lands, he was finally relieved of command in 1800. Napoleon, however, soon found that he could not do without the martial services of the gifted warrior. Within a year, Vandamme had resumed active service and, apparently repentant (or perhaps merely less brazen), managed to stay out of trouble for the remainder of his remarkably active military career under the empire. Vandamme rallied to Napoleon on his return from Elba and was rewarded with a short-lived peerage during the Hundred Days. For having accepted this dignity—or perhaps for having returned to his old habits during the confusion (he was accused of stealing 2 million francs from army funds during the interregnum)—the Bourbons placed Vandamme's name on the proscription list of 24 July 1815. He first fled to the Low Countries and then to the United States. He arrived in Philadelphia in July 1817, hoping his exile would be short.

The exiled generals were joined in America by a handful of prominent civilians whose connections to the imperial or revolutionary regimes made them targets of Bourbon proscription. Like the generals, the civilian exiles owed their prominence to the Revolution, without which they would have remained small-time lawyers (Réal, Garnier des Saintes, and Pénières) or, in the case of Lakanal, a clerical schoolteacher.

The most powerful of them was Pierre-François Réal, one of Napoleon's internal security advisers and police chief of Paris during the Hundred Days.[44] A lawyer in the Paris criminal court before 1789, Réal embraced radical politics during the Revolution. A close collaborator of Danton, he had nearly shared his bloody fate before linking his fortunes to the Directory's brightest young star, General Bonaparte. One of the organizers of the coup that brought Napoleon to power, Réal was rewarded with appointment to the Council of State, where he was one of several men entrusted with overseeing the police of the empire. Réal's vast bailiwick encompassed the north of the country and the all-important city of Paris. As one of the empire's leading lawmen, Réal incurred the wrath of the royalists for his role in prosecuting the royalist conspirators Georges and Pichegru, as well as for acquiescing in the execution of the prince d'Enghien. Named in the ordinance of 24 July 1815, he left France with his wife and nephew (a former police commissioner) and arrived in New York in early August 1816.[45]

Another refugee whose political life spanned the Revolution and empire was Jacques Garnier (known as Garnier des Saintes).[46] Like many revolutionaries, Garnier had been a lawyer before 1789. When the Revolution broke out, he became an enthusiastic advocate of the new regime. Elected to the National Convention in late 1792, Garnier gravitated toward the radical fringe. He not only voted for the immediate execution of the king but also pushed through a draconian law banishing the émigrés and putting to death those who dared to return. Although these actions alone would have been enough to seal his fate in 1815, Garnier's subsequent political career reinforced his radical reputation. He helped organize the notorious Committee of Public Safety and applauded its most bloodthirsty activities. After Robespierre's downfall and the end of the Reign of Terror, Garnier continued to uphold revolutionary positions, among them the exclusion of nobles from public office and the deportation of counter-revolutionary journalists. After Napoleon seized power, he employed Garnier in the administration, as president of the criminal court of Saintes. During the Hundred Days, Garnier was named to the short-lived Chamber of Representatives, where he urged measures of total war—notably the appointment of commissars to the armies—which recalled those of the Terror. Targeted by the ordinance of 24 July 1815, he fled to Brussels with his son, a decorated cavalry captain of the Imperial Guard. There, he published a radical journal, *Le Surveillant,* and wrote a degrading biography of the Bourbon family. Under pressure from the French government, the local authorities ordered him out of the country. Garnier and his son arrived in the United States in the summer of 1816.

The law of 12 January 1816 drove other regicides into exile in America. One of the best-known was Joseph Lakanal.[47] Destined from a young age for a career in education, then controlled by the church, Lakanal entered the Pères de la Doctrine, a Catholic teaching order. Although an ordained priest, he claimed that he never actually performed his sacerdotal functions, but instead devoted himself exclusively to his pedagogical calling. Elected to the Convention in 1792, Lakanal established himself as both a radical republican and an educational authority. President of the Committee of Public Instruction, he soon found himself ideally placed to give both tendencies free rein. He proposed a fundamental reform of the education system aimed at imbuing the new generation with republican morality. An idealist, Lakanal nonetheless possessed many of the vices he sought to extirpate in the young. Trained in rhetoric (if not possessed of discernible gifts in this field), he was given to such verbosity that a reputation for "unparalleled pedantry" preceded him across the Atlantic.[48] Napoleon had no time for the pompous former terrorist and declined to employ him. Only during the Hundred Days was Lakanal allowed to return to public life, as inspector of weights and measures at Rouen. Had it not been for his vote at Louis XVI's trial more than twenty years earlier, this revolutionary relic would have been left alone to live out his life in provincial obscurity. Instead Lakanal was swept up in the general repressive measures and exiled. He arrived in the United States with his wife and two teenaged daughters in March 1816.

The final regicide to take part in Vine and Olive was Jean-Augustin Pénières-Delors.[49] From a long line of lawyers and feudal judges, Pénières was destined from birth for the legal profession. But to take his family's occupational stability as a sign of stagnation would be a mistake. On the contrary, Pénières' father and grandfather had taken great strides toward advancing the status of the family in the decades before the Revolution. By 1775 it had acquired several *seigneuries* for itself and become the largest landowner in its native parish. His family's regional standing made Jean-Augustin an obvious choice for election to the Legislative Assembly in 1791 and, the following year, to the Convention. There, his already-moderate views grew more pronounced as the political situation became more anarchic. Although he voted to find the king guilty of treason against the nation, he also pleaded to suspend the death sentence that crime entailed. Pénières was one of the few deputies to dare to take public stands against the deepening radicalism of the Convention. He denounced Marat, defended the Girondins, and, after the overthrow of Robespierre, became one of the most ardent opponents of the former terrorists. For this, he was attacked on the streets of Paris. But unpopularity with the sansculottes of the capital did not indicate disfavor at home. Repeatedly reelected by his constituents, Pénières remained a deputy throughout the 1790s and thereafter sat in several of the emasculated legislatures permitted to survive by Napoleon. When word reached him of the law of 12 January 1816, he set out for Bordeaux to take passage to the United States. A series of grave accidents punctuated his journey into exile. Struck unconscious by a falling bale of hay at a country inn, he was hustled out of the country in spite of his serious injuries by Bourbon authorities fearful of his substantial local influence. Once under way, his ship was wrecked off the coast of Africa, and he spent a week in a lifeboat before being rescued. On 16 July 1816 he finally arrived in Philadelphia. His son joined him soon thereafter.

The military and political exiles described above were all important men who played significant roles in the Revolution, empire, and Hundred Days. In so doing, they earned the wrath of the Bourbons. It is less clear why Louis-Marie Dirat and J. Jerome Cluis were deemed worthy of inclusion on the proscription list of 24 July 1815. From the Bordeaux region, Dirat had been a military officer and served as aide-de-camp to his relative Marshal Perignon before being appointed subprefect of his hometown of Nérac.[50] During the Hundred Days he dabbled in radical journalism, serving as accountant (and, the police suspected, editor) of the left-leaning *Journal des Arts* or *Nain Jaune*. Placed under surveillance and forced into internal exile, he petitioned the royal government to remove his name from the proscription list and even offered to become a police informer.[51] But his pleas went unanswered. With the passage of the law of 12 January 1816, he was expelled from France. In February 1816 he left from Bordeaux with his wife and two children and arrived in Philadelphia a short time later. Cluis was even more obscure than Dirat.[52] A military officer and aide-de-camp to General Savary, Cluis had once been the jailer of Ferdinand VII, the Bourbon ruler of Spain who briefly lost his throne to Joseph Bonaparte.[53] After Waterloo, Cluis was arrested in Paris where he was recovering from wounds and ill health. Expelled from the city by the ordinance of 24 July 1815, he acquired a passport at Le Havre from the sympathetic American consul and departed for the United States in March 1816, leaving behind his wife and children.

The New Children of Israel

Not all who came to the United States after Waterloo were fleeing capital charges—or even formal proceedings of any sort.[54] Given the climate of reaction in France, a number of officers who felt themselves to be compromised by their actions during the Hundred Days or their proximity to the former imperial power elite decided to take themselves out of harm's way. Others made their way to America for less honorable reasons; gamblers, embezzlers, and forgers, these wayward officers would have been in serious trouble under any regime. But probably the majority of the officers who came to the United States faced neither political retribution nor criminal charges. Rather, they were young men who, having enlisted too late to win their laurels on the Napoleonic stage, preferred adventure in the New World to garrison routine in the Old. Finally, along with these different types of voluntary military exiles came a number of civilians who, as had Europeans since the seventeenth century, sought better lives in America. To these economic migrants, the great military and political events of 1815 probably meant no more than the reopening of trans-Atlantic sea-lanes.

For many of the officers who voluntarily left for America, fear of political retribution was an important factor in their decision. Particularly prominent among them were those who had accompanied Napoleon to Elba and led the way back during the Hundred Days. One of them was Nicholas-Louis Raoul.[55] Son of a revolutionary general, Raoul followed his father's footsteps into a military career. Graduate of the Ecole Polytechnique in 1809, Raoul had risen to the rank of captain in the Imperial Guard artillery by 1814. After the emperor's first abdication, Raoul followed him into exile, was named commander of the artillery of his diminutive Elban army, and claimed to have served as the former emperor's aide-de-camp. It was Raoul who led the vanguard during Napoleon's march up the Rhône during his return to France in 1815.[56] Rewarded for his devotion with a battalion of the reformed guard, Raoul was wounded at Waterloo. On the strength of his eleventh-hour promotion, he henceforth styled himself "colonel," prompting one French diplomat to grumble that "every day we learn that those who call themselves colonels were captains at most, and that the captains were only lieutenants, soldiers, or servants."[57] This conceit was not Raoul's only compromise with the truth. Although he later claimed to have been "swept up" in the general measures of repression, he actually resigned his commission voluntarily. He first went to Italy, where he was charged with overseeing the education of one of Napoleon's nephews. But a scandalous dalliance with a married Italian woman forced him to leave for America, where he was one of the first exiles to lend his sword to the insurgency of the Spanish colonies.[58]

Another Elban in American exile was Michel Combe.[59] Son of a shopkeeper turned revolutionary officer, Combe himself enlisted at the age of fifteen and rose through the ranks. Captain in the Imperial Guard in 1814, he joined Napoleon in his first exile and returned to France with him in 1815. Like Raoul, Combe was promoted for this display of fidelity—leading to similar pretensions about his rank—and served at Waterloo. Removed from active service in September 1815, he retired to his family's home in a village near Lyon where he and his younger brother (also a former imperial officer) soon fell under suspicion of spreading Napoleonic propaganda among the troops of the nearby garrison. Because of his "boundless fanaticism for the usurper," an arrest warrant was issued, prompting Combe to flee to the United States where he renewed contact with other former members of Napoleon's Elban guard.[60] These included Antoine Taillade, who served briefly as commander of Napoleon's navy on Elba and as captain of its largest ship before running it aground. This mishap did not prevent him, however, from successfully conveying Napoleon from his Elban exile to France, an act that brought upon him the wrath of the Bourbons.[61] Other Vine and Olive participants who had served in Napoleon's Elban army were Etienne Merle and Pascal Luciani.[62]

Others felt compelled to emigrate because of their compromising service in the Napoleonic satellite kingdoms. Among these were Fabius Fourni, Louis Gruchet, and an officer named Lavaudray. Former lieutenant-colonel of artillery in the royal guard of the kingdom of Naples—a puppet state ruled by Napoleon's marshal and brother-in-law Joachim Murat—Fourni fled to America on the failure of Murat's attempt to recover his throne in 1815.[63] Gruchet, who had commanded a cavalry squadron in the Neapolitan service, and Lavaudray, one-time aide-de-camp to Murat himself, probably also took part in this ill-fated expedition and, like their comrade Fourni, had to flee abroad.[64]

Perhaps the exiles with the least to lose were the officers of Napoleon's Polish legions, men without a country for whom the cause of international revolution offered the only hope of liberating their homeland. The best known of the Polish officers to take part in Vine and Olive was Capt. Jean Schultz.[65] Born in Warsaw in 1768, he had begun his military career as a cavalry cadet at the age of fifteen. With the third (and final) partition of Poland in 1794, Schultz lost his homeland. Like many Polish patriots of his generation, he would spend the rest of his life fighting to re-create Poland or, if that failed, to get revenge on those who had destroyed it. For Schultz, this initially meant lending his sword to the Turks, traditional enemies of the Russians. But in 1796 he transferred his services to the French Republic, which was raising legions of Polish volunteers. He rose steadily through the ranks before being captured in Spain in 1809 and sent to England as a prisoner of war. Released in late 1813, he returned to France too late for the final campaign that ended with Napoleon's abdication, but in time to be appointed commander of the Polish Lancers of the Elban army. In this capacity, he took part in the return to France, fought at Waterloo, and tried to accompany Napoleon into his second exile. But the British forcibly separated Schultz from the emperor and imprisoned him on Malta with Gen. Charles Lallemand. Released in mid-1816, Schultz took passage for America to join his comrades in exile, including Col. Constantin-Paul Malezewski, last commander of the Second Legion of the Vistula, one of Napoleon's storied Polish units, and "Col." Ambroise Jourdan, an officer in the Polish Lancers.[66]

The political motivations behind the American odyssey of another military exile, Louis-Jacques Galabert, are more difficult to fathom. Galabert was an enigmatic figure whose career literally took him around the world.[67] Youngest son of a mercantile family in the sleepy town of Castelnaudary, Galabert left home at the age of sixteen to make his fortune in the French sugar colony of Saint-Domingue. But the year was 1789 and the Caribbean island soon experienced a massive slave rebellion. Appalled by the violence, Galabert returned to France in 1791. For reasons that are unclear, he was arrested soon thereafter, imprisoned in Paris, and barely escaped the guillotine. He sought anonymity in the army, but was discovered and denounced—once again it is unclear why. To save himself, as well as strike back at a revolution that had treated him so roughly, Galabert fled to England where he joined a unit of French émigrés under Maj. Count Williamson.[68] In 1796 this corps was part of the disastrous Quiberon expedition in which the émigré forces landed by the British were captured and then executed to a man. As his unit was held in reserve and never disembarked, Galabert survived the debacle. But the spectacle of what he considered to be the cold-blooded abandonment of his countrymen by the perfidious English left him with a profound hatred of that nation, a hatred that colored his subsequent actions.[69]

As a virulently Anglophobic counterrevolutionary émigré, Galabert's options were limited. Fortunately for him, there was still Spain, where family connections may have helped him gain employment, possibly as a secret agent.[70] In 1798 he was sent on a mission by the Spanish government (under cover of employment with the Spanish Philippines Company) to British-controlled Bengal. Upon arrival in India, however, he was arrested by the British governor-general first as a French spy and then as a Spanish one. On the point of being shipped to London as a prisoner, Galabert escaped in a Danish vessel that then spent several months trading in the South China Sea. During the trip, he wrote poetry that blended classical form, lachrymose pining for his lost love, and rabid Anglophobia.[71] From November 1800 to March 1802, Galabert sailed to Europe heading eastward via Mexico and Cuba, thereby circumnavigating the globe. On his return to France, Galabert entered government service under Napoleon and undertook a series of mysterious trips to Italy from 1803 to 1806. In April 1806 he was commissioned as a lieutenant in the newly activated Tour d'Auvergne regiment, a unit intended to attract former émigrés and other counterrevolutionaries to Napoleon's army. Galabert apparently never joined his new corps.[72] Instead, from 1806 through 1809 he was employed in various diplomatic and covert missions in the Adriatic and Aegean region, notably Turkey, Dalmatia, Albania, and the Ionian Isles. Because of his profound knowledge of the country and its language, Galabert was next attached to the headquarters staff of the Army of Spain in 1809 as Marshal Soult's aide-de-camp. After Waterloo Galabert was exiled to Pau and placed under surveillance. Although he tried to win the confidence of the government—he even began one of his letters to the Duke d'Angouleme with the proud declaration, "I am an émigré"—the Bourbons remained suspicious of this man who had so effortlessly transferred his loyalty from the English to the Spanish to Napoleon. Frustrated by what amounted to house arrest, Colonel Galabert (as he now called himself) resigned from the army in 1817 and sailed for the United States. A new adventure was beginning for this restless man of action.

If Galabert's professional trajectory was unorthodox, the careers of a number of other officers who took part in Vine and Olive were frankly criminal. One of these was Col. Pierre Douarche.[73] Having enlisted in the patriotic surge of volunteerism of 1791, Douarche rose steadily through the ranks—thanks to his bravery, seniority, and numerous wounds—in spite of serious character flaws. Noted in an undated report as "too weak to command a regiment" and "requiring the general's authority to have himself obeyed," Douarche would probably have ended his career in the middling ranks had it not been for the advancement opportunities created by the bloodletting in Russia and Spain.[74] An uncultivated man with a weakness for games of chance and no income apart from his salary, Douarche could not resist dipping into unit funds to support his habit. But in spite of admitting to having lost twenty-five hundred francs of regimental money at the gaming tables of Paris, he was nonetheless promoted to command of a regiment during the dark days after the retreat from Russia. When his unit was demobilized after Waterloo, military accountants found ninety thousand francs missing from the unit's pay chest but could not locate Douarche.[75] The last anyone at the war ministry heard from him was a letter from Bordeaux, dated 8 February 1817, in which the fugitive former colonel explained that family affairs urgently required his presence at Bourbon Island, a French possession in the Indian Ocean. He then boarded a ship headed in the opposite direction and arrived in the United States several weeks later.

In America, Douarche joined forces with another fugitive officer, Jean-Philibert Charrasin, a younger, better-bred version of himself.[76] From a comfortable Burgundian family, Charrasin entered the officer corps directly (that is, without serving as a soldier in the ranks) at the age of twenty or so. A veteran of Spain like so many of his fellow exiles, he served briefly as a staff officer under Marshal Exelmans and then as an Imperial Guard lancer. Retained in this unit, now renamed Lancers of the Royal Guard, after Napoleon's first abdication, he soon ran afoul of his new commander, Colonel Colbert. Accused by Colbert of manifesting "a constant desire to elude the authority of his superiors," Charrasin offered his resignation, citing the seven wounds he had suffered (including a lance thrust through the chest) during his short career.[77] What Charrasin did not say was that he still held more than two thousand francs of regimental money. The matter was still pending when Napoleon returned from Elba. Promoted to the rank of captain during the Hundred Days— by virtue of which he would henceforth style himself "colonel"—Charrasin did not wait for the Bourbons' second coming to clarify his financial conduct, but hastily boarded a ship for America.

A final fugitive from justice was Paul-Albert Latapie.[78] After having risen to the rank of colonel and commanded the 17th Light Infantry Regiment at Waterloo, Latapie was retained on active service by the Bourbons after Napoleon's second and final abdication. But by 1816 he found himself in serious legal trouble. Charged with forging the war minister's signature to financial documents, undoubtedly with the intention of diverting military funds into his own pocket, he shot to death the gendarme sent to arrest him. He then fled to Belgium where he worked briefly with Louis-Marie Dirat editing the opposition paper in exile, the *Nain Jaune*. He then proceeded to the United States, landing in Charleston under an assumed name inscribed in a false passport.

Although the Vine and Olive colony harbored a number of political exiles and lawbreakers, most of the officers associated with it faced neither proscription nor criminal charges. Rather, they were typical young officers of the late empire—albeit perhaps a bit more ambitious and adventurous than most—who chose expatriation for a combination of professional and political reasons. The steep cuts in the size of the military, the return of counterrevolutionary émigrés seeking to recover their former military positions, hints that the Bourbons would favor nobles for promotion, and the new regime's pacific foreign policy all presaged the slowing of advancement. For young men who had embraced the profession of arms in pursuit of martial glory, the prospect of spending the next twenty years sunk in the drudgery of garrison life seemed worse than death itself. For those removed from active service, civilian life could mean disorientation and decline—exacerbated by alcohol, tobacco, gambling, and penury, what Balzac termed "all the bad tendencies of the disbanded trooper."[79] For these thwarted soldiers, professional frustration flowed into and gradually fused with political opposition. Anger at the Bourbons for military downsizing and slowing advancement easily mutated into political opposition. For none was the imbrication of professional and political grievances more total than for officers who were sons of the proscribed generals and legislators—the Grouchys, Garniers, and others—for it was clear that the Bourbons sought to punish the children for the sins of the fathers.[80]

The trinity of professional frustration, political disgust, and youthful adventurism surfaces again and again in contemporary literary depictions of the self-exiled officers.[81] One of several to publish an account of his adventures in America was an anonymous officer writing under the pseudonym Just Girard. A boy who had "dreamed of nothing but military honors," Girard had enlisted in the army at the age of seventeen and risen through the ranks.[82] Promoted during the Hundred Days, a common characteristic of those officers who turned up in America, he was placed on the half-pay list after Waterloo. Defeat, abdication, and inactivity—all combined to deal him "a blow that destroyed every hope of my heart, for I was fit for no career but the army. I had no home ties, no interest even, to keep me in France, and my first idea was to leave a country which, according to my political opinions, I could no longer serve, and from which I could not expect any consideration."[83] The reaction then taking shape reinforced his determination to leave France. "The country was in a ferment, there was violent ill-will on the part of the government against all those who had in any way been connected with Napoleon's return from Elba or who had helped to uphold his falling throne. . . . The lives of the Bonapartists were

in danger and those who had been lucky enough to escape the decree of proscription had gladly exiled themselves, in hopes of better times."[84] Taking passage on the first available ship, Girard arrived in Baltimore in April 1816, met
some of his exiled compatriots, and became involved in their projects.[85]

Apart from the handful who published memoirs of their experiences in
America, the adventure-seeking junior officers have left scant documentary
trace. Of little interest to the government because of their low rank and political insignificance, these officers rarely generated official paperwork other than
laconic service and pension records. A few, however, have left evidence of their
motivations. One of these was Charles Haraneeder, a junior officer. Son of a
banker, Haraneeder wrote to Stephen Girard at the end of 1817 asking to draw
money on his father because his own funds had run out, as he "had not expected to stay long in this country."[86] An impetuous rich kid in search of adventure, Haraneeder would eventually become involved in the most desperate
schemes of the more hardened exiles. One of his peers, Hyacinthe Gerard, refused to take part in these activities and suffered the consequences. Harassed
by the Bonapartist exiles for having expressed the intention of returning to
France, the destitute half-pay lieutenant turned to the French consul at Philadelphia for help. Expressing "repentance and regrets," Gerard sought to obtain
pardon "for whatever could be deemed reprehensible in his conduct" by informing on his former companions.[87] Another young soldier, the navy aspirant Jean-
Baptiste Néel, was "turned" in a similar manner, also in exchange for a pardon
and repatriation.[88] It was largely through the revelations of these double-agents
that the French diplomatic corps in America was able to keep tabs on the activities of the exiles.

The most important group of post-1815 French emigrants—in terms of both
numbers and long-term historical significance—was composed not of military
men, but of economic migrants. Although no exact figures are available, contemporary estimates suggest that in the three years following Waterloo as many
as thirty thousand French came to the United States.[89] It would be a mistake
to interpret this surge in emigration in political terms. Rather, it reflected the
end of the British blockade of French ports and the resumption of regular
trans-Atlantic shipping that allowed would-be emigrants to put their plans into
action. Moreover, the harvest of 1816 had been so disastrous in eastern France
that famine swept through the region during the first six months of 1817. As a
result, more than five thousand Alsatians and a smaller number of Lorrains left
for the United States in that year.[90] The magnitude of the emigration was so
great that Bourbon police officials even considered the possibility that it was

the result of a "perfidious" plot to depopulate entire areas of the French country-side.[91]

It is true that some efforts were made after 1815 to bring skilled European workers to the United States. By revealing the weakness of America's domestic manufacturing sector, the English blockade of the United States during the War of 1812 convinced a number of observers of the need to strengthen this area by facilitating the immigration of European craftsmen. One official particularly involved in this was William Lee, U.S. consul at Bordeaux. In the months following Napoleon's second abdication, Lee issued hundreds of passports to "the most valuable manufacturers of [France], Switzerland, and Germany," and, on his return to the United States in 1816, founded two textile mills employing more than a hundred skilled European workers. But despite these efforts, Lee was no supporter of mass immigration. On the contrary, he assured James Monroe, then secretary of state, that he had no intention of opening the floodgates to Europe's huddled masses, only to "a few useful ones" who "would in time of war lessen our dependence on foreign nations."[92]

Of no interest to even the strongest advocates of European immigration, the thousands of poor French emigrants who flooded into America's ports from 1815 to 1818 unfortunately remain largely faceless.[93] It is very difficult to get at the experience of these economic refugees as they strove to make their way in the strange new land. Impoverished, with no grasp of English, and few (if any) special skills, their daily struggle for survival rarely made an impression on the public archival record. Nor did they have the time, education, or inclination to keep diaries or maintain any regular correspondence with their families back in Europe. Indeed, many were so desperate that they were only able to secure passage to America by entering into contracts of indenture, reducing them to near-slave status. One French consular official reported in August 1817 that such immigrants were "rented or sold" by the ship captains "in order to reimburse the cost of their voyage."[94] Those emigrants with enough money to pay for their own passage to America often chose to settle in New Orleans, a bustling port city where French was still the dominant language. So popular was the city as a destination among French immigrants that at least fifteen hundred out of a total population of twenty-seven thousand in 1820 were actual French citizens fresh from Europe.[95] Thus, added to the native francophone Creole population and the ten to twelve thousand Domingan refugees who arrived in 1809, French speakers in the 1810s constituted at least 75 percent of the city's population.[96] So French was the city that Hyde de Neuville confidently assured the foreign minister in January 1817 that "if ever we find ourselves at war with the Americans, nothing would be more effective than a landing in Louisiana; we would certainly not be welcomed like the English!"[97]

For new arrivals from France, the benefits of linguistic and cultural familiarity available in New Orleans were counterbalanced, however, by the highest mortality rate of any major American city. Each summer, yellow fever would make its appearance. At least eight hundred died in 1817 (3–4 percent of the population) and as many as two thousand in 1819 (7–8 percent).[98] Recent immigrants from Europe proved especially susceptible to these annual epidemics. But what was once the bane of the immigrants is now the boon of the historians, for each rumor of a new epidemic provoked a surge of anxious letters from France to the French consul, inquiring about the health of relatives who had emigrated to that plague-ridden city. These letters, scrupulously conserved by the French consulate and now available for consultation at the Centre des Archives Diplomatiques in Nantes, offer a glimpse into the lives of some of the economic migrants who ultimately took part in the Vine and Olive venture. One of these, Joseph Truc, arrived in the city in 1816, hoping to make his fortune. After various speculations, of which acquiring Vine and Olive land was among the most honorable, Truc was jailed in the New Orleans municipal prison as a "fraudulent bankrupt." He died there in 1819, owing more than two hundred thousand francs to enraged French and American creditors.[99] Another, known only as Bistos, eked out a precarious living as an apprentice candymaker on Royal Street before joining Vine and Olive. Allotted a small parcel of land in the settlement, a mere forty acres, Bistos tried to support himself from this holding but had to give up the struggle after a few years of thankless labor. Leaving the colony, this unfortunate individual disappeared once again from the historical record.[100]

The Refugees from Saint-Domingue

Upon their arrival in the United States, the Napoleonic exiles and other French expatriates gravitated toward the substantial French communities already established in the major cities of the eastern seaboard, as well as New Orleans. French immigrants had been coming to what would become the United States since the seventeenth century when a number of Huguenot refugees settled in Charleston, South Carolina. But their numbers were never great. Like the United States, France had historically been a destination for, not a source of, migrants. The troubles of the French Revolution, however, caused a sharp upsurge in emigration. About 150,000 people left France during the 1790s for political reasons.[101] A portion of these took refuge in the United States. There they were joined by a much larger contingent of French citizens who had fled from the great slave rebellion that had broken out in Saint-Domingue in 1791 and, in lesser numbers, from revolutionary disturbances in the other islands of the French Antilles. Although most of the political émigrés from France returned during the early 1800s, many refugees from the Caribbean remained in the United States. The typical French expatriate in the United States after 1800 was thus a merchant, artisan, or planter from Saint-Domingue.

On the eve of the Revolution, the French island of Saint-Domingue was one of Europe's richest colonies. Reexported to Europe and North America, the products of its plantations—primarily sugar, but also coffee and indigo—represented fully 40 percent of French foreign trade.[102] A small elite of often-absent planters—some of whom had parlayed their fortunes into marriage alliances with metropolitan families of the court aristocracy—dominated Domingan society. Attending to its economic interests, basic needs, and comforts was an intermediate group of about 75,000 whites, mulattoes, and free people of color. The richest of these owned coffee plantations in the highlands and had interests in the island's extensive seaborne import and export trade. Others oversaw the great sugar plantations of the lowlands, managed their complex financial and legal affairs, and regularly purchased slaves from Africa—37,000 annually during the decade 1783 to 1792—to replace those who succumbed to the infernal regimen of the cane fields.[103] Other members of this intermediate group were the skilled craftsmen and shopkeepers who provided objects of beauty and utility to the resident elite, as well as to the intermediate group itself and the floating population of sailors, soldiers, and ne'er-do-wells.

Domingan society rested on the labor of enslaved Africans.[104] By 1789 about 500,000 toiled on the island's steaming plantations. For slaves on Domingan sugar plantations, the routine was grueling and eventually lethal. The best estimates place the annual rate of mortality among the entire slave population of the colony at 5 to 6 percent and at 50 percent for newly purchased Africans within three to eight years of their arrival. Subjected to a harsh, quasi-industrial work routine that reached a killing pace during the cane harvest, slaves not only suffered extreme hardship but also lived under psychological and material conditions that strongly discouraged childbearing. Rather than slow the murderous pace and allow the slaves a touch of normal life, plantation managers deemed it more profitable to work the slaves mercilessly until they died and then purchase replacements. Realizing that newly imported slaves typically survived only a few years under the plantation regime, the managers factored the cost of replacing part of their workforce each year along with their other annual operating expenses like the maintenance of machinery, the payment of salaries, and the purchase of equipment.[105]

On 22 August 1791, the world's only successful slave rebellion began with an uprising in the north of Saint-Domingue. With the colonial administration wracked by revolutionary factionalism and the island's garrison pulled apart by the same forces, the French were unable to bring the growing rebellion under control. Fighting raged across the island, characterized by horrendous massacres of civilian men, women, and children by both sides. The first mass exodus of whites began in the summer of 1792 when ten thousand refugees fled from the burning city of Le Cap on board a flotilla hastily assembled from stray ships at anchor in the harbor. In early July it arrived in Chesapeake Bay.[106] Some whites, however, still dreamed of seeing the old colonial order restored and remained on the island, clinging precariously to the shards of their former lives. As violence and disorder continued throughout the 1790s, most eventually gave up hope. Departures occurred both individually and in waves, culminating in 1803 when Napoleon renounced his attempt to reconquer the island—henceforth know as the Republic of Haiti.

Many of the fleeing Domingans sought refuge in the United States, generally settling in Philadelphia and other eastern port cities.[107] Their numbers increased substantially in 1808–9 when, in retaliation against Napoleon's invasion of Spain, the government of Cuba expelled the thousands of French refugees who had fled there from the troubles of Saint-Domingue.[108] Many of these unfortunates made their way to the United States, especially Louisiana.[109] Between May 1809 and January 1810 the city of New Orleans alone received more than ten thousand refugees, most of whom remained in the city where they formed a "distinct ethnic group" into the 1830s.[110] The lack of studies of the refugee experience in the other cities where they congregated—especially Philadelphia, whose Domingan exile community rivaled that of New Orleans in size, cohesiveness, and cultural weight—makes it impossible to advance firm general conclusions about the scope and nature of the French Caribbean influx.[111] Suffice it to say that, at least in these two cities, the Domingans formed the nucleus of large, culturally distinct francophone communities toward which the exiles from Bourbon France gravitated.

Some of the refugees came with very little and were forced to subsist on charity from French benevolent societies and aid from the American government. It would be a mistake, however, to exaggerate the poverty of the refugees as a group. Their large numbers and lengthy span of time during which they departed give lie to the myth that the Saint-Domingue revolution was a "nightmare of gore" in which the colonists had to flee precipitously, with just the clothes on their back, from ravening hordes of bloodthirsty ex-slaves.[112] In fact, many refugees left in a relatively orderly fashion, with at least some of their moveable property. More valuable, however, than the commercial merchandise, sacks of coffee and sugar, household furniture, and family heirlooms that packed the holds of their departing ships were the slaves the refugees took with them. Of the Domingans who disembarked at New Orleans in 1809, more than one-third were slaves—some of whom were owned by the mulattoes and free people of color who also fled from the uprising.[113] But probably the most precious assets the refugees took with them were their skills, experience, and family relations. These would provide them with the means of rebuilding their lives and prospering.

Although many of the refugees—both white and mulatto—were slaveholders, few were members of the true plantocracy. While a few were coffee planters from the highlands, there were almost no *grand blanc* (great white) sugar planters. Notarial records from New Orleans indicate that most of the refugees (62.6 percent) who came to that city were involved in commerce—as merchants, retailers, or mariners—and that almost all the rest practiced a craft (15.6 percent) or profession (9.4 percent).[114] While it gives a rough idea of the Domingan community during the first two decades of its American exile, socioprofessional quantification of this sort is not an entirely satisfactory method of getting at the multifaceted activities of the refugees.[115] This method of analysis reduces what were in fact complex occupational trajectories to single, static categories. Because of the oversimplification that socioprofessional quantification entails, it will be set aside here for an admittedly more impressionistic, but also more textured, anecdotal approach. Even so, the cases of specific individuals and families presented below roughly conform to the socioprofessional pattern suggested by the New Orleans figures—that the Domingan refugees in the United States came mainly from the worlds of commerce and craftsmanship.

Most of the Domingan families associated with the Vine and Olive colony had been active in the vibrant mercantile and artisanal sectors of the island's economy before the uprising. Thomas Noël, who would become one of the colony's principal landowners, had been a large-scale merchant in Port-au-Prince before leaving for the United States around 1800.[116] An importer and exporter in the busy port, Noël's entire life was commerce, so much so that he married the daughter of a business associate and neighbor, Grégoire Hurtel. From Noël's marriage with Anne-Déolice Hurtel issued one of the Vine and

Olive colony's two largest kin groups. Prosper Martin du Columbier, another refugee, established a successful iron foundry in Philadelphia after his flight from Saint-Domingue. Other future members of the colony, like Jean-Baptiste Herpin, had engaged in trade on a smaller scale, and one, Auguste-Firmin Follin, successfully combined a career in commerce with his veterinary practice.[117] There were a few doctors as well, such as Placide-Laurent Faurès, who also dabbled in business, but the representatives of the liberal professions among the Domingan Vine and Olive colonists were outnumbered by both businessmen and skilled craftsmen.

At least five Domingan watchmakers, jewelers, and goldsmiths held allotments in the Alabama settlement: Jean-Simon Chaudron and his son Pierre-Edouard, Alexandre Fournier, Pierre Gallard, and Théodore Guesnard.[118] Of these, the most famous was the Swiss-trained Chaudron, a watchmaker, as well as a skilled gold- and silversmith, who produced objects of great beauty. Like many of the finer craftsmen of the Enlightenment, Chaudron was also a man of letters who served as chief orator of the French freemasons of Philadelphia, wrote poetry, and published a French-language newspaper, *L'Abeille Américaine*. Fournier, also a mason in the Philadelphia lodge, probably shared Chaudron's Enlightenment tastes and attitudes. Other Domingans who may have had similar inclinations were Jean-François Hurtel and Louis-Descoins Belair, Philadelphia printers who specialized in publishing French and Spanish language books. Men such as Chaudron, Fournier, Hurtel, and Belair would find that they had much in common with the political exiles—Garnier des Saintes, Lanakal, and Pénières—who arrived after 1815.

Occupational diversification was the norm, not the exception, among the Domingan Vine and Olive colonists, but business was nearly always well represented among an individual's varied pursuits. The skilled craftsmen discussed above, for example, were also retailers who owned their own shops in Philadelphia, advertising and selling their wares to the public. Even the handful of Vine and Olive families that had managed to ascend into the lower ranks of planterdom on Saint-Domingue could trace their roots to commerce and, to a lesser degree, skilled craftsmanship. More significant still, they did not abandon these roots even after having acquired coffee estates. The Stollenwerks, for example, had begun as watchmakers. Even after the family patriarch and one-time Paris businessman Pierre-Hubert purchased a coffee and indigo plantation near Le Cap, he continued to engage in a wide variety of commercial affairs: fitting-out ships, trading in slaves, and exporting colonial goods to the United States with the aid of his son-in-law, Jean-Simon Chaudron. All the while,

Pierre-Hubert's younger brother, Pierre-Martin, worked as a jeweler and watchmaker in the city.

The family of Jean-Marie Chapron, who would eventually become the largest French landowner in the Vine and Olive colony, shows a similar mixture of urban and rural tendencies. While various branches of his family—including the Nidelet branch—owned coffee plantations around Port-de-Paix in the southern part of Saint-Domingue, Chapron himself pursued a career in business and married into a commercial family. His father-in-law, Francis Teterel, ran a large bakery that employed sixteen slaves. After the Haitian revolution, all these families—Chaprons, Nidelets, and Teterels—fled to the United States, established businesses in Philadelphia and Saint-Louis, and eventually joined the Vine and Olive colony. Frédéric Ravesies, whose family had known the Chaprons on Saint-Domingue, was the son of a coffee planter established on the northwestern tip of the island. In 1787, however, he sold his plantation, and Frédéric devoted himself thenceforth entirely to business. Only one Domingan member of the Vine and Olive colony came from anything approaching a grand planter background. This was Anne-Gilbert-Marc-Antoine Frenaye. Although coffee planters like the rest, the Frenayes did not sully their hands by dabbling in commerce, but were magistrates in the sovereign courts of France.[119] The Frenayes, however, resembled the other families described above in that they all pursued urban occupations while at the same time possessing substantial rural properties. Typical of both Old Regime France and colonial Saint-Domingue, this pattern of bourgeois landownership was maintained by the wealthier members of the Vine and Olive colony.

Stripped of their coffee plantations—or of the possibility of acquiring such estates—the Domingans in America threw themselves wholeheartedly into business. In this, they benefited enormously from their close relations with the existing French business community. For some, such as Pierre-Hubert Stollenwerk and Jean-Simon Chaudron, their mercantile pursuits in Saint-Domingue had already taken them on business trips to America where they made valuable contacts with American merchants. Chaudron transferred much of his wealth into U.S. banks. Others, after going into exile, were able to forge useful links with the existing French business community in America, especially in the Philadelphia area that was home to two tycoons of Gallic ancestry. One of these, the shipping magnate Stephen Girard, had himself lived in Saint-Domingue before emigrating to the United States. He employed two future Vine and Olive colonists—Pierre-Edouard-Côme George and his son Edouard—as supercargoes on his China ships. Many other Domingan refugees turned to

Girard with requests for employment, favors, or handouts, but their solicitations were uniformly ignored by the tight-fisted millionaire. Another capitalist of French ancestry in the Philadelphia area was E. I. du Pont de Nemours. At various times, his gunpowder factory entered into contracts with smaller businesses run by the Domingan exiles, including the firm of Curcier and Ravesies. They, in turn, employed two refugees who would later become Vine and Olive members, François Melizet and A. C. Salaignac, and did business with two others, Auguste-Firmin Follin and Romain Parat.

Other refugees in Philadelphia formed business partnerships with each other, partnerships sometimes reinforced by bonds of friendship and family forged years earlier in Saint-Domingue. The firm of Fontanges and Frenaye, for example, rested in part on the marriage of Piere-Frédéric Fontanges's sister, Thérèse-Antoinette-Margueritte, to Anne-Gilbert-Marc-Antoine Frenaye. The partnership between Jean-Marie Chapron and his cousin Etienne Nidelet—who worked as silk merchants—offers another illustration of how the Domingan refugees mixed family and business. And by way of a third example, the durable mercantile partnership between the brothers-in-law Charles Bruguière and Antoine Teisseire was further strengthened by the marriage of their children—Charles Charles Bruguière Jr. and Hester-Héloise—to each other in the following generation.[120] But others reached beyond the exile community to forge a potent mix of familial and business ties with the large population of non-Domingan French resident in the city. Examples of these include the partnership of the Domingan merchant André Farrouilh with the French emigrant Jean-Baptiste Lapèyre or the marriage of Louise-Françoise Beylle, daughter of a French-born confectioner, wine merchant, and distiller of Philadelphia, to Jean-Baptiste-André Herpin, son of a Domingan merchant who had fled to the same city. In the first decades of their exile few of the refugees seem to have established links with Anglo-Americans.

Although Philadelphia and New Orleans were the undisputed centers of the Domingan diaspora in the United States, refugees settled throughout the country. Every major city on the East Coast of the United States was home to at least a few Domingans, some of whom eventually joined the Vine and Olive colony. One of these was Pierre Drouet, who had established himself as a merchant in Williamsburg, Virginia, after arriving in America. Other Virginians were Pierre-Edouard Chaudron and Pierre-Solidor Millon of Norfolk. New York City was also home to a Domingan community, which included the family of the merchant Pierre-Hyacinthe-Baptiste Hurtel, as well as the Stollenwerk clan.

More surprising perhaps than the concentration of Domingan refugees in the urban centers of the Atlantic seaboard was their strong presence in the interior of the country, especially along the arc formed by the Ohio and Mississippi rivers. This area had been French territory until 1763, when Great Britain acquired it through the Treaty of Paris. In spite of the rapidly growing American presence in the first decades after U.S. independence, the Ohio and Mississippi valleys retained a noticeable French character into the 1810s. Some of the Domingan exiles took advantage of cultural, linguistic, and religious affinities to establish familial and business ties with the old French families of the area. The most successful in this regard were the Nidelets, who settled in Saint Louis and contracted advantageous business and marriage alliances with the Chouteaus, Laclèdes, and Prattes, important mercantile families of French ancestry in the city. Another group of Domingans settled nearby, on the rich lands at the confluence of the Mississippi and Ohio rivers that had been part of the French settlement of Illinois before 1763. There the refugees married into local French families, thereby constituting two of the family groupings associated with the Vine and Olive colony: the Audiberts and Delaroderies, and the Bogys, Vaugine de Nuisements, and Villemonts. Although the older French inhabitants of these regions had always been active in trade, the arrival of the Domingans gave a new, international dimension to their business activities.

Other refugees sought success in the economically vibrant Ohio Valley, particularly in Kentucky. Two of these were Joseph Barbaroux, who settled near Louisville, Kentucky, and his cousin, L. J. F. Martin Piquet, who lived across the river. Barbaroux eventually married Piquet's sister Julia and the two families went into business together. They bought shares in steamships plying the river between Cincinnati and New Orleans and imported a wide range of goods—including Haitian coffee and French wine—into the region via Piquet's father, also a merchant, who had remained in Philadelphia. In the course of their partnership, Barbaroux and Martin Piquet transacted business with other French and Domingan merchants active in the West—Lecoq de Marcelay, Cadet Bergasse, Anne-Gilbert-Marc-Antoine Frenaye, and François-Hyacinthe Teterel (who, in 1820, owned a store in Louisville), Etienne-François Nidelet, Jean-Marie Dubarry, André Curcier, and the Bujac brothers—as well as other merchants with Gallic names—Tarascon, Colmesnil, and Turcas—who may have also been Domingan.[121]

Life in America, especially in the western states, could be difficult for the Domingan refugees who were used to a more urbane lifestyle. One who found it particularly trying was Alexandre Fournier, son of the goldsmith mentioned above, who moved from Philadelphia to Demopolis, the town on the south-western corner of the Vine and Olive grant. Although a prosperous shopkeeper and a prominent local citizen, Fournier never really felt a part of America and tried desperately to remain in touch with Europe. He read the latest French novels and histories—in 1841, for example, he devoured works by Alexandre Dumas, La Tour de Nesle, and Gaillardet.[122] He also followed European poli-tics, speculating, for example, in 1841 about the Eastern question, the growing Franco-Russian-English struggle for influence in the eastern Mediterranean.[123] He aired his feelings of cultural isolation in a letter he wrote the following June. Characterizing his recent trip to New Orleans as "a sort of compensa-tion for the privations we have been forced to suffer year after year in Demopo-lis," Fournier related, "how much my heart and soul felt revived by contact with the good French creoles of Louisiana. . . . It seems to me," he reflected, "that the enormous difference in habits, education, and an infinity of little things between the French and the Americans, especially those of the southern states, . . . engenders true repugnance and renders impossible any veritably so-ciable *rapport.*. . . . Leaving aside my business connections, I feel enveloped in solitude, like an exile deprived of all society."[124] Fournier's feelings of separation from and distaste for American culture remained with him until the end of his life. In one of his last surviving letters, written in 1845, he lamented that his daughter Louise's education was "unfortunately more English than I would have liked."[125] By that time, she had already married George B. Hayden; soon, the only trace of Frenchness in the Fournier family would be its name.

Intermarriage and acculturation would be the ultimate fate of all the Do-mingan families that remained in the United States. But intermarriage with Anglo-Americans did not take place on any large scale until the second or third generation. From the arrival of the first waves of refugees in the early 1790s until the 1830s, Domingan society in the United States remained largely endogamous. Cast upon the shores of a strange land by a shared tragedy, this inward-looking group of exiles at first grew increasingly interconnected through a proliferating web of marital alliances. This tendency to marry within the Domingan community was even more pronounced among the refugees who joined the Vine and Olive colony. The member families were a self-selected lot, often related to one another by ties dating back to Saint-Domingue or the days of exile in Philadelphia. These thick webs of marriage alliances, friend-ships, and business partnerships likely gave them the courage and wherewithal to venture together into the Alabama wilderness. As a result of these intercon-nections, the Vine and Olive colony was dominated by several distinct groups of interrelated families. Their ability to call upon an extended kin group for support may well have been instrumental to their success. But it is equally plausible that success on the grant—whether as a land speculator, planter, politician, magistrate, or merchant—was the key that opened the door to advantageous marriages with other successful families in the area. Did family connections underpin success, or did success make those connections possible? Whatever the case, clearly the settlement's real backbone was not the highly visible revolutionary and Napoleonic exiles, most of whom returned to France as soon as they could. Rather, at the heart of the Vine and Olive colony were interlocking groups of Domingan families.

Some of these groupings were quite small, involving the alliance of only two families, as with the Frenayes and Fontanges, Bruguières and Teisseires, Combes and Lacombes, Ducoings and Robards, or Coquillons and Marchands. Other groupings were somewhat larger, such as the successful mercantile families of Chapron, Nidelet, and Teterel, which had forged their mutual links back in Saint-Domingue. Through the subsequent marriage of Marie Drouet, daughter of the Williamsburg merchant Pierre Drouet, with François-Hyacinthe Teterel, another future Domingan Vine and Olive family was added to this group. A larger network of marital alliances connected another group of future Vine and Olive colonists, forming a clan of six families. At its center was the French-born confectioner, wine merchant, and distiller Joseph Beylle, who had emigrated to Philadelphia in the 1790s. There in 1797 he married a young Domingan refugee, Marie-Françoise Sévelinge, from a family of former coffee plantation owners, whose brother, Joseph, also a Philadelphia distiller, later signed up with Beylle for Vine and Olive allotments. Although the couple had no children and Marie-Françoise died after only a few years, relations between Beylle and Sévelinge remained close. Joseph Beylle remarried in 1804 to the widow Marie-Madeleine-Louise-Thérèse Lemaistre and had several children with her. Their second daughter, Josephine-Irma, later married another Domingan Vine and Olive colonist, the shipowner Jean-Baptiste-François Tête, and their fourth daughter, Louise-Françoise, married Jean-Baptiste-André Herpin, son of a Domingan tradesman. The daughter of this last-named couple, Marie-Zéline-Angélique, married the Domingan goldsmith Théodore Guesnard, and Ursule-Céphise Godichaux, the daughter of Madame Beylle née Lemaistre by her first marriage, married Alexis Tardy, the son of a former coffee planter in Saint-Domingue. With these two peripheral marriages, the Beylle, Sévelinge, Tête, Herpin, Guesnard, and Tardy clan of Vine and Olive shareholders was completed. A business partnership between Joseph Beylle and Alexis Tardy, on the one hand, and between Beylle and the influential Batré brothers of Mobile, on the other, gave the group a solid financial base.

Despite its impressive size and connections, this family was dwarfed on both counts by the two principal clans that dominated the Vine and Olive colony. The first and largest of these orbited around the allied Stollenwerk and Chaudron families.[126] The alliance was based on the marriage of the coffee planter Pierre-Hubert Stollenwerk's first two children, Jeanne-Geneviève-Mélanie and Pierre-François, to Jean-Simon Chaudron and Geneviève-Antoinette Dagneaux, respectively. From the Chaudron line issued nine children, of whom five married into the families of Vine and Olive grantees. These were Jules de la Garda, who married Anita Duval, daughter of a Domingan merchant in Philadelphia; Caroline, who married Félix-Achile George, son of Stephen Girard's supercargo and his formidable wife, Victoire; Sylvanie, who married Adolphe Batré, successful merchant and prominent citizen of Mobile; Octave-Pierre, who married his first cousin Louise-Estelle Stollenwerk, the fourth child of Pierre-Francois and Geneviève-Antoinette; and Félix B., who married Merceid Duval, sister of Anita. The Chaudrons' youngest child, Melanie-Victoria, married Nicholas Weeks, an Anglo-American businessman from Mobile who obtained final patent on two allotments in the Vine and Olive grant bordering Chaudron property. With seven children, the Stollenwerk line was only slightly less prolific, although it showed a more pronounced tendency to marry outside of Vine and Olive circles. Only two of the Stollenwerk children married into the families of other grantees. These were Sylvanie-Geneviève, who married Eduouard-Auguste Bayol, and Louise-Estelle, who married her first cousin Octave-Pierre Chaudron.

While the marriages of the Chaudron and Stollenwerk children formed the inner core of the clan, more distant relations obtained through the marriages of the children of allied families—like those of the Georges and Batrés—gave it more layers. In addition to Félix-Achile, who married Caroline Chaudron, the Georges had another child, their only daughter, Victorie, whose two marriages—the first to the French-born Philadelphia engraver Isaac Butaud and the second to the French-born Philadelphia merchant Nicholas-Elisée Thouron—added two more Vine and Olive families to the clan. The marriage of Thouron's sister Marie-Anne-Ursule to Pierre-Corneille Roudet brought not only the Roudets into the web, but also the Melizets, the family of Pierre-Corneille's mother. The Batré connection contributed a final family to the mix through the marriage of brother Charles Batré to Adèle Macré. In all, ten additional Vine and Olive families—the Dagneaux, Duvals, Batrés, Weeks, Macrés, Georges, Butauds, Thourons, Roudets, and Melizets—branched out from the Stollenwerk-Chaudron trunk.

The second great Domingan clan of the Vine and Olive colony centered on three allied families, the Noëls, Follins, and Bayols. The patriarch of the clan was Thomas Noël, the former merchant from Port-au-Prince who settled in Virginia after the slave uprising. He married Anne Déolice Hurtel, from another family of Domingan merchants that, after first fleeing to Cuba, settled in the United States and joined the Vine and Olive colony. The Noël-Hurtel marriage produced six children of whom two daughters, Eliza and Déolice, married their Hurtel cousins Jean and Firmin. These marriages undoubtedly strengthened the ties between the two families but were also a missed opportunity for them to establish links with other families. But Thomas Noël had come to the United States with his three sisters, who more than made up for the insularity of his own children's marital alliances. The eldest, Marie-Perrine, contracted a highly advantageous first marriage to Jean-Paul Bouttes d'Estival, a nobleman who owned a substantial estate in Saint-Domingue, and had two daughters with him. After Bouttes d'Estival was killed in the slave uprising, Marie-Perrine married her former estate manager, Honoré Bayol, and fled to Philadelphia with him and his bachelor uncle, the goldsmith Pierre Gallard. Once in America Marie-Perrine's eldest daughter from her first marriage, Adèle, married Alexandre Fournier, the homesick shopkeeper of Demopolis. Her second daughter, Josephine, married Jules Martinière, the son of a former Domingan coffee planter and, like Fournier, a successful Demopolis merchant. One of Thomas Noël's other cousins, Marie-Jeanne-Mélanie, established a link with the Follin family by marrying its patriarch, the veterinarian-merchant Auguste-Firmin. One of their daughters, Alameïde-Eugénie, married Lemuel Sanderson, a patentee of the Vine and Olive colony who may himself have been a Domingan, and another, Virginie, married her cousin Louis-Edouard Bayol, the only son of Honoré and Marie-Perrine Bayol née Noël. After Virginie's untimely death, Louis-Edouard married Sylvanie-Geneviève Stollenwerk, daughter of Pierre-François and his wife, Geneviève-Antoinette née Dagneaux, thus establishing a bridge between the Vine and Olive colony's two largest clans. Taken together, they accounted for twenty of the settlement's principal families and shaped its character. Many of their descendants still live in Alabama today.

2

The Society for the Cultivation of
the Vine and Olive

The post-1815 exiles from France were welcomed as heroes by the
American population at large. Bonapartist sentiment, however, had little to do
with the enthusiastic reception. While citizens of the United States recognized
Napoleon as one of the great figures of the age, they also understood that his
regime was based on principles antithetical to their own. So why were the exiles, who included prominent servitors of that alien regime, received so warmly?
The answer has more to do with American antipathy toward England than
with American admiration for Napoleonic France. "Hatred of Great Britain or
apprehension of her enormous power," Albert Gallatin (then the American ambassador in Paris) assured the Duke de Richelieu in 1816, "was the true cause
of whatever might . . . be written in favor of Bonaparte."[1] At no time was
American Anglophobia more pronounced than in the period 1815–18.[2] The bitter hostilities of the War of 1812 were fresh in everyone's mind, and no amount
of self-congratulatory chest-pounding over Jackson's defense of New Orleans
could efface the memory of American failure in Canada, the English blockade
of the eastern seaboard, and the sack of the nation's capital. In the eyes of
Americans, still smarting from these humiliations, the great virtue of the exiles
and their main claim to the Republic's gratitude was that they had spent their
lives fighting America's most feared adversary. The bittersweet legacy of the
War of 1812 was the single greatest factor shaping the welcome accorded the
French exiles.

At Loose Ends in America

With the fall of Napoleon, the specter of unchecked English hegemony
haunted the nightmares of not only American statesmen but also the diplomats
of the Old World monarchies—France, Spain, and Russia—that had recently
been her allies. So suddenly and completely did this fear replace that of Napoleonic thralldom that in April 1817 the French government even proposed to the
United States that it enter into a "triple alliance" with France and Spain. If these

three countries joined forces and established a common Atlantic policy, the advance of British power into Spain's rebellious American colonies might be checked and "advantageous commercial results might be secured to the three nations from which England could be excluded."[3] For Americans, the new sense of vulnerability was felt even more acutely than by the Europeans because they were painfully aware that theirs was one of the few republics left in a world dominated by monarchies. Not content with having defeated Napoleon, these seemed determined to extinguish the last flames of revolution wherever they still flickered, notably in the rebel provinces of Spanish America. Urging an all-out national effort on behalf of the beleaguered Spanish patriots, Edward Livingston, one of General Jackson's lieutenants at the Battle of New Orleans, painted a grim, but widely shared, picture of American isolation. On the struggle for Latin American independence, he wrote to Andrew Jackson in November 1816, depended "the very existence of freedom on the globe." "Republicanism has not even a man left in Europe, and if the despotism of Spain is established in one half of North America, the other half will very soon have to contend alone against the coalesced tyrants of the world for their existence." At this critical juncture, Livingston continued, it was necessary to fan "the flame of liberty that is now rising in the southern continent and thus provide for our posterity." Circumstances demanded nothing less than "a coalition of republics to resist the holy league of kings."[4] From this perspective, the French exiles appeared not as servants of a defeated tyrant, but as valiant warriors in an epic struggle for liberty.

The exiles were thus welcomed to America with pomp and circumstance. A succession of parades, banquets, and toasts heralded their arrival in the cities of the eastern seaboard. In May 1816, for example, the "principal" French and American citizens of Philadelphia held a banquet for the refugees—among whom were Marshal Grouchy and Generals Clausel and Lefebvre-Desnouettes— who had just arrived in the city. Presided over by Pierre-Etienne Duponçeau, president of the American Philosophical Society, the assembly drank numerous patriotic toasts, was addressed by Charles Ingersoll (attorney general for Pennsylvania), and was treated to several odes written for the occasion by Jean-Simon Chaudron. The festivities, described by Chaudron in his paper as an "homage to persecuted merit," closed with a rousing rendition of the "Marseillaise."[5] A year later Gen. Charles Lallemand was greeted with equal enthusiasm in Boston, a city of a far different political character and cultural outlook than Francophile Philadelphia. On his arrival from France in April 1817, Lallemand was welcomed by some of the leading figures of the state of Massachusetts including gubernatorial candidate General Dearborn, the former U.S. ambassador to Sweden Jonathan Russel, and Commodore Bainbridge, captain of the U.S. frigate *Independence* then stationed at Boston. Befriended by Pierre-Paul-François Degrand, a wealthy and well-connected Boston merchant and business journalist of French birth, Lallemand was soon introduced to "a grand and numerous circle . . . composed of the most distinguished and richest among both the federalists and democrats."[6] Wherever they went, the French exiles (at least the prominent ones) were greeted with warm admiration.

On occasion these celebrations gave vent to rhetorical sallies against royalty in general and the Bourbons in particular. One such outburst even led to a diplomatic tiff between France and the United States.[7] At Baltimore's Fourth of July banquet in 1816, the city postmaster, James Stuart Skinner, proposed a toast—to "the generals of France in exile" who could never be "dishonored by the proscriptions of an imbecile tyrant"—that was printed in the national newspapers. The French ambassador Hyde de Neuville was furious—especially because Skinner's barb was aimed at "the brother of Louis XVI in a ceremony that should rather have recalled what the United States owed to the generous alliance of the Bourbons." Although he had lived too long in America not to understand the principle of liberty of the press, Hyde asserted that Skinner's status as a public official required his immediate dismissal.[8] The American government rejected the demand, an incredulous President Madison characterizing it as "very extraordinary."[9] Secretary of State Monroe elaborated in official instructions to Gallatin. "From the nature of our institutions [which make no distinction between government employees and ordinary citizens in the arena of free speech]," he explained, Skinner's removal was "[im]practicable." But "the peremptory tone" of the demand "renders it utterly impossible." "If a foreign minister can dictate measures to the U.S., especially in a case so intimately connected with the vital principles of their government, their independence is gone."[10] Hyde did not concur and, as an expression of his government's anger, suspended the French consul at Baltimore. The stalemate dragged on through the fall, poisoning relations between the two countries. But ultimately their shared interest in trade and mutual suspicion of the English led to a rapprochement and the incident was forgotten.

Public demonstrations of support for the exiles occasionally turned violent. This was especially so in New Orleans, where the combination of weak federal authority, local involvement in the Spanish American independence movement, a large French population, and the presence of foreign sailors proved highly combustible.[11] An explosion occurred on 18 March 1817 when French sailors in the port, "some Barataria men" (pirates in the employ of the notorious Lafitte brothers), and "a few Bonapartists from amongst the French population" attacked the Liverpool ship *Hamilton* on the pretext that its captain had insulted the tricolor flag of revolutionary and imperial France.[12] According to the horrified consul of Bourbon France, rioting crowds spilled out of the port and poured through the streets of the Vieux Carré shouting "Vive Napoléon!"[13] During the following weeks, Zephir Canonge (the cousin of future Vine and Olive member Pierre-Auguste Canonge) caned the Spanish consul, Diego Morphy, as he was relaxing in the Exchange Coffee House.[14] At the same time, several French citizens "known for their attachment to the monarchy" were attacked by crowds.[15] The climax of the agitation came on 4 May with the staging of a hastily written Bonapartist play, *The Day of the Three Emperors.* Announced with great fanfare in *L'Ami des Lois,* a left-leaning paper published by Jean-Théophile-Victor Leclerc, a radical journalist who had attempted to assume Marat's mantle (and editorship of his famous *L'ami du peuple*) after his assassination, the spectacle attracted "an immense throng," many of whom wore tricolor cockades.[16] Preceded by equestrian exercises and augmented by a third act crammed with scenes from Napoleon's military career, the spectacle ignited the passions of the audience. Repeatedly interrupted by cries of "Vive l'Empéreur!" and "Vive Napoléon!" as well as famous revolutionary airs sung heartily by the entire crowd (including the mayor Nicholas Girod), the chaotic play finished with an orgy of Bourbon bashing. To the repeated "bravos" of the crowd, the actors stood on the edge of the stage and recited vulgar couplets "injurious to the person of the King, the royal family, and all the classes of people who now compose His Majesty's government." In the eyes of Hyde de Neuville, these displays of sympathy for the exiles and their lost causes only served to reveal the "anarchical delirium" to which "a numerous class of Americans had abandoned themselves."[17] And to make matters worse, the administration in Washington responded to his appeals for action by pointing out that the Constitution granted it no power to police the separate states of the Union.[18]

But when the speeches had been pronounced, the toasts drunk, and the rioters gone home, the exiles had to confront an unavoidable question: what were they to do with themselves now that they were in America? It is true that some of them—Joseph Bonaparte and Marshal Grouchy, for example—held letters of credit that allowed them to draw on their substantial European resources.[19] And others had letters of introduction, usually provided by the Marquis de Lafayette, to influential Americans such as Thomas Jefferson and Henry Clay.[20] In a letter to his family in France, Pénières even boasted that he had a "large drawer" full of such missives.[21] But open doors did not necessarily fill pockets and, still less, satisfy souls. Even Lakanal—who probably possessed more letters of introduction than any of his compatriots, as well as thirty thousand francs that he had carried with him into exile—had to do something to replenish his respectable, but finite, resources and give purpose to his existence.[22] After all, the exiles—especially those who had been formally expelled from France—did not know when or if they would be able to return. And a few never wanted to. The challenge the exiles faced was that confronting all immigrants: to adjust to life in a strange new country.

They tried to make their way as best they could. Since many of the exiles had been career officers in the renowned armies of Napoleon, they naturally expected to find places in the armed forces of their host country. Some notable exceptions—such as General of Engineers Simon Bernard, whose fortifications still stand at points on the American coast—succeeded in entering the American army.[23] But for most of the officers, confident expectations that the Americans would be awed by their Napoleonic credentials and welcome them into the military were soon put to rest. They had counted on neither the large number of American officers, demobilized after the War of 1812, who wanted their places back, nor the chauvinism of their hosts, which ensured that "preference would not be given to foreigners" were the army to return to a war footing.[24] Moreover, the United States—a mercantile nation—displayed a fundamental "indifference" to those whose only contribution to society was "the service of their swords."[25]

Thwarted in their attempts to enter the American army, some of the military exiles offered themselves to the cause of Latin American independence. Here they encountered similar obstacles as in the United States, but now on an international scale. The end of the Napoleonic Wars and War of 1812 had put thousands of veterans out of work, as the enormous armies raised for those conflicts were demobilized. With this mass of career soldiers seeking employment wherever they could—in Egypt, Turkey, Persia, and especially the insurrectionary armies of the Spanish colonies—competition for the limited number of positions was keen.[26] Nonetheless, some French officers managed to impress insurgent recruiters in the United States. One of these was Colonel Raoul. Appointed to the rank of general in the army of Buenos Aires in 1816, he served there several months before accusations of malfeasance forced him to return to the United States.[27] Another possible Vine and Olive member who found service—and misfortune—with the Spanish American patriots was François Durant. Forced to flee France after Waterloo for "political reasons," Durant arrived in New Orleans with no other "means of procuring [his] existence than [his] sword." He joined an insurgent expedition to Mexico, was badly wounded and captured by the royalists. Imprisoned for thirty months in the infamous dungeons of Morro Castle in Havana, he was eventually released, an impoverished invalid, to the United States.[28]

The lure of participating in the movement for Latin American independence tempted even the most prominent exiles and drew them into unsavory contacts with the international community of revolutionaries, mercenaries, and spies drawn to the struggle between Spain and the colonies. Persistent rumors named Grouchy and Clausel as the designated leaders of an imminent invasion of New Spain to liberate it from Spanish rule.[29] There is evidence that Grouchy also held talks with Gen. Jose Miguel Carrera, a Chilean rebel leader, about the possibility of taking command of insurgent military operations there.[30] Two more generals established a relationship with the insurgents. In the summer of 1816 Henri Lallemand and Lefebvre-Desnouettes left Philadelphia under the pretext of visiting the hot mineral baths of Virginia, where Lallemand could soothe the wound he had received at Waterloo. But no sooner had they arrived than they headed west over the Appalachians and into the Ohio Valley.[31] Although their ostensible purpose was to descend the Ohio and Mississippi rivers to Louisiana, where they spoke of purchasing land, the British ambassador suspected that the "real object of this journey might be . . . to put themselves . . . in connection with the insurgents in Mexico." Reports from British consular officials confirmed that the generals were "deeply engaged in some design now carrying on in this country for the assistance of the revolutionists in the Spanish settlements."[32] The British diplomatic corps was well informed—perhaps it even knew more than it was telling about these doings. Upon their arrival in New Orleans, Lallemand and Lefebvre-Desnouettes were reportedly approached by an English agent who sought to enlist them in a rival scheme to conquer New Spain. His offer of arms was tempting, but disguised neither his lack of manpower nor the fragility of the Mexican insurgency. The two generals did not merely decline his proposition, but even contacted the French consul in the city with an offer to report on his maneuvers.[33] Anglophobia apparently ran deeper in French souls than political difference.

Lallemand and Lefebvre-Desnouettes were not averse, however, to serving the insurgent cause under the banner of the Mexican Congress, a fugitive body that spent most of its energy trying to evade the royalist forces on its trail. The generals would have had difficulty making contact with representatives of the nomadic Congress had it not been for the good offices of Jean-Joseph-Amable

Humbert—a former general of the French Republic now established in New Orleans.[34] Humbert had won a reputation for bravery for having been the only commander to gain a foothold in Ireland during the failed French invasion of 1798.[35] Napoleon, however, dismissed him several years later for his eccentric character and outspoken republicanism. Undaunted, he settled in New Orleans where he embraced the cause of Mexican independence and played a leading role in several unsuccessful invasions. In 1814 he was even named general-in-chief of all the republican armies of Mexico and presided over a governing junta based in New Orleans that included among its membership future Vine and Olive shareholder Louis Bringier.[36] After a brief interlude in 1815—when he fought under Jackson in his famous defense of the city—Humbert returned to his earlier endeavors on behalf of the Mexican insurgency, serving as its representative in New Orleans.[37]

Thanks to his introduction, Lallemand and Lefebvre-Desnouettes were able to send an emissary, Colonel Charrasin, into Mexico to explore the possibility of collaborating with the insurgents.[38] The results of his mission are unclear. The French diplomatic corps in the United States intercepted documents suggesting that the colonel had brought back discouraging news: the insurgent forces lacked everything—except officers. Although there were "more than 400 French officers in the United States . . . who would like nothing better than to serve this cause," the patriots did not need more "headquarters staff" but rather "disciplined European soldiers to lend consistency to military operations." As a result, the French government believed, Lallemand and Lefebvre-Desnouettes had concluded that their participation would be "useless" or "impractical."[39] Other sources, however, suggest that Charrasin's mission bore fruit. Although he arrived at the insurgent base at Galveston too late to meet General Mina, the Spanish insurrectionary who had just departed to make a landing farther south along the Mexican coast, he encountered several other important figures in the shadowy world of Latin American revolutionaries.[40] One was Pierre Lafitte, the privateer and smuggler of New Orleans currently in charge of Galveston, who made Charrasin "some proposals" (unfortunately not specified) that the French officer reportedly accepted. He also met there Louis-Michel Aury, another privateer chieftain, and his right-hand man, Colonel Joseph Savary, a mulatto refugee from Saint-Domingue and leader of the New Orleans–based Battalion of Free Men of Color. It is not clear what Charrasin discussed with Aury and Savary, who departed soon thereafter for another insurgent base that had just been established by Gregor MacGregor on Amelia Island, just off the northeastern coast of Florida.[41] Charrasin also made contact with several northern Mexican mine owners who assured him of their desire for independence and their willingness to contribute men and money toward that end.[42]

As Lallemand and Lefebvre-Desnouettes discovered in New Orleans, the number of foreign officers seeking employment with the Spanish American insurgents was so great that even illustrious veterans of Napoleon's army might find it difficult to obtain service on good terms. By mid-1817, it was reported, the patriots' recruiters in the United States had even stopped paying the southbound passage of those who joined up. In the armies of Bolivar and San Martín, already top-heavy with officers from the local Creole elite, there was simply no need for more infantry and cavalry cadres, even if these had earned their spurs in the great battles of Napoleon.[43] Disappointed by the "scant welcome" they received from the Latin Americans, most of the expatriate officers remained in North America, idle and unemployed, their meager resources rapidly dwindling.[44]

Some—whether out of frustration or a thirst for action—threw themselves into adventures ranging from freelance military operations undertaken in the name of Latin American independence to undisguised acts of piracy. Often the slide from insurgency into sheer adventurism, impelled by the gradual closing of more legitimate avenues of subsistence, was barely perceptible. Take, for example, the case of Dreyer and Dubois, two young officers who left France to serve the cause of Latin American independence. Upon arriving in the United States, they tried to join MacGregor's expedition against Amelia Island, but were offered only vague promises. They then attempted to speak with Joseph Bonaparte, but he refused to meet them. Increasingly desperate, the young men encountered a French officer named Labatut who asked them to join an expedition against Mexico. The two would-be freedom fighters balked at this highly dangerous mission and, penniless, threw themselves upon the mercy of the French ambassador, begging for repatriation.[45]

Other officers were more determined than these hapless young men. One was future Vine and Olive grantee, Col. Paul-Albert Latapie. Upon learning that Pernambuco in Brazil had revolted against Portuguese rule in early 1817, Latapie hired a ship, recruited more than thirty adventurers, and set sail for the new republic. His expedition was rumored to be part of a larger operation to rescue Napoleon from Saint Helena, which lay in the middle of the South Atlantic, several hundred miles to the east of the city.[46] Others were even more reckless, such as the French officers who hijacked the ship carrying them from Anvers to New York and tried to force the captain to take them to a rendezvous with Mexican insurgents.[47] Some sought to join one of the many privateers commissioned by representatives of the Latin American republics in the ports of the Eastern seaboard. Although authorized to cruise only against Spanish shipping, the privateers often proved less than discriminating in their choice of victims.[48] In the wars of Latin American independence, as in revolutions more generally, the line between idealism and profiteering was often blurred. The confusion generated by what was, in effect, a civil war fought on a global scale opened many opportunities for adventurism. This was readily apparent to apprehensive European and American statesmen who perceived that "the military reputation and desperate fortunes of the French officers" made them "the fittest and readiest instrument" for intervention—whether official, covert, or piratical—in nearby Spanish America.[49]

While the military exiles could hope to enter the service of a foreign power or, in the last resort, take up the life of a condottieri, the civilian exiles did not always possess such easily transferable expertise. Many had to make do as best they could by selling whatever skills they possessed, generally in the form of lessons, publications, or formal education. For some, cosmopolitanism was their most valuable asset. René de Perdreauville, once a tutor to the pages of Queen Marie Antoinette in the court of Louis XVI, opened a girls' finishing school in New Orleans.[50] Another Vine and Olive member, Henri-Antoine Saignier, founded a school of equitation for women and children in Philadelphia, offering as well to stable and train horses. The business did not go well. In December 1822 he described himself as "the father of a family who is in great trouble, with a wife who is ill and about to be confined; children, two of whom are ill, all including himself without the indispensable necessities at this season of the year."[51]

Other future Vine and Olive participants tried to make a living by teaching, writing, or publishing. But according to some accounts, their efforts were not always appreciated. Some French travelers blamed capitalism: America's all-consuming love of money undermined the development of a cultural elite, a decent system of education, and, above all, "that refinement of taste . . . which was the soil necessary to nourish intellectual and artistic excellence."[52] Texier de la Pommeraye, self-described "chief of the general staff of the army of France," wrote a grammar textbook but had to borrow money to have it printed.[53] Garnier des Saintes wrote (in French) a two-volume, thousand-page work titled *Les Emerides de Socrates* and advertised it for sale in *L'Abeille* for three dollars for subscribers and five dollars for the general public.[54] Edouard de Montulé, a former Napoleonic officer touring America in 1817, met Garnier at his home on the Ohio River and had a chance to read "a few pages" of this "entirely philo-sophical" book. He found it "well thought out" and "admirably written," al-though somewhat marred by "prolixity"—not exactly the kind of work likely to appeal to a large audience.[55] Under the direction of Jean-Simon Chaudron, the struggling *L'Abeille* provided employment for a number of literary-minded exiles. The exiled journalist Dirat was invited to write a column, and Pierre Pagaud, a peddler by trade, was ostensibly taken on as a printer (although he seems to have spent most of his time on suspicious voyages between France and the United States during this period).[56] *L'Abeille* itself barely scraped by, ceasing publication in mid-1817 before being resuscitated by a subsidy from Joseph Bonaparte.[57] The refugees who became educators seem to have achieved greater success.[58]

Some of the more promising schemes concocted by the exiles involved speculation in land. Joseph Bonaparte purchased a magnificent estate in New Jersey, not far from Philadelphia—as well as several outlying properties in which to house his mistresses. Soon after arriving in America, Réal and Marshal Grouchy also investigated the possibility of buying land in a colony being set up in upstate New York for French exiles by James LeRay de Chaumont, a speculator of French origin who had already founded one such establishment, Asylum, in the 1790s.[59] Réal was impressed and purchased 1,760 acres there.[60] Other refugees, no doubt inspired by Enlightenment literature extolling the American wilderness, set their sights on more distant lands. Soon after his arrival in the United States (in late February or early March 1816), General Clausel was described as "waiting for the good season" to settle on the banks of the Ohio.[61] At the same time, the ostentatiously savant Lakanal announced his resolution to conduct "geological research" in the West.[62] By May he had arrived in the Ohio Valley and acquired an estate on the Kentucky side of the river, opposite from the viticultural colony of Vevay, founded ten years earlier by Swiss immigrants. In identical letters, the proud pioneer announced his new situation to both Jefferson and Madison, proclaiming his intention to balance agricultural with literary pursuits. He would ultimately fulfill neither, notably failing to produce the comprehensive history of the United States of which he boasted in his letter.[63] A more successful "westerner" was Lecoq de Marcelay. An elderly man who came to America from Nantes in 1815 with his wife, daughter, and son, Lecoq established himself in Louisville where his principal activities concerned trade and land speculation.[64] In early 1817 he even tried to interest Stephen Girard in one of his schemes, effusively detailing the satisfaction the stingy plutocrat would feel at seeing "a budding Stephentown or

Girardville" springing up on the banks of the Ohio or Mississippi.[65] Although Girard did not take the bait, the idea of a French settlement in the West would soon capture the imagination of the expatriates and, more importantly, win the support of the U.S. Congress.

A Field of Common Repose

In the 22 August 1816 issue of *L'Abeille,* an anonymous article appeared urging the exiles to join together to establish a community of their own. While thanking America for its hospitality and acknowledging the "superiority" of its "republican institutions" over those of "old and degraded Europe," the author warned of dangers that lay ahead. Without taking on a grand new challenge that would end their idleness, the exiles would fall into the pernicious French habits of "inconstancy" and "turbulence"—and eventually wear out their welcome. Without a "homeland to cherish," they would be like the "children of Israel," condemned to wander in a strange land. For readers inculcated with the Enlightenment's ethos of social utility or familiar with the Biblical allusion, this cautionary picture was well calculated to spur them to action. Only by "going together, hand in hand, into a mild region to found a new Thebaide," the author concluded, could the exiles "prove themselves excellent citizens of a happy republic." The region he had in mind was the vast area between the Ohio, Mississippi, and Natchez rivers. Healthy, well-watered, fertile, and temperate, this area was additionally recommendable, the author assured, because it "was still without inhabitants." In this desert paradise, the French exiles would "implant their mores, usages, [and] customs." Far from cities—"political sodoms" where "corruption forges the chains of enslavement"—the exiles would be reborn as "republicans of the New World."[66]

Although the author of this article is unknown, the image of harmonious rustic community he sought to evoke was rooted in familiar cultural soil—to wit, Rousseauist notions associating moral regeneration with a return to nature and physiocratic ideas extolling the benefits to society of the agricultural life—likely to have appealed to educated French readers in the early nineteenth century.[67] Moreover, the article published in *L'Abeille* did not represent the first time the Enlightenment's vision of America had captured the imagination of French immigrants. In 1816 New Atlantic France could look back to the precedent of several agricultural colonies—Gallipolis, Asylum, and Vevay—that had been founded by previous waves of French (or Francophone) expatriates.[68] Gallipolis was the first of these settlements. Founded in Ohio in 1790 under the leadership of the Marquis de Lezay-Marnesia, Gallipolis (City of the Gauls) soon counted a population of about a thousand, But composed almost exclusively of middle- and upper-class members, the top-heavy colony suffered from a lack of laborers and competent farmers. By 1795 fewer than one hundred of the original French settlers were left. By 1807 only one remained—probably future Vine and Olive grantee Pierre Legris Belleisle, a former magistrate in a Norman commercial court.[69] A second French colony was established in Pennsylvania in 1793. Known as Asylum, it was briefly home to liberal royalists—courtiers, noble officers, and refractory clergy of both sexes—who had fled to America from the excesses of the Revolution. Although counting illustrious inhabitants like the Viscount de Noailles (from ancient nobility), Marquis Omer Talon (of esteemed magisterial lineage), and Aristide du Petit-Thouars (a celebrated naval officer), the settlement broke up soon after Napoleon's rise to power made it possible for these sorts of people to return to France.[70] The final colony, Vevay, was founded in Indiana in 1805 by French-speaking peasants from the Vaud, a wine-growing Swiss canton. Conceived as a viticultural enterprise, the town flourished. By 1816 it contained 75 dwellings, 8 stores, 3 taverns, 31 mechanics, 2 lawyers, 2 physicians, a carding machine, and even a 300-volume library.[71] By the fall of 1818 Vevay could boast of "prosperous vines" and an "excellent" harvest.[72] It, more than Gallipolis or Asylum, would serve as the model for the colonial association that began to take shape in Philadelphia following *L'Abeille*'s appeal of 22 August 1816.

Throughout the summer and fall of 1816, Chaudron devoted the pages of *L'Abeille* to publicizing the idea of a new French colony in the West. Thanks to its wide-ranging circulation and its network of subscription agents (in Montreal, Boston, New York, Philadelphia, Baltimore, Norfolk, Richmond, Charleston, New Orleans, and Saint Louis), the newspaper was an ideal instrument for reaching the French diaspora in America and beyond. In the issue of 14 November 1816, readers learned that a "Colonial Society" composed of "some of the most enlightened men of the century" had been formed in Philadelphia with the aim of "forming an establishment on the banks of the Ohio or Mississippi." A number of "naturalists, agriculturalists, manufacturers, artists, and artisans" had already signed on to the project, and commissioners had been chosen to "visit the countries of the West and there identify an expanse of land sufficient for the importance of the enterprise." This enterprise, readers were informed, would consist primarily in the cultivation of the vine and olive. All French interested in joining the society were asked to contact the former consul of Bordeaux, William Lee, now vice president of the society, or Nicholas-Simon Parmentier, its secretary.[73]

In the issue of 23 January 1817, Chaudron described in glowing terms the progress of the venture. More than a hundred French exiles in America had become shareholders in what was now being referred to as the Colonial Society of French Emigrants. More encouraging still, letters had arrived from France and Belgium that augured "an entire success." As soon as a suitable site could be found, assured Chaudron, more than three hundred individuals—"men of all mechanical professions, proprietors, laborers, [and] manufacturers"—would leave Europe for the settlement, contributing to it all their "pecuniary means and industry." Planted with vine, olive, silk, and cotton, the flourishing new community would "console the refugees for their expatriation and reward their adoptive homeland for its noble hospitality."[74] Word of Vine and Olive even reached such unlikely places as the remote French colony of Guyana and the Paris offices of the Bourbon war minister Gouvion Saint-Cyr, who reportedly exclaimed: "My goodness! I am happy to let whoever is discontent with life here go to Mobile."[75]

Although the correspondence and records kept by the society have been lost or destroyed, it is possible to trace its early organizational activities through the glowing progress reports published regularly in L'Abeille. The first meeting for which an account survives took place in October 1816 under the chairmanship of Garnier des Saintes. After approving the minutes of the previous meeting, the assembly was treated to a letter from Lakanal, then residing in Kentucky. In it, Lakanal expressed his desire to become a citizen of "Demopolis," thereby coining the name that would be given to the principal town of the Vine and Olive settlement. Then Pénières, previously chosen as one of the society's "exploring commissioners," informed the assembly of his imminent departure for the "South West." He was sent off with the good wishes of the society, promises that his expenses would be reimbursed, and instructions to maintain a regular correspondence with the society. In case Pénières could not complete his mission before Congress adjourned on 4 March 1817, the assembly resolved to ask William Lee to conduct parallel research in the Land Office in Washington to find a suitable tract for which the society might submit a collective petition. This, it was decided, was to be drafted by a "permanent bureau" composed of Garnier, Parmentier, Dirat, and Joseph Martin du Columbier (a Philadelphia-based Domingan physician), in conjunction with the politically savvy and well-connected Lee. The assembly recognized that the success of the venture would "depend entirely on the terms that the government of this happy country would be willing to grant to unfortunates in search of a homeland."[76] These terms would be most generous indeed.

Another meeting was held on 2 January 1817, under the chairmanship of Lee, still vice president of the society. After approving the minutes, the assembly considered several letters, including one from an inhabitant of Louisville, Kentucky (probably the Francophile F. S. Brown mentioned by Pickett in his classic account of the Vine and Olive colony[77]) that recommended that the society ask for a grant in the territory recently conquered from the Choctaw and Creek Indians, between the Mississippi and Tombigbee rivers, in what would become the state of Alabama. A long discussion ensued. Advocates of the Tombigbee option assured the assembly that it was a "healthy country, enjoying a temperate climate," easily accessible by land and sea, and not far from the "great establishments of the Tennessee and New Orleans." It had the additional advantage of being situated near a "navigable river"—a river, the assembly was told, "whose amelioration already entered into the forward-looking and benevolent views" of the government. Eager to gain possession of lands in such a desirable location, the assembly agreed to abandon its initial inclination for the Ohio Valley and instead ask Congress for a concession—"upon the most advantageous conditions"—on either bank of the Tombigbee. The permanent bureau, now minus Garnier who had moved to Kentucky, was directed to draft an appropriate petition in collaboration with Lee. The assembly concluded its meeting by resolving to ask Thomas Jefferson, "the Sage of Monticello," to provide the society with a "social pact"—in effect a particular constitution that would not only give a foundation to the "local laws" of the new community, but also serve as a "monument to the centuries."[78]

This odd démarche—akin to the Poles' invitation to Jean-Jacques Rousseau in 1773 to draw up a constitution for their state (Rousseau accepted)—has been cited as evidence of the French exiles' incomprehension of the American political system.[79] Thomas Jefferson naturally saw the impossibility of establishing separate constitutions for distinct communities within the American republic and had to turn down their request. He explained his reasons for declining to William Lee. "There are some preliminary questions . . . which are particularly for their own consideration. Is it proposed that this shall be a separate state? Or a county of a state? Or a mere voluntary association, as those of the Quakers, Dunkers, Menonites? A separate state it cannot be because, from the tract it asks, it would not be of more than 20 miles square, and in established new states, regard is had to a certain degree of equality in size. If it is to be a county of a state, it cannot be governed by its own laws, but must be subject to those of the state of which it is a part. If merely a voluntary association, the submission of its members will be merely voluntary also, as no act of coercion would be permitted by the general law."[80] Could the exiles, many of whom had already lived for decades in the United States, have really been so ignorant of American constitutional government? Did the more recent arrivals really find the American political system so different from that which they had known in republican France? In fact, the monarchical regime of privilege (distinct laws creating and determining the rights of corporate bodies such as provinces, cities, and guilds) had been abolished at the outset of the French Revolution and replaced, as in America, by a single constitution that applied uniformly to all France. Familiar with the principles of undivided republican government, it is hard to believe that the exiles could have really expected Jefferson to provide them with a constitution of their own. What then were they really after in making their unorthodox request?

Rather than revealing their ignorance of the American system of government, the exiles' approach to Jefferson shows, on the contrary, a great deal of political savvy.[81] It allowed them to link the great man's name to their venture. The fact that he had been consulted on the organization of the colony was trumpeted not only in the pages of *L'Abeille* but also noted in the pages of English-language newspapers such as the influential *Niles' Weekly Register* and *National Intelligencer.* Legitimated by the public association of Jefferson with the project, as well as attracting substantial public curiosity in its own right, the Vine and Olive venture began to draw journalistic comment—much of it positive. The press campaign was just the most visible part of the broader effort to win support for the project.

More than favorable reports in the nation's newspapers, what would ultimately prove decisive in deciding the fate of the proposed settlement would be the support it enjoyed in Congress. To this end, the society launched a major lobbying effort facilitated and probably masterminded by William Lee. Whether undertaken directly by himself or arranged through his good offices, critical power brokers—the former president Thomas Jefferson, Pres. James Madison, Secretary of State James Monroe, Speaker of the House Henry Clay, Gen. Andrew Jackson, and William Pickering—were contacted about the project and urged to use their influence on its behalf.[82] Thanks to these lobbying efforts, Chaudron was able to report as early as January 1817 that "all appearances are in favor of our national establishment."[83]

The intensive lobbying succeeded in having the society's petition placed on the congressional agenda, no small feat given the flurry of activity that attended the final month of the fourteenth Congress and the Madison administration. The Senate's Committee on Public Lands presented a bill to grant lands to the French expatriates on 10 February 1817.[84] After several amendments, which are unfortunately unspecified in the scant congressional records for the period, the bill was passed on 21 February by a large majority and reported to the House the same day.[85] Six days later the House began to debate the measure, now described as an act "disposing of a tract of land, to embrace four townships, on favorable terms to the emigrants, to enable them successfully to introduce the cultivation of the vine and olive, etc." Although the lack of detailed accounts makes it difficult to reconstruct what appears to have been a heated discussion, the normally laconic *Debates and Proceedings in the Congress of the United States* found the fireworks impressive enough to summarize what it termed a "considerable debate." Opponents of the bill, led by Mr. King of New York (a notoriously Anglophile federalist), argued that the grant would fall prey to speculation and deprive the government of revenue it could expect were the land to be sold to the public in the ordinary way. The supporters of the measure—spearheaded by the Francophile republican Henry Clay, Speaker of the House—countered these objections with a veritable barrage of arguments. The "general principles of hospitality," the "advantages of the particular culture proposed to be introduced," the "advantages which would accrue to the United States from the introduction of so much industry and such improvement into [its] midst," and the resulting increase in the value of the "public lands" thus improved—all these motives were marshaled on behalf of the bill. On a vote that echoed the sharp divisions between pro-English federalists and pro-French republicans during the 1790s, the bill, slightly amended, passed by a "large majority."[86]

The resulting "Act to set apart and dispose of certain public lands, for the encouragement of the cultivation of the vine and olive" was signed into law by President Madison on 3 March 1817, his last day in office. It authorized the society to select for itself four contiguous townships located in the so-called Creek Cession, the lands conquered by Andrew Jackson from the Creek Indians in 1814. Thus designated, this expanse of land, totaling 144 square miles or slightly more than 92,000 acres, was to be taken out of the public domain and "reserved from public and private sale." This was significant not only because it gave the exiles first pick of the valuable lands within the cession before they were made available at auction to the general public, but also because it exempted the grant from the general laws on public lands. In return for these favorable considerations, the society was bound, as a collectivity, by several requirements. First, its membership had to equal or surpass the number of half sections in the four townships: 288. Second, no individual could be issued a patent for more than 640 acres. And finally, a certain amount of the land—as determined by a contract to be negotiated between the secretary of the treasury and the society—had to be devoted to the "cultivation of the vine, and other vegetable productions," as appeared "reasonable." Only after a term of fourteen years, should these conditions be met, was the society to pay the United States government anything. At $2.00 per acre, the total bill (to be paid in a single lump sum) would come to approximately $184,000. Given the rate at which land values in the area were increasing during the period 1817 to 1819, the height of Alabama Fever, and the fourteen-year grace period during which the French were expected to have begun reaping a handsome reward from their desirable Mediterranean products, the grant was almost a free gift.

Why Did Congress Make the Grant?

This act of congressional generosity did not go unnoticed. Despite the popularity of the French exiles, the sympathy their plight evoked, and the powerful political support they enjoyed, Congress's munificence raised hackles as well as eyebrows. As early as 1816, in the midst of *L'Abeille's* publicity campaign, questions were already being raised about the fitness of the French to undertake a colonial settlement. In its issue of 19 November 1816, the Philadelphia *Aurora* suggested that the recent exiles—"persons of cultivated minds, accustomed to the refinements and social enjoyments of the most polished nation in Europe"—would not easily support "the privations, labor, and exposure of the western world." "How will those aged men of letters, those men accustomed to the pursuits of philosophy in the well-furnished cabinets," the article's anonymous author asked, "learn to fell trees, to square them into timbers, to raise the log house, level the floor, clear the corn patch?" Rather than "seek seclusion in the wilderness," the author concluded, the exiles ought to establish a settlement near Philadelphia.[87] The *Columbian Centinel* of Boston expressed similar doubts. While applauding the agricultural efforts of Swiss and German settlers—"the right sort of emigrants"—the paper forecast the quick failure of the French colony. It gloated that the exiles would find that "something very different from fiddling, dancing and book reading" was required to "subdue a wilderness." "Made up of Princes, Generals, Legislators, Counts, school masters, and scholars—bred in the refinements of luxury and many of them advanced in years, we are confident they will find themselves better qualified to shine in a Court in Paris than in a forest in Indiana; to set a battalion in array in the garden of the Tuilleries or regulate the etiquette of a ballroom than to level trees, grub up roots, and open the earth for the reception of seeds; and that finding their sylvan anticipations wholly disappointed, on the first promulgation of an act of general amnesty and grace by the Bourbons, they will pack up stakes, joyfully recross the Atlantic, and embrace with rapture the enjoyments of their beloved Paris."[88] In spite of the author's Francophobia and distortion of the sociopolitical character of the exiles—as former revolutionary generals and politicians, they could hardly be described as courtiers—his prediction would turn out to be reasonably accurate.

More serious concerns were raised as the development of the colony progressed. In a letter to the editor of the *Huntsville Republican,* published in the issue of 28 October 1817, one inhabitant of the Alabama Territory denounced the "special and peculiar privileges" Congress had granted the exiles. "While American citizens with their little hard earned gains are compelled to go into the market, not only in competition with one another, but also with foreign capitalists of immense wealth (and many French emigrants are said to possess this), we very naturally inquire why these latter have peculiar preferences to favorite selections."[89] In a subsequent letter to the editor, published in the 4 April 1818 issue of the *Alabama Republican,* this same critic detailed the excessive advantages Congress had given the French. By "inconsiderately granting to a company of foreigners 92,000 acres of the *choicest selections*" in the territory, the government was effectively "giving away" a tract presently worth more than $1 million on the open market. Particularly galling was the fact that, in a region where good town sites were scarce, the French had been allowed to select "the most eligible situation for a town on the waters of the Tombeckbee river." Far from fulfilling the agricultural conditions of the grant, predicted the author, "French speculators" would sell their town lots to Americans "at an incredible price." There would be no "extensive vineyards," just "cotton fields."[90]

Several months later *Niles' Weekly Register* added its influential voice to the growing chorus of criticism. In a scathing front-page article, Hezekiah Niles branded the grant one of the most "splendid fooleries" ever inflicted upon the American people. Given the "license of selection" the emigrants had enjoyed in their choice of land, the congressional grant was "much better than a mere gratuity." By now worth at least $2 million, he asserted, the tract had already fallen prey to speculation. In addition to the familiar charges of financial malfeasance, Niles added a new criticism. As a "large and compact settlement of emigrants," the colony threatened the "national character" of the United States by introducing "manners and prejudices . . . repugnant to our rules and notions of right." The only good immigrants, Niles asserted, were those who renounced their former culture, entered the "common stock," and became "Americans." It was too late to revoke the ill-considered law of 3 March 1817, but a "rigid" congressional inquiry was necessary to determine if the French were adhering to its letter and spirit.[91]

Given the serious public objections raised against Vine and Olive, the question arises of why Congress was willing to run such a political risk for the benefit of several hundred French immigrants. The emotional and ideological reasons for its act of generosity—hospitality, the influence of Lafayette and other patrons of the exiles, and sympathy for fellow republicans in distress—are not sufficient to explain congressional largess. Nor do Congress's economic calculations—to plant the seeds of a domestic wine industry that would free the United States from its dependence on the productions of Europe—fully explain its actions. In addition to these considerations, a set of strategic concerns underlay the act of 3 March 1817. These concerns—to consolidate the westward expansion of the Union, resolve in a satisfactory manner the borderland conflict with Spain, and remedy the grave military weaknesses revealed during the War of 1812 with England—intersected to form one great imperative: to secure America's hold on the Gulf Coast, especially Spanish Florida. In itself, this remote and disease-plagued region was, in the estimation of Secretary of States Monroe, "comparatively nothing." But if occupied by a hostile naval power, he continued, it was "of the highest importance." "Commanding the Gulph [sic] of Mexico, and all its waters, including the Mississippi with its branches, and the streams emptying into the Mobile, a vast proportion of the most fertile and productive parts of this Union, on which the navigation and commerce so essentially depend, would be subject to its annoyance, not to mention its influence on the Creeks and other neighbouring Indians."[92] If Florida fell into the hands of a hostile nation, frontier settlements from Georgia to Louisiana would find themselves even more exposed to attack by Indians and escaped slaves—who already had a long tradition of conflict with the land-hungry Anglo-American pioneers. More critically, an enemy naval power could use its harbors to maintain a close blockade of New Orleans, the only port through which farmers in the Mississippi and Ohio Valleys could profitably export their productions, thereby strangling the economies of the trans-Appalachian United States. American statesmen feared that if this transpired, it would only be a matter of time before the suffering westerners submitted to the power controlling their access to the sea. Until the country's vulnerable Gulf flank was secure, the federal government's hold on the West would remain shaky and the Union itself face the specter of dissolution.[93]

Only two years before Congress made the Vine and Olive grant, the War of 1812 had underlined the dangers foreign control of this strategic sector posed to the United States.[94] Reinforced by seasoned troops released for American service by the end of the war with Napoleon, the British commander Admiral Cochrane planned a southern campaign for 1814 that, he hoped, would bring the United States to its knees. As British-backed Indians and escaped slaves waged guerilla warfare against American settlements from the sanctuary of Spanish Florida, amphibious forces would launch a series of surprise attacks against the Gulf ports culminating in the capture of New Orleans and the closing of the Mississippi River. The operation began in the summer of 1814 when British military advisers were landed in Florida with the acquiescence of local Spanish authorities. Equipped with thousands of modern firearms and amply supplied by sea from Jamaica and the Bahamas, this group of about a hundred Royal Marines led by Maj. Edward Nicolls helped organize a formidable guerilla army of Indians and blacks. Their raids spread terror among the American inhabitants of Georgia and the Mississippi Territory. The mere existence of this force not only encouraged American-held slaves to escape to Florida but also fed rumors of the imminent uprising of slaves throughout the Gulf South. The raiding, runaways, and rumors created a climate of near-hysteria that forced the United States to garrison the frontier with thousands of troops. For a small investment of men and resources, the British had managed to tie down a large part of the American army in the South.

Despite the success of these guerilla operations, the second part of the British campaign did not go as planned. Trouble began when an unexpectedly large American garrison of regulars beat off the British attack against Mobile, forcing Cochrane to attempt a direct amphibious assault on New Orleans without the benefit of a nearby port from which to launch the operation. The story of the resulting Battle of New Orleans is well known. Arriving in the nearly un-defended city only days before the British expeditionary force, General Jackson hastily assembled an army of regulars, militia, friendly Indians, Colonel Savary's Battalion of Free Men of Color and other free-black militia units, a contingent of Barataria pirates under Jean Lafitte, Creoles, and even French citizens—including at least one future Vine and Olive member[95]—and prepared defensive positions. Given the multiplicity of waterborne approaches to the city and the mobility of the British expeditionary force, this was no small task. Indeed, in

December 1814 the British were able to move their main assault force to within several miles of the city itself, largely undetected by the Americans. Here, however, they committed a critical error by launching a frontal assault on the main American line of defense. Executed on 8 January 1815, the attack caused crippling casualties to the British, who were forced to withdraw. Thanks to the steadiness of his ragtag army, the bad judgment of the British commander, and good luck, Jackson had saved New Orleans, allowing the United States to claim victory in the War of 1812. But thoughtful observers—such as John Quincy Adams, who urged Americans "to remember more studiously than our triumphs" the "defeats and disasters" of the conflict—understood that the war had been a close-run thing.

Along with crash programs of coastal fortification and road building, the creation of the Vine and Olive colony was intended to help shore up America's Gulf flank, whose vulnerability had been revealed by the recent war. One of the strategic purposes of the settlement—composed, in principle, of Napoleonic veterans—was to act as a military barrier against cross-border raids like those that had been mounted by the British-backed guerillas from their bases in Spanish Florida. This was not merely a preventive measure, adopted in case a new war should break out, but also a response to the fact that hostilities had not ceased in the Southeast even after the signature of the Treaty of Ghent became known. When the British expeditionary force in the Gulf withdrew in June 1815, its commanders in Florida—notably Major Nicolls—promised that England would never abandon the Indians and escaped slaves it had recruited during the war. Encouraged by these assurances (later repudiated by the government in London) and furnished from stores the departing British officers left behind, the guerillas continued to launch raids into the United States from their principal base in Spanish Florida. Known to the Americans as Negro Fort, this fortification on the Apalachicola River at Prospect Bluff was not only surrounded by swampland and armed with a daunting array of cannon but also situated within Spanish territory. It therefore lay across an international boundary, which should have sheltered it from American reprisals. Nonetheless, pressure from southern slaveholders—worried that the fort presented a continual inducement to their slaves to escape or, worse, rise up in insurrection—finally forced the United States government to act. After an ultimatum to the Spanish military commander at Pensacola failed to spur the Spaniards to action, General Jackson ordered American forces to cross the border and attack it.[96] Negro Fort was destroyed on 27 July 1816 by a lucky cannon-shot from a United States gunboat.[97]

The demise of the Negro Fort did not end hostilities in the Southeast. Vicious cross-border raiding—in effect, an undeclared guerilla war—continued throughout 1817 and 1818.[98] The violence touched the entire Southeast, including the new territory of Alabama, where Governor Bibb mobilized part of the militia, "the regular troops being inadequate to afford the necessary protection."[99] It is not clear if the militia company of the Vine and Olive colony led by Captain Lajoinie, Lieutenant Butaud, and Enseign Roudet participated in these operations.[100] The settlement was placed on a war footing in 1818, however, when a party of Indians passed nearby.[101] Although the role it actually played in frontier defense could not have been great, the implantation of a colony of experienced soldiers in this newly acquired border zone was a step toward implementing Jackson's recommendation to Monroe that the area be peopled with settlers "competent to its defense."[102]

In addition to providing a barrier to raids mounted from Spanish territory against American frontier settlements, Vine and Olive also played a role in ensuring that the western interior of the country would have access to the Gulf of Mexico, even in the event of renewed war with Britain and naval blockade. The recent conflict had illustrated all too clearly the West's dependence on the vulnerable port of New Orleans. Although Jackson's defense of that city had saved the Union from a severe trial, sober statesmen could imagine the catastrophic consequences likely to have ensued had the British attack been successful. One overarching lesson emerged from this brush with disaster: it was imperative to obtain additional Gulf ports with good riverine access to the interior. Fortunately for them, the Americans had acquired such a port during the war with Britain: Mobile. Having seized it from Spain in April 1813—on the grounds that that country was too weak (or simply disinclined) to prevent the British from occupying it—the United States unilaterally annexed it.[103] The American government considered possession of the port vital to the demographic and economic development of the interior areas that had just been opened to American settlement by the Creek Cession, as well as to the security and prosperity of New Orleans and the vast territories that depended upon it for their livelihood.

As it had been taken by an act of naked military aggression, however, no country in the world recognized American sovereignty over the city and its hinterland.[104] One of Congress's probable reasons for settling the French exiles on a substantial tract only a hundred miles upriver from the disputed city was to solidify the dubious American claim to the territory—to create "facts on the ground," as it were. The Spanish government certainly saw the Vine and Olive colony in this light. Its ambassador in Paris, the Duke de Fernán Núñez, tried to associate the French government with his king's protest against the French settlement. First, he claimed that it deserved to be opposed because it was an "establishment [that] obviously announces the [American] design of remaining in possession of West Florida." The ambassador recognized that the government-sponsored influx of French settlers into the lands of the Creek Cession signaled the determination of the United States to retain possession of Mobile. Moreover, the character of the grantees raised the gravest suspicions. For the most part Bonapartists and revolutionaries, they were "all known for their principles, subversive of the social order, and their aversion for the august Bourbon house." Spain "could not look indifferently upon . . . a colony composed of such elements in the neighborhood of a country stolen from Spain, bordering on Spanish possessions, and on the shores of the Gulf of Mexico."[105] To make matters worse, the Vine and Olive colony was situated in territory that had only recently been part of Spanish West Florida, territory that the Spanish government still coveted. Taking advantage of the "ruinous war" into which the French Revolution had plunged Spain, the United States had acquired through the Treaty of San Lorenzo (1795) the "best lands" of the province, situated on the Tombigbee, Pearl, and Alabama rivers. Although the Spanish Cabinet realized that there was no prospect of regaining this vast tract of territory in the near future, perhaps dramatic changes on the international diplomatic scene might one day reverse Spain's present impotence.[106]

Spanish remonstrations to the Americans fell on deaf ears. Committed to achieving their broader strategic goal, the opening of a second Gulf port, American planners pushed forward the fortification of Mobile and even contemplated constructing a network of canals to link the city with the Mississippi-Ohio-Tennessee river system.[107] Situated on the high ground commanding the confluence of the Tombigbee and Black Warrior rivers, the Vine and Olive colony controlled an important choke point along the projected waterway. Although the state of Alabama began surveying operations in 1819 in preparation for the canal, the Tennessee-Tombigbee Waterway would not be opened until 1984.[108]

Acquiring a second port on the Gulf—especially if it required the construction of a vast system of canals to connect it with the great waterways of the interior—was a roundabout and expensive way of freeing the West from its dependence on the sole port of New Orleans. Why did the United States pursue such a circuitous path toward this strategic end when a simpler, more immediate, and less costly solution lay in the acquisition of Florida from Spain?

Although a current of opinion headed by General Jackson demanded the out-right conquest of the province, the cooler heads of the Monroe administration prevailed. While sure to overwhelm the feeble Spanish garrison, explained John Quincy Adams, an invasion of Florida would "plunge us into a new contest with [England]."[109] Invaluable to the United States in the event of renewed hostilities with Britain, Florida was worth almost any price to the Americans—except a new war with that formidable naval power. This then was the challenge facing the United States government: to acquire Florida from Spain without provoking war with England, a challenge that could only be accomplished across a baize-covered table, not on a battlefield.

Therefore, as it began to move ahead with plans to improve the port of Mobile, the United States government entered into negotiations with Spain for the purchase of her strategically priceless—but economically stagnant and mili-tarily indefensible—colony. Keenly aware of the great value the Americans attached to Florida, however, the Spanish refused to trade it for mere gold. They drove a much harder bargain. If the Americans wanted Florida, they would have to relinquish in favor of Spain their claim to all lands west of the Mississippi, including the hotly contested province of Texas. This demand—equivalent to a renunciation of the Louisiana Purchase (which Spain had never recognized) and an end to the westward expansion of the country—was too much for the Americans to accept. By early 1817 the negotiations had clearly reached a deadlock. "Here we are about as we were ten years ago," grumbled Rufus King on 23 February.[110] Less than two weeks later, in this "thickening atmosphere" of diplomatic stalemate over Florida, Congress approved the Vine and Olive grant.[111]

Reassessed in this context, it becomes clear that the French settlement on the Tombigbee was intended to put additional pressure on Spain to resume nego-tiations for the sale of Florida. By encouraging settlement in the Gulf region, the American government hoped not only to solidify its hold on the area but also to demonstrate to Spain that the prevailing demographic trends made it inevitable that the United States would eventually absorb Florida. By making it see the writing on the wall, the Americans hoped to convince the Spanish government to sell Florida while it still could. President-elect Monroe was the first to formulate the idea that Spanish Florida could be obtained through the weight of demography alone. He explained this strategy at the end of 1816 in an important letter to the military commander in the South, General Jackson. "In extending our settlements along the Mississippi and toward the Mobile, . . . great strength will be added to our union in quarters where it is most wanted.

As soon as our population gains a decided preponderance in these regions, East Florida will hardly be considered by Spain as part of her dominions, and no other power would accept it from her as a gift. Our attitude will daily become more imposing on all the Spanish dominions, and indeed on those of other powers in the neighboring islands. If it keeps them in good order in our relations with them, that alone will be an important consequence."[112] Although often at odds with Monroe over Gulf policy, Jackson approved wholeheartedly of these views and in his response reiterated the need to strengthen the frontier "by a permanent settlement of all the lands acquired from the Creek Indians."[113] Congress's decision to approve the society's petition for lands may be understood as an expression of this demographic approach to the problem of Spanish Florida. Promising the rapid creation of a compact settlement composed partly of French soldiers, as well as holding out the possibility of attracting additional refugees from Bourbon France and British-held Quebec, the act of 3 March 1817 was part of the postwar effort to populate the Spanish-American frontier.[114] Once the Gulf South was properly settled and fortified, Andrew Jackson predicted, "all Europe will cease to look at it with an eye to conquest" and the United States would, at long last, enjoy "permanent security."[115]

Preparing to Move South

These strategic concerns were far from the minds of the emigrants as they readied themselves for the move south. Under the direction of Clausel and Lefebvre-Desnouettes, who effectively assumed leadership of the society in the months following the passage of the act, preparations progressed rapidly. A new group of commissioner-explorers and an advance party of colonists was dispatched, this time to the site of the grant itself. There they were to conduct a survey of the terrain and make preparations for settlement.[116] Headed by Parmentier, the group of about twenty set sail from Philadelphia in a small chartered schooner, the *McDonough,* in late April or early May.[117] After an uneventful voyage whose monotony was only broken by grounding at the entrance to Mobile Bay, the party arrived at the port after a one-month voyage. There they were welcomed by public officials and leading citizens of the town, who held a banquet in their honor and invited them into the "first houses" of the city. The tax collector of the port, Addin Lewis, generously offered to transport the French upriver in his revenue cutter. They accepted and several days later departed. During their rather long journey, Parmentier and his companions stopped at the few settlements that then existed along the river: Fort Stoddard, Fort Montgomery, and the small town of Saint Stephens, where they made contact with the leading Anglo-American citizens of the western Alabama territory. One of these, Judge Harry Toulmin, eventually became a patentee in the Vine and Olive colony. Another, Gen. Edmund Gaines, had scouted the area around the junction of the Tombigbee and Black Warrior rivers for the American military and confirmed that it was an excellent location for the colony. On 14 July the exploring party arrived at the site they had chosen for their town, a point of high land overlooking the Tombigbee River know as White Bluff. There they began to mark off the outlines of a town site and, in early August, informed the surveyor general that they were ready for an official survey.[118]

By midsummer, their encouraging reports detailing the site's many advantages —"fertility, healthfulness, and navigation"—convinced Clausel and Lefebvre-Desnouettes back in Philadelphia that the time was right to move the main body of colonists to the grant.[119] The generals purchased agricultural equipment and imported vine cuttings and olive seedlings from France. They also made arrangements with ship captains to carry the colonists from the East Coast around the tip of Florida to Mobile, from whence they would proceed upriver to their new home. It is difficult to retrace the emigrants' precise movements because they did not set out all at once, in a single body, but in stages. Some—like the former maid of Madame Lefebvre-Desnouettes, Léontine Desportes, who was suspected of acting as a liaison agent between Bonapartists in France and America—even traveled alone, taking passage as individuals on ships bound for Mobile.[120] And not all the colonists made the journey by sea. According to articles published in the major national papers, the summer of 1817 saw upward of a hundred French emigrants making their way to the Tombigbee grant through the Ohio Valley.[121] By the end of August, Clausel and Lefebvre-Desnouettes felt ready to make the trip themselves. Satisfied with their preparations and confident that they were leaving behind only a few unimportant loose ends to tie up, they sailed for Mobile on 27 August 1817.[122] Accompanying them were Capt. Victor Grouchy, eight other officers, two French women (one of whom was Clausel's relative, Madame Desmares), thirty German indentured laborers whose services the generals had purchased, and a cargo of supplies worth about three thousand dollars.[123] In their haste to depart and get established on the grant before the onset of winter, however, they made one serious mistake: they left unfinished the potentially divisive task of distributing allotments to the members of the society.

Hyde de Neuville observed the proceedings of the French exiles with great interest. Although considered a staunch reactionary, Hyde displayed more sympathy toward them than one might expect given their sharp political differences. Like them, Hyde had been a political refugee in the United States, where he had fled to avoid the excesses of the French Revolution. Because he had walked in their shoes, he "experienced a profound sentiment of commiseration for these French exiles who, like me, had been cast into this land by the tragic fluctuations of politics."[124] Thus, despite his reputation, his attitude toward them was clement. Whatever their schemes, whatever their pronouncements, Hyde never forgot that the refugees were "expatriated and unhappy," and that it was "pity" and "charity" that could alone "cure them" of their incorrect political sentiments.[125] If the more desperate among them wanted to "throw themselves into the abyss" by engaging in dangerous adventures, it was the duty of the French diplomatic corps to try to dissuade them. "The paternal hand of the King must be everywhere."[126] Instructing his consuls never to close their doors to the exiles, for whom the hope of forgiveness should ever be before their eyes, preserving them from the temptation of rash behavior, Hyde laid down the cardinal rule to guide their conduct toward these unfortunates: in a monarchy, there should be no "limits to royal clemency."[127]

Because he was so interested in seeing the exiles put aside their turbulent ways, return to the bosom of civilized society, and there redeem themselves by tranquil and productive habits, Hyde looked with favor on the Society for the Cultivation of the Vine and Olive. It would not only channel the restless energies of the exiles toward useful ends, Hyde hoped, but also generate commercial possibilities for French manufacturers. Enumerating all these benefits, Hyde in early 1817 even tried to convince his government to support the venture. "I would regard as an advantage the success of this project. I even believe that it should be supported. These individuals will bring their bad opinions to the banks of the Ohio, but they will also bring our tastes, our habits, and the commerce of France can only gain from establishments of this type. Moreover, in looking at it from a purely commercial point of view, I also see it as a good investment which would not involve considerable expense and would work toward a goal that all paternal governments should always strive for, to avoid reducing to total despair men to whom it has dealt only half-blows."[128] Richelieu believed that Hyde was being too optimistic. Although he recognized the benefits the Vine and Olive settlement might bring to French industry, he believed that various considerations—especially the "situation of Spanish America"—demanded that the government tread cautiously. "If an influential man formed around himself a body of refugees, founded with them a considerable establishment, and linked his views and projects to those of the insurgent colonies, it is prudent and appropriate to appear not to have lent any aid whatsoever to that establishment."[129] In fact, as Richelieu was dictating these words, the man destined to realize his fears—Gen. Charles Lallemand—had just embarked for America.

3

Double and Treble Treachery

The European diplomatic corps in the United States followed closely the activities of the French expatriates.[1] The French ambassador feared that, unless occupied in some wholesome enterprise like the Vine and Olive colony, the exiles might give in to the temptation of adventurous or revolutionary pursuits. Other European ambassadors shared his concern that men such as Clausel, Lefebvre-Desnouettes, and the Lallemands would not meekly accept their banishment and settle into inconspicuous new lives in America. Mindful of the abundant opportunities for mischief presented by the troubles of Spanish America, the diplomats found it hard to imagine that such desperate and capable men as these would refrain from joining the fray. Lending their swords to the cause of Latin American independence—or the more unsavory enterprises that cloaked their true nature in its banner—would be simple since, by 1815 the United States had become the headquarters, arsenal, and sanctuary for blows against Spain's crumbling empire. In American seaports, reported Hyde de Neuville, representatives of the insurgency "readily found sailors and adventurers . . . to cruise under the insurgent flag against the Spanish royalists." "It is of the utmost importance," he urged, "to find out exactly what is going on in this part of the world."[2] On the frontiers of Louisiana, he found the situation positively explosive. "There is talk of war and plans of conquest are afoot. The states of the West, above all, want to take up arms; everyone sees Mexico as a new promised land."[3] To the diplomats of the Old World, the prospect that Spain's venerable American empire might be replaced by a confederation of hostile republics was bad enough. That the Bonapartists might bend the Latin American revolutions to their own ends conjured up visions almost too terrible for these sentinels of legitimacy to contemplate. "The revolution of America is the revolution of Europe," declared the Spanish government in an official communiqué to the great powers of Europe. "To complete it, all that remains is for the Bonaparte family to enter directly into its machinations."[4]

The "New Algiers"

The conflict in Spanish America attracted to the United States an international community of revolutionaries, mercenaries, and scoundrels whose plots and exploits threatened to upset the delicate calculations and negotiations of the established powers as they maneuvered to gain an advantage from the breakup of Spain's empire.[5] The Concert of Europe would have preferred to restrict the scramble to pick up the pieces to its own exclusive membership, but this was not to be. The end of both the Napoleonic Wars in Europe and the conflict between Great Britain and the United States in North America swelled the ranks of this shifting population of "adventurers of all nations" and, if anything, increased their desperation.[6] In the postrevolutionary and postwar world, the United States—with the exception of Haiti, the world's only remaining republic—had become the principal "rendezvous of all the enemies of government."[7]

While all the European governments instructed their diplomatic agents in the United States to keep close tabs on the activities of these people, those of France and Spain had special reason for concern. Within the ruling circles of Bourbon France, the presence of prominent Bonapartists among the international desperadoes gave rise to speculations of the wildest kind. To this was added another less evident cause for concern. Their political proclivities aside, the participation of so many renegade Frenchmen in the privateering and filibustering expeditions undertaken from American territory was a source of deep national embarrassment.[8] Renegades they might be, but Frenchmen they remained in spite of their crimes against the ruling dynasty. Although ardent monarchists like Hyde de Neuville would not have admitted it, the Revolution had triumphed in at least one way: a sense of national belonging transcending even the sharpest political differences had taken root, even in the most reactionary minds.[9]

For its part, the Spanish government felt the menace of these foreigners even more sharply than the French, for they posed a direct threat to Spain's tottering colonial authority. Don Luis de Onís, the Spanish ambassador to Washington during the critical period 1815–19, recalled that "increased associations of adventurers were immediately formed at various points of the Anglo-American territory to assist the malcontents of Spanish America.... Those who were proscribed and banished from the society of other European nations, vagabonds without the means of subsistence, or who were stimulated by the hope of amassing large fortunes in the rebellious provinces of our America, hastened to reinforce the auxiliary bodies that were organized in the United States to cooperate with the rebels."[10] Spanish officials viewed these European adventurers as vectors of the revolutionary contagion that was leading astray their American vassals. In a typical formulation of this widely held view, Jose Cienfuegos, the captain-general of Cuba, denounced the "impunity with which a multitude of French, English, and American adventurers introduce themselves into [our colonies]" and disseminate "false, seditious, and alarming ideas." Their activities, he claimed, were "one of the most powerful causes of the spread of insurrection in the Americas."[11] Although the military and ideological role of foreigners in the movements for Latin American independence is well documented, even if it is underemphasized in the scholarly literature, another contribution they made has been overlooked.[12] By providing a convenient scapegoat for the insurrection, they enabled the cabinet in Madrid to avoid acknowledging that its own policies were helping to foment discontent in the colonies.

Thanks to the tireless efforts of its agents in the United States to counter insurgent operations mounted from the sanctuary of that country, the Spanish government should have known just how simplistic this characterization of the international adventurers really was. Rare was the mercenary, privateer, or ideologue driven purely by republican sentiment. For most, the lines between political engagement, profit, and glory-seeking were blurred. Rather than forming a disciplined legion bound together by a shared ideological commitment, the international supporters of Latin American revolution formed a shifting population of individualistic men of action. Easily forging temporary alliances for specific projects that promised mutual benefits, they just as easily moved apart. They often betrayed each other, revealing information about each other's machinations to the spies and diplomats of the established powers in exchange for personal advantage. The masters of this game were the notorious Lafitte brothers, Jean and Pierre, citizens of France who had settled in New Orleans. Effortlessly fusing the occupations of insurgent privateer, smuggler, slave trader, pirate, and fence, they secretly served the cause of Spain (and possibly the United States as well) by informing upon the projects of their partners in revolution and crime—men who, not coincidentally, happened to be their business competitors.[13] Keeping abreast of the plots, alliances, and deceptions of this mercurial community of international adventurers was one of the greatest challenges facing the European diplomatic corps in the United States after 1815. And as the machinations of these international activists threatened to destabilize further relations between the United States and Spain—and possibly disrupt negotiations for a peaceful settlement of their territorial disputes—American authorities finally began to view their activities with concern. But gaining a clear picture of their designs was no easier for the Americans than for the Europeans. "There is so much double and treble treachery in the speculations of these auxiliaries to the South American Revolutions," wrote a frustrated John Quincy Adams as he tried to uncover the true aim of Gen. Charles Lallemand and his followers within the Vine and Olive group, "that the principal difficulty is to discover on which side the chief acting personages are."[14]

The activities of the international adventurers peaked in 1817.[15] By the end of that year, expeditions mounted from American soil had seized bases at Galveston, on the coast of Spanish Texas, and on Amelia Island, at the mouth of the Saint Mary, the river dividing Spanish east Florida from the state of Georgia.[16] From these havens, insurgent privateers not only preyed on Spanish merchant shipping but also introduced into the United States contraband, particularly slaves brought from the Caribbean and Africa in violation of the constitutional prohibition on the slave trade. Moreover, as borderland posts, Amelia and Galveston gave the insurgents ideal launching pads from which to attack east Florida and New Spain. None of this—nor the participation of some of the French exiles—escaped the attention of the foreign diplomatic corps and American authorities.

The establishment of the privateering base at Galveston coincided with the ill-fated attempt of Francisco Xavier Mina to liberate Mexico from Spanish rule.[17] Although a veteran of the guerilla war against the Napoleonic occupation of Spain, Mina opposed the restoration of Ferdinand VII's absolutism in 1815. Forced to flee Spain, he took refuge in England where members of its government and the American general Winfield Scott encouraged him to seize New Spain and declare its independence. With aid from English merchants and letters of introduction furnished by Scott to leading American supporters of Latin American independence, Mina sailed in May 1816 for the United States at the head of a small, multinational band of followers. Upon arrival, he garnered additional support from American merchants and attracted more recruits, including some of the expatriate French officers. Spanish diplomatic agents, who followed every step in the organization of this highly public (and publicized) expedition, even reported that Mina received money from Joseph Bonaparte.[18] In November 1816 Mina's force, now numbering several hundred, arrived off the coast of Texas and landed on Galveston.

Several months earlier Louis-Michel Aury, the French privateer captain, had taken possession of the island in the name of the Mexican Congress and set up a government—consisting principally of an admiralty court to condemn Spanish prizes.[19] Formerly of the French imperial navy, Aury had offered his services to the cause of Latin American independence as the Napoleonic Wars drew to a close. Cited for heroism, he was given command of a squadron by Simon

Bolivar, under whom he served with distinction before squabbling with his patron and deciding to seek his fortune in the Mexican revolution.[20] Although the lofty title of "civil and military governor of Texas" granted him by the Mexican Congress gave his piratical activities a veneer of legality, Aury's authority at Galveston rested on a more substantial basis—the troops of Colonel Savary whose Battalion of Free Men of Color had fought for Jackson at the Battle of New Orleans. When Mina arrived, relations between the young Spanish insurgent and seasoned French privateer were strained. But in early April 1817, Aury agreed to convey Mina's force to Soto la Marina, a port farther south on the coast of Mexico, from where it launched its invasion of the interior. Despite its initial success, Mina's army was destroyed later that year, and he died before a royalist firing squad.

Having disembarked Mina and his followers, Aury wisely abstained from any further participation in the ill-starred adventure. Abandoning Galveston to the Lafitte brothers, Aury set sail in July 1817 for Florida, to rendezvous at Amelia Island with Gregor MacGregor.[21] MacGregor was a Scots Catholic nobleman who had joined Bolivar's insurgent army in 1811. Rising rapidly through the ranks, thanks in part to his marriage to the Liberator's cousin, he had served with Aury before, at the siege of Cartagena. Like Aury, MacGregor fell out with Bolivar soon after this great battle and departed for the United States, where he hoped to continue the fight for Latin American independence on his own terms. During the spring of 1817 he scoured the eastern seaboard, securing commissions from the agents of the insurgent governments, soliciting financial assistance, seeking out recruits, and ensuring himself of the neutrality—if not active support—of the American and English governments. In secret meetings with an intermediary of Richard Rush, then serving as secretary of state, MacGregor revealed his plans for the conquest of east Florida. From the latter, he received hints that the United States government might be interested in purchasing this strategic province once he had wrested it from Spain.[22] He also visited Charles Bagot, the British ambassador in Washington, to assure him that the expedition was in no way directed against His Majesty's interests. This meeting gave rise to rumors that the Scots adventurer was in the pay of Great Britain. MacGregor also encountered leaders of the Bonapartist exile community in America, notably Regnault Saint-Jean d'Angely, Joseph Bonaparte's close political adviser. According to MacGregor, Regnault tried unsuccessfully to recruit him for a most fantastic expedition: to rescue Napoleon from Saint Helena and place him on the throne of Mexico.[23] MacGregor also held talks with the recently arrived Charles Lallemand—who knew east Florida well from having been shipwrecked there—and invited him to join the projected expedition to Amelia Island. But occupied with his own schemes, Lallemand declined to take part, although he did prepare a memoir for MacGregor with advice on how to conquer that province.[24] Perhaps because of these meetings with Regnault and Lallemand, other rumors began to circulate that MacGregor was involved in Bonapartist projects against New Spain and even that he was seeking to incite a general slave uprising in the Caribbean in order to undermine the British colonial economy.[25]

By the end of June 1817 MacGregor was ready to strike. With a small force composed mainly of demobilized American veterans recruited in Charleston and Savannah, MacGregor bluffed into surrendering the small Spanish garrison at Fernandina, the principal settlement on Amelia Island. Hardly a shot had been fired. Flushed with this easy triumph, MacGregor hoisted the green flag of the Republic of Florida and proceeded to set up a provisional government. Although he had originally planned to liberate the entire province of east Florida, the expedition got no farther than Amelia because it lacked followers, money, and support from local inhabitants. Indeed, MacGregor and his dwindling band were hard pressed to feed themselves, let alone beat off a Spanish counterattack in September. American reinforcements brought to the island in late August by Ruggles Hubbard, the former high sheriff of New York City, and Jared Irwin, a former Pennsylvania congressman, only served to weaken MacGregor's authority and dispel forever his hopes of liberation. Under the influence of the newcomers, the establishment gave itself over to new occupations—privateering and large-scale slave smuggling across the Saint Mary's River into the United States. Frustrated, MacGregor took passage with Woodbine, one of the English agents who had been operating since the War of 1812 with the Indians and slaves of east Florida, to New Providence in the British Bahamas. There they reportedly hoped to recruit a new force from a demobilized regiment of black colonial marines and land at Tampa Bay the following year.[26]

With MacGregor out of the picture, Amelia Island was left to the Americans under Hubbard and Irwin. But their rule was to be short-lived, for only one week after MacGregor's departure, Aury arrived from Galveston with 130 men of Savary's legion. While Aury was probably pleased to find that the establishment had cast off the pretense of liberation to get down to the business of smuggling, he was not inclined to let the Americans remain in charge of such a lucrative venture. Tensions soon flared between the "American party" of Hubbard and Irwin and the largely black "French party" of Aury.[27] After a period of treacherous factional maneuvering, Aury succeeded in gaining control of the establishment. His success, however, marked the beginning of the end for the "independence" of Amelia Island, for the planters of southern Georgia had little stomach for the presence of an encampment of armed blacks in their neighborhood. The pressure they brought to bear on the U.S. government ultimately helped convince the Monroe administration to break up Aury's establishment with military force.[28] But it is significant that during the several months while he ruled Amelia, Aury and his crew of mulattoes, free people of color, and former Haitian slaves reportedly smuggled into the United States more than a thousand Africans and sold them as slaves to the Georgia planters.[29] This little-studied commerce suggests not only the accommodating plasticity of racial solidarities—on the part of both blacks and whites—when it came to the business of slavery but also the interconnection between the slave trade and the movement for Latin American independence. The lines between patriot and profiteer, liberator and enslaver were easily blurred.

Pinpricks and Sword Thrusts

The governments of Europe and the United States followed closely the goings-on at Galveston and Amelia, but reacted toward them differently according to their general policies on Latin American affairs.[30] Together with the ebb and flow of the insurgency in the revolted colonies, these policies defined the context within which the international adventurers—including the French exiles—had to plan and conduct their operations. The following paragraphs provide a broader view of the international political framework that shaped the French exiles' opportunities for action.

As the activities of Mina, MacGregor, Aury, and others of their ilk directly threatened the territorial integrity and maritime commerce of her crumbling empire, Spain was both afraid and outraged—especially at the impunity with which the American government allowed the adventurers to conduct their preparations. Through its legation in Washington, the Spanish government issued a series of formal protests—to little effect—and conducted a secret campaign of intelligence gathering and counterespionage.[31] But while Onís and his subordinates, particularly the Spanish consul at New Orleans, Felipe Fatio, achieved notable successes in "turning" notable figures in the independence movement like the Lafittes and Gen. Jose Alvarez Toledo, these victories had little impact on Spain's effort to defeat the insurrection. Still exhausted in 1817 by the bitter war against the Napoleonic occupation, Spain had little money, few troops, and, most importantly, no large flotilla to transport them to the Americas.[32] Given that at least thirty-seven privateers mounting a total of three hundred cannon were reported in 1818 to be operating from American ports alone, even warships of the Spanish royal navy had to fear being outgunned on the high seas by the insurgents.[33] Recognizing their country's weakness, a number of Spanish diplomats and statesmen concluded that a policy of compromise and reconciliation was the only way to salvage something from the shipwreck of the empire.[34] Ideas presented to the cabinet in 1817–18 by the moderate prime minister Jose Garcia de Leon y Pizarro included allowing the colonies to trade freely with foreign merchants, offering amnesty to the rebels, and ending discrimination against Creoles.[35] Perhaps the most daring move advocated by Pizarro—possibly at the urging of Onís who strongly supported the idea—was to grant independence to the Spanish viceroyalties in America under the sovereignty of Bourbon princes.[36] The creation of intermediate, independent kingdoms, it was hoped, would not only take some of the steam out of the rebellion but also raise on the frontier with the United States a barrier to American territorial ambition.

Although their willingness to contemplate concessions has earned Pizarro, Onís, and Toledo reputations for moderation, it would be a mistake to draw too sharp a distinction between them and the hard-liners—a group dominated by military men—who insisted that force alone could restore the colonies to obedience. Even Pizarro, the leader of the moderate faction, was willing to consider muscular policies—such as Toledo's plan for the cession to France of peripheral colonies in exchange for direct military aid in crushing the rebellion in the imperial heartland—or risky schemes likely to provoke international war— such as the old Burr-Wilkinson design for the secession of the western states of the Union.[37] At one point, Pizarro even recommended hiring as mercenaries the international adventurers who were causing such trouble for Spain in Mexico, Florida, and on the high seas—an approach to colonial defense recalling Rome's use of barbarian auxiliaries to guard her vulnerable frontiers against barbarian invasion.[38] Elements of these schemes for independent buffer states, Burr-like subversion against the territorial integrity of the United States, and the use of foreign legions would soon combine in unlikely ways in the adventures of Charles Lallemand and his followers.

The difference between the moderates and hard-liners did not lie in the reluctance of the former to adopt extreme and violent measures, for, if anything, they proved more willing than their inflexible opponents to consider unorthodox responses to the rebellion. Rather the difference lay in the fact that while the moderates were willing to take a hard look at the actual state of Spanish power and adjust their policy accordingly, the hard-liners were not—with tragic results for Spain's colonial empire, for they wielded enough influence to block even the most timid moderate concession.[39] Their unwillingness to adjust policy to the crippling financial and military situation of Spain did not, however, make those weaknesses go away, but only served to limit Spanish options. Without the means of raising and dispatching sufficient forces to crush the rebellion, the cabinet's only hope was to convince the European powers to intervene in America on Spain's behalf.[40] To persuade England or the Holy Alliance to send armies across the Atlantic to pacify the rebellious colonies was a tall order indeed. Yet, unable to agree on any other policy, the cabinet charged Spanish diplomats with the task of winning support for European intervention. They had to find arguments likely to convince potential European partners, while at the same time trying to thwart insurgent intrigues that might derail the diplomatic initiatives or destabilize the situation on the ground.[41] Some observers mistook Spain's delaying strategy as confirmation of its decrepitude, but others recognized it for what it was. "The more things drag on," noted Hyde de Neuville, "the greater chance Spain has of interesting Europe in its cause."[42]

Keenly aware of Spain's efforts to enlist the great powers in its colonial struggle, the American administration was alive to the possibility that, should it embrace too openly the cause of Latin American independence, the wrath of Europe might descend upon it.[43] Even if the bid for intervention failed, the Spanish Cabinet realized, the mere discussion of it would suffice to prevent the American government from openly recognizing Latin American independence.[44] Spain calculated correctly. Fear of European involvement compelled the Monroe administration to proceed gingerly on the question of Latin America—more gingerly, indeed, than American ideological sympathies, public opinion, commercial interests, and undisguised hunger for contiguous Spanish territories might otherwise have dictated. Many American citizens saw their country as a revolutionary republic with an obvious interest—and possibly even a moral obligation—in supporting other struggles for freedom from monarchy. The "disposition already existing in the nation to embark in the civil war now raging between Spain and her colonies is already sufficiently strong," observed the secretary of war William Crawford in September 1816, that "the power of the executive would be exerted in vain to restrain that disposition" were any new provocation to inflame the American public.[45]

Sentiment in favor of the rebellion drew additional strength from business interests that saw in the establishment of independent Latin American republics an end to Spanish trade restrictions and the opening of new markets for American commerce.[46] Many European statesmen believed that Americans were drawn to the cause of independence more by the lure of profit than the love of freedom. "This enterprising, mercantile nation," noted Hyde de Neuville, "looks to the liberty of other peoples less than to the interest of its commerce."[47] The Spanish general Toledo—who, like Hyde, had lived in the United States for many years—was blunter. "The dream of making a colossal fortune is the unique object that moves Angloamerican hearts."[48]

Even these observers realized, however, that another motivation was pushing the United States to support the struggle for Latin American independence: the desire to expand westward. With the exception of Portugal—which seized upon the revolt of Buenos Aires to wrest from Spain the Banda Oriental (present-day Uruguay)—only the United States enjoyed the geographical contiguity necessary to parlay Spanish colonial troubles into territorial aggrandizement. The strategic significance of Florida, the growing commercial importance of the Columbia River, the extent of fertile land in Texas—together with the debility of Spanish authority and scant population in these areas—exerted a nearly irresistible pull on the American government and citizenry. As James Lewis has shown, a handful of far-sighted American statesmen did worry about the effects of dramatic expansion on the cohesion of the Union and successfully restrained more impatient figures like Andrew Jackson. But their caution had little influence on public opinion.[49] Restraining the more zealous partisans of Latin American independence—who tried more than once to mobilize public sentiment in favor of the insurgents to force the administration's hand—was the greatest challenge the administration had to face in implementing its policy of prudence.

The American government had not always handled Latin American independence so cautiously. Before 1815 first Jefferson and then Madison had come close to proffering recognition and even sponsored filibustering expeditions against Spanish provinces, notably the Floridas and Texas.[50] But after the return of peace to Europe and the United States in 1815, a note of hesitation began to color American policy. President Madison signaled this shift with a proclamation delivered on 1 September 1815, prohibiting "illegal expeditions" against the Spanish domains and enjoining all "good and faithful citizens" to inform the government of plots that came to their attention.[51] Many considerations underlay this newfound caution. One, of course, was the fear of European intervention—a fear deftly reinforced by the British government's hints that it might take military action should it determine that the United States was "pursuing a system of encroachment" against the provinces of Spanish America.[52] Renewed conflict with Great Britain was the last thing the United States needed, as it was still trying to recover from its efforts in the War of 1812.[53] Other reasons for caution included concern that the opening of Spain's former colonies to foreign trade would lead to British economic hegemony in the New World, doubts about the character of the republican governments of South America, and perhaps the personality of the new American secretary of state, John Quincy Adams.

To ensure that the actions of reckless individuals did not sabotage its emerging policy of prudence, the administration began to keep close tabs on the international revolutionaries and adventurers gathered on American soil and pressed Congress to grant it new powers to maintain neutrality. Passed over the opposition of a powerful minority led by the influential Speaker of the House Henry Clay, the Neutrality Bill signed on 3 March 1817—the same day as the Vine and Olive legislation—was the first in a series of measures to curtail unauthorized American participation in the movement for Latin American independence. Because of the widespread sympathy for the cause of independence, however, the government had great difficulty in actually enforcing these laws. Some local port and judicial officials, on whose exactitude enforcement depended, turned a blind eye to recruiting and armament taking place openly within their jurisdiction. Worse, government agents ignored the administration's policy of caution and themselves flaunted the provisions of the new law. The rabble-rousing Baltimore postmaster John Stuart Skinner and the accredited American representative in Buenos Aires Thomas L. Halsey were both eventually charged with involvement in privateering ventures.[54] Col. Thomas S. Jessup, the American commander on the sensitive Louisiana frontier, sought to maneuver the administration into a war with Spain by fabricating intelligence of Spanish preparations to attack New Orleans.[55] And at least one cabinet member encouraged MacGregor's invasion of east Florida by dropping hints of eventual American recognition and annexation. Despite the difficulties experienced by the government in enforcing American neutrality, even within its own ranks, the fact that violations were increasingly exposed and sometimes prosecuted underlines the growing determination of the administration to proceed cautiously after 1815.

If the United States was more reserved in practice toward the revolutions of Latin America than its history, ideology, and economic interests seemed to dictate, Great Britain proved significantly warmer to the cause of independence than might have been expected.[56] Britain was the country that had led the long struggle against revolutionary and Napoleonic France, ultimately triumphing through its naval power and tireless efforts to preserve a coalition of continental powers willing to fight the proficient Gallic legions. And after having achieved victory, Britain had been instrumental in the efforts of the great powers to establish a new world order that would eliminate the possibility of future revolutions. If the United States appeared after 1815 to be the arsenal of revolution, Great Britain—thanks to its strong financial system, burgeoning industry, and worldwide empire—seemed to be the foundation upon which the peace and prosperity of conservative Europe would rest. But it was precisely the economic forces underlying its strength that pushed Britain to favor discretely but powerfully the cause of Latin American independence. Barred during the early 1800s from its traditional European outlets by Napoleon's continental system and from American markets by Jefferson's embargo, British domestic manufacturing and seaborne commerce had developed alternative outlets in the Spanish empire.[57] Occupied and entirely dependent on British aid for its fight against the French invaders, royalist Spain tolerated this trade, which amounted to an unprecedented violation of the regulations that had barred foreign merchants from Spanish America since the fifteenth century. With peace in 1815, British business interests showed no intention of disengaging from this lucrative market. Far from hurting British commerce, noted the Duke de Richelieu, first war and then revolution in Spanish America had "vivified the factories of Great Britain."[58] A substantial sector of the British economy had thus come to depend on trade with Spanish America—a market that would be lost if Ferdinand VII crushed the rebellion and restored his authority.[59] If it did not necessarily favor outright independence, the British mercantile lobby demanded a solution to the Latin American crisis based on the principle of free trade.

The challenge facing the British government was to achieve this goal without favoring the insurgency so brazenly as to antagonize the conservative powers and wreck the framework for postwar European stability so painstakingly assembled at the Congress of Vienna. Reconciling these contradictory ends was rendered more difficult by the Spanish king's opposition to a moderate approach, a position that foreclosed creative solutions—the creation of intermediate, independent kingdoms and British mediation in exchange for commercial privileges—that the British government had considered. In the face of such intransigence, the British Cabinet had to steer a narrow course between the breakers of revolution and the shoals of reaction. Too pronounced a drift toward the independence movement could jeopardize Britain's relations with Europe. But equally, too conservative a policy might so alienate the emerging republics that they would turn to a rival power for support. That power—the United States, British statesmen believed—would reap the economic benefits of trade with Latin America that Britain presently enjoyed. Caught on the horns of this dilemma, Whitehall tried to postpone the inevitable decision by delaying tactics in the councils of Europe and covert aid on the battlefields of Latin America. British diplomats in the courts of continental Europe maneuvered ceaselessly to keep Spain, France, Russia, and Austria from forging a joint plan of intervention that might end the rebellion—and in so doing terminate Britain's trade with the rebel-held ports of South America. In London, the government parried Spanish requests for unilateral British mediation—to be backed by British arms should the rebels fail to agree to the arbitrated settlement—by demanding terms, notably the opening of the Spanish colonies to British commerce, that it knew Ferdinand VII would reject. The Spanish Cabinet was bitterly aware of the "Machiavellian principles" shaping "the mercantile policy of England," but lacking both flexibility and resources, could only continue its hopeless pursuit of British support while raging secretly at its hypocrisy.[60] As long as it avoided openly flaunting the conservative principles of the postwar order—by recognizing the independence of the rebel colonies, for example—Britain could keep its supposed European partners in a state of fuming impotence. With Europe neutralized, the only remaining threat to British plans was the possibility that the Spaniards might succeed in overcoming the rebellion by force. By 1817 this outcome seemed within reach of the royalist armies.[61] To keep the flame of rebellion alive and maintain British influence with the rebels, Great Britain unofficially tolerated on its soil fund-raising, naval outfitting, arms purchases, and recruiting on behalf of the insurgents. In addition, many British subjects—generally demobilized veterans of the Napoleonic Wars—served the revolutionary cause as volunteers.[62] By providing covert aid to the rebellion and subtly sabotaging all moves toward European intervention (while persuading the United States it was pursuing the opposite course), Britain did more than any other country to seal the fate of Spain's American empire. "The fact is," observed Hyde de Neuville in 1817, "that while the Americans are openly giving pinpricks the English are secretly delivering sword thrusts."[63]

With the United States edging away from its earlier embrace of the independence movement and Britain adopting policies increasingly favorable to the rebellion, the years after 1815 saw a gradual rapprochement of their respective policies toward Latin America. This convergence, however, did not reflect a growing recognition of shared interests, but rather deepening rivalry between the two powers. Afraid that independence would result in British economic and political hegemony in the Western Hemisphere, the American administration began to cool its ardor for the revolutionary cause. Worried that too conservative an approach would undermine its influence in the emerging republics and permit the United States to monopolize trade, the British government looked with increasing favor on the independence movement.

The rivalry between Great Britain and the United States did not escape the notice of the Spanish government, which perceived the possibility of playing on it to neutralize both countries and achieve its own ends in Latin America. Toledo articulated clearly this possibility in a memoir presented to the Spanish government in 1816. "From this rivalry and opposition of interests between Great Britain and the United States," he wrote, "Spain can obtain great advantages."[64] Pizarro agreed with his assessment and presented to the cabinet a detailed plan for fomenting conflict between the two powers. By ceding Florida to Great Britain, Pizarro argued, Spain could establish in North America "a kind of political equilibrium in which both the Americans and English would serve as safeguards for us, the ones impeding the aggressions of the others." With the United States caught in a vise between the British possessions of Canada in the north and Florida in the South, suggested the minister, it might even be possible to recover Louisiana.[65] But thwarted by the hard-liners, Pizarro was unable to put these plans into effect. This failure, however, did not prevent him from repeatedly pointing out all the disadvantages English interests would sustain should weak Spain be left to face the United States without British backing.[66] "In truth," Pizarro noted in June 1817, "the English government has the same interest as us in containing the Americans."[67]

The possibility of manipulating Anglo-American distrust to advance their country's own interests in Latin America also struck French diplomats.[68] Unlike the Spanish, who had turned somewhat uncomfortably to Great Britain for help against the territorial ambitions of the United States, the French did not hesitate to seek the support of the United States in thwarting England's bid for hegemony in Latin America. The traditional rival of Great Britain, France after 1815 remained wary of her old enemy. The defeat of Napoleon may have even raised French sentiment against England to unprecedented heights. By signaling the definitive triumph of England in what had amounted to a 150-yearlong struggle for world domination, Waterloo and the subsequent occupation of their country filled the French of all political tendencies with a deep sense of humiliation. Foreign observers were struck that Bourbon France burned with a hatred of Great Britain just as fierce as at the height of the Revolution. "England is for France the pole of repulsion," noted the Russian ambassador in

1816. "Neither reason, policy, nor even the force of circumstances will diminish the bitterness and distrust that rivalry excites between these two countries."[69]

Directed in his general instructions to attend closely to divisions between Great Britain and the United States and exploit them to French advantage, Hyde de Neuville wasted little time in warning the American government of the fast-approaching day when Britain would control the commerce—and destiny—of the Western Hemisphere.[70] In a series of conversations with Richard Rush at the end of April 1817, Hyde hammered home the point that "England would be likely to run away with the chief profit of their [the Spanish colonies'] independence."[71] Although it is impossible to know exactly how the French ambassador elaborated on this theme, his dispatches from the same period illustrate the vehemence of his feelings and depth of his fears. Two weeks after his meeting with Rush, Hyde wrote to Richelieu that England wanted to exempt itself from "the general equilibrium." "England wants to remain absolute, or at least without rivals, on the high seas. It wants above all that its commerce becomes universal and that the colonies all fall under its influence or domination. What it accomplished in the Indies, what it is trying in Africa, what it obtained in Saint-Domingue, it wants to take in South America. Thus, if the great powers do not make haste to stop this invasion of world commerce, nothing will remain for them but miserable debris."[72] After another year observing Latin American developments from his post in the United States, Hyde was more convinced than ever that English ambition, if unchecked, would turn South America into a "second Hindustan."[73] In December 1818, he was still at work, trying to convince John Quincy Adams to join an international coalition to counterbalance "the commercial despotism of England."[74]

Rivalry with England colored the foreign policy of France and dictated its approach to the Latin American crisis—to find a solution to the conflict between Spain and its colonies that would keep English commerce out while letting French commerce in. Neither outright independence nor the integral restoration of Spanish dominion could achieve this ambitious end. The first, French statesmen feared, would lead to the rapid consolidation of British economic hegemony over the newly independent republics. To avoid this, Hyde de Neuville repeatedly urged Onís to sign a boundary treaty with the Monroe administration before American public opinion forced the United States to recognize Latin American independence.[75] The second, by leading to the reimposition of the old regime of exclusionary trade regulations in the Spanish colonies, would exclude French manufacturing from the Latin American outlets believed necessary to offset England's economic lead.[76] In working for a resolution to the Latin American conflict that would avoid the extremes of total independence and total subjugation, French diplomats concocted schemes similar to those proposed unsuccessfully by Pizarro and the Spanish moderates. One recurrent hope was that the insurgents could be satisfied by offering independence to the colonies under Bourbon princes, preferably from the French branch of the family.[77] The foreign minister, Richelieu, was convinced that such an arrangement could "give another direction to the American spirit of independence" and ordered the Marquis d'Osmond, French ambassador in London, to broach the subject with Castlereagh.[78] In the United States, Hyde de Neuville repeatedly pressed upon his colleague, Onís, the desirability of establishing independent monarchies as "veritable ramparts between the Spanish possessions and the United States," particularly in Texas and Northern Mexico.[79] Onís hardly needed convincing—he had already suggested a similar solution to his court—but his hands were tied by its intransigence.

The French government, however, possessed more freedom of maneuver. Frustrated by Spanish rigidity, the French went ahead with their own plans for setting up independent Bourbon kingdoms in Latin America. In the spring of 1818 Richelieu dispatched a secret agent, a Colonel LeMoyne, to South America where he was to "sound out the dispositions of [the insurgents of] Buenos Aires on the adoption of a monarchical government." This agent, however, had to be disavowed when, on his own initiative, he proposed the politically unacceptable Duke d'Orléans as a potential king.[80] During the same period, the French government entered into secret negotiations with a renegade Spanish general, Mariano Renovales, who was in England preparing a military expedition against New Spain. If France agreed to support his venture, Renovales promised, he would install a "French monarchy in Mexico" and grant French commerce a 50 percent tariff reduction. Should a new revolution break out in France, moreover, he was prepared to grant "asylum" to the ruling family of France.[81] Despite the chilling implications of this odd sales pitch, Osmond was favorably impressed. Renovales, he reported to Richelieu, was an ideal man to carry out such a venture. "He wants neither a republic nor the Bonapartes," reported the ambassador, "and prefers France to England."[82] Moreover, Renovales had pledged that, were his invasion to succeed, "nothing would be changed . . . [and] the elements of society would remain as they are."[83] As negotiations continued throughout the spring of 1818, Richelieu, however, began to experience growing doubts about the general and his project. Although the prospect of commercial advantages kept Richelieu from breaking off contact, he thought Renovales's glib assurances of the ease with which he would "replace Spanish domination with an independent monarchy" smacked of "charlatanism."[84] When Renovales sent Osmond an ultimatum demanding a two-hundred-thousand-franc advance, Richelieu decided that enough was enough. "Something in his conduct stinks of the adventurer," the foreign minister concluded.[85]

Although the French government aborted its exploratory mission to Buenos Aires and declined to associate itself with Renovales's scheme, its willingness to consider such options in spite of the opposition of the Spanish court underlines the independence of France's Latin American policy after 1815. To a certain extent, its independence had been obscured by the reactionary tone of its public pronouncements. Restored to his throne by Europe's conservative powers, Louis XVIII had been the principal beneficiary of reaction and was expected to become one of its staunchest defenders. Moreover, he was related to the Spanish king by ties of blood and pledged to uphold his rights by the so-called Family Compact. At the very least, this solemn accord seemed to demand that the French government support Spain's policy toward its American possessions and respect its colonial regulations—including the restrictions barring foreign commerce. France did neither. Indeed, its persistent efforts to mediate the boundary dispute between Spain and the United States evoked bitter protests from Spain. While the French government believed it imperative to find a mutually acceptable solution to this issue in order to prevent the further deterioration of relations between Washington and Madrid, American recognition of Latin American independence, and even open warfare, the Spanish court viewed France's attempt to engineer compromise as a betrayal of its legitimate interests. By promoting compromise, complained the Spanish government, France was not only implying that the American claims possessed merit but also failing to uphold her sacred obligations to a sister kingdom. A true friend would forthrightly take Spain's side to thwart the "ambitious aims" of the American government. Only by presenting a common Bourbon front to the United States could Spain obtain a "satisfactory resolution" of the territorial dispute.[86] France's refusal to bend before these blandishments helped keep alive Spanish-American negotiations— negotiations that ultimately resulted in the so-called Transcontinental Treaty of 1819.

Napoleon's Ghost

Haunting the shadowy labyrinth of the Western question after 1815 was an almost surreal fear: that Napoleon would escape from Saint Helena, take over the independence movement, carve out a New World empire, and wage war on the established powers of Europe.[87] Having seen him rise so high so quickly, contemporary observers had difficulty assimilating his sudden fall from power. Having accomplished so much already, it was easy to imagine that he was still capable of great things. And the revolt of the Spanish colonies seemed to offer a perfect stage for his genius. "With regard to South America," wrote Hyde de Neuville to Richelieu, "I persist in thinking that only one man, Bonaparte, can effect a grand revolution there. The Spanish insurgents will do anything to have him at their head."[88] From the moment of his incarceration on Saint Helena, fantastic rumors of his escape began to circulate throughout the Atlantic world and beyond.[89] While trawling for cod off Newfoundland, Captain Leborgne, master of a fishing boat sailing from Dieppe, heard that Bonaparte had escaped.[90] A captain just arrived at Marseille from Malta claimed to have read in a Maltese newspaper that the great man had been spirited away by a Mexican corsair and given command of the insurgents.[91] An English inhabitant of Orléans, in the heartland of France, reported that the town was abuzz with word that Napoleon had escaped from Saint Helena aboard a steamboat.[92] Variations on this rumor—apparently spawned by Colonel Latapie's failed attempt to mount a rescue from Pernambuco—spoke of balloons and submersibles, fitting conveyances for a man who, more than any other figure, embodied the idea of modernity during the first decades of the nineteenth century.[93] Some of the rumors even connected the embryonic French settlement on the Tombigbee with these projects.[94] Although most of these stories were spread deliberately to foment panic and confusion among the established authorities, as well as to keep up the hopes and retain the attention of the political opposition, European governments took the prospect of Napoleon's escape seriously. Richelieu's official instructions to his ambassadors were explicit in this regard. Wherever they were posted, they were to keep "their telescopes constantly fixed on Saint-Helena, because that little black point on the horizon might still give rise to storms."[95]

Since the United States was the most likely place from which a rescue expedition would be planned, prepared, and executed, keeping a close watch on suspicious Bonapartist activities was of particular concern to Hyde de Neuville. Indeed, a special clause in his instructions directed him to "seek to learn if any enterprise or intrigue is afoot . . . to spirit Bonaparte away from [Saint Helena]."[96] Hyde took this charge very seriously. "The increasing activity of the refugees during the past six months," Hyde wrote to the French consul in New York in May 1818, "should make you more vigilant than ever and increase the diligence with which you send me all the information you can gather. We must investigate everything that is possible and even what is unlikely."[97] The consuls scrupulously collected even seemingly insignificant bits of information about the Bonapartist exiles and shared it both horizontally with their colleagues in other cities and vertically with the consul-general and legation. Guillemin, the consul at New Orleans, even began on 1 January 1817 to keep records of all French citizens entering the United States through that port.[98] Although no other consulate seems to have adopted such thorough measures as this, they all regularly forwarded to the Ministry of General Police in Paris lists of all French citizens in their jurisdiction leaving the United States for Europe. Collated by Hyde and sent on to Richelieu, their reports on the activities of local Bonapartists also found their way to this ministry. In turn, it periodically shared with the Ministry of Foreign Affairs the intelligence it had gathered in Europe about Bonapartist activities in America. The Ministry of War also cooperated frequently with Foreign Affairs, both sharing information on the Napoleonic officers in America and asking for intelligence on them procured by the diplomatic agents in the United States. The impressive coordination that characterized French interministerial relations sometimes even extended to relations with other governments. For example, Hyde worked out a system with the British ambassador in Washington for keeping tabs on French citizens and naturalized Frenchmen in America who sought to sneak into Europe on English passports.[99]

Although this feverish activity produced much information on the French refugees and exiles in America, it did not penetrate the mystery of their designs—if such designs existed at all. Hyde was convinced they did, but was frustrated by his inability to uncover their purpose. "If the nature of the danger escapes me," he wrote to Richelieu a year into his term as ambassador, "everything I learn convinces me that it exists."[100] The first real breakthrough came on 23 July 1817 when an apparently repentant Colonel Raoul presented himself to French diplomatic officials in Philadelphia and made the following, startling revelations. He claimed to have been charged by Joseph Bonaparte with organizing a plan for rescuing Napoleon. Lefebvre-Desnouettes and Stephen Girard were to procure and arm the ships; indeed, confided Raoul, they had already done this—one was sitting at Baltimore and the other at Annapolis. The Lallemand brothers were to serve as recruiters, vetting the troops and passing them on to Galabert, Douarche and Adolphe Pontecoulant (a nephew of Marshal Grouchy) who would hold them in readiness. Latapie had already gone to Pernambuco with an advanced party to prepare a forward staging base on the island of Fernand de Morunka, 210 miles off the coast of Brazil. There the party from the United States was to rendezvous with a similar group being raised in Buenos Aires by General Brayer, another proscribed Bonapartist who had sought refuge in South America, as well as a naval contingent from England under the command of the renegade admiral Lord Cochrane. Counting nearly 500 Napoleonic officers, 800 sailors, and 3 vessels—including Cochrane's 74-gun flagship—the assembled force would proceed to Saint Helena, destroy the English cruisers guarding the island, overwhelm the garrison, and whisk Napoleon to safety in the United States. Once in America, he would embark for France with a small force, land at Cherbourg, and march on Paris, just as he had when he escaped from Elba. While all this was going on, another party of officers assembled in Italy would rescue Napoleon's infant son and carry him to safety in America. Even if Napoleon himself perished in the desperate scheme, his dynasty would live on.[101]

Treating Raoul's revelations with the utmost seriousness, Hyde wasted no time in adopting countermeasures. Within days he had informed the Spanish and Portuguese ambassadors of the plot, sent a courier to Europe with a warning about the plan to kidnap Napoleon's son, and retained a fast ship to dispatch to Saint Helena the moment the rescue expedition departed from the Chesapeake.[102] The consul at Baltimore was directed to observe the port for signs of suspicious activity and, above all, to keep an eye on the ships indicated by Raoul.[103] As he reflected on the exile's story, however, Hyde began to doubt its veracity. As reports arrived contradicting some of Raoul's claims—including information that one of the ships indicated by Raoul was actually a coasting vessel manned by four sailors and loaded to the bridge with crates of porcelain—Hyde's suspicions grew.[104] Had there not been other indications from other sources that something was afoot in the exile community, Hyde informed Richelieu on 4 August 1817, he "would see in the proceedings of this man [Raoul] only the exaggerated and, above all, self-interested zeal of an adventurer who, not knowing where to turn, was trying to give himself an air of importance."[105] But the comings and goings of Bonapartist messengers, the meeting of the leading exiles at Joseph's estate, the gathering of officers in East Coast ports, the arrival of new officers from Europe, and the sense of confidence that seemed to have infused the exile community in recent weeks, all these signs made it impossible for Hyde to disregard Raoul. As he thought about the situation, Hyde became convinced that Raoul was a plant sent by the plotters to obscure their true aims. His talk of Saint Helena was "only a point of diversion or rather an imaginary goal masking another project and serving to seduce, to motivate, the common soldiery for whom the name Napoleon will always be a fatal talisman."[106] More sure than ever that an insidious plot was in the making, Hyde redoubled his vigilance.

Although Hyde initially suspected that the real aim of the conspiracy was to effect a landing in France, documents intercepted at the end of August, probably on the same day Clausel and Lefebvre-Desnouettes left for Alabama, convinced him otherwise. Transmitted to him by an unidentified friend of the French monarchy, these papers—soon identified by a troubled William Lee as written on Lakanal's stationery, in his hand, and bearing his signature— outlined a grandiose plan for a "Napoleonic confederation" to place Joseph Bonaparte on the throne of Mexico.[107] The first phase of the plan called for the secret formation in the western United States of an army of nine hundred men (supported by a mere two pieces of artillery) to accomplish the inva- sion. One hundred fifty commissioners—presumably the core members of the confederation—would be dispatched to the Ohio and Mississippi valleys where they would each secure the services of five individuals from the local popula- tion. Accustomed to "hunting, fishing, and adventurous enterprises," the tough westerners would make ideal soldiers. Increasingly lost in bizarre digressions— on the "vegetative force" of corn, the dietary preferences of Indian warriors ("horsemeat that their women prepare with wild cayenne pepper . . . and a sort of pea that grows on a tree resembling a willow"), and the guidelines for a Latin-based code titled "Enigmatic Vocabulary"—Lakanal never spelled out ex- actly how such a tiny and lightly equipped force was to conquer Mexico, nor how Joseph's royal authority might be established throughout that rebellious country once it was. He did not neglect, however, to request a "Spanish distinc- tion" to lend him "a degree of political importance" in the eyes of the Mexi- cans. Nor did he forget to ask for money—seventy-five thousand francs to be exact.

That Hyde took these ravings seriously is telling testimony to the influence that the prospect of a Bonapartist restoration continued to exert over the mind of reactionary Europe. Despite its similarities to what he termed "Colonel Burr's conspiracy," Hyde believed that the design of the Napoleonic confedera- tion was far more dangerous because it was "linked to Saint-Helena and per- haps to other, even more dangerous plans."[108] Within days of its discovery Hyde had informed Richelieu in Paris and the representatives of the European diplomatic corps in Washington, and had demanded a meeting with the Ameri- can secretary of state to discuss "a matter that interests the United States much more than France."[109] Just about to step down from his interim office, Richard

Rush happily passed on to John Quincy Adams an affair whose "extraordinary character baffles all my conjectures."[110] In a series of meetings that took place during September, Hyde sought to persuade Adams to take legal action against the men implicated by the documents.[111] While offering Hyde the vague assurance that the president would take "every measure within the competency of the government and compatible with the rights of individuals" to counter activities "tending to disturb the public tranquility," he refused to institute proceedings. As the "repressive powers of the government" were limited to "cases of actual transgression and do not extend to projects which, however exceptionable in their character, have not been matured at least into an attempt or commencement of action," Adams explained, the administration could do nothing, despite the "friendliness of its disposition" toward France.[112] Hyde, whose years of exile in the United States during the French Revolution had given him an understanding of its constitutional principles, did not insist.

Instead, he suggested an alternative course: the publication of the intercepted documents. "A notice pointing out not only the consequences, but also the ridiculousness of the plot" would suffice to destroy it.[113] The administration came close to adopting this course, even going so far as to draft an introductory note to the documents "in the form of an editorial article." Crafted by Adams, it underlined the wickedness concealed by the laughable insanity of the plan. "That foreigners scarcely landed upon *our* shores should imagine the possibility of enlisting large numbers of the hardy republicans of our western states and territories in the ultra-quixotism of invading a territory bordering upon their country for the purpose of proclaiming a phantom king of Spain and the Indies is a perversity of delirium, the turpitude of which is almost lost in its absurdity."[114] President Monroe approved the draft, but before going ahead with the publication, decided to consult the other members of the administration on the wisdom of this course. "Much connected with South American affairs generally," what Monroe referred to as "Mr. [Hyde de] Neuville's business" was the immediate precipitant of the historical cabinet meeting of 30 October 1817 in which the government reaffirmed its commitment to a policy of prudence vis-à-vis the Latin American independence movement.[115] In the course of the wide-ranging discussion, the decision was made not to publish the documents. Like the other options considered and rejected at that meeting—recognizing independence, sending ambassadors to the insurgent republics, allowing the piratical establishments at Amelia Island and Galveston to subsist—the publication of the Lakanal documents at this sensitive moment in Spanish-American relations was deemed too explosive a measure to authorize.[116]

The administration had other reasons as well for keeping the intercepted documents under wraps. In the event of publication, Lakanal might deny authorship, complain noisily about government persecution, and perhaps even institute libel proceedings. Even if things did not go this far, Adams wrote to Monroe, publication risked exposing the government to public censure.[117] Other concerns reinforced the administration's wariness. As Adams reflected on the astonishing ease with which the papers had fallen into Hyde's hands, he began to wonder if they had been deliberately leaked for some secret purpose. Perhaps Lakanal—or a clever forger—had written the documents "to obtain his own pardon by entrapping or implicating in criminal enterprises a more important personage."[118] Perhaps the documents had been fabricated to compromise Joseph Bonaparte or to justify the conservative powers' "arbitrary detention" in Europe of Bonaparte family members.[119] Given his persistent doubts about the real provenance and purpose of the documents, Adams gradually became convinced that their publication—or indeed, any public statement on the part of the administration—ran the risk of making the United States the unknowing accomplice of an obscure maneuver.

The administration's growing hesitancy did not escape Hyde's notice. In a series of letters to Richelieu, he speculated on its cause. In his meetings with Adams and the president on the Lakanal affair, Hyde believed he had detected in their words an undercurrent of embarrassment that he attributed to their foreknowledge of the French exiles' plot. Surely the American government, he wrote, "could not ignore certain movements, certain agitations in the western provinces and among the French refugees; and perhaps it entered into its secret policy that, without openly participating, it could give several new worries to Spain by these adventurous bands, in order to make that power more pliant" in the ongoing boundary negotiations.[120] He also suspected that Henry Clay, the powerful Speaker of the House from Kentucky, was one of those "whom the intercepted papers would deeply embarrass." In a meeting requested by Clay—the day after Hyde had shared the Lakanal papers with the president—Hyde was struck by the Speaker's "preoccupied air, the length of his visit, the pains he took to tell me that he had just arrived from the West, but kept at home by domestic affairs, had been unable to travel around the country." While Clay, the "Grachus of the United States" would never hesitate to "avow an enterprise against Spain," the secret monarchical purpose of the Napoleonic confederation would, if exposed publicly, place him in a very awkward situation indeed.[121] Despite these suspicions, Hyde was nonetheless confident that the American government was "taking serious, albeit secret, measures to thwart the conspiracy, at least insofar as it might compromise itself and certain personages closely linked with its leaders."[122]

Hyde was correct in his judgment. His revelations had indeed spurred the Monroe administration to action. It initiated an investigation into the rumors of levies in the West, an investigation that failed to turn up evidence of the secret army described in the Lakanal papers.[123] It also began to show new determination to enforce the provisions of the Neutrality Bill of 3 March 1817.[124] When that law proved to be insufficient to curtail the outfitting of insurgent privateers in American ports, Monroe went to the Congress and demanded new powers—a request that was granted by Congress on 20 April 1818.[125] And it also moved to break up a gathering of armed men in the Mississippi Territory, which had been denounced to Judge Toulmin by the Spanish governor of Pensacola as a filibustering expedition intended to take over west Florida.[126]

The clearest measure of the administration's newfound firmness came when, after heated debate, the president ordered the U.S. military to break up the insurgent bases on Amelia and Galveston Islands. First broached at the critical cabinet meeting of 30 October 1817, the decision to act vigorously reflected the administration's determination to eliminate sources of instability that might complicate relations with Spain and jeopardize its delicate Latin American policy. Other considerations also contributed to the decision: the presence of armed blacks at these establishments, the fear that they might provoke unrest among the slaves of neighboring Georgia, their involvement in smuggling Africans into the United States, the persistent rumors that the takeover of Amelia Island had been sponsored by a foreign power, and the fact that Aury had claimed both points for the Mexican Republic. Moreover, the administration had recently learned of the connections between MacGregor and Woodbine and of their plans for leading an Indian revolt in Florida the following spring. In November 1817 American naval forces were ordered to occupy Amelia Island.[127] Congress approved this action despite political opposition led by Henry Clay, who wanted the insurgents to keep these valuable bases, and protests from the Spanish government, which suspected the entire affair had been orchestrated by the administration to give it a pretext—the restoration of order and suppression of smuggling—to occupy Spanish territory.[128]

Despite his satisfaction with the administration's resolve, Hyde also prepared his own measures against the Napoleonic confederation. He had, of course, immediately informed Onís, so that he could warn the Spanish military posts in the west and sent word to the French consul at New Orleans to be on the lookout for suspicious activities. He also dispatched the Chevalier de Mun, a

French royalist officer living in the United States, to travel through the western states and look into the rumored levies of troops.[129] With passports and lines of credit opened for them by Hyde in New Orleans, the chevalier and his traveling companion, another royalist officer by the name of Lavaud, departed in early September. Although they encountered no sign of a secret levy of frontiersmen during their seven-month trip, they did learn that a number of Bonapartist officers who had been staying in the principal cities of Ohio and Kentucky had suddenly embarked on riverboats for New Orleans. Dispatched to investigate their activities, Lavaud discovered that the growing assemblage was involved in purchasing supplies. Although he had no hard evidence of it, his sense was that these preparations were being directed against Mexico.[130]

As de Mun and Lavaud were setting out on their reconnaissance mission, Hyde was also laying plans to put a fright into the conspirators. Through highly visible meetings with the captain of the French warship *Eurydice,* which had just put in at New York on its way from the Caribbean to Brest, Hyde managed to give rise to wild speculation among the French exiles and their allies within the broader community of international adventurers. According to one rumor, the warship had been redirected to Amelia Island where it was to attack the insurgents and liberate a French merchantman recently taken by the privateers. According to another, the *Eurydice* had been ordered to overtake the vessel carrying Clausel and Lefebvre-Desnouettes to Mobile and arrest them on the high seas. For his part, Hyde believed that his stratagem had not only forced the abandonment of the Napoleonic confederation's plans but also induced MacGregor to abandon Amelia Island.[131] The high hopes with which the international community of adventurers had begun 1817 had, by the final months of the year, all but evaporated. But not all of them were willing to admit defeat and renounce their schemes.

4

Ultra-Quixotism: The Bonapartist Invasion of Texas

The discovery of the Lakanal papers effectively killed the plot to put Joseph Bonaparte on a Mexican throne—if such a plot ever really existed.[1] But not all the French exiles abandoned the idea of intervening in the turbulent affairs of New Spain. In the summer of 1817 the recently arrived Gen. Charles Lallemand set in motion an audacious plan to establish a fortified camp in the disputed Texas borderlands, a region claimed by both the United States and Spain. At the time, many observers suspected that it would become a base from which to invade Mexico proper. Aided by an inner circle of talented lieutenants—his own brother Henri, Gen. Antoine Rigau, and the seasoned colonial administrator George Jeannet—the charismatic General Lallemand assembled a group of followers among the military expatriates to undertake this dangerous adventure. Lallemand intended the Society for the Cultivation of the Vine and Olive to play a role in this endeavor.

The Bonaparte of the New World

Like so many of his fellow officers-in-exile, Gen. Charles-François-Antoine Lallemand had passed his entire adult life under arms.[2] He had enlisted in the army at the age of seventeen and risen rapidly through the ranks. His remarkably active career took him through some of the most storied military campaigns of the age: Napoleon's invasion of Italy, the expedition to Egypt, the attempted reconquest of Haiti, and the guerilla war in Spain. In 1815, when General Lallemand learned of Napoleon's return from Elba, he attempted to lead a military uprising he had previously coordinated with two other generals, his younger brother, Henri, and Lefebvre-Desnouettes. Although the revolt failed and the plotters were imprisoned, Lallemand's actions earned him Napoleon's gratitude and the hatred of the Bourbon regime. Back in power, Napoleon rewarded the intrepid general with the command of a mounted regiment of the Imperial Guard, at whose head he was lightly wounded at Waterloo. Returning to France with the remnants of the army, he caught up with the indecisive former emperor at the Atlantic port of Rochefort. Lallemand urged his wavering chief to escape to America. To arrange for Napoleon's flight, Lalle-mand went to Bordeaux where the local military commander, General Clausel, put him in contact with the sympathetic American consul, William Lee, about hiring a fast ship to undertake the hazardous mission.[3] But on his return to Rochefort, Lallemand found that Napoleon had decided to place himself in English custody. In a gesture of loyalty, Lallemand and other members of Na-poleon's retinue embarked with him on the warship *Bellerophon* and sailed for England. The date was 16 July 1815.[4]

For Lallemand this was the beginning of a two-year anabasis that would take him halfway around the world before finally reaching the United States.[5] In what Lallemand considered a breach of trust, the British refused to release him after arriving in England, but instead dispatched him, General Savary (an-other of Napoleon's eleventh-hour stalwarts), Major Schultz, and several other officers to a fortress dungeon on the island of Malta. Lallemand's incarceration was actually a blessing in disguise, for it saved him from the Bourbon military court in France, which condemned him to death in absentia on charges of treason, rebellion, and attempting to overthrow the monarchy. When finally released, Lallemand boarded an English merchant ship bound for the Turkish port of Smyrna.[6] There, after being rebuffed by the Sultan and evading arrest by French agents, Lallemand headed for Persia where he hoped to gain employ-ment in the Shah's army.[7] This and a subsequent attempt to enter the service of Egypt having failed, Lallemand decided to join his younger brother, Henri, in America. Upon arriving in Boston on 11 May 1817, he was feted by enthusiastic Americans who had followed in their newspapers the hair-raising odyssey of a man portrayed in the press as one of the most heroic victims of "English Machiavellianism."[8]

Lallemand was soon joined by several other late-arriving refugees from Bour-bon France who would play key roles in the planning and execution of the Texas expedition. His second-in-command was Gen. Antoine Rigau, a career soldier of a socially modest, small-town background who had enlisted as a pri-vate in the infantry in 1779.[9] For young men who, like himself, lacked wealth and pedigree, promotion to officer rank in the royal army was a near impossi-bility. But with revolution came opportunity, especially for experienced military professionals who could train and lead the revolutionary levies. Named captain in a hussar regiment in 1793, Rigau served in many of the great battles of the revolutionary decade and acquired a reputation for courage, a reputation en-hanced by the wounds that "covered his entire body."[10] The worst was a gunshot to the jaw that had crushed his mandible and so mutilated his tongue that he had lost the power of intelligible speech. Appointed general in 1807 at the age of forty-eight, Rigau remained what he had always been: a no-nonsense, fighting soldier. During Napoleon's return from Elba, however, Rigau abandoned his apolitical professionalism to hide the fugitive conspirator Lefebvre-Desnouettes and—thanks in part to the liberal distribution of drink—induce two passing royal regiments to betray their oath to the Bourbons and acknowledge Napoleon as emperor. To make matters worse, Rigau had paid for the drink by taking ten thousand francs from the local civil administration. For these acts, Rigau was named in the proscription ordinance of 24 July 1814 and forced to flee the country. At first he found safety in Sarrebruck, just across the Rhine River in Germany, where he was joined by his two sons—also military officers—Narcisse-Périclès and Dieudonné. Together they began to foment discontent among French troops stationed across the border by circulating seditious pamphlets among them and encouraging them to desert. When the Bourbon government of France instituted extradition proceedings, Rigau fled with his son Narcisse-Périclès and daughter Antonia for the United States. They arrived in New York in November 1817 and joined the Lallemand brothers soon thereafter.

Lallemand's chief administrative and financial deputy was Georges-Nicholas Jeannet-Oudin, sometimes called Manchot (sleeve) because he had only one arm.[11] Jeannet was raised in a prominent mercantile family of Arcis-sur-Aube, a market town in the Champagne region of France. As a young man he followed his father into business and became a successful cotton merchant. When the Revolution broke out, the Jeannet clan placed itself at the forefront of the movement and, thanks to its local stature, found itself well placed to secure office and advancement. Jeannet's uncle, Danton, became a political figure of national importance; his brother Louis-François became a general; and he himself held a variety of important public positions. Although he was elected mayor of his hometown in 1790, most of Jeannet's political career was spent in appointed offices. After serving as agent of the Executive Council (over which his uncle Danton presided) at the siege of Thionville, Jeannet was sent to French Guyana where he was charged with overseeing the emancipation of the slaves. He spent most of the 1790s there, earning a reputation as a radical for his treatment of the conservative legislators deported there after the coup d'état of 18 fructidor year V (4 September 1797) and his institution of a social regime in which (according to his enemies) former slaves were encouraged to terrorize the white colonists. In the late 1790s he was posted briefly to Guadeloupe (this time with his brother Gen. Louis-François Jeannet) before being recalled to France by Napoleon. Under the emperor, Jeannet served in the War Ministry and also founded a sugar-beet refinery in his hometown. Having incurred royalist wrath for his actions as a colonial administrator, Jeannet fled to the United States after 1815 with his wife and children.

It is impossible to reconstruct with certainty the inner calculations of Charles Lallemand as he seized upon and carried into execution the idea of invading the Texas borderlands. It is not clear that even his closest lieutenants ever knew the real aim of the desperate undertaking.[12] What is clear is that, by September 1817, he had resolved to lead an expedition to Spanish America and begun his preparations accordingly. His trusted lieutenants Rigau and Jeannet, as well as Galabert, were charged with finding recruits among the expatriate officers adrift in the cities of the Atlantic seaboard. Prospective candidates were informed of neither the destination nor goal of the expedition, but were assured that it would be launched on a grand scale, that it had government backing, and that it would strike Spanish America—the Floridas, Panama, Buenos Aires, Mexico, or even Texas depending on who was doing the telling.[13] There were even rumors that its true purpose was to liberate Bonaparte from Saint Helena.

Lallemand did not confine his recruiting activities to the East Coast of the United States. He dispatched agents to Louisiana and the Gulf Coast, as well as to the French Caribbean colonies of Guadeloupe and Martinique—Jeannet's old stomping ground—where they sought to entice soldiers in the local garrisons to desert their units and join the expedition.[14] It was also rumored that emissaries had been sent to Europe, where they were scouring the ranks of the Bonapartist disaffected for reinforcements. Lallemand's widely cast net failed to land the catch of eager veterans he expected and needed. Potential participants recognized the perils of a freelance attack on Spanish possessions; the chilling example of Mina and his followers—executed only months earlier—was still fresh in their minds. Lallemand's assurances that he had official support from the United States or some other government did little to calm their fears. As the French consul in New York City put it, many officers gave Lallemand a wide berth because "they do not want to get themselves hanged."[15] In addition, his recruiters faced competition from other adventurers who were also seeking followers in the United States, particularly Gregor MacGregor who had tried to recruit Lallemand himself to join his Amelia Island expedition.[16] Because of these obstacles, Lallemand had barely more than 150 recruits by the end of 1817.

Lallemand's shortage of funds hampered his recruitment effort. Lacking the wherewithal to provide enlistment bounties, he could not attract and retain large numbers of followers, let alone provide them with supplies adequate to their perilous mission. And without a large, well-equipped force at his disposal, Lallemand found it difficult to convince potential financial backers that his expedition could succeed. Even those close to the general, like Pierre-Paul-François Degrand and Stephen Girard, were loath to risk their money on such a desperate (and vague) adventure.[17] Breaking this vicious cycle—no money no men, no men no money—was beyond his power when simply providing for the upkeep of his followers while waiting for an opportune moment to launch his expedition stretched his resources. To meet even these modest expenses, Lallemand was forced to adopt extraordinary fund-raising measures—measures that involved bending the Society for the Cultivation of the Vine and Olive to his own ends.

Lallemand perceived in the society—now bereft of its forceful leaders, Generals Clausel and Lefebvre-Desnouettes—an opportunity to obtain money for his expedition. On 9 September 1817 the members of the society met in Philadelphia to carry out the long-awaited distribution of allotments in the grant.[18] From the outset, trouble was in the air, plainly visible in the seating arrangements. All the military officers clustered at one side of the hall, a disposition intended to "signal the predominance that the officers wanted to exercise in the group's deliberations." The meeting opened with a motion by members of the military faction to exclude from the society all those who had come to the United States before the overthrow of Napoleon—in essence, the civilian refugees from Saint-Domingue and France. Refusing to be intimidated by the officers, they responded so vigorously that the officers took insult. The meeting quickly degenerated into a verbal free-for-all, replete with "insults and filthy, dishonorable appellations." At the height of the tumult, General Vandamme brandished his sword, threatening the civilians with violence if they did not accept the officers as "masters at the Tombigbee." They retorted that the military men were "no longer at the head of their battalions," and some of the bravest took up Vandamme's challenge to duel the next day. In vain did the current president of the society—Charles Villars, an immigrant from France who had resided in the United States for twenty years—attempt to restore order. Only by dousing the lights in the hall did some of the more quick-thinking members prevent violence from breaking out on the spot. The meeting ended with the society on the verge of schism and the distribution of allotments paralyzed.

If the fireworks of the previous night nearly shattered the internal cohesion of the society, the following day's events almost destroyed its public credibility.

The twelve men who had taken up Vandamme's invitation to duel concocted a plan to humble the general and teach him a lesson he would not soon forget. Instead of convening at the agreed-upon dueling ground, they would each lodge a formal complaint against Vandamme with a different justice of the peace. These officials, it was hoped, would turn up simultaneously at the general's doorstep and together lead him through the town to appear before their respective district magistrates. This humiliating procession would teach the choleric general that the classical axiom, "cedant arma togae" (swords cede to citizens' robes) was the rule in the United States. But calmer heads among the Domingans persuaded their colleagues to abandon a scheme certain to make a mortal enemy out of Vandamme, deepen the society's internal divisions, and heap public ridicule on all the expatriates. It was resolved instead to send two delegations, one military and the other civilian, to Washington to present their respective cases to the secretary of the treasury, whose department was responsible for the public lands in general and those of the Vine and Olive grant in particular.[19]

At the same time, tension within the military faction distanced prominent figures who could have served as counterweights to Charles Lallemand. The most serious of these intermilitary disputes pitted Vandamme and his friends against Lallemand's cadre of would-be adventurers. Having learned that Lallemand was planning some sort of blow against the Spanish colonies, Vandamme became incensed. Such a provocation, he feared, would cast discredit on the exiles, poison their relationship with their American hosts, and jeopardize their chances of obtaining clemency from the king of France. Denouncing Lallemand's machinations to William Lee (who promptly informed John Quincy Adams), Vandamme vowed that "he would never suffer that the last asylum offered to himself and his countrymen by the American people should be endangered by the conduct of boys, fools, and madmen."[20]

The incipient conflict between the Vandamme and Lallemand cliques burst into the open at the next meeting of the society, on October 22, when the secretary of the treasury's ruling was to be announced and the allotments finally distributed. Trouble began when Vandamme's chief lieutenant, "Colonel" Taillade, had some words with Henri Lallemand. As tempers flared, the "most vile insults" were exchanged, and Taillade challenged the younger Lallemand to a duel, a challenge that was promptly accepted. The next morning, before setting off for his dawn encounter with Taillade, Lallemand sent his fiancée, Henriette Girard (Stephen Girard's niece), a lachrymose farewell note melodramatically dated "the day of my death." In it, the younger Lallemand mourned that "on the eve of my marriage, a fatal duel has transformed my nuptial bed into a tomb."[21] Lallemand's prediction was far from accurate, although what actually transpired may have left him wishing for an honorable exit from this world. Instead of fighting to the death, the two myrmidons were arrested by local constables before they could even draw their swords. "Followed by a crowd of people," the hapless pair was led through Philadelphia in police custody and taken before a magistrate who made them bail a substantial bond. This public scandal marked the end of Vandamme's active involvement in the society. Although he and Taillade retained their shares of land in the colony, they never again figured in its deliberations. A major obstacle to Lallemand's hold over the society had been eliminated.

It was on the occasion of his younger brother's wedding that Charles Lallemand definitively secured his predominance. The leading exiles—Joseph Bonaparte, Marshal Grouchy, the generals who had not yet left for Alabama, and dozens of officers—were all invited to the ceremony, held at the house of the bride's wealthy uncle. Fearful that attendance at such a public gathering of so many proscribed Bonapartist exiles would hurt his chances of obtaining a royal pardon—which he had been soliciting ever since arriving in the United States—the aristocratic Grouchy hesitated to attend. The Lallemands insisted, however, and the marshal reluctantly agreed, albeit with the proviso that his presence be kept a secret. One can well imagine his shock and outrage when he learned that major American newspapers had run descriptions of the wedding noting the presence of "Marshal Grouchy and son."[22] Suspecting that the mendacious, upstart Lallemands had wanted "to place themselves on the same line as himself," as well as undercut his efforts to obtain Bourbon clemency, Grouchy thenceforth distanced himself from the activities of the society— although he, like Vandamme and Taillade, retained his share of land.[23] Grouchy, moreover, was not the only officer to fall out with the Lallemands in the course of the wedding. At a well-lubricated postnuptial banquet, one of Charles Lallemand's closest confidants and self-described author of his Texas plan, Colonel Galabert, reportedly "stupefied everyone" not only by his "rantings against the Bourbon family" but even more so by his outbursts against "France, the French people, and everything French." Probably a reflection of growing tensions between the two, Galabert's tirades certainly gave Lallemand a pretext for sidelining his former collaborator. Like Vandamme, Taillade, and Grouchy, as well as the absent Generals Clausel and Lefebvre-Desnouettes, Galabert would not take part in Lallemand's expedition. Swerving from scandal to scandal, Hyde de Neuville wryly remarked, the exiles could be "safely entrusted with the task of their own discredit."[24]

With his potential military opponents out of the way, Charles Lallemand set in motion a scheme for raising badly needed cash through the Society for the Cultivation of the Vine and Olive. This shadowy operation appears to have rested on a mutually beneficial arrangement worked out between the general and the influential merchants who spoke for the civilian faction in the society. The merchants, for the most part Domingan exiles resident in Philadelphia, agreed to elect Lallemand to the presidency of the society, a position from which he could carry out the long-delayed distribution of allotments—and ensure that his followers received land. In return, Lallemand promised to have his men sell their allotments to the merchants at the price of a dollar per acre. Both sides stood to gain from the deal: Lallemand would raise money for his expedition, and the merchants would acquire more land than allowed by the terms of the Act of 3 March 1817.

This plan was carried out with scarcely a hitch.[25] Presenting himself as a peacemaker who could bridge the gap between soldiers and civilians, Lallemand was elected president of the society at the end of October. From this position he presided over the committee charged with assigning allotments in the grant. The committee promptly approved the distribution of 160-acre allotments to a number of Lallemand's followers. For the most part officers interested in neither agriculture nor settlement, they had not put their names down on the original subscription list. Some, moreover, were not even French, but Poles, Neapolitans, Germans, Piedmontese, and Spaniards who had served in the armies of Napoleon's satellite kingdoms and puppet states.[26] The records of the General Land Office suggest that there were fifty to sixty latecomers.[27] Most of them signed a document granting power-of-attorney to Georges Jeannet, whom Lallemand had entrusted with arranging the transaction with the Philadelphian-Domingan merchants. In a complicated series of transfers carried out during the first two weeks of December 1817, more than eleven thousand acres changed hands, raising more than eleven thousand dollars for the expedition.[28] Although this sum was not very large, it was sufficient to pay off outstanding debts, purchase last-minute supplies, and charter a vessel to carry the bulk of Lallemand's men to Texas.

Not all of Lallemand's followers gave up their grants willingly. One of the recalcitrants, Pierre Palmerani, a former second lieutenant from Parma who had served in the Empress Maria-Louisa Regiment, was summarily stripped of his allotment. Indignant, he wrote to John Quincy Adams imploring the "paternal protection" of the American government and its help in obtaining "reparation" for the injustice he had suffered.[29] A second officer stripped of his allotment, Hyacinthe Gerard, turned to French diplomats for help, offering his services as an informer in exchange for a pardon and passage back to France.[30] And it was through the revelations of another repentant young officer in Lallemand's orbit, the naval cadet Jean-Baptiste Néel, that French diplomats in America first learned of the expedition.[31]

The Germans and the Don

Lallemand's preparations went beyond recruitment and fund-raising.[32] No less important was his effort to obtain official backing for his endeavor or, failing that, to create the illusion that he enjoyed such support. This involved Lallemand in dizzying rounds of discussion with representatives of various governments—as well as with figures in the Atlantic underworld of privateering and adventurism. These dealings fueled wild speculation among European diplomats in the United States. None of his machinations, however, caused as much surprise as his negotiations with the Spanish ambassador, Don Luis de Onís. It is in these contacts between Bonapartist adventurer and Bourbon spymaster that the secret of Lallemand's purpose began to disclose itself.

Naturally, however, Lallemand turned first to the Americans for support. Some time prior to October 1817, he held discussions with influential politicians—probably including the Speaker of the House, Henry Clay—who wanted more decisive measures to aid the cause of Latin American independence. These politicians assured Lallemand that, in its winter 1817–18 session, Congress would "give an opening to all those who wished well to the revolution in Spanish America" by repealing the Neutrality Act of 3 March 1817.[33] But having caught wind of these machinations, the administration dispatched William Lee to warn off Lallemand. In an interview with the former consul, Lallemand expressed surprise that the American government could view him as "an object of anxiety" and sought to justify himself. Although he had met "with members of the American government," he admitted, they had exchanged only "personal opinions and desires." Swearing that he would never "cause any embarrassment to a country to which we owe gratitude," Lallemand promised that he had never intended "to violate its laws in order to organize within it an expedition against Mexico."[34]

Stung by the rebuke and worried about how the administration's suspicions—let alone the likelihood that his expedition would not be receiving official American support—would affect his plans, Lallemand turned at this juncture to a most unlikely source of aid: the Spanish ambassador. The genesis of the negotiations between Lallemand and Onís is unclear. According to Onís, it was he who initiated the contact by arranging a secret meeting with Lallemand's then-trusted lieutenant, Galabert. The succession of events that led to these unlikely discussions went something like this. In early October, Lt.-Col. Geraud-Calixte-Jean-Baptiste-Arsène Lacarrière Latour, a royalist French officer who had established himself in Cuba, informed the Spanish ambassador that he had recently encountered Colonel Galabert on a trip to Philadelphia and had learned from him that, despite the discovery of the Lakanal papers, the exiles were still contemplating a "vast plan" against the Spanish possessions.[35] When Onís learned that the Spanish consul in Philadelphia had once been Galabert's "intimate friend," the ambassador saw a way to arrange a secret, face-to-face meeting with the Frenchman. He directed the consul to renew his friendship with Galabert and invite him to his home. During this visit, Onís would drop by "casually," as if he were paying an innocent social call. The consul would then withdraw, leaving Galabert alone with the ambassador. No one would know of their meeting, and the two men would be able to speak in confidence. American sources suggest, however, that it was Lallemand and Galabert who, by a "masterstroke" of intriguing, induced Onís to make overtures to the French exiles.[36]

Whatever the case, Onís met with Galabert in early October and asked him about his compatriots' intentions.[37] In their three-hour discussion, Galabert explained that, although the United States had given them land, the French expatriates were dissatisfied. The officers were restless, in a state of "desperation," because they "knew no other life than war making." It was true, Galabert admitted, that there had been a plan—detailed in the intercepted Lakanal papers—to invade Mexico. But it had collapsed, largely because the officers had grown disillusioned with the Bonapartes. The passive, soft-living Joseph was an object of their disgust, and they had come to realize that his brother, even if freed from Saint Helena and restored to power, lacked the "qualities necessary for the well-being of France." At the same time, however, they had also become disenchanted with the United States because the "character of the Americans is opposed to their own." These complaints were music to the ambassador's ears. Sensing that Galabert was amenable to working for Spain and might even be able to divert the entire body of French officers from their perilous course, Onís solicited his ideas on how to prevent them from mounting attacks on Spanish possessions.

Aiming not merely to stop the French officers from acting against Spain, but, more ambitiously, to induce them to "embrace the interests of His Majesty [the king of Spain] with all their hearts," Galabert's plan was breathtakingly audacious.[38] This was its essence: in exchange for lands in the border province of Texas, the French would defend the frontiers of Mexico against expeditions launched from the sanctuary of the United States. If given the means, Galabert boasted, they could train and lead an army that would "defy that Republic and the entire world." At present, Galabert assured the ambassador, there were more than six hundred seasoned officers, all regretting their previous adventurism and all eager to redeem themselves by serving Spain with "honor and fidelity." Their numbers would soon surpass two thousand, as others were arriving daily from Europe. Funds were running out, and it was becoming increasingly difficult to restrain their energies. A small grant of four to six thousand dollars, Galabert explained, would be enough to keep them in check for the moment. In the absence of such aid, however, necessity would force them to take more vigorous measures to "provide for their subsistence."

Onís responded to Galabert in neutral, noncommittal tones, but his dispatches to Madrid suggest that he was actually quite taken with the French officer's plan. To Galabert, he explained that he did not possess the authority to approve the formation of a French satrapy in Spanish Texas. He could do nothing more than present the idea to his superiors and await their response. He also lacked the funds necessary to provide the officers with money while waiting to hear back from Madrid. But he would write to the intendant of Havana—in effect, the treasurer for the Spanish Caribbean—to see if he would advance the funds. Meanwhile, Onís concluded, Galabert and the other officers would have to wait. From the ambassador's perspective, this result alone would have amply justified his unorthodox discussions with Galabert. And if six thousand dollars could ruin the French officers' plans for invading Mexico or "at least put off their execution," it would be money well spent. But it would be wrong to assume that Onís saw in Galabert's proposition only a pretext for delaying the French. The ambassador had long urged the formation of a buffer zone to insulate the Mexican heartland from the dangerous influence of the North Americans and now saw in Galabert's propositions a chance to raise the issue again. In the accounts of the meetings he addressed to Madrid, Onís praised the idea of a French establishment in the Texas borderlands as the best "antidote against the ambitious views of this Republic."[39] The Napoleonic veteran would make an excellent border guard not only because of his exemplary martial virtues but also because he "hated the Anglo-American, . . . could not stand his pride, . . . [and] could not adapt to his customs and religion." Indeed, Onís went on, other foreigners should be encouraged to immigrate not only to the meditated Texas establishment but to all the Spanish possessions. In this way—and in this way alone—Spain might be able to keep pace with the superior demographic and economic growth of the United States. Only Protestants and Anglophones should be excluded. Of course, he "did not dare recommend this plan absolutely," but it is clear from the tone of his confidential dispatches that Onís did not dismiss Galabert's scheme out of hand.[40]

The ambassador, however, lacked the authority to make any decisions on the matter and, as he had explained, had to await direction from his government. This was slow in coming. Suspecting that the delay was a deliberate attempt to paralyze his expedition, Lallemand tried to pressure the Spanish by ostentatiously renewing his contacts with the American administration. In early November the general tried to secure an interview with John Quincy Adams but was rebuffed.[41] Undaunted, Lallemand turned up uninvited the next day and obtained a long audience with the reluctant secretary of state. The general spent much of the meeting denying that he had ever "contemplated engaging in any project contrary to the laws of the United States." He claimed to have already declined a role in MacGregor's invasion of Florida, as well as "some other projects of a similar nature." Although he had "an ardent love of liberty and a warm sympathy with the South Americans," his respect for the laws of the United States was even greater. If suspicions had been raised about his character and intentions, Lallemand protested, they must have been planted by the French and Spanish ambassadors who, "much alarmed at the new projected French settlement on the Tombigbee," were scheming to destroy it by slandering him, its current president. He took leave of Adams, reiterating his determination to avoid any action that would offend the government and asking for a meeting with President Monroe.[42] For his part, Adams was relieved, for Lallemand had given him "the strongest and most satisfactory assurances that he will engage in no project or military adventure forbidden by the laws of this country."[43]

In visiting Adams, Lallemand had never expected to find support for his expedition. Rather, his purpose was simply to be seen conferring with the administration, thereby convincing the watchful Onís that the Spanish government had better approve Galabert's proposition or that a more advantageous offer—one inimical to Spanish interests—might be forthcoming from the American government. To reinforce the point, Lallemand sent an intermediary—the naval cadet Jean-Baptiste Néel—to convey the exiles' impatience to Onís.[44] In his November meeting with the ambassador, Néel explained that the officers were getting restless, that they truly wanted to serve the king of Spain and thereby win amnesty from his French cousin, but that this was not the only course open to them. The implication was clear: if Spain refused to employ them, they would be forced to take desperate measures against Spain. In the absence of a better alternative, the French would lead an expedition of "discontented Mexicans, Spanish patriots, [and] American, English, and French adventurers" against Spanish possessions.[45] But because they preferred an honorable career in the Spanish service to the unsavory cause of insurgency, Lallemand would endeavor to restrain his impetuous followers until the response of the Spanish government arrived. But time was running out.

Lacking funds and direction from his government, but still hopeful that he could restrain the officers a little longer, Onís responded with "nice words and phrases to delay their relocation to the Tombigbee for a little."[46] Once installed in their remote grant, there was little else he could do to prevent them from organizing a military expedition and carrying out their plans. These, he suspected, would involve an attack on Pensacola, capital of Spanish West Florida, which would then be turned over to the Americans under the pretext of restoring order—a restaging of the Amelia Island comedy.[47] In a panicky dispatch he shot off the day after he learned of the officers' departure from the East Coast, the ambassador even urged the viceroy of New Spain, Don Ruiz de Apodaca, to launch a preemptive attack against the Vine and Olive colony.[48]

On 27 December, a final meeting took place between Onís and one of Lallemand's couriers.[49] The general's emissary explained that, with the number of his followers increasing and their resources dwindling, it had become "infinitely difficult" to contain them any longer. Moreover, the government of the United States was beginning to wonder why the French officers were still putting off their move to Alabama. To keep his men occupied, provide them with the means of subsistence, and alleviate the suspicions of the Americans, Lallemand had determined to lead them to the Tombigbee. There they would take up their plows while awaiting the Spanish government's reaction to Galabert's proposition. They still preferred to settle in Spanish Texas, the emissary assured Onís, albeit under "certain just and liberal conditions." To discuss these, Lallemand desired a passport for the principal Mexican port of Veracruz and a letter of introduction to Viceroy Apodaca. Onís acceded to this request on the grounds that the viceroy himself was in the best position to weigh the advantages and disadvantages of a French military settlement in Texas. Besides, prolonging discussions with Lallemand was the only way to further delay the French. This was a vain hope for, even as these discussions were under way, Lallemand's expedition had already put to sea.

The Champ d'Asile

On 17 December 1817, a hired ship, the *Huntress,* left the port of Philadelphia for Mobile, crammed with the bulk of Lallemand's force under the command of General Rigau. Newspaper accounts put the number of passengers at around 150, but eyewitness testimony indicates that only 80 or 90 men were aboard.[50] While almost all were officers who had fought for Napoleon, a significant minority—one authority has estimated as many as one-third—were not French.[51] Piedmontese, Polish, Swiss, Italian, Belgian, Dutch, Irish, Spanish, and German, they had served Napoleon's satellite kingdoms until the bitter end. With the collapse of the empire, these soldiers had been branded traitors, stripped of their positions, and hounded out of Europe. Even more than the expatriate French Bonapartists, who were at least free of the stigma of having betrayed their country, these lost children of empire had little hope of clemency. That men such as these formed such a large part of the expedition suggests the desperation of the endeavor.

It soon became apparent that this was going to be no ordinary sea voyage.[52] Only two days from Philadelphia, even before the *Huntress* had cleared the Delaware estuary, a man suspected of being a spy was assassinated.[53] The following day, December 20, a severe storm struck the ship, breaking a mast and carrying off the rudder. After repairs were effected at sea, the ship continued southward along the Atlantic coast. Only Rigau and possibly a few of his lieutenants knew its real destination. The ship had been hired for Mobile, and most of the officers on board expected to launch an attack from the Tombigbee settlement against Spanish Florida.[54] When the ship rounded the Florida Keys and turned westward, Rigau ordered the ship's captain to make for Galveston, the notorious lair of insurgent corsairs off the Texas coast. Captain Matthews refused and responded to threats by letting the ship drift aimlessly. Only the promise of a thousand-dollar bonus and indemnities for his crew convinced him to accede to Rigau's demands.[55]

The *Huntress* was now in the Gulf of Mexico, sailing perilously close to the Spanish coast guards and privateers based in Cuba. Fearful that the Spaniards had divined their hostile intentions, Rigau ordered his men to hide in the hold every time a sail was spotted on the horizon.[56] This precaution was unnecessary. The *Huntress's* only encounter with a Spanish ship was with a prize that had been recently captured by an insurgent corsair and was being taken to Galveston to be condemned. The two vessels proceeded together to the island where they arrived in the middle of January.[57] At that time, the master of Galveston was the notorious Jean Lafitte who, in addition to his privateering and smuggling operations, had recently become a secret agent in the service of Spain. Worried that the presence of the Napoleonic exiles would draw unwanted attention to his lucrative contraband business and perhaps place him in a difficult position vis-à-vis his Spanish spymasters, he could not have been pleased at their arrival. Nonetheless, as they outnumbered and outgunned his followers, Lafitte was forced to put on as cheerful a face as possible and welcome the newcomers to his domain. They erected tents and lean-tos on one side of the island—plagued by tropical heat, thirst, torrential downpours, and swarms of mosquitoes—and there awaited the arrival of Charles Lallemand. Under these harsh conditions, with nerves frayed by uncertainty and friction exacerbated by national differences, Rigau had difficulty maintaining discipline. As one participant recalled: "Disunity was the rule between the leaders and their subordinates. Every day there were duels; one of my friends was assassinated. The ill-conduct and misunderstanding of the superior officers gave rise to the most complete lack of discipline; we were more than once on the point of cutting each other's throats. We were fed up with this life and reduced to the last degree of despair when Lallemand arrived."[58] This would not be the last time Lallemand's commanding presence would be required to hold together the fractious expedition.

Instead of traveling to Galveston with the main body, the Lallemand brothers had remained on the East Coast, in New York City, where they engaged in a flurry of eleventh-hour negotiations. The Lallemands' ultimatum to the Spanish ambassador failed to get him to issue official authorization for a French settlement in Texas, although it did convince him to give Charles a passport for Veracruz and a letter of introduction to the viceroy. At the same time they were trying to squeeze a commitment (or at least a few thousand dollars) out of Onís, the Lallemands were also speaking with agents of the Latin American independence movement about the possibility that Captain Aury collaborate with them for a blow against the royalists in Mexico. Aware that the American administration had just ordered the occupation of Amelia Island, the agents urged him to abandon the base and accept the Lallemands' proposition.[59]

Aury's response has not survived, but the Lallemands claimed to have had an agreement with the privateer chieftain. Aury, according to Henri Lallemand, "was to give us transportation and supply us with powder, lead, cannons in case of need, [and] captured negroes to till the soil regularly and produce provisions." But a storm caught his fleet as it was sailing into the Gulf, which forced it to take refuge on the island of Santo Domingo and miss the planned rendezvous.[60] Aury's absence would be cruelly felt.

On December 31 the Lallemands left New York in the brig *Actress,* bound for New Orleans. They were accompanied by three trusted young subordinates: Louis Lauret (Charles Lallemand's aide-de-camp), Emile Pénières (son of the regicide, who disapproved of his son's participation in the expedition), and Jacques Barraud. They arrived at the mouth of the Mississippi River on 4 February 1818.[61] One of Henri Lallemand's first acts was to write to Stephen Girard to explain why he had abandoned his new bride—Girard's niece—just weeks after their marriage. In phrases calculated to appeal to the self-made millionaire, Lallemand boasted that he was "the architect of the fortune which I acquired in France and, to restore that fortune, I am ready to go through danger, trouble, and privation."[62] There would be danger, trouble, and privation in abundance, although not for Henri who remained in New Orleans to seek out new recruits and provide logistical support for the expedition.

The Lallemand brothers remained together in New Orleans for two weeks. During that time they sought recruits—without much success—and purchased additional supplies and equipment. In addition to small amounts of flour, arms, and gunpowder, the Lallemands also obtained goods suitable as presents for the Indians they expected to encounter in Texas, as well as two antique bronze cannon.[63] But their efforts to equip the expedition were hampered by a shortage of funds, a problem compounded by the dramatic rise in prices experienced in New Orleans during the winter of 1817–18. "Just living in this place is terribly expensive," wrote Henri Lallemand ten days after his arrival, "and nothing can be done except for its weight in gold." To pay for their purchases, the Lallemands relied on a letter of credit from Stephen Girard that allowed them to borrow four thousand dollars.[64] Rumor transformed this modest loan into unlimited financial backing from the famous capitalist. In fact, the Lallemands' money ran out in April, and local merchants stopped extending them credit.[65] In desperation, Henri took passage back to Philadelphia—he had to borrow money to pay for the voyage—to plead with Girard for assistance. He begged, unsuccessfully for a two-thousand-dollar loan to repay various creditors, as well as to purchase 150 barrels of flour required to prevent the expedition from failing "for lack of provisions."[66] After this disappointment, Henri seems to have given up on the expedition. The French consul-general was surprised by his inactivity. The younger Lallemand, he noted in June, "has neither booked passage back to New Orleans, . . . nor is he seeking, at least ostensibly, to recruit adventurers to go to Mexico."[67]

While Henri remained behind in the United States to wage his losing battle to meet the expedition's logistical needs, Charles left for Galveston on 19 February to take charge of his followers, restore their discipline, and revive their sinking spirits. Accompanied by eight officers, he traveled by land to join Rigau, passing through the Attakapas district of south Louisiana.[68] Within days of his arrival, one eyewitness reported, "everything changed; he reestablished order and obedience."[69] Wasting no time, he ordered the expedition to leave the insalubrious quarters on the island and head up the Trinity River to a place the Spaniards called Cayo de Gallardo, or the Oroquisiac bluffs, the site he had chosen for their permanent encampment.[70]

The first leg of their journey involved rowing the length of Galveston Bay, a deceptively calm lagoon made treacherous by unpredictable tides and fierce winds.[71] On the first day, sudden gusts kicked up huge waves that swamped one of the tiny boats, drowning six of the men on board, including Col. Emile Vorster. At night the men drew their boats onto sandbanks and tried to shelter themselves from the elements. After three days and nights, they finally arrived at the mouth of the Trinity River. There Lallemand divided his men into two groups. He would reach the Cayo de Gallardo by water, leading the provision-laden boats and a small contingent of rowers up the meandering watercourses of the Trinity delta. The bulk of the force, again under Rigau's command, would take a more direct, overland route. The groups were to rendezvous three days later, but things did not go as planned. Lallemand almost immediately became lost in the mazelike wetlands and took six days to arrive at his destination. Rigau had better luck finding the site and arrived on time, although his men—who carried only three days' rations—suffered terribly from hunger as they waited for their tardy leader.

Lallemand's arrival brought them only temporary respite, for the boats carried rations for only eight more days. A new detachment was hastily sent back to Galveston to procure more food, while the men at Cayo de Gallardo had to reduce their rations to only one biscuit a day. As the days passed and the boats did not return, the men ran out of biscuits and were forced to subsist on only four ounces of rice and two handfuls of corn a day. When the boats finally appeared at the end of March, they brought with them only ten days' rations and fifteen new followers, "comrades in misfortune" who had been recruited by Henri Lallemand in New Orleans. The boats were thus dispatched back to Galveston again, and rations maintained at starvation levels. Desperate with hunger, many of the men ate a wild plant that resembled lettuce but produced "terrible convulsions which seemed like attacks of epilepsy" in those who ate it. Fortunately the poisonous plant, called fools' grass (*l'herbe aux fous*) by the party, was not fatal. Food shortages continued for two more months until Lallemand finally worked out a reliable system of bringing up food from Galveston. Throughout the short existence of his settlement, it remained dependent on the island's master, Jean Lafitte, who reportedly supplied it—on credit—with more than three hundred thousand francs worth of provisions.[72]

Lallemand's first efforts at organizing the settlement were intended to put it on a war footing. He divided his men into three cohorts, each with a distinct military specialization.[73] The first, commanded by Colonel Douarche, was designated infantry; the second, led by Colonel Charrasin (until his desertion) and then by Major Schultz, cavalry; and the third, under Lieutenant-Colonel Fourni (who also deserted), artillery. There was, in addition, a small staff, including Georges Jeannet, who took the imposing title of "intendant-general." Lallemand imposed military discipline on the cohorts, drilled them, and set them to work building a wooden fort. Additional cannon were brought up from Galveston, and munitions were fabricated on site. From 4 A.M. to 8:30 A.M., and then again from 5 P.M. to 7 P.M., everyone labored on these collective tasks. Only in their spare time were the men allowed to build huts for themselves and tend their gardens. Some accounts mention attempts to trade with local Indians. But even the most sympathetic descriptions agree that the colonists' energies went mainly into warlike preparations. The establishment in Texas was a military camp, not a colony.

The former general took great pains, however, to paint a different picture for public consumption. In a proclamation released to the press and widely reprinted under the title "Extract of a Letter from a French Settler," Lallemand stressed the pacific, industrious character of his establishment.[74] Victims of misfortune and persecution, the manifesto began, the French had come to Texas to seek a field of asylum, a Champ d'Asile.[75] As Texas had been "abandoned by civilized man," the unfortunate exiles felt justified in claiming it for themselves under "the rights granted to man by the author of nature."[76] The exiles sought only shelter for themselves, the proclamation continued, and harbored no malice toward any person or power. "We will attack no one, we have no hostile intention; we ask only for peace and friendship . . . and will be grateful for the goodwill that is shown us. We respect religion, law, morality, and the customs of civilized nations. We respect the independence, habits, and lifestyle of the Indian nations whom we will disturb neither in their hunting, nor in any other point of their existence. . . . Our existence will be peaceful, active, and laborious." But, warned the proclamation, the men of the Champ d'Asile would not hesitate to defend themselves if "persecution followed us into the deserts where we have sought our retreat." If attacked, they were prepared to defend themselves to the death. "We have arms. . . . Here we will live free and honorably, or find our graves." Signaling the determination of the French to assert the independence of their establishment, these ill-considered threats could not help but raise the hackles of the Spanish and American governments, both of which claimed this part of Texas as their own. In the judgment of the French consul-general, it was this "maladroit" proclamation that was Lallemand's undoing.[77]

The proclamation was the first salvo in a veritable barrage of propaganda. While the Lallemand brothers did not possess the fund-raising, recruiting, and political skills necessary for the success of their endeavor, they sought to compensate for these deficiencies by skillful public relations. Even diplomatic officials, themselves experts in the arts of disinformation and propaganda, could not help but admire the Lallemands' mastery of these techniques. As he followed the activities of the brothers in early 1818, the French consul in New Orleans was impressed by "the publicity they are giving their enterprise in the newspapers."[78] Their propaganda efforts were not limited to the press. The Lallemands also disseminated rumors by word of mouth and, through deliberate actions to lend them credence, magnified their scope and encouraged their spread. Many of these rumors were reported by consular officials. At various times the French consul in the city heard that, in addition to having unlimited financial support from Stephen Girard, the Lallemands enjoyed official Spanish or American backing, that they had already enrolled thousands of men for their expedition, that the generals who had gone to Alabama (Lefebvre-Desnouettes and Clausel) would soon be bringing up reinforcements, that they were expecting massive naval support from insurgent privateers, that secret arrangements had been made with rich Mexican mine owners, and, of course, that the ultimate aim of the expedition was to rescue Napoleon from Saint Helena.[79] Even the French ambassador, no stranger to political intrigue, marveled at how many "diverse rumors these adventurers have circulated."[80]

Naturally the brothers did not neglect the printed word. They employed newspapers controlled by friendly editors—particularly French-language publications like Chaudron's *L'Abeille* and Leclerc's *L'Ami des Lois*—to disseminate glowing descriptions of the Champ d'Asile. As was the custom at the time, other editors, including those of the major English-language papers of the United States like *Niles' Register* or the *National Intelligencer,* would then translate and reprint these stories, making them available to their American readership. For example, on 18 June 1818, *L'Abeille* published what was supposed to be an "extract of letters from the French Colony on the Trinity River," which boasted of the good living to be had in the burgeoning settlement. The land was of the "best quality" and "easily cultivated"; vast tracts had already been planted with "sugar, cotton, and indigo"; the forests swarmed with game; docile herds of cows, bulls, and horses were there for the taking; the "beautiful lakes" were "full of fish"; and relations with the Indians, who regularly brought tribute in the form of fresh meat, were excellent. In short, the "colony" was a veritable Garden of Eden.[81] This piece of naked boosterism was picked up by *L'Ami des Lois* and reprinted both in the original French and in English translation.[82] *Niles' Register,* which had already published a translation of Lallemand's proclamation in its issue of 8 August 1818, published a variety of notices based on this and other equally exuberant descriptions. On 26 September, Niles wrote that the colony was "gathering strength very fast," and on 7 November that "the number of Lallemand's followers still keeps increasing" and that "neither provisions, money, or arms are said to be wanting."[83] Similar reports filled the pages of American newspapers during the summer months and into the fall of 1818.[84] The crowning achievement of the propaganda campaign, however, was not to be found in the United States, but rather in France, in the pages of the *Minerve Française,* one of the leading liberal opposition papers. Reprinting the Lallemands' communiqués, issuing vehement editorials praising their steadfastness, publishing rousing songs by the Bonapartist bard Berenger, and sponsoring a nationwide collection drive for the exiles, the *Minerve* made the Texas expedition a symbolic rallying point for the political opposition and forged an image of the Champ d'Asile that has lasted down to the present day.[85]

The Lallemands' propaganda served several functions. First, it was intended to persuade one or more established governments to extend official sanction to the expedition or, failing that, to sow so much mistrust among them that they would be unable to share intelligence and coordinate countermeasures. By fabricating accounts of the vast material and political resources at their disposal, the Lallemands hoped to convince either the American or Spanish government that their force could be a powerful ally—or a dangerous enemy—and thereby win formal recognition and concessions. When negotiations with Adams and Onís failed to produce the desired result, the Lallemands spread another rumor: that they had been commissioned by the French government to conquer Texas "to form a new colony called New France under the auspices of Louis XVIII" not merely "to indemnify him for the loss of Louisiana" but eventually to "revolutionize" the former French colony and "attach it to the so-called New France."[86] The rumor was taken seriously not only by veteran filibusterer Joshua Childs, who warned the administration that "if New Spain should be revolutionized by a second Napoleon, the United States will have to dispute their title to Louisiana with him," but also by John Quincy Adams, who grilled the French ambassador about it.[87] In addition to raising American suspicions of French intentions, it also "sowed discord" between the Spanish and French embassies, preventing them from acting together to nip the expedition in the bud.[88] In the confusion and mistrust generated, the Lallemands hoped promising new opportunities would arise for their expedition.

Another function of the Lallemands' propaganda campaign was to secure financial backing and recruits. If the real state of their finances and following were known, the brothers reasoned, few would be willing to risk life and limb on their behalf. But if no one would back an obvious loser, they might flock to join an apparent winner. The appearance of wealth, resources, diplomatic support, and manpower, they hoped, would place these very things at their disposal. The rumor of Stephen Girard's unconditional financial backing was intended to unlock the purses of the capitalists, that of armies of thousands assembling in the ports of Europe and North America to attract new recruits, and that of a plan to rescue Napoleon to mobilize the support of the enemies of legitimacy the world over.[89] To conjure the reality of power from its illusion was the main goal of the Lallemands' propaganda efforts.

As the toilsome days in Texas dragged on for Lallemand's followers, rumor also began to play an important role in holding together the weary band. The testimony of survivors of the Champ d'Asile all agree that Lallemand deliberately nourished the most brilliant hopes, for only hope could keep his exhausted, starving men from giving up their seemingly pointless efforts. He told them that reinforcements were en route from Guadeloupe and Martinique, as well as France itself. In Baltimore and New York, hundreds of foreigners had assembled to join them. The Creoles of Louisiana were riding to join them, as were the frontiersmen of Kentucky and Tennessee. A force of veteran insurgents would soon be joining them, and they would then march together on the legendary mines of San Luis Potosi. Sympathetic merchants were on the point of sending them vast funds. An attack on the heart of Mexico was imminent. They would be joined on the coast by an insurgent fleet of dozens of ships. Napoleon would be rescued, spirited to America, and personally lead them to new glory. These and other rumors seem to have kept the expedition in hand, a real testimony to Lallemand's reputation and personal magnetism. But they could not conceal the true circumstances of the venture indefinitely. "In hiding the nullity of his means and resources under a great air of importance, and seeming prouder as he became weaker, he succeeded for some time in hiding from them his embarrassments and worries—in a word, everything in their position that was frightful for them and dishonoring for him."[90]

The reality of the Champ d'Asile was indeed frightful. Food remained in short supply, so the expedition remained dependent on the treacherous Jean Lafitte—who, in late June or early July, submitted a plan to the Spanish government for the destruction of the encampment.[91] The promised influx of reinforcements from North America and Europe never materialized. "Not a single Frenchman," a French diplomat wrote in August 1818, "has left for the new colony."[92] To prop up their flagging spirits, or at least prevent them from dwelling on their increasingly bleak prospects, Lallemand kept the men working constantly on extending the fortifications.[93] By the time of the camp's dissolution, it was reported by one survivor that more than two thousand defenders would have been required to man the ramparts that had been constructed.[94] And Lallemand continued to plant rumors and nourish false hopes to buck up his dispirited followers. That he managed to prevent a "general revolt" by these expedients, a French diplomatic official wrote, was "proof of his eminent talents in the art of leading men."[95] Even so, "discontent and disunion manifested themselves," and "duels became frequent and murderous."[96] One fugitive from the Champ d'Asile, a Belgian peddler who had been lured to the settlement by the promise of being made its commissary officer, reported that four men had died at the hands of their comrades before his escape.[97] In this tense climate of forced labor, factionalism, and violence, desertion was rife. In a bid to stop it, Lallemand stationed twenty of his most loyal stalwarts around the encampment every night with orders to shoot anyone who tried to leave.[98] Even this draconian measure did not entirely check the outflow. At least eleven people escaped, including Charrasin and Fourni, commanders of the second and third cohorts.[99] By the beginning of April, one survivor reported, only sixty men were left.[100]

The End of the Champ d'Asile

The fate of the Champ d'Asile ultimately rested with Spain and the United States, the two powers that claimed the area in which it lay. Although the question of ownership had yet to be definitively resolved—the exact demarcation of the boundary between Spain and America in the Southwest would not be determined until the signature of the Transcontinental Treaty in 1819—it was clear that neither government was indifferent to the presence of an armed camp of Frenchmen in the disputed zone. Despite the glowing reports propagated by Lallemand, his agents, and allies, public opinion in the United States was not wholly swayed. Significant currents of dissent, ranging from the merely skeptical to the downright hostile, made themselves felt in the pages of the American press. Much of the suspicion and anger stemmed from the perceived ingratitude of the French exiles. They had been treated as heroes and given a generous grant of land to help them make new lives for themselves in America. But instead of showing appreciation, they had sold their Alabama tracts to raise money for an armed expedition of the most dubious nature.[101] Although John Quincy Adams's friend and informant, the Franco-American publisher and entrepreneur Degrand, was not surprised that the "French military emigrants should barter away their vines and olive-trees for the chance of gathering fresh laurels," others were both shocked and outraged.[102] In his influential journal, Niles lambasted Congress for granting land to the French exiles because the gift had only been used to fund Lallemand's mysterious expedition—an expedition that Niles assumed was "another speculation."[103] If Niles was skeptical and somewhat bemused, reassuring his readers that there was little chance Lallemand would "conquer the United States, as some seem to apprehend," the *National Intelligencer* adopted a far grimmer tone. In claiming sovereignty over Texas, establishing a "military form of government," and announcing their intention to "justify the occupancy of the territory by arms," the French emigrants, the paper proclaimed, had shown their true colors and revealed their "hostility to our laws."[104] Spurred by editorials such as these, Congress ordered an investigation of the proceedings of the Society for the Cultivation of the Vine and Olive in December 1818.[105] It would not be the last.

In the absence of personal correspondence, minutes of private conversations, or records of formal cabinet deliberations, it is difficult to retrace the steps of the Monroe administration as it sought to define a policy toward the Champ d'Asile. Among the foreign diplomatic corps, however, there was much speculation—at times verging on conviction—that the Americans were going to use the Bonapartist incursion into Texas as a pretext for seizing that disputed territory. The United States had used this tactic before. In 1810 American forces occupied most of Spanish West Florida after a revolt, secretly encouraged by the United States government, broke out in Baton Rouge. Such tumult, the Madison administration claimed at the time, not only violated the laws and threatened the security of the United States, but also demonstrated that Spain was incapable of maintaining order and had thus lost all legitimate claim to sovereignty over the territory. Abortively in 1812 and then with more success in 1817, the administration had adopted a similar course toward Amelia Island, invoking the disorderly consequences of MacGregor's invasion—slave-smuggling and piracy—to justify American military occupation. Given these precedents— and the Monroe administration's announcement in December 1817 that it would suppress the "piratical establishment at Galveston"—foreign observers expected to see this now-familiar scenario played out in Texas.[106]

While dismissing the notion that the United States had instigated Lallemand's expedition, Hyde de Neuville had little doubt that the administration would take advantage of the Bonapartist incursion to occupy the disputed land in Texas as it had on Amelia Island. Even worse in his view was that the Spanish ambassador had let himself be drawn into a trap whereby he had furnished the Americans with diplomatic "arms against Spain."[107] Since Onís appeared through his negotiations with Lallemand to have invited the French into the disputed territory, effectively occupying it for Spain, the Americans could now justify their own military intervention there on the grounds that they were only responding to Spanish provocation. At the very least, the Monroe administration could invoke Spain's involvement with Lallemand to justify General Jackson's recent conquest of East Florida. Hyde's suspicions were confirmed at a dinner party where Henry Clay laughingly whispered in the ambassador's ear that the Champ d'Asile was "a trick on the Don."[108] The French consul at New Orleans had a different sense of the considerations shaping American policy toward the exiles in Texas. He wondered if the Americans might actually fear Lallemand's settlement because it had been "undertaken by Frenchmen in the neighborhood of a former French colony." If the Champ d'Asile grew and prospered, he mused, it might eventually "threaten the influence and perhaps the sovereignty of the United States in this part of their domains."[109]

Satisfied with Charles Lallemand's assurances that the expedition was in no way aimed against the United States nor detrimental to its interests, the administration had at first adopted a hands-off attitude.[110] But members of the foreign diplomatic corps continued to question the beleaguered secretary of state, and on 6 May 1818 Onís transmitted a formal protest complaining about the impunity with which the United States had allowed Lallemand to equip and recruit his expedition.[111] This finally spurred the administration into action. A week later, President Monroe held a cabinet meeting at which the matter of the Champ d'Asile was discussed for the first time. Although the laconicism of the Adams diary—the best available source—does not detail what exactly was discussed, it is clear that the meeting resulted in the determination to send a special envoy to Texas. Accordingly, on 19 May 1818 Adams summoned Maj. George Graham, a career officer who had served as acting secretary of war, and entrusted him with the mission.[112] Graham was instructed to gather as much information as he could about Lallemand's mysterious expedition, especially its "precise and real object," and then order the intruders to leave.[113] After some haggling over his per diem allowance, Graham left Washington on 6 June.

Traveling down the Mississippi and then overland via Natchez, Natchitoches, and Nacogdoches, Graham arrived in Galveston on August 27 only to learn that the French had precipitously abandoned their encampment on the Trinity weeks ago.[114] On 23 July 1818 a messenger sent by Jean Lafitte had informed them that a body of Spanish troops were moving toward them.[115] Lallemand had ordered his men to break camp and, within two hours, they had loaded their boats and departed down river. They had been encamped on Galveston Island ever since. There, Graham met with Lallemand.[116] At first, the Frenchman appeared uncomfortable to the American, respectful but displaying "considerable embarrassment and evident uneasiness of mind." To Graham's queries, Lallemand responded with old explanations: that the Champ d'Asile was intended only as "a place of refuge for those Frenchmen who had been obliged to leave their country," that "his objects in making the establishment were agricultural," that "he wished to be at peace with the whole world."

As the two men continued their talks, however, they developed a rapport and began to exchange confidences. Lallemand claimed that he had entered into a treaty with the insurgent Congress of Mexico and had been on the point of declaring war against Spain when Graham had arrived. He had delayed this step until the envoy had conveyed to him the wishes of the United States. It was at this point that Graham dropped a bombshell of his own. Disregarding his written instructions to evict the French, but perhaps obeying a verbal directive from President Monroe, he made an audacious proposition.[117] After he returned to the United States, the French should remain in Galveston—apparently in open defiance of his orders. The administration would thus have to send military forces to drive the lawless trespassers from American territory—and in the process take control of the Texas coast. In return, Graham promised them "the greatest advantages, both political and pecuniary."[118] Lallemand readily agreed and, to prepare for the great stroke, turned over command to Rigau and returned to New Orleans with Graham. As the foreign diplomatic corps had suspected, it looked as if the Lallemands were about to "stage at Galveston the same drama that Aury performed at Amelia."[119] But it was not to be. Upon learning of Graham's secret proposal, John Quincy Adams disavowed the negotiation as "unauthorized," "all of his head," and "not much to the credit of its wisdom." Perhaps daunted by the looming sectional crisis over slavery, Adams ultimately dissuaded the administration from its Texas adventure.[120]

The Champ d'Asile Exists No More

Meanwhile, Spanish authorities were making their own arrangements to deal with the French establishment in Texas.[121] While Onís seems to have held out hope that Lallemand and his followers could be enticed into royalist service, the viceroy of New Spain did not. He was convinced that the entire negotiation between the general and the ambassador—whom he considered a fool—was a "fiction" designed to advance the insurgent cause in Mexico. At the very least, the presence of "subjects of this class" would provoke "an extraordinary sensation and revive the causes that have been taken as a pretext for rebellion."[122] But Apodaca suspected that Lallemand's bizarre proposal to establish a barrier settlement in Texas was more dangerous than this. It was either a ruse, he surmised, to gain entry into the viceroyalty in order to reconnoiter its defenses in preparation for a full-blown invasion, or a diversion to get him to withdraw troops from counterinsurgency operations in the interior and wear them out in costly, pointless redeployments to the northern frontier. Stripped of troops, central Mexico would be defenseless in the face of renewed, internal rebellion.[123] Under no circumstances, Apodaca ordered, were the French to be allowed to enter Mexico. If their leader, General Lallemand, appeared, presenting a passport from Onís and demanding an audience with the viceroy, his documents were to be confiscated and he himself expelled.[124] When word arrived that the French had entered Texas and were building a fort on the Trinity River, Apodaca determined to crush them. It was, he thought, an excellent opportunity to give an example to all those contemplating action against royalist authority in Mexico.

The problem was that the French on the Trinity would be difficult to attack. Their establishment was located in a remote and trackless region at the farthest extremity of New Spain. Following an agreement with the Americans to designate the disputed area a neutral zone, the Spanish government had ordered the area depopulated several years earlier. All these factors made it difficult for a military force to traverse the area; progress would be slow, and it would have to take with it everything it might need—food, spare horses, munitions. To approach the French encampment by sea was no less difficult. A naval force would have to seize Galveston, key to the entire Texas coastline. In addition to being defended by the Gulf pirates, Galveston was protected by natural barriers. Ships approaching the harbor had to wind their way through a treacherous maze of narrow channels and shifting sandbars so complex that only a few experienced pilots—all of them apparently corsairs—could navigate it successfully. And even if the island could be seized by a naval assault, it was a near desert—a windswept sand spit lacking flora, fauna, and water. An occupying force would have to be supplied at great cost and risk (given the corsairs' presence in those waters) by sea. In these respects, Lallemand had chosen a nearly impregnable site, protected by remoteness, barrenness, and isolation.

Apodaca realized, however, that these geographical advantages also constituted the weak point of the French position. Just as it was impossible for troops converging on the Trinity to subsist off the land, so too was it impossible for Lallemand and his men to survive without provisions brought in from outside. If these could be cut off, the viceroy reasoned, it would not even be necessary to attack the French; starvation would soon force them to abandon their untenable position in the middle of the wilderness. These same thoughts had occurred to Jean Laffite who, eager to remove the inconvenient Bonapartist intruders while winning further favor with the Spanish government, had communicated a detailed plan for a combined land and sea blockade to Spanish diplomatic officials in New Orleans in a secret meeting in the house of Father Anonio Sedella, the legendary secret agent known as Père Antoine.[125] Laffite believed that only a small force would be required to dislodge the French. A party of forty or fifty men posted on the bank of the Trinity, upriver from the encampment, would suffice to seize any supply-laden canoes that local Indians might be tempted to bring to the French. If Lallemand sent out boats to seek provisions from the Indians directly, they would be intercepted and destroyed by the same detachment. At the same time, shallow-draft Spanish naval vessels would enter Galveston Bay, sail to the mouth of the Trinity, and there land a force of three or four hundred marines, thereby cutting off the flow of supplies from Galveston, as well as Lallemand's most likely escape route. Apodaca had been thinking along similar lines and adopted Laffite's plan as his own.[126]

There was, however, a major obstacle to carrying it out: the viceroyalty of New Spain had no navy to speak of. The only significant Spanish maritime forces in the Gulf region were concentrated in Cuba. Apodaca therefore resolved to request naval reinforcements from the island. To this end, he sent his aide-de-camp, naval lieutenant Don Joaquin Zayas, to Havana with orders to ask for the loan of four barks or at least two corvettes. If this request was denied, Zayas was to purchase two well-armed ships using Apodaca's personal credit to secure the required funds.[127] Zayas found passage on 27 May 1818 and, after convincing the naval authorities in Cuba of the seriousness of the situation on the Texas coast, returned to Veracruz on 15 June with two vessels of the Real Armada, the corvette *Flora* and the bergantine *Consulado*. Joined by the goelette *Belona,* which had just been purchased in Veracruz, the flotilla proceeded to Galveston under the command of naval lieutenant Don Francisco de Villavisencio and tried to impose a "rigorous blockade."[128]

On 9 August, after the tidal effects of the equinox had passed, the squadron finally left the port of Veracruz.[129] It arrived in the waters off Galveston two days later. For the remainder of the month and into early September, Villavisencio struggled to maintain a blockade on the island. His operations were hampered, however, by the fierce storms that regularly battered the Texas coast and errors in the naval charts that threatened to send the ships aground. Nonetheless, he considered his mission a success because not a single ship was spotted entering or leaving Galveston during the period of the blockade. Villavisencio interpreted this as a sign that his presence had been noted and was so dissuasive that it had effectively cut communications between New Orleans and the corsair base. With dangerous weather approaching—a hurricane would soon batter the Texas coast—Villavisencio lifted the blockade and returned to Veracruz.

As the storm finished pounding the coast, the land-based component of Apodaca's plan finally got under way. On 16 September a force of 240 soldiers commanded by Capt. Don Juan Castaneda left the capital of Texas, San Antonio de Bexar, on its long march to the Trinity.[130] His orders from Colonel Arredondo, commander of the eastern internal provinces, were not only to evict the French and destroy their fortifications but also to cow hostile Indians on the frontier and sack the town of Nacogdoches to punish its lawless, smuggling inhabitants. In a word, Castaneda was to show the flag and remind the population of the east Texas frontier that they were vassals of Ferdinand VII, subject to his law and, if necessary, his wrath. On 12 October, after a grueling journey that took its toll on men and horses, Castaneda's force arrived at the French fortifications at Cayo de Gallardo only to find them empty. Two Anglo-American settlers who had established themselves by the Trinity were captured. They informed Castaneda that the French had abandoned their establishment more than two months ago and fled to Galveston. Castaneda therefore continued his march down river, established a temporary camp near its mouth at a place called Punto de Busto, and sent a party to the island to parlay with the French.

Led by Lt. Don Jose Sandoval, this detachment set out for Galveston in a small boat and, after a hazardous journey across the windswept bay, arrived on the island several days later. They were met by French officers who brought Sandoval to Rigau's headquarters, a dismasted vessel beached in the sands. Sandoval presented Rigau with a letter from Castaneda announcing that his party was just the vanguard of a much larger force and ordering the French to leave if they wanted to avoid a fight. After conferring with his advisers, Rigau responded that he and his men wished for nothing more than to leave Galveston, but that General Lallemand, who had returned to New Orleans to arrange transport back to the United States, had not been heard from since. Protesting yet again that they had only come to Texas to establish a peaceful, agricultural colony, Rigau begged that he and his men be allowed to remain on Galveston until Lallemand's return. Given that his provisions were running dangerously low, that he had no means of attacking the French on the island, and that Spanish naval forces were nowhere to be seen, Castaneda was forced to accept this arrangement. After destroying the fortifications at the Cayo de Gallardo, he marched his exhausted and hungry men back to Bexar.

Upon learning that his subordinate had not evicted the French, let alone executed his orders to castigate the hostile Indians and raze Nacogdoches, Arredondo was furious and tried to bring Castaneda up on charges of disobedience.[131] Arredondo need not have worried. By the time the Spanish had arrived on the Trinity, the French expedition on Galveston was short of food and water, disunited, and demoralized. The hurricane of 13–15 September had covered the island in three to four feet of water, filling the few wells with saltwater and destroying the flimsy huts the French had constructed for themselves.[132] Accentuated by physical hardship, the indiscipline and fractiousness that had characterized Rigau's first attempt at command returned with a vengeance. Desertion mounted, with some men daring to attempt the journey back to Louisiana by land.[133] In their desperation to leave, some even signed on with the corsairs as menial laborers.[134] Discontent and disunion had already reached new heights when Lieutenant Sandoval disembarked on the island bearing Castaneda's ultimatum. The arrival of the Spanish forces precipitated an open schism in the expedition. A group of fifteen Lallemand stalwarts led by Lt. Pierre Guillot considered Rigau's willingness to parlay a betrayal of their cause and tried to overthrow him. Rigau, who had become increasingly resentful of Lallemand and weary of the hopeless expedition, resisted with five of his loyalists. A tense standoff ensued, and only the withdrawal of each group to a different part of the island averted bloodshed. Disgusted with this fratricidal behavior and tired of enduring pointless hardships for leaders in whom they had lost confidence, the largest part of the men coalesced into a third, neutral faction that rejected the authority of both Lallemand and Rigau and sought only to return to the United States.[135] Above all, they were furious at Lallemand for having "deceived them with the most misleading hopes, imposed on them an iron yoke, and condemned them to all sorts of privations only to abandon them in their moment of danger." With the help of Jean Laffite and General Humbert, who was then at Galveston, these "unfortunates abandoned by Lallemand on a foreign shore" were able to take passage back to New Orleans on an old prize taken from the Spanish.[136] Although a few of the French seem to have remained on Galveston Island into early 1819, with the arrival of these refugees, the French consul was able to announce that "the Champ d'Asile exists no more and its inhabitants are dispersed."[137]

Why had Lallemand thrown himself into a remote corner of Spanish Texas with few followers, little money, and no political support? What was the real purpose of the expedition? As word of the Champ d'Asile spread, the diplomats of the Old World and the New struggled to divine the purpose of the puzzling establishment. Given its strategic location in the disputed Texas borderlands, it seemed to have an important bearing on the question of American-Spanish relations, as well as on the course of the Mexican insurgency. With minds dizzied by the swirl of rumor, confounded by Lallemand's promiscuous intriguing, and made mistrustful by the great international rivalries that formed the backdrop to their thinking, the diplomats endeavored to penetrate the secret of the former French general's enterprise. Spanish authorities—as well as those of France and Great Britain, who viewed U.S. expansionism with hardly less concern—suspected a replay of the Amelia Island farce or an even more audacious territorial grab. Traditionally fearful of European intervention in the Americas, officials of the United States were concerned that the expedition might enhance the power of the Old World over the New—by bolstering Spanish frontier defenses, creating a new French buffer colony, checking American territorial ambitions, provoking a crisis in the Latin American independence movement, or some other disastrous result. The injection of the dreaded Bonaparte name into the mix led to even wilder speculations about rescue attempts, Mexican thrones, and world conquest. But while the diplomats considered, reported, and occasionally believed these rumors, they had to admit that they did not fully grasp Lallemand's aims. "All of [his] intrigues," wrote the French consul at New Orleans, "are cloaked in a profound darkness."[138]

As accounts of the true state of the Champ d'Asile filtered back from Texas, however, a different interpretation began to take shape in the European diplomatic dispatches from America. Lallemand was a loner, an adventurer, a con man who had tried to make himself formidable by bluffing. Isolated and weak, he sought to win the material and moral backing of an established government by claiming to have already secured the support of its enemies. By inserting himself between the mutually antagonistic Spanish and Americans and manipulating their suspicions, he sought to win recognition from one, the other, or both, and perhaps spark a bidding war between them for his loyalty. Although this strategy failed, Lallemand was not dissuaded. If war broke out between the United States and Spain and he happened to be occupying vital ground between them, he would become "necessary and useful to one or the other."[139] Armed with this hope, but with little else, he launched his incursion into Spanish Texas confident that, as he bided his time and waited for political developments to turn in his favor, he could attract the men and money he lacked by bluffing. Upon his arrival in New Orleans, he began to let slip word of the impressive resources at his disposal: official backing from Washington and Madrid, thousands of reinforcements on the way, unlimited sources of money and credit, munitions, treaties with the Latin American insurgents, naval forces in the Gulf, and even a secret conspiracy to spirit Napoleon from Saint Helena. No one would join a fool's mission, he reasoned, but even the faint-hearted would not hesitate to stake their lives and property on a force such as the one he was conjuring from thin air. Only with hindsight did Lallemand's strategy become clear to the diplomats. "Supposing a reality in order to produce it," observed one French diplomatic official with a Bourbon-scented air of disdain, "that is the ordinary tactic of all our revolutionaries."[140]

5

The Vine and Olive Colony

While Lallemand had been engaged in his fool's mission, the Society for the Cultivation of the Vine and Olive persisted with its plans. By 1822 close to 70 of the original grantees had spent some time on the grant—a figure nowhere near the 347 who had received allotments. Conditions there also fell short of the settlers' expectations. The difficulty of clearing the forested terrain, shortage of labor, lack of infrastructure, oppressively hot climate, and diseases that ravaged the area all conspired against them. By the mid-1820s many had abandoned their grants. To a great extent, Anglo-American settlers purchased the allotments of those who left, consolidated them into contiguous holdings, and established cotton plantations. But some of the wealthier and better-connected French grantees also profited from their compatriots' failures to found their own estates. With two nationally distinct groups of large-scale planters precipitating out of the original mass of French grantees, the Vine and Olive colony had by the mid-1830s evolved into something quite different from what its founders had envisioned.

From Optimism to Abandonment

As the drama of the Champ d'Asile moved toward its tragicomic denouement, the remaining members of the Society for the Cultivation of the Vine and Olive moved ahead with their settlement plans. The first two contingents of grantees—those who had come in the spring of 1817 with Parmentier and those who had arrived that fall with Generals Clausel and Lefebvre-Desnouettes—were reinforced the following year by a steady trickle of settlers. By the end of 1818 the society informed the secretary of the treasury that 34 grantees and 7 other individuals (most of whom would receive forty-acre reserve allotments the following year) were established on the grant.[1]

Popular accounts of the Vine and Olive colony describe the settlers as Bonapartist or Napoleonic officers, but these are inaccurate labels.[2] In fact, relatively few soldiers came to Alabama. Of the 65 imperial veterans whose names appear on the membership lists of the Vine and Olive Association, 33 (51 percent) sold their allotments and followed Lallemand to Texas. Others retained their allot-

Table 5.1 Background of the Settlers on the Grant in 1818 and 1819

	1818	1819
Domingans	19 (28)	26 (24)
Metropolitan French	12 (17)	14 (13)
Military	9 (13)	12 (11)
Unknown	29 (42)	56 (52)
Total	69 (20)	108 (27)

Note. Numbers in parentheses equal percent of total settlers.

ments, but remained on the East Coast while awaiting Bourbon clemency. Among these were Galabert, Grouchy, Vandamme, and Taillade. Thus, many of the Napoleonic veterans never set foot on the Vine and Olive colony, and even those who did—only 12—had little desire to make the United States their permanent home. Like their comrades on the East Coast, what they really wanted were pardons from the French government. Lefebvre-Desnouettes, the highest-ranking officer to settle on the grant, was no exception.[3] Until he obtained clemency, he wrote in mid-1821, he had no choice but to "vegetate in this country and make myself the least miserable possible."[4] His reiterated invitations to Clausel, who had settled temporarily in Mobile but refused to visit the grant, are eloquent testimony to Lefebvre-Desnouettes's loneliness on the Tombigbee.[5] Although their correspondence has not survived, it is likely that the other military men on the grant felt the same way about their sojourn in the Alabama wilderness; by 1830, every one of them had departed.[6]

In exaggerating the military and Napoleonic character of the settlers, existing works on Vine and Olive tend to overlook the civilian expatriates from France and Saint-Domingue who actually formed the backbone of the Alabama settlement. Even so, most civilian members of the Society for the Cultivation of the Vine and Olive never came to Alabama. In fact, only 61 of the 285 civilian grantees inscribed on the society's original membership list of 1818 (21 percent) ever set foot on the grant. This is not to say, however, that the absentees were indifferent to the fate of the colony in general or their own holdings in particular. Many, especially the Philadelphia-based Domingan merchants, treated their land as an investment and employed agents to improve it and meet the conditions (such as vine cultivation) required by the society's contract with Congress. Not all the civilian absentees, however, had the same degree of business acumen, deep pockets, and patience, and instead they sought to sell their allotments at the first opportunity—usually for nominal sums. Among these were Laurent Astolphi and Victor Hamel, French immigrants who had been working together as confectioners in Philadelphia since the early 1800s. On 11 June 1818 Astolphi and Hamel sold their 480-acre allotments (no. 51 and no. 245) to the Philadelphia merchant Thomas Newman for $738 each, or $1.54 per acre.[7] For Astolphi and Hamel the transaction represented a quick infusion of cash and for Newman, the addition of two large allotments (960 acres) to the 12 (2,130 acres) he had already acquired from other grantees.[8] Others, like Marshal Grouchy, who owned enormous estates in France, seem to have forgotten about their Alabama lands altogether, neither arranging for the required improvements to be made nor seeking to sell.[9] Because these nonperforming, neglected allotments failed to meet even the minimum conditions stipulated by the law, they were eventually taken from their original grantees and sold at public auction.

Of those who moved to Alabama and took up their grants in person or who remained on the East Coast but provided for the upkeep of their allotments, the most numerous, as well as the most determined to succeed, were the refugees from Saint-Domingue. At least 26 Domingan grantees are known to have come to the grant. More than the others, they tended to regard Alabama as their permanent home, adapt to conditions there, and achieve success. As the others left, the percentage of Domingans among the remaining French grantees rose, accentuating their influence on the cultural tone and economic character of the settlement. This is perhaps because these former coffee cultivators, merchants, craftsmen, shopkeepers, and clerks could at last achieve in Alabama the planter status denied them—but long envied—in Saint-Domingue. If life in the Alabama wilderness was a purgatory for the handful of military and political exiles who went there, for the Domingans it offered a way of achieving long-held social aspirations.

Achieving the planter lifestyle, however, was not easy. When the first French settlers arrived in 1817 and 1818, they found that their lands were covered with dense forest and cane, sometimes flooded in wet weather, and often parched in the oppressive Alabama summer. One of the townships was even transected on a southwest to northeast diagonal by a swath of destruction caused by a recent tornado. It was, as one of the principal colonists put it, "a rough and hardly explored country."[10] Before anything could be planted, the settlers had to clear the terrain and prepare the soil for cultivation. Some of the grantees threw themselves into these tasks—cutting down trees, hauling away fallen timber, removing rocks, and plowing the land—with alacrity and abandon. One of these was Edouard George Jr., son of the mercantile Domingan family that had come to Philadelphia in the 1790s. Although he worked "harder than a day laborer," wrote his concerned mother, he had cleared only fifteen acres after seven months of work.[11] Two years later, the George family had only cleared another eighty-five acres.[12] Like the other French settlers, they soon realized they needed additional sources of labor.

The settlers looked for workers wherever and however they could. A few of the grantees—Lefebvre-Desnouettes, Lintroy, and possibly others—may have brought recent European immigrants with them as indentured servants or redemptioners.[13] Others allowed Anglo-American pioneers to farm their allotments rent-free provided that all improvements made reverted to the owner when the lease expired.[14] Still others sought wage labor—not merely hired hands, but also slaves rented out by their masters—to perform specific tasks.[15] And at one point, *L'Abeille* even printed an appeal urging workers, both skilled and unskilled, to come to the grant.[16] None of these methods proved satisfactory. As in other regions of the frontier South, the abundance of cheap land and the scarcity of manpower conspired against the formation of a viable market in free labor. Potential farmhands generally preferred to work their own lands and would only sell their labor to others at a cost few could afford. The impossibility of relying on wage labor soon became apparent to the grantees. "I see it more and more," wrote Victoire George within weeks of arriving on the grant. "The whites who come here ask more wages than we can possibly give them; they all want to be farmers on their own account and they are quite right to do so if they can." The solution was equally obvious to the former inhabitant of Saint-Domingue: "we absolutely must have Negroes to cultivate our land."[17]

To generalize from Madame George's voluminous correspondence, acquiring slaves was the grantees' most pressing concern. In her very first letter from Mobile, written no more than a day or two after her arrival there in December 1819, she described finding "a Negro woman who is to be sold" and considered purchasing her on credit.[18] Immediately after reaching the grant in early February 1820, she wrote another letter, this one emphasizing even more urgently the need for slaves. Slaves were essential, she explained, because "servants and day laborers would devour us entirely."[19] Over the next two years, she returned to this theme again and again. "The white laborers are ruining us," she wrote one week later.[20] The following month she complained that the wages of the cheapest day laborer, eighteen to twenty dollars a month, were "ruinous."[21] The approach of 1821 and a new year seem to have brought Madame George little relief. "Without Negroes," she worried, "it will take all our efforts just to subsist."[22] At the end of February 1821, she asked Stephen Girard for a three thousand dollar loan to purchase some slaves who a notable Anglo-American settler, George Strother Gaines, had informed her were on auction at Saint Stephens.[23] Eventually the George family managed to acquire at least twelve slaves.[24]

Slaves represented a substantial capital investment without which a landholder on the southern frontier could not hope to make a profit. This was not lost on the French settlers and visitors. When he went to the grant briefly at the end of 1821 to determine if it made sense to settle there, Henri Lallemand calculated that he would need to make an initial investment of at least six thousand dollars, including the purchase of seven to twelve slaves, in order to establish himself profitably on the Tombigbee. "A man with fewer Negroes would do no more than vegetate," he concluded.[25] It was difficult, however, for the French settlers to obtain slaves in the numbers they desired. During the late 1810s and early 1820s, demand for slaves in the fast-growing state of Alabama consistently outstripped supply, driving up their price to six or seven hundred dollars, if they were available at all. "It is only occasionally that one has an opportunity to buy one or two," Henri Lallemand noted with concern, and wondered if it might be possible to seek slaves in Virginia where they were reportedly cheaper.[26] Although Lallemand never carried out this project and—daunted by the high startup costs—did not settle on the grant, some of those who did made slave-purchasing trips farther north. In 1821 Charles Villars traveled to Tennessee to buy slaves; Lefebvre-Desnouettes bought slaves the following year during a trip to Washington.[27]

Although the purchase of slaves was probably the single greatest startup expense the French settlers had to bear, other essential expenditures were also heavy. While waiting for their lands to be cleared, they had to purchase food locally, at prices inflated by distance from markets and the sudden concentration of consumers in such a remote area. To keep these costs to a minimum, recommended Jean Pénières, settlers should bring at least a six months' supply of food with them on their move to Alabama.[28] Few did so.[29] To reduce the expense and difficulty of obtaining food, many of the settlers at first planted corn—instead of the required vines and olive trees or lucrative cotton.[30] Whether obtained at great cost through middlemen or planted in lieu of these other crops, grain represented a major expense for all settlers during the first years of the colony.

The same was true of another basic necessity, shelter. The first French settlers had to build houses without delay, a vital task that competed for their time and resources with the equally pressing work of clearing land and planting corn. And as with these agricultural activities, the construction of houses was rendered both slow and costly by the scarcity of labor and necessary materials. Yet, while exorbitantly expensive, these first houses—really little more than lean-tos and log cabins—were "not fine, nor do they last long."[31] Ten years after the first settlements, the grandest structure on the grant was a log cabin measuring nineteen by twenty-three feet.[32]

In addition to obtaining food and shelter, the settlers had to get vine and olive cultivation under way. Grape vines and olive saplings had to be imported, often from Europe and always at great expense. Although carefully packed in earth-filled barrels, many of the precious vine cuttings perished en route. Most of the olive trees succumbed to frost. These agricultural diversions resulted in nothing but frustration, wasted time, and financial loss. The cost of establishing oneself on the Tombigbee in the 1810s was enormous. Only those with enough financial staying power to weather the initial years of outlay had a chance of making a successful establishment.

An enterprising few perceived in the chronic scarcity of both necessities and luxuries an opportunity for enrichment. Dearth and distance may have been the bane of the consumer, but these same conditions also made it possible for importers, transporters, middlemen, and shopkeepers to reap enormous profits. Having experienced to the detriment of their own pocketbooks the killing made by Mobile merchants, riverboat captains, and local suppliers, some of the French settlers decided to try their hand as middlemen, hoping to defray their own high startup costs by selling at a steep markup to their struggling compatriots. Even Lefebvre-Desnouettes decided to pursue this potentially lucrative, but essentially selfish, course.[33] His business plan—based on a partnership with Clausel in Mobile—was sound in principle. Clausel would purchase goods wholesale at the port and ship them by riverboat to the grant where Lefebvre-Desnouettes would sell them there from his general store.

There are no surviving papers documenting Clausel's end of the operation, but Lefebvre-Desnouettes's correspondence indicates that he had no head for business. Instead of managing his store personally, the general hired another grantee, the junior officer Lucien Enfelders, to take care of inventory and sales. The result was "a disaster," as Lefebvre-Desnouettes found during a rare inspection in January 1819. The store had not only sustained financial losses of 50 percent, but also lost its entire inventory—devoured by rats according to the charming but untrustworthy Lucien. To make matters worse, not a cent was left in the till, and money was still owed to creditors for goods that had been purchased.[34] The general's attempts to get to the bottom of the matter failed to uncover the "least scrap of information." Angry and frustrated, he decided to cut his and Clausel's losses by selling what was left of the concern to another inhabitant of the grant, a Monsieur Drouin, in February 1819.[35] Lefebvre-Desnouettes continued to import modest quantities of goods from Mobile for resale, but with a similar lack of success. In July 1819 he complained to Clausel that a shipment of thirty hats actually contained only twenty-two. The following month, he was at it again, this time demanding that his partner share some of the losses he had suffered from a barrel of salted herrings that had arrived rotten.[36] Only a few years earlier, when they had held the lives of tens of thousands of soldiers in their hands, these two generals could not have imagined that they would one day be haggling over spoiled fish on the Alabama frontier.

Like struggling farmers the world over, the French settlers had to become jacks-of-all-trades, each pursuing a wide range of activities to increase their meager earnings. A number of those for whom information is available were involved in transportation. Colonel Raoul operated a ferry across one of the many creeks that crisscrossed the grant.[37] The villainous Enfelders, when he was not robbing Lefebvre-Desnouettes, also ran a ferry service.[38] And Jacques Lajoinie had a barge that plied the Tombigbee River between the grant and Saint Stephens.[39] Grantees also worked as tavern- and innkeepers. For several years Jean-Jerome Cluis and his wife ran a tavern in Greensboro, a town just northwest of the grant. When they left for Mobile, Alexandre-Léonard Descourts and his wife, Aimée—who, while living in New York in 1816–17 had run a similar establishment popular with Bonapartist exiles—took over the tavern.[40] Colonel Raoul and his wife, the former Marquise de Sinabaldi and once lady-in-waiting to Napoleon's sister Caroline, briefly operated an inn famed for Madame Raoul's delicious "pancakes" (probably crepes).[41] Others practiced various trades, like Pierre Mangon, who worked as a wheelsmith.[42]

These activities were intended to supplement the grantees' principal livelihood, agriculture, which, however, did not get off to a good start. The crop of 1818, planted at great effort and expense, was a total failure.[43] Those counting on the first harvest to see them through were bitterly disappointed. Even Lefebvre-Desnouettes, who seems to have done more than anyone else to clear and plant his land, was forced to buy seed corn in 1819.[44] The following year, a late hard frost damaged the crop, and 1821 saw extensive flooding that covered most of the allotments in water.[45] The year 1822 began well, but a severe summer storm destroyed half of the nearly mature crop. "It is very hard after having worked so much to lose the whole in a moment," lamented Edouard

George Sr., whose first substantial harvest of cotton was ruined by the deluge.[46] A combination of heavy downpours and drought promoted rot that again damaged the cotton crop in 1823.[47] On top of these annual disasters, the persistent lack of water on many allotments—even the deepest wells failed to penetrate to the water table—hindered the agricultural efforts of many allottees.[48] "We have nothing in this miserable country," George Sr. wrote at the end of 1822.[49]

The hardship of life on the grant was exacerbated by the difficulty of communication with the outside world. Until the opening of steamship service on the Tombigbee, there were only two methods of traveling to the grant. The first was by water, on heavy barges that had to be dragged upriver from Mobile. Lasting up to twenty-five days, the journey was considered uncomfortable and unhealthy.[50] The other was by land, through what one grantee termed "trackless dessert."[51] Nonetheless, many of the settlers seem to have preferred this method of travel, presumably because it was more rapid. It did, however, have serious drawbacks. The condition of the roads, to the extent they existed at all, was appalling, and they were cut at various points by unbridged creeks that had to be forded.[52] This could be very dangerous. Isaac Butaud, a French engraver who had married Victoire George's daughter Victorie, fell into a stream while traveling to the grant. He was saved, but his horse was drowned. Other victims were Jacques Garnier des Saintes and his son, both drowned when their steamship sunk.[53] The son of Charles Villars also perished in a riverboat accident.[54] It is hard to resist the conclusion that the French settlers were uncommonly prone to waterborne disasters. Madame George lost personal provisions and salable commodities worth six thousand dollars when the *Alabama Packet* sank off Long Island in January 1820.[55] Madame Frenaye endured an agonizing seventy-day passage from the East Coast to Mobile and then lost all her baggage (and nearly her life) when her ship foundered at the bar of the harbor.[56] And Lefebvre-Desnouettes would drown in a shipwreck off the Irish coast when returning to France in 1822.[57]

Transportation to and from the grant may have been sporadic, fatiguing, and sometimes fatal, but disease was by far the greatest threat to the colonists. Pierre-Ange-Chevalier Stollenwerk, the first society member to die, fell victim to an unspecified disease at Saint Stephens in September 1817, while en route from Mobile to the grant. He was eulogized in the pages of *L'Abeille,* but as more and more colonists fell ill and perished, Jean-Simon Chaudron stopped this practice, which threatened to give readers—potential colonists—the unfortunate (but correct) impression that the nascent colony was unhealthful.[58] During the colony's first years, there were seasons when nearly every inhabitant was sick with what they termed "fever."[59] By 1825 at least twenty-two of the grantees who had actually set foot on the grant—more than 20 percent of those who did so—were dead. As Victoire George so succinctly put it, "this country is very far from being as healthful as was believed."[60]

If nature did not help the French settlers to gain a foothold on the land, neither did their fellow human beings. First, a surveying error forced the grantees to relocate their town site. In 1817 the settlers had originally chosen the high ground above the juncture of the Tombigbee and Black Warrior rivers for their town and named it Demopolis, city of the people. Their choice of location was excellent but premature, because the definitive township-grid survey of the vast territory recently acquired from the Creeks was still under way. When the survey was finally completed in August 1818, it was discovered that Demopolis lay just outside the grant's boundaries.[61] Thus, only a year after the first parties of settlers had arrived, the French had to abandon their promising riverside town and begin anew farther inland. They named their new capital Aigleville (Eagle City), a name that evoked both the Napoleonic empire and the Republic of the United States.[62] One of the leading civilian settlers, Frédéric Ravesies, later founded a second town—named Arcola after a Napoleonic military victory—on his original allotment on the bank of the Black Warrior.[63] Neither Aigleville nor Arcola, however, ever rivaled Demopolis or Greensboro, which became the political and commercial centers of the region. Many of the grantees themselves moved to these towns and Aigleville itself was soon abandoned. Today a concrete plant sits on the land it once occupied.

The relocation of the town site sparked a spate of contentious property transfers that embittered feelings in the colony. The problems began when General Lefebvre-Desnouettes, who had drawn a 480-acre allotment in a remote corner of the grant, sought to exchange it for an equivalent amount of more valuable land on the edge of Aigleville. Invoking the seventh article of the contract between the U.S. government and the society, which allowed grantees who had improved lands not their own before August 1818 to retain those lands, he had the original owners (Nicholas-Cadet Bergasse and Pierre Gallard) evicted from the tract he coveted and removed to his own, distant allotment. To round out his new holding to a complete section (640 acres), Lefebvre-Desnouettes also appropriated an unoccupied 40-acre reserve in the section and again tried to evoke the seventh article to evict Victorie Butaud née George, from her 120-acre allotment. Victorie fought back. In a sharp rebuke, she pointed out that Lefebvre-Desnouettes had no right to claim her land under the article as he had already used it to exchange his original allotment for those of Bergasse and Gallard. Thus, the attempted eviction was "unjust and arbitrary," devoid of any legal justification whatsoever. A compromise was finally reached, whereby Butaud agreed to sell the rights to both her originally assigned and replacement allotments to the general for three hundred dollars.[64] By similar legal maneuvers, as well as outright purchases, Lefebvre-Desnouettes had acquired more than 2,000 acres of grant land by the time he left in 1822.[65]

Other disputes over land flared up between the settlers. As they dragged on, they generated bad feelings and left the legal status of the contested allotments in doubt. One of the largest landholders, the speculating Philadelphia merchant Thomas Newman, was accused of having sold one of his allotments (no. 93, 480 acres) twice, first to William Stevenson in 1819 and again in 1838 to Anne-Gilbert-Marc-Antoine Frenaye. Litigation persisted into the 1840s.[66] Another dispute over ownership of an allotment (no. 71, 480 acres) this one pitting the Ravesies clan against the Follins, also lasted for years, generating more than fifty motions, affidavits, depositions, legal opinions, and rulings.[67] In another, astonishing case the owner of one of the 40-acre reserves seems to have forgotten about his land and failed to obtain a patent for it. A prison was eventually established on land bordering the vacant reserve, now overgrown with trees. During his daily walks in the prison yard, an observant convict noticed that no one seemed to be cultivating this parcel of land. Upon his release in 1933 he applied to the federal government for a patent on the land under the terms of the century-old Vine and Olive legislation. Surprised officials in the General Land Office confirmed that the unclaimed reserve had reverted to the federal government and was indeed available for someone to purchase according to the terms of the grant. At the end of 1933, a patent was issued to the sharp-eyed former convict L. M. Lowery, the last Vine and Olive patentee.[68]

Disillusioned by infighting, demoralized by the forced relocation of their town, their health broken by disease, their spirits oppressed by physical hardship and isolation, fatigued by the challenge of planting the wilderness into which they had moved, and reaping nothing but financial ruin from their fruitless efforts, numbers of settlers gave up in frustration and left the grant. Françoise Rivière, who departed in 1823 or 1824 to start anew with her husband in Tennessee, felt that her life's "misfortunes began on the Tombigbee," where she spent "almost five years, constantly struggling with poverty."[69] Although much wealthier and more comfortably established, Victoire George explained her decision to leave the grant in similar terms. She described her family's "five-year sojourn" on the grant as "a long ordeal of labor, patience, and perseverance."[70] "Everybody is discouraged," she wrote, "French as well as Americans, and everybody wants to sell."[71] By 1830 few French people were left on the grant.

From Collective to Private Property

Adding to the difficulties of the Vine and Olive landholders as they tried to establish successful plantations were the government regulations setting forth various requirements that had to be met before definitive title to the land could be issued. Among the most irksome were the principle of solidarity, requiring *all* allottees to fulfill the conditions of cultivation, settlement, and payment stipulated by the act of 3 March 1817 before *any* could receive patents for their land, and the requirement of grape vine and olive tree cultivation. In its efforts to have Congress release it from these different requirements, the society never lost sight of its ultimate object: to convert the Vine and Olive allotments into unencumbered, individual private property. Such a transformation, the society's leaders believed, would increase the value of the allotments by liberating them from the restrictions imposed in 1817. But in certain instances, such as its fight to exempt the grant lands from federal preemption laws, which gave squatters ownership rights, the society did not hesitate to claim privileged treatment on the grounds that its lands were not ordinary, individual properties but formed a special collective establishment governed by a unique contract between Congress and the shareholders. Employing a high degree of logical dexterity and moral flexibility (if not actual hypocrisy), the society was nothing if not determined to achieve a single, unwavering goal: the imposition of the legal framework most advantageous to its landed interests.

The grantees' lobbying efforts began within a year or two of their arrival on the Tombigbee. In late 1819 or early 1820 leading grantees, headed by the Philadelphia-based Domingan merchant Jean-Marie Chapron, petitioned Congress to abolish the principle of solidarity.[72] Instead of penalizing the diligent majority of the grantees for the neglect of a few, the petitioners argued, Congress should reward and encourage individual effort by confirming the land titles of those who personally fulfilled the requirements of the law. Those who failed to perform should have their allotments confiscated by the government, the petitioners concluded, but in no case should their sloth disadvantage the settlers who had faithfully met their obligations. William H. Crawford, the secretary of the treasury, was not persuaded. "The principal object of the grant is not that a small number of tracts of land should be cultivated in vines and olives," he reported to Congress, "but that the whole tract should be settled by persons understanding the culture of those plants." This was the only way the government could establish a domestic wine industry. To grant the prayer of the petitioners, Crawford feared, would fragment the colony, thereby preventing it from achieving the critical viticultural mass it would need to influence surrounding areas. If the collective obligations of the society were abolished, poor allotments would be abandoned and the best tracts, having become "individual property," would enter the general land market and lose their special viticultural vocation. Deferring to Crawford's recommendation—and very likely mindful of unfavorable commentary in the press, which viewed the petition as an attempt to open "a new door . . . to further speculation"—Congress rejected the colonists' request.[73]

Regarding this rebuff as no more than a temporary setback, the society prepared a new memorial requesting the abolition of solidarity.[74] This time, however, they chose Lefebvre-Desnouettes, a more weighty presence than Chapron, to present the petition to Congress, which he did in early 1822.[75] The new petition began by explaining that most of the settlers had expended great efforts and substantial resources to comply with the terms of the contract. Despite much hardship, 81 grantees and their families—a total of 327 persons—were currently established on the Tombigbee. They had 1,100 acres in direct cultivation and another 1,500 acres being farmed by lease. Moreover, they had already planted nearly 10,000 vines. The cost of these accomplishments had been heavy: $160,000 and the lives of 23 individuals who had perished in accidents or from disease. Yet, while they had proven their good faith and determination by these hard-earned achievements, the laziness of a handful of irresponsible individuals put their titles in jeopardy. As long as the solidarity clause remained in force, the petition read, the settlers would face "the sad prospect of being turned out on account of the neglect or bad will of some individuals." This created a permanent state of anxiety detrimental to the grantees' morale and productivity. In threatening to strip them of their land for the faults of others, faults beyond their control, the petitioners concluded, "the mere idea of solidarity slackens our energy."

Although this second petition was essentially the same as the first, Crawford, perhaps swayed by the personal entreaties of Lefebvre-Desnouettes, who had met with him in Washington, now urged Congress to grant the colonists' request. Since many of the grantees showed no sign of ever meeting their responsibilities, he noted, all the settlers—even the most diligent ones—would lose their land if the solidarity clause remained in force. Would it be fair, he asked, would it be in the national interest, to allow "the object contemplated by the act of the 3d of March 1817 [to be] abandoned, to the great injury, if not entire ruin, of that part of the French emigrants who have made great exertions" to show themselves worthy of the American government's unparalleled generosity?[76] After much debate and "considerable opposition," Congress took Crawford's recommendation and abolished the condition of solidarity on 26 April 1822.[77] Henceforth, grantees or their heirs who had planted the requisite amount of vine and olive on their allotments would be allowed, as individuals, to obtain patents for their specific parcels of land.[78]

With the abolition of solidarity, the society set its sights on overturning the conditions of vine and olive cultivation, the last major hurdle standing between the grantees and outright ownership of their allotments. According to the third and fourth clauses of their contract with the secretary of the treasury, the settlers were supposed to have planted at least 576 acres of vines and 500 olive trees by January 1826. Accordingly, Pres. John Quincy Adams directed the secretary of the treasury, Richard Rush, to send a special agent to the Tombigbee to investigate the progress the grantees had made. In September 1826 Rush designated William G. Adams, of Tuscaloosa, Alabama, to carry out the inspection.[79] From the outset, Adams's mission was hampered by ill-health and tainted by excessively close collaboration with the grantees. When his letter of appointment finally reached Adams in November, it found him too sick to leave his bed. But reluctant to delay what promised to be an arduous surveying operation, Adams forwarded his official instructions to Ravesies, the current agent of the society, to enable the grantees to prepare for his inspection. According to Ravesies, the society eagerly sought "to afford every facility to enable [Adams] to obtain the correct information upon the subject of his mission." In his final report, Adams would express gratitude to Ravesies for "the constant and friendly aid which he rendered me in this work." The extent to which this aid influenced the report is evident in its generous conclusions.

When he finally arrived in Aigleville at the end of November, Adams sought to carry out a detailed survey of vine and olive cultivation on the grant but was laid low by another bout of illness. For six weeks, he lay in bed, unable to visit the allotments. In February 1827, when he had finally recovered sufficiently to set pen to paper, Adams prefaced his findings with significant caveats. Because of his long spell of ill-health, he admitted, the report could not be "so full as to every point as may be wished for." In a tacit admission that some of the information it contained was inaccurate, he stated that it contained "no errors that will materially injure the rights of either of the contracting parties." When the report finally reached Congress in December 1827, Adams was dead, victim some months earlier to the stubborn ailment that had so hampered his mission.

The Adams report presented an unexpectedly positive view of the grantees' progress. Despite numerous allotments that had shown no performance, nearly seventy-five hundred acres had been cleared and were currently being cultivated with all manner of crops, mainly corn, cotton, and small grain. These more orthodox agricultural pursuits, Adams concluded, had not distracted the French from making a determined attempt at viticulture. More than a hundred allotments were already bearing grapes, the vines generally strung up between the rows of cotton. More would be planted as soon as spring arrived. Substantially more acreage would have already been planted in vine, Adams explained, had not so many of the specimens ordered from Europe perished in transit. The state of olive tree cultivation was not so promising. Although dozens of allotments had been planted with olive trees, the grantees had informed the agent, they perished every winter. In an additional setback, two hundred trees recently imported from Europe had all perished in shipment. The report reluctantly concluded that "the tree will not succeed in this climate."

Richard Rush was suspicious of the Adams report because it did not provide sufficient information. To note (as the report did) that a given allotment was planted in vine or olive trees, the secretary complained, did not indicate the actual extent of that cultivation. Thus, on 17 May 1827, he wrote to Adams in Tuscaloosa directing him to obtain further information, specifically the number of acres cultivated in vine and the quantity of olive trees planted in each allotment.[80] By the time the letter arrived, Adams had already died. Another copy, addressed to the society's headquarters in Aigleville, was opened by its secretary, Charles D. Conner, who took it with him on a long trip to North Carolina. Yet another copy sent to Ravesies, at the time in Philadelphia on business, failed to elicit immediate action. Waiting until he returned home to the grant, Ravesies first applied to the administrators of the Adams estate for the original copy of his instructions and, only when further delaying tactics began to appear counterproductive, did he proceed to gather the information requested by the secretary of the treasury.

The society's reluctance to provide more precise data is understandable, given the discouraging picture that could not help but emerge from it. Where the Adams report could be interpreted as confirmation that 160 allotments had been planted in vine, Ravesies had to admit that this amounted to only three hundred acres actually under cultivation.[81] To make matters worse, these few acres were not concentrated in one area, but scattered throughout the grant. Ravesies's supplementary report made clear that little progress had been made toward establishing Mediterranean-style agriculture in the United States.

Dreading the unfavorable impression these results were likely to produce, Ravesies penned a letter explaining why the grantees had performed so poorly.[82] Progress had been slow, he explained, because the settlers were "chiefly composed of officers and merchants, possessing extremely limited knowledge of either the science or practice of agriculture." Even if they had been expert farmers, they would still have struggled because their Tombigbee lands were "a perfect wilderness" when they arrived. During the crucial first years of their establishment, therefore, their efforts had been diverted from the cultivation of vine and olive by the more immediate challenge of obtaining "the common necessaries and means of support." The sudden concentration of so many people in such an isolated spot drove the price of indispensable items, such as food, to an intolerable level. In the early days, Ravesies recalled, corn had cost five dollars a bushel, and cows forty to fifty dollars a head. Disease ravaged the settlers, and a chronic shortage of water afflicted many of the allotments. To make matters worse, the grantees had to contend with squatters who encroached on their allotments and, "threatening the most violent and determined vengeance upon any person who would interfere with their settlement," prevented them from entering their land. Despite a ruling in 1825 rejecting the squatters' claims, they remained on the grant in defiance of the law. Finally, Ravesies concluded, it had proven more difficult than anticipated to cultivate grape vine. Only by a costly process of trial and error had the grantees made progress in identifying the types of vine that could grow in Alabama. But a real breakthrough remained elusive. Although expressing confidence that viticulture could succeed on the grant, Ravesies cautioned that it would take seventy years, rather than seven, to ascertain the ideal mode of cultivation.

In fact, the grantees had recognized almost immediately that cotton, not grapes or olives, was the key to agricultural prosperity in antebellum Alabama. Some, like the brothers-in-law Marc-Antoine Frenaye and Pierre-Frédéric Fontanges, had never intended to cultivate vine seriously, but had always planned on becoming cotton planters.[83] Even those settlers who may have genuinely wanted to pursue viticulture soon realized that cotton offered much brighter prospects. The temptation of cotton afflicted all but the most stubborn of the would-be winegrowers. Cotton from western Alabama, Madame George wrote in 1820 within days of arriving on the grant, was "considered as fine as that of New Orleans," but "we do not know whether the vines will succeed or not."[84] After more than a year in residence and plenty of bitter experience, she had concluded what she had already suspected upon her arrival, namely that cotton "was the only way to make an income."[85] Like many of the other grantees, however, the George family continued to grow some vines on their cotton fields. The reason they did not simply abandon this costly and unsuccessful crop, Madame George explained, was to secure their titles to the allotments, making them more attractive on the real estate market. Prospective buyers, particularly newly arrived Americans, would not purchase lands without at least some vine for fear that they would be deemed in noncompliance with the contract and have their lands confiscated by the government.[86] Without vines, land on the grant was not easily marketable, so many grantees found themselves forced into a nominal viticulture in order to preserve the value of their allotments.

There were, however, a few eccentrics whose commitment to unorthodox crops set them apart from their cotton-minded peers. One was Corneille Roudet, who stayed faithful to the vine and published a newspaper editorial in 1831 arguing for its viability.[87] Another was the Philadelphia silk merchant Jean-Marie Chapron. Although he had devoted most of his extensive holdings in the grant to cotton, he remained interested in the possibility of raising other crops. During the late 1830s he became involved in sericulture, subscribing to *Silkworm Grower* magazine, planting mulberry trees, and ordering batches of eggs from suppliers on the East Coast.[88] Like his attempts to cultivate the vine and olive, his experiment with silk production was a failure. Cotton, as even Chapron had to admit, was the only way to go.

During the late 1820s, therefore, the executive committee of the Society for the Cultivation of the Vine and Olive—by now composed of a roughly equal number of French and Anglo-American planters—lobbied Congress to further relax the terms of the contract. In 1827 and again in 1828, it petitioned Congress for an extension of the deadline for fulfilling the agricultural conditions.[89] The Alabama delegation, led by Senator King, the powerful member of the Committee on Public Lands, took up the grantees' cause but failed to win the desired concessions during the winter session of 1828.[90] The committee did not lose heart, but returned to the charge the following year by asking Congress for even more far-reaching changes. As well as seeking additional time for delinquent grantees to make settlements and plant vines, it requested in its petition of November 1829 that all those noted as having already fulfilled the contract in the indulgent Adams report be allowed to obtain patents for their allotments without further delay, upon payment of the now-standard price for federal land, $1.25 per acre rather than the $2.00 agreed upon in 1817.[91] After wending its way through both houses of Congress, a law emerged on 19 February 1831 that granted the petitioners' prayer and then extended to them concessions even more generous than those they had originally sought.[92] According to the new legislation, not only would the grantees noted by Adams as having performed their obligations be eligible to receive patents upon payment of $1.25 per acre, but so would those who were in "actual occupancy and cultivation"—not necessarily of the vine and olive—at the time of the law's passage. Moreover, the widows and heirs of grantees who had died "without performing the conditions required" would be allowed to purchase their allotments purely and simply, without having to meet any agricultural or residency requirements whatsoever. And in addition to these changes, the new law did away with the provision barring any individual from owning more than 640 acres of grant land. Two years later, on 19 February 1833, Congress amended this law to extend the deadline for payment until 15 May 1834.[93] After this date, lands left unpatented would be offered at public auction. The French and American planters of the society welcomed these laws as a triumph: they had finally succeeded in transforming their special grant lands into ordinary private property unfettered by any onerous obligations or restrictions.

When it suited their interests, however, the leaders of the society did not hesitate to invoke the special character of the grant. The most striking example of this occurred in the late 1830s, when they sought to prevent squatters from claiming ownership of certain parcels of land under the general preemption laws of the nation. Squatters had always been present in the grant, but in the 1830s they began trying to take formal possession of the plots they occupied under the right of preemption. The society countered that the act of 3 March 1817, having withdrawn the four townships of the grant from the public domain, had exempted their land from the general land laws of the federal government. Theirs was a privileged sphere, administered according to a contract between their private association and the secretary of the treasury. Federal laws regulating public lands that had been passed subsequent to the acceptance of this contract had no effect on the grant lands because, at the time such changes to the public land legislation had been made, the Vine and Olive lands were no longer part of the public domain. The U.S. attorney general, Felix Grundy, agreed. In his 1839 ruling, he rejected the squatters' attempts to apply the preemption laws to the allotments they were occupying on the grounds that the

grant had "been reserved and taken out of the class of public lands and conse-
quently withdrawn from the operation of those laws."[94] The Society for the Cultivation of Vine and Olive thus enjoyed the best of both worlds, assimilating
its land to ordinary private property when seeking profit in the marketplace
and claiming exemption from the general laws of the United States when seeking to avoid the public obligations land ownership entailed.

Patterns of Sale and Speculation in Vine and Olive Land

These legal changes came too late to help most grantees. By the early
1820s many had already sold their allotments and left Alabama. Analysis of
land sales between 1817 and 1834, when Congress finally fixed the legal status of
the Vine and Olive allotments, reveals three distinct stages in the evolving market in grant lands. The first, from December 1817 through the end of 1818, was
characterized by brisk sales at low prices, generally a dollar per acre. This pattern reflected the mass liquidation of their allotments by Charles Lallemand's
followers, as well as by other grantees seeking a quick profit. The principal
beneficiaries of this first wave of sales were a tight-knit group of Philadelphia
merchants, almost all Domingans, interested in land speculation The second
stage, stretching from 1819 to 1829, was characterized by a decline in the pace
of sales, but a perceptible rise in the price of land to about three to five dollars per acre, a level at which it would remain well into the 1830s. It is easy
to account for the slowdown in sales during these years—the economic crisis
of 1819 (known simply as the Panic) led to a shortage of credit that burst the
speculative bubble that had inflated the western land market in the years after the War of 1812. But why land prices rose during this period of slump-
ing sales is not clear. The majority of buyers during the second stage were
Anglo-Americans, who for the first time began to make inroads into the French
grant, although more gradually than often assumed. The third phase, from 1830
on, saw the real estate market rebound, with a sharp increase in the pace of
sales. As the nation emerged from the economic doldrums of the 1820s, those
who had had the wherewithal to maintain their position or even expand their
holdings now found eager buyers for their allotments. A decade of agricultural
improvement, construction, and road building, as well as the growth of riverine
commerce on the Tombigbee, began to have an impact and helped push up
demand for the Vine and Olive lands. Many property holders, both French
and Anglo-American, who had acquired land cheaply in earlier years were
now able to reap handsome profits during this period, mainly by selling to

Table 5.2 The Vine and Olive Land Market

Year	Acres sold	Avg. price per acre (in dollars)
1817	15,760	1.05
1818	15,672	1.58
1819	6,490	3.77
1820	7,610	3.04
1821	4,243	2.49
1822	4,250	4.20
1823	4,160	5.23
1824	3,376	4.33
1825	1,960	3.01
1826	780	4.77
1827	1,230	3.80
1828	2,480	5.17
1829	6,800	2.25
1830	12,160	4.14
1831	14,666	3.55
1832	15,460	4.82
1833	11,196	4.05
1834	11,120	4.38

Source: NARA, RG 49, 234–38.

Anglo-American newcomers who began to enter the grant in significant numbers. Yet, despite the robust demand for grant lands, prices in the 1830s remained at the levels they had reached in the 1820s. This apparent disjunction between demand and price is the greatest mystery of the Vine and Olive land market.

The sale of allotments began in earnest at the end of 1817, before most of the future settlers had even left for Alabama. In fact, during the first two weeks of December 1817 the pace of the Vine and Olive land market reached its all-time peak with forty-nine confirmed and eleven probable sales during this brief period. This surge reflected the mass sale of the allotments of officers preparing to embark for Texas. The purchasers were a group of about ten Domingan-Philadelphian merchants who had struck a deal with Charles Lallemand and worked out the mechanics of the transaction with his lieutenant, Georges Jeannet. Only six of the sixty-six Vine and Olive shareholders known to have taken part in the Champ d'Asile did not sell off right away but, perhaps suspecting

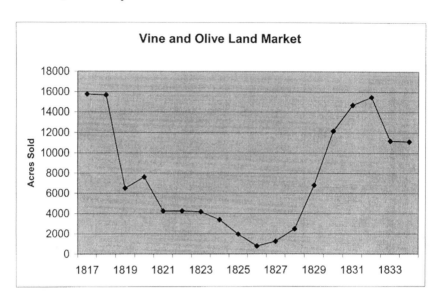

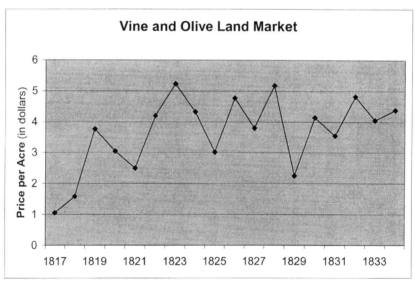

that the mission to Texas would fail, retained their allotments.[95] Tellingly, the Lallemand brothers were among them.

The principal buyers were Pierre-Frédéric Fontanges, Marc-Antoine Frenaye, Jean-Marie Chapron, Etienne-François Nidelet, Frédéric Ravesies, André Curcier, François-Hyacinthe Teterel, Jacques Duval, Charles Villars, and Thomas

Table 5.3 Merchant Purchases of Champ d'Asile Allotments, December 1817

Buyer	No. of allotments	Acres
Fontanges/Frenaye	12	2,400
Duval	8	1,280
Chapron/Nidelet	7	1,020
Curcier	5	800
Newman	4	1,010
Villars	3	640
Ravesies	2	640
Teterel	3	520
Jeannet power-of-attorney	11	2,640

Source: NARA, RG 49, 234–38.
Note: In addition to the buyers shown here, other shareholders bought allotments from another seven members of the Champ d'Asile. Those transactions are not included in this table nor are those involving the six members of the Champ d'Asile who sold their allotments after December 1817.

Newman.[96] With the exception of Curcier and Newman, all were founding members of the society, and only one, Newman, was not French.[97] The group was tight-knit, bound together by familial ties forged on Saint-Domingue. Fontanges and Frenaye were brothers-in-law; Chapron and Nidelet were cousins; and Chapron was married to Teterel's daughter. A dense web of business partnerships also connected the members of the group. Frenaye was not only a business associate of his brother-in-law, Fontanges, but also of Chapron and Teterel. Curcier and Ravesies were partners, as were Chapron and Nidelet who had occasional business dealings with Curcier, Duval, and Ravesies. But perhaps stronger than ties of blood, friendship, and business partnership was the lure of profit that drew these merchants to the Vine and Olive venture. With the price of land in the newly opened Alabama territory rising rapidly in 1817 and 1818, the so-called Alabama Fever, allotments in the promising colony seemed like an excellent investment.[98]

Lallemand's followers were not the only shareholders to seek easy profit by selling their allotments. Indeed, by the end of 1818, no fewer than seventy-four other shareholders who were *not* part of the Texas adventure had also sold their allotments.[99] Generally, these sellers were civilian immigrants from France or Saint-Domingue. Given the speculative boom of the time, there was no lack of buyers eager for their land. The same merchants who had bought out Lallemand's men were happy to acquire these other Vine and Olive lands, confi-

Table 5.4 Merchant Purchases of Non–Champ d'Asile Allotments, 1817–18

Buyer	No. of allotments	Acres
Newman	14	3,100
Fontanges/Frenaye	5	1,440
Teterel	4	1,040
Ravesies	3	880
Gratz	3	680
Duval	1	160

Source: NARA, RG 49, 234–38.

Table 5.5 Total Merchant Purchases, 1817–18

Buyer	No. of allotments	Acres
Newman	18	4,110
Fontanges/Frenaye	17	3,440
Teterel	7	1,560
Ravesies	5	1,520
Duval	9	1,440
Chapron/Nidelet	7	1,020
Curcier	5	800
Gratz	3	680
Villars	3	640
Jeannet power-of-attorney	11	2,460

Source: NARA, RG 49, 234–38.
Note: Numbers reflect purchases from Champ d'Asile participants as well as nonparticipants.

dent that they would continue to rise in value. Although most of these transactions seem to have been arranged on an individual basis between the buyer and the seller, some sales were conducted en masse through powers-of-attorney in the same manner as those supervised by Jeannet. In the most obvious example of this, Ravesies brokered the sale of seven allotments of 160 acres each to Newman on 5 December 1817.[100] This pattern of rapid sales caught the attention of the treasury secretary, William Crawford, who denounced it as "sheer speculation" in a report to Congress at the end of 1818.[101]

Not all the allotments offered for sale in 1817–18 were snatched up by this group of speculating businessmen. Some were purchased by shareholders, again predominantly Philadelphia Domingans, who were committed to establishing themselves as planters in Alabama. They jumped at the opportunity of cheaply acquiring large holdings for themselves by buying the allotments of their lukewarm or profiteering compatriots. These would-be planters included the formidable Chaudron-Stollenwerk-George clan. The Georges purchased six allotments totaling 760 acres; the Stollenwerks, two allotments totaling 720 acres; and the Chaudrons, two allotments totaling 320 acres. While these families were determined to found plantations on the grant, they were not averse to acquiring a parcel of land at a good price and reselling it at a handsome profit. Although settlers and planters, they, no less than the absentee merchants in Philadelphia, had a direct interest in land speculation and proved adept at it. The example of speculating settlers like Victoire George or settling speculators like Frédéric Ravesies illustrates Daniel Feller's pertinent observation that the "dichotomous images of settler and speculator were essentially fallacious and did more to obscure the real interests at stake than to explain them."[102]

By the end of 1818, 134 grantees out of the 347 originally belonging to the Vine and Olive Association had sold their allotments. A little more than one-third of the total land initially allotted had thus changed hands within a year of the initial distribution—29,416 out of 87,936 acres. The clique of Philadelphia merchants—most of whom never intended to move to Alabama—benefited disproportionately from these sales, taking 85 of the 134 allotments (63 percent) and 17,950 of the 29,416 acres sold (60 percent) during this first year.[103] For those who hoped that the Vine and Olive grant would become the center of a domestic wine industry, these trends did not augur well.

The Panic of 1819 dashed the speculating merchants' hopes for making a quick profit. The collapse of credit burst the speculative bubble that had fueled the dramatic rise in both the pace of sales and the price of land since 1815. With credit now unavailable and the meteoric rise in land values a memory, potential buyers had neither the ability nor the desire to invest in the stagnant market in western land. These national trends were apparent for all to see in the Vine and Olive colony. In contrast to the one-year period from December 1817 to December 1818, when 134 allotments were sold, the entire decade of 1819–29 saw just 184 allotments change hands, more than a sevenfold decrease in the pace of sales. Because of the downturn, some Vine and Olive landholders who wanted to sell out could not find buyers. Others like Chapron, Duval, and Ravesies, who possessed some financial staying power, battened down their hatches and waited for an economic recovery. Others like Curcier and Villars, who had overextended themselves during the boom of 1817–18, were forced to sell out—in both cases to their respective business partners and fellow share-holders, Thomas Badaraque and Ravesies.[104]

Although not until the very end of the decade did signs of recovery first appear, the Vine and Olive land market did not dry up completely during the 1820s. Throughout the decade, settlers continued to sell their allotments and leave the grant, often in ill-health and usually in dire financial straits. Given the desperate circumstances of their departure and the prevailing economic gloom, one would expect to see the price of land fall. This, however, was not the case. During the decade, prices rose as high as $5.23 per acre on average (1823) and never dropped lower than $2.25 per acre on average (1829). The persistence of these robust prices in the midst of a poor national economy and a sluggish local land market is difficult to explain. One possible answer to this conundrum is that these annual averages conceal a wide range in the price of land in any given year. Given the small number of transactions in these years, the sale of a parcel or two of choice land could skew the annual average upward.[105] Another pos-sible explanation for the relatively high prices of the 1820s is that the few buyers interested in purchasing land were only interested in acquiring choice parcels. Although the existing surveys—which describe the quality of land only along boundary lines between townships and sections—paint an impressionistic pic-ture of the quality of individual allotments in the grant, there is some evi-dence that this was the case. In 1823, for example, the two contiguous allot-ments (no. 2 and no. 28, totaling 640 acres) sold by Fontanges and Frenaye to Charles D. Conner for $10 per acre were described as "first rate . . . level land" by the surveyor.[106] If this single transaction were deducted from the total sales in that year, then the average price per acre in 1823 would fall from $5.23 to $3.65. Even this, however, was a respectable price for western lands at the time. While difficult to explain, the fact remains that the price of Vine and Olive lands resisted the general downturn of the 1820s.

During the decade of the 1820s Anglo-Americans first began to purchase the allotments of French settlers. In 1827 William Adams reported that the new-comers had already acquired "the most extensive and profitable farms" in the grant. This idea—and the related notion that a massive influx of Americans in the 1820s diluted the French character of the grant—has made its way into even the best histories of the Vine and Olive colony.[107] In his *Days of Exile,* for ex-ample, Winston Smith states that by 1823 "great caravans of white settlers from Virginia and the Carolinas were pouring into the new state of Alabama, and many of them were eager to buy French land." Engulfed by this demographic

Table 5.6 Price of Vine and Olive Land, 1819–29

Year	Acres sold	Avg. price (in dollars)	Range (in dollars)	Median price (in dollars)
1819	6,490	3.77	1.25–6.00	2.06
1820	7,610	3.04	.96–12.50	2.00
1821	4,243	2.49	.27–7.58	1.79
1822	4,250	4.20	1.00–10.00	4.00
1823	4,160	5.23	1.00–12.10	3.33
1824	3,376	4.33	.25–10.00	2.50
1825	1,960	3.01	.38–6.25	2.28
1826	780	4.77	1.00–9.55	5.54
1827	1,230	3.80	.50–9.07	3.37
1828	2,480	5.17	.83–12.19	7.00
1829	6,800	2.25	.67–6.00	2.08

Source: NARA, RG 49, 234–38.

onslaught, the Vine and Olive colony began "disintegrating."[108] Not only were the Americans flooding in by the 1820s, according to this interpretation, but they were rending the French fabric of the settlement.

This view is misleading in several ways. First, it obscures the fact that a significant number of departing grantees actually sold their allotments to fellow French shareholders, rather than to newly arriving Americans. Of the 184 sales of land from 1819 to 1829, 89 (48 percent) were French-to-French transactions.[109] The original French grantees, in other words, were nearly as likely as American newcomers to purchase the allotments of their failing compatriots. A second problem with the notion of a massive American influx in the 1820s is that it exaggerates the magnitude of the transformation. Anglo-Americans certainly began to buy up allotments from French sellers during the decade but never to the extent implied by Smith and others. Rather than a flood, the growing American presence on the grant more closely resembled a rising tide. In the most active years during the decade (1823, 1824, and 1829), American purchasers never acquired much more than 2,500 acres from French sellers and in the slowest years (1820, 1826, and 1827) did not even surpass the 500-acre mark. Nor was it unknown for Anglo-Americans to sell their holdings back to French buyers.[110] In the course of the 1820s American buyers acquired 15,203 acres, only 35 percent of the 43,379 acres offered for sale during the decade.

Table 5.7 Anglo-American Land Acquisitions, 1819–34

Year	Total acres sold	Acres acquired by Anglo-Americans	% of total acres sold
1819	6,490	600	9
1820	7,610	320	4
1821	4,243	983	23
1822	4,250	1,840	43
1823	4,160	2,520	61
1824	3,375	2,480	73
1825	1,960	1,840	94
1826	780	280	36
1827	1,230	420	34
1828	2,480	1,360	55
1829	6,800	2,560	38
1830	12,160	2,560	21
1831	14,666	8,090	55
1832	15,460	5,120	33
1833	11,196	2,940	26
1834	11,120	4,840	44

Source: NARA, RG 49, 234–38.

While these purchases represented a noticeable inroad into the grant, they only brought the Americans' total share of grant lands to around 20 percent by the end of 1829. Only in the 1830s did the pace of American acquisitions in the grant begin to increase significantly and the composition of the colony's land-holders change noticeably (see table 5.7).

Far from adulterating the character of the colony and destroying its cohesion, the American newcomers in the 1820s seem to have adapted to the institutions and practices of their new neighbors. In acquiring allotments, they became shareholders in the society, adopted its interests as their own, and began to play an active role in its governance. By 1829 the French and Americans had worked out a power-sharing arrangement—with an executive committee of five members, composed of three American (Robert Withers, John Marrast, and Samuel Strudwick) and two French representatives (Honoré Bayol and the ubiquitous Ravesies, its president and chairman).[111] A petition addressed by the society to the House of Representatives at the end of 1831 reveals a similar balance. Of its thirty-nine signatures, twenty-three were of American shareholders and sixteen of French.[112] The most surprising indication of the Americans' easy integration into the life of the colony was the assiduousness with which they pursued the frustrating task of viticulture. Americans were responsible for planting with vine 139 acres of the approximately 300 under cultivation by mid-1828.[113] Far from undermining the Vine and Olive colony, the Americans who acquired allotments in the 1820s generally became active, upstanding members of the society, apparently living in relative harmony with the original, French settlers. Rather than "disintegration," what was happening was the consolidation of scattered, individual allotments in the hands of an emerging Franco-American landholding elite, an elite made more homogenous by the failure and departure of the poorer and less successful among the French settlers.

A sharp upswing in the pace of sales occurred in 1830 as the land market emerged at last from the doldrums of the 1820s. Some large landholders who had patiently held on to allotments they had purchased in previous years now determined that the time was right to sell. Among the largest profit-takers were the merchant speculators of 1817: Ravesies, Chapron, Teterel's widow, Fontanges, Frenaye, Duval, Newman, and Gratz. From the beginning of 1830 to the end of 1834, they sold 11,740 acres—20 percent of the 57,950 acres sold during this period—and made a total profit of $32,597.[114] To counter accusations of speculation, they launched a bold preemptive strike. Far from damaging the colony and diverting it from its viticultural goals, they claimed, the hope for resale at a profit was responsible for "the most thriving settlements and valuable improvements" in the grant.[115] Not all, however, totally liquidated their stake in the Vine and Olive colony. Chapron, Duval, and Ravesies retained a substantial portion of their property and remained important landholders in the area for some time to come.

The rejuvenation of the Vine and Olive land market accelerated the consolidation of landholdings in the hands of fewer and fewer families, both American and French. Whereas in 1817 the Vine and Olive lands had been divided among 347 individual owners and, with the allocation of the reserves in 1819, to 384, by 1834 this number had fallen to 170.[116] To a great extent, this development reflected the purchase of land by incoming Anglo-American planters who, by the early 1830s, had become the majority landholders in the grant. By 1834 they controlled 58,745 acres, almost two-thirds of the 89,741 acres of grant land for which information is available. Much of the Americans' property was concentrated in the hands of a few large planters. The 12 leading Anglo-American families on the grant owned 21,460 acres, almost 37 percent of the total land

Table 5.8 Profits of Philadelphia Merchants, 1830–34

Merchant	Allotments sold	Acres sold	Profit (in dollars)
Teterel (widow)	11	3,660	12,066
Ravesies	9	2,640	9,240
Newman	9	1,920	4,033
Chapron	6	1,720	298
Fontanges/Frenaye	3	960	5,024
Gratz	3	680	909
Duval	1	160	1,027

Source: NARA, RG 49, 234–38.

Table 5.9 Allotments Patented by Philadelphia Merchants, 1830–34

Merchant	Allotments patented	Acres patented
Chapron	12	4,000
Duval	8	1,600
Ravesies	7	1,280
Fontanges/Frenaye	2	520

Source: NARA, RG 49, 234–38.

held by their fellow countrymen. The remaining 60 percent was shared by 108 additional families. In other words, among the Anglo-American allotment-holders, the top 10 percent owned nearly 40 percent of the land.

A similar pattern of concentration occurred among the most prominent French families, who like their Anglo-American counterparts, took advantage of the revival of land sales in the 1830s to expand their holdings. Together, the top 12 French landholding families controlled 17,676 acres, 57 percent of the 30,996 acres of grant land still in French hands. The remaining 44 percent was shared among 38 additional families. To put it another way, while the French planter elite comprised a bit less than a quarter of the French land-holders on the grant, they owned more than half of the total land in the hands of their compatriots. Of the leading French landholding families, seven were Domingan—Chapron, Ravesies, Butaud/George, Nidelet, Noël/Follin, Stollen-werk, and Chaudron—and the rest had marital connections with these or other Domingan families.

Table 5.10 The Twelve Leading Anglo-American Landholders

Family name	Acres owned
Glover	3,080
Withers	2,500
Manning	2,360
Cocke	2,240
Witherspoon	1,680
Pickens	1,640
Robertson	1,440
Strudwick	1,400
McRae	1,360
Purnell	1,280
Young	1,280
Greer	1,200

Source: NARA, RG 49, 234–38.

Table 5.11 The Twelve Leading French Landholders

Family name	Acres owned
Chapron	4,000
Duval	1,600
Melizet/Roudet	1,480
Ravesies	1,440
Butaud/George	1,320
Nidelet	1,320
Thouron	1,240
Noel/Follin	1,220
Stollenwerk	1,160
Promis	1,136
Beylle	960
Chaudron	880

Source: NARA, RG 49, 234–38.

These two groups of landholding elites, one Anglo-American and the other Franco-Domingan, were bound together by shared financial interest. They served together in the administration of the society and spoke with one voice when seeking to influence the policy of the U.S. government toward the grant. Their shared landed interest went far toward fusing the most prominent French and American shareholders into a single, binational elite. Yet, the connections between these groups ran deeper still, as ties of marriage, friendship, and business began to be forged. Perhaps the best examples of the multidimensional bonds that came to link the leading families of the grant, even across the cultural, linguistic, and religious divide, can be found emanating from Frédéric Ravesies. His sister Marie-Angelique married a fellow grantee, François Plaidaut, but most of the Ravesies family connections reached out to the world of Anglo-American elites. Through the marriages of his three children, Ravesies became father-in-law not only to Isabella Strudwick and John McRae, both from families of large Anglo-American landholders, but also to George N. Stewart, a respected attorney and influential public figure in western Alabama. Stewart himself owned substantial holdings in the Vine and Olive colony, some individually and some jointly with his business partner Francis Strother Lyon, another prominent lawyer who would become a leading Alabama statesman. Lyon, moreover, was married to the daughter of Allen Glover, the largest Anglo-American landholder on the grant. In addition, Ravesies's stepdaughter, Cecilia-Agnès Davide, was married to Col. John Foy, a substantial Vine and Olive patentee. Between them, the Ravesies, Strudwicks, McRaes, Stewarts, Lyons, Glovers, and Foys owned nine thousand acres of land in the grant, about 10 percent of all the Vine and Olive land. In his efforts to forge ties with the leading Anglo-American families of Vine and Olive, Ravesies did not neglect to maintain his connections with his French counterparts. To this end, he could count on relations of family, business, and friendship the Ravesies had established with the Nidelets and Chaprons when all were living in Saint-Domingue before the French Revolution. In fact, Chapron, the leading French landholder on the grant, acted as Ravesies's business agent in Philadelphia, and it is likely that Ravesies had a hand in overseeing Chapron's substantial interests in Alabama. The Nidelets, who had moved to Saint Louis and married into the leading French mercantile families of that important riverine city, added another dimension to Ravesies' dense network of connections.

It is tempting to conclude that the ability to make connections with other families in the Vine and Olive colony was the key to success on the grant. Clearly all successful grantees could and did mobilize networks of in-laws, business partners, and friends to help them endure hardship and prosper in good times. Yet, it is equally plausible that it was success—whether measured in terms of land, liquid assets, public office, education, or pedigree—that opened the door to advantageous familial alliances and business partnerships. Therefore the difficult problem of cause and effect arises when trying to ascertain the reasons why some of the French grantees succeeded in Vine and Olive and others failed. Did connections breed success, or did success breed connections? Choosing between these possibilities is not easy and, in any case, is probably of little use. What is clear is that by the 1830s, a binational planter elite joined by ties broader and deeper than those forged by its common landed interest was emerging as the dominant force on the grant.

Gen. Charles-François-Antoine Lallemand, president of the Society for the Cultivation of the Vine and Olive and founder of the Champ d'Asile. Photo reproduced with the permission of the Bibliothèque Nationale de France.

Gen. Charles Lefebvre-Desnouettes, the highest-ranking Napoleonic exile to settle on the Vine and Olive grant. Photo reproduced with the permission of the Bibliothèque Nationale de France.

Gen. Bertrand Clausel never took up residence in the colony; instead he settled in Mobile as a merchant. Photo reproduced with the permission of the Bibliothèque Nationale de France.

S CONTEMPORAIN

(D'après un médaillon de David d'Angers.)

LAKANAL, Conventionnel (1762-1845)

I. ORIGINE — ÉTUDES
PUTÉ A LA CONVENTION

Un de ses oncles maternels,
Font, ancien curé de Serres, et qu

The former *conventionnel* Joseph Lakanal was a founder of the Vine and Olive colony and alleged architect of a Bonapartist plot to conquer Mexico. Photo reproduced with the permission of the Bibliothèque Nationale de France.

1841-1862

Jean-Simon Chaudron

à l'âge de 40 ans.

Known as the Blind Poet of the Canebrake, Jean-Simon Chaudron was a refugee from Saint-Domingue who settled on the grant and founded one of its most prolific lineages. Photo reproduced with the permission of the Bibliothèque Nationale de France.

As secretary of state, John Quincy Adams had to deal with the activities of the French exiles within the tricky context of the Spanish-American boundary disputes. Photo reproduced with the permission of the Bibliothèque Nationale de France.

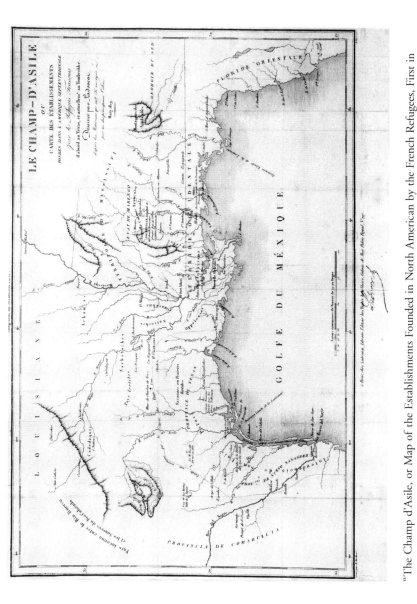

"The Champ d'Asile, or Map of the Establishments Founded in North American by the French Refugees, First in Texas and Presently on the Tombechbé." Photo reproduced with the permission of the Bibliothèque Nationale de France.

An artist's impression of the construction of Aigleville, described in the original caption as: "Construction of Aigleville, Capital of the State of Marengo, on the Banks of the Tombechbé, Directed by General Lefebvre-Desnouettes." Photo reproduced with the permission of the Center for American History, University of Texas, Austin.

An artist's impression of the construction of Aigleville. Photo reproduced with the permission of the Center for American History, University of Texas, Austin.

An artist's fanciful rendition of the Champ d'Asile. The caption says, "We see in this camp those brave men who, for twenty-five years, astonished the universe with their brilliant exploits." Photo reproduced with the permission of the Bibliothèque Nationale de France.

An artist's impression of the Champ d'Asile, described in the original caption as "This Texan Colony Founded by Unfortunate Heroes." Photo reproduced with the permission of the Bibliothèque Nationale de France.

A metaphorical evocation of the Champ D'Asile, centering on the embrace of farmer and solider surrounded by symbols of Napoleon's final battles. Photo reproduced with the permission of the Bibliothèque Nationale de France.

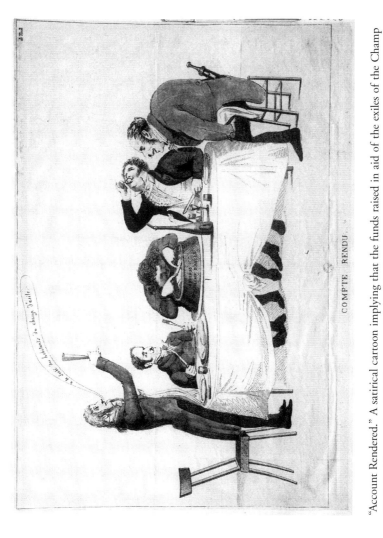

COMPTE RENDU.

"Account Rendered." A satirical cartoon implying that the funds raised in aid of the exiles of the Champ d'Asile had been embezzled. Photo reproduced with the permission of the Bibliothèque Nationale de France.

6

The Fate of Vine and Olive

What became of the grantees of the Vine and Olive colony? Some would lead lives of action and adventure; others would enjoy the comforts of family and wealth; and still others would pass the remainder of their days in laborious obscurity. But whatever course their lives took, for only a few did it lead to western Alabama. To be sure, many Vine and Olive shareholders remained in the Gulf South, but they tended to settle in Mobile and New Orleans. Another large concentration remained in Philadelphia, where they had been established for many years, and a substantial number eventually returned to France. And even most of those who settled on the grant left in the 1830s or 1840s. By the time of the Civil War, little was left in Marengo County of the former French presence.

Unlike the interconnected families of Domingan refugees who made up the bulk of the colony's resident French population, the most prominent grantees—the officers and political figures who had been exiled in 1815—never intended to settle on the grant, much less remain in the United States. Even before the foundation of the Vine and Olive colony, they had begun to seek amnesty from the Bourbon government and permission to return to France. The passage of the "Act to set apart and dispose of certain public lands, for the encouragement of the cultivation of the vine and olive" and the beginning of actual settlement on the grant did nothing to alter their determination. Few of the proscribed exiles ever left the East Coast. Instead they remained in Philadelphia, where they enjoyed the comforts of civilization and proximity to the French diplomatic corps, whom they assailed with protestations of repentance and petitions for clemency. Even the two generals who settled briefly in Alabama had no intention of staying in America. Clausel seems to have gone to Mobile because he had several relatives—his cousin Constance Ogé (the widow Demerest), nephew Louis-Edmond Bourlon, and relative Odele-Marie Desmares née Pitot—already established there. From his home on the grant, Lefebvre-Desnouettes regularly addressed statements of contrition to the French legation and, on one of his trips to Washington, met with Hyde de Neuville to beg for a royal pardon.[1] Few of the exiles ever reconciled themselves to living in the United States. Most hoped to recover their former lives in France.

Their hopes were not ill placed. Indeed, it is striking how rapidly the royal government reversed the proscription measures of 1815–16 and allowed the exiles—some of whom had been sentenced to death for treason against the throne—to return to France and resume their military service. Nothing better illustrates the extent of Bourbon clemency than the postexile career of General Clausel.[2] Pardoned in 1820, he immediately returned to France and was placed on the general officers' active list. In 1829 he was elected to the legislature as a deputy of the Ardennes. Having already recovered some of his former prominence under the Bourbons, Clausel was virtually catapulted to the summit of the French military profession after the July revolution of 1830, which brought Louis-Philippe, Duke d'Orléans to the throne. Three weeks after the revolution, he was appointed general-in-chief of the Army of Africa, which had just begun the conquest of Algeria. The following year, the regime bestowed on him the rank of marshal of France and in 1834 named him governor-general of Algeria. While serving in this capacity, he proposed the implantation at strategic points of agricultural colonies of demobilized soldiers, as a way of exerting French control over Algerian territory.[3] Military historians have noted the Roman antecedents of this Napoleonic idea but have not recognized Clausel's more immediate inspiration: the Vine and Olive colony. During his service in Algeria, which ended in 1837, he continued to win reelection to the legislature, for the last time in 1839, just three years before his death. Clausel's brilliant career demonstrates not only the desire of the Bourbons to rehabilitate their former enemies, but also the extent to which the July Monarchy favored former servants of the Napoleonic regime.

One category of exile, however, was excluded from Bourbon clemency—the regicides, barred from France for having violated the sanctity of kingship in the most unforgivable way. But of the three former members of the Convention who became Vine and Olive grantees, only one of them, Joseph Lakanal, had to endure years of exile. The other two, Jacques Garnier des Saintes and Jean-Augustin Pénières-Delors, died after only a few years in America. Garnier perished with his son in 1818 in a steamboat accident on the Ohio River. Pénières succumbed to yellow fever in 1821, soon after becoming the U.S. agent to the Florida Seminoles.[4] For his part, Lakanal made a promising start at establishing himself and his family in New Orleans. His daughter Alexandrine first married a prominent Louisiana educator, Lucien Charvet, and when he died, contracted a new marriage with Henri Germain, a Vine and Olive grantee, former member of the Champ d'Asile, and by the 1820s, vice-consul of France in New Orleans.[5] Lakanal himself mobilized his friendships with American political figures, notably General Livingston, to secure the presidency of the city's Collège d'Or-léans. The Creole families that had traditionally patronized the institution, however, recoiled at the thought of having their sons educated by a defrocked, regicide priest and gradually withdrew from it.[6] By 1825 it was forced to close its doors for good, and Lakanal left the city for Mobile. There, in a small house on the shores of the bay, he lived in almost total obscurity until his death in 1837.

Lakanal was joined in the town by a number of other Vine and Olive grant-ees, for the most part former settlers on the grant, who, while retaining and even expanding their holdings, had left it for the more comfortable surround-ings of Mobile. The core of this group was the Chaudron-Stollenwerk-George clan, which soon established durable connections with the French elite of the city.[7] Their shift to Mobile began in 1823, when Victoire George's niece and ward, Eugénie le Grand de Boislandry, and Sylvanie Chaudron went to the city to find matches for themselves. The following year Eugénie married Lazare Chieusse, a prominent local medical man who had recently been widowed. Sylvanie secured an even more advantageous match, to Adolphe Batré, a grantee himself and brother of Charles Batré, the prominent merchant and French con-sular agent at the port.[8] By 1825 or so, the rest of the George and Chaudron families had joined the young women in the city. Edouard George Jr. became a ship captain and, like his father, Edouard Chaudron, worked as a merchant, watchmaker, and jeweler. The family patriarch, Jean-Simon Chaudron, who was now approaching the age of seventy, continued his Masonic activities in Mobile, in the course of which he could not have helped but encounter fellow grantee Amand Pfister, his son Amand Jr., and his brother-in-law Nicholas-Basile Meslier, important masons in the city.[9] Other prominent Vine and Olive families also moved to Mobile. Among them were the Hurtels, who contributed a mayor, Alphonse Hurtel, to the city in the 1870s, as well as Corneille Roudet and Frédéric Ravesies. With the relocation of these large planters to Mobile, five of the twelve leading French patentees of Vine and Olive land could be found in the city.

Not all the grantees who settled in Mobile enjoyed such success. Of the twenty-seven original grantees known to have ended up in the city, many lan-guished in poverty or, worse, fell victim to the diseases that periodically swept through the city.[10] By 1823, three had died: Clausel's kinsman Bourlon (1819), Dechoule (1821), and the Domingan Jean Jeandreau (1823). Others seem to have barely made ends meet. Prosper Baltard, who had been one of the first to settle on the grant, finally gave up his agricultural efforts in 1821 and moved to Mobile. There, he sold his 120-acre allotment to the wealthy Batré brothers for $200.[11] At only $1.66 per acre, the price Baltard got was lower than the average price of Vine and Olive land in that year, $2.49 per acre, perhaps a sign of financial difficulty and desperation to sell. In 1824 F. Romain Parat, a self-described merchant, left the grant for Mobile, selling his 40-acre reserve for a mere $10.[12] The same year, Charles Prudhomme, a Domingan-Philadelphian tinman who had settled on the grant in 1818, also came to Mobile. One can only imagine what sort of life awaited him there. But perhaps the former Vine and Olive colonist who found himself in the most difficult circumstances in the city was Col. Jean-Jerome Cluis, one of the few proscribed exiles not to return to France.[13] He had settled on the grant with a Frenchwoman, Louise-Emilie de Mazières, whom he married after being exiled to the United States. They farmed, operated a tavern in Greensboro, and had two children, but by the mid-1820s they had left the colony for Mobile. They were clearly not rich: the 1830 census indicates that they owned only one slave. After Cluis's death in Mobile in 1834, it was discovered that he had left another family in France. For the next several years, his two wives engaged in a legal tug-of-war over his miserable fortune.

Mobile was not the only Gulf Coast city that attracted former members of the Vine and Olive colony. French emigrants and expatriates seem to have gravitated to the entire region, drawn in no small measure by the cultural and linguistic legacy of French and Spanish colonialism that still lingered there in the first decades of the nineteenth century. Two even went to Florida— Nicholas-Simon Parmentier, who left the grant for Pensacola to take up a minor post in the customs service, and Pénières, who became an Indian agent.[14] But most former Vine and Olive colonists who settled in the Gulf region went to New Orleans or its environs. At least forty-two settled in the city, and many more passed through at one time or another.

As with the colonists who settled in Mobile, those who ended up in New Orleans spanned the entire social spectrum. Near the summit was grantee Pierre-Auguste Canonge, nephew of the prominent New Orleans judge and freemason Jean-François Canonge.[15] Louis-Etienne and Victor Tulane, while not particularly successful in their own right, could boast of their younger brother Paul, who soon joined them in the city. Paul became a wealthy merchant and ultimately founded the university that bears his name.[16] Aimée Valcour, whose Point Coupée sugar plantation earned him the nickname the Prince of Planters, was another former Vine and Olive member who scaled the heights of Creole society.[17] And at the very pinnacle of the Louisiana plantocracy was Paul-Louis Bringier, eldest son of Marius-Pons Bringier, perhaps the largest planter in the entire state.[18] The Bringiers had come to Spanish Louisiana from Guadeloupe in the mid-1780s and lost no time acquiring vast tracts of land. By the 1820s they had turned these into some of the most celebrated plantations in the state—Maison Blanche, Bocage, Union, and the Hermitage. As a young man, however, Paul-Louis seemed set on squandering the family fortune and ruining its good name. A gambler and adventurer, Paul-Louis was an Indian trader on the Missouri frontier before the War of 1812, fought in that conflict (although his brother, who served as Andrew Jackson's aide-de-camp at the Battle of New Orleans, had a more distinguished military record), and then joined the governing junta of the so-called Republic of Mexico. In 1818 he disappeared from view for a time, possibly as part of the Champ d'Asile, before reemerging to explain that he had been involved in a scheme to take over Mexican silver mines. By the 1830s, however, he seems to have cast off his youthful restlessness and achieved public respectability and power as the surveyor general of the state of Louisiana. For Bringier, whose family already owned fine plantations long before the creation of the Vine and Olive colony, a 240-acre allotment in Alabama could not have meant much. He never set foot on the grant and simply abandoned his parcel. It was auctioned off with other nonperforming allotments in 1834.

At the other end of the social spectrum, the bustling international seaport of New Orleans attracted a floating population of speculators, con men, and criminals. One was Vine and Olive grantee Joseph Truc.[19] In 1816 he left Marseille, where he had incurred large debts, for New Orleans, where he hoped to make a new start. Borrowing money there, he opened a store, but the endeavor soon ran into difficulties and his store failed. He was jailed for fraud and died in prison in 1819, still owing French creditors two hundred thousand francs. A similar fate befell fellow grantee Abel Farcy Sainte-Marie.[20] As a young man, Farcy traveled to London where he contracted debts. After the Napoleonic Wars, he left for the United States, partly to escape his English creditors. When he learned of the formation of the Society for the Cultivation of the Vine and Olive in Philadelphia, he signed up for an allotment, but then fell under the sway of Gen. Charles Lallemand. By late December 1817 Farcy had ceded his share to Georges Jeannet and was on board the *Huntress*, sailing for Galveston. He survived the debacle of the Champ d'Asile and returned to New Orleans only to engage in new speculations. When these failed, leaving him even more deeply in debt, he moved to Baton Rouge where new schemes only brought him further losses. He returned to New Orleans, declared bankruptcy, and

found work as a beadle. In 1822 he was described as living in "the most profound misery."[21] A final example is provided by Mathieu-Ferdinand Manfredi,
another member of both the Vine and Olive colony and the Champ d'Asile.[22]
Nothing is known of Manfredi's background, but upon returning to New Orleans from Galveston he asked Louis Lauret, a young officer who had also gone
to Texas, to invest $860 in a warehouse he wanted to open on the Mississippi
River. At the urging of Charles Lallemand, Lauret—who was the nephew of
the wealthy New Orleans merchant Paul Lanusse—agreed to advance the
money. Manfredi promptly fled to Havana, contracted an illness, and died in a
charity hospital, leaving Lauret in the lurch.

Lauret was a hardworking individual who, after his involvement in the Lallemands' Texas adventure, seems to have made a genuine attempt to establish
himself in New Orleans.[23] Aided monetarily and socially by his uncle, Lauret
contracted a good marriage with Josephine Rousseau, the daughter of a Creole
ship captain. He then acquired slaves and set to work clearing a small plantation for himself upriver from New Orleans. He was contentedly engaged in this
endeavor—"happy and independent in my own humble hearth" as he put it—
when General Lallemand, who had also settled near New Orleans, came to see
him. Lallemand not only urged him to invest in Manfredi's bogus venture, but
also asked the gullible young Frenchman to endorse one of his own notes in
the sum of $2,327. Lallemand soon defaulted, and Lauret was forced to pay the
general's obligation. On top of this setback, four of his slaves perished in 1823,
and the following year brought floods that inundated his field. By 1826 Lauret
had given up and gone to Philadelphia, unaccompanied by his wife (who may
have died). He then disappeared for several years, only to resurface in 1830. In
that year he wrote a farewell note to Henriette Lallemand, at whose wedding
to Gen. Henri Lallemand he had served as best man. In it, he explained that
he had been wandering in the Georgia wilderness and was currently living in a
cabin on the shore of a bayou. Although "difficult and disgusting," he explained, this lifestyle allowed him to "avoid the sight of the world, which fills
me with horror." He further announced that, as his retreat became uninhabit-
able during the cold winter months, he was going to camp in Florida for the
season, taking with him only his musket and a small sack, and there "write the
story" of his life. He was never heard from again.

Most of the grantees who settled in New Orleans led more conventional
lives.[24] Antoine Barbe moved there from Philadelphia in 1822 and became a
merchant. The Domingan Bujac brothers, also merchants, followed the same
path from Philadelphia to New Orleans, where they were still living in the

1850s. The Domingan-Philadelphia merchant Jean-Juste Nartigue joined them there with his wife in 1819. And the following year, the Philadelphia handwriting teacher Lintroy also moved to the city, although by 1831 his widow had left for Mobile. Even Jean Quésart, who had been living in Philadelphia for at least two decades, joined the internal movement of French expatriates in America from their old center of Philadelphia toward New Orleans and became a successful tobacco and chocolate manufacturer there in the early 1820s. A number of those who joined in the migration had been living on the grant. Julie Delpit, who settled in Alabama for about one year in 1819, soon left for New Orleans, where she opened a tobacco store. Pierre-Maxime Manoury also left the grant in 1819, after a short stay, and became a dry goods merchant in New Orleans. Jacques Pueek stuck to agriculture a bit longer, remaining on the grant until 1821, when he left to open a hardware store in the city. Even Michel Mestayer, the archivist of the society, abandoned the grant in 1824 to go into business in New Orleans.

After the failure of the Champ d'Asile, its survivors also made their way to New Orleans, where some remained to become upstanding citizens of the city. Félix-Marie Formento, the Piedmont-born French army doctor, opened a medical practice after returning from Texas and in 1820 purchased a pharmacy in the Vieux Carré where he lived until his death. The Savoyard officer Henri Germain stayed to marry Alexandrine Lakanal and become vice-consul of France in the city. Former imperial artillery lieutenant Pierre Guillot became a teacher of French, Latin, and mathematics at the Collège d'Orléans, perhaps with the help of its president, Joseph Lakanal. Dublin-born Samuel Stephens, who had been an officer in Napoleon's Irish Regiment, married a widow and settled in Saint Tammany Parish, an Irish neighborhood in the city. The surgeon Charles Monnot founded a plantation, Napoleonville, and marched in Napoleon's grand funeral procession in December 1821. Other medical veterans of the Champ d'Asile settled in the city, no doubt attracted by the numerous opportunities afforded by the disease-plagued metropolis. François Canobio and François Violle (accompanied by his wife, Léontine Desportes) both practiced medicine in the city. And even Jean-Baptiste Campardon, the modest Philadelphia tailor who had provided uniforms to Charles Lallemand's departing adventurers, settled in New Orleans.

Those Vine and Olive members who settled in Mobile and New Orleans were outnumbered by those who remained in Philadelphia. In fact, the largest single group of shareholders whose destinies are known, sixty-two in all, stayed put in Philadelphia where many had lived since the 1790s. They included many of the large merchants prominent in the history of the Vine and Olive colony. Apart from a trip to Mexico in the mid-1820s, Pierre-Frédéric Fontanges remained in the city, as did his brother-in-law and business partner Marc-Antoine Frenaye. In addition to accompanying Fontanges to Mexico, Frenaye sojourned briefly on the grant and in New York City. But by the early 1830s he had returned to Philadelphia, where he served as a confidential agent to the Roman Catholic bishops of the city and was one of the founding members of the cathedral cemetery. Joseph Beylle also remained in Philadelphia, although he co-owned a store in Mobile with the Batré brothers. Others who stayed, but nonetheless maintained business relations with relatives in Alabama, were François Melizet, whose brother-in-law Corneille Roudet had settled on the grant, and Jacques-Séraphin Duval, who was related by marriage to the Chaudron family. Most of the Philadelphia merchants, however, quickly sold their allotments and severed their ties with the Vine and Olive colony, ties that were never very strong. These included the china merchant Joseph-Hilaire Gubert; merchants Nicholas-Cadet Bergasse and Léonard Engelbert; shipowner Pierre Lacombe and his brother-in-law, the physician and druggist Germain Combes; Dr. Joseph Martin du Columbier Sr. and his son, owner of an iron foundry; and even businessman Joseph-Thomas Badaraque, who had once been the director of the Society for the Cultivation of the Vine and Olive. Also remaining in Philadelphia were many more grantees who, while respectable, were of a lower social level. These included a contingent of bottlers and distillers—Elie Forestier, Philippe Knappe, and Joseph Sévelinge. There were also a number of artisans, among whom the more skilled or intellectual trades were well-represented. These included the dealer in foreign books Louis-Descoins Belair, the jeweler Louis Brechemin, and the confectioners Laurent Astolphi and Victor Hamel. Others included hairdresser and perfumer Charles Condé, barber Mathieu Dutertre, baker Guillaume Caillebaux, and Jean-Vincent Vernhes, who was in the textile business.

If the largest single group of grantees remained in Philadelphia until the end of their lives, another smaller group—almost all military officers—chose a more daring course. Whether from adventurous inclination, the habit of living by their swords, love of glory, or ideological commitment, they spurned the tranquility craved by their fellow grantees and instead threw themselves into the upheavals of the Atlantic world. The civil strife within the Spanish dominions continued to exercise the strongest attraction on these men of action, many of whom had already served there under the empire. Perhaps for these veterans of the bitter guerilla fighting in Spain, serving the Latin American insurgency was a way of getting revenge for the defeat they had suffered ten years earlier.

Of those who took up arms against Spanish royalism, the artillery officer "Colonel" Raoul was undoubtedly the most successful.[25] Having briefly served the Republic of Buenos Aires in 1816, Raoul was an old hand at Latin American insurgency. His experience in Argentina, however, had been brief and not entirely satisfactory. During the early 1820s he eschewed adventure and even settled briefly on the grant where he ran a ferry service, and his wife, the former Marquise de Sinabaldi, served up delicacies at an inn they ran together. But by 1824 the lure of adventure overcame Raoul's resistance, and he left with his wife for Central America, where opportunity could be had for men with expertise in the technical branches of the military. The details of his military service there are unknown, but by about 1830, he had risen to the rank of major-general commanding the artillery of the Guatemalan Army. He had also divorced his first wife, remarried a local woman, and then divorced her as well. When news of the 1830 Revolution finally reached him, he lost no time petitioning the new government for reinstatement in the French army. He was welcomed back and given his old rank of lieutenant-colonel. Within a year his career began to take off. Called in to help suppress the uprising of the silk weavers of Lyon, Raoul took a page out of Bonaparte's book and ruthlessly turned his cannon against the working-class quarters. The July Monarchy rewarded him with rapid promotion, ultimately to the rank of general, and directorship of the artillery school at Besançon. His professional success paved the way for a third marriage, this time to the daughter of a wealthy bourgeois family of the same city. Raoul died several years later, in 1850, an influential military technician, a wealthy man, and a respected member of provincial elite society.

Other Vine and Olive grantees took part in the Spanish constitutionalist movement that began in 1820 when liberals succeeded in limiting the power of Ferdinand VII and ended in 1823 when invading armies from Bourbon France restored absolutism. During Spain's short experiment with constitutionalism, many foreign volunteers flocked to the country to support the Spanish legislature, the Cortes, in its trial of strength with the king and then the French. Among them were Louis-Jacques Galabert, Bartolo Colona d'Ornano, and Paul-Albert Latapie, all of whom served as colonels in various formations of foreign volunteers. With the success of the French invasion in 1823, their hopes of rebuilding new military careers in Spain were dashed. Worse, they found themselves in the awkward situation of having borne arms against the armies of Bourbon France. Their respective attempts to deal with this problem met with varying degrees of success, but in all three cases, their attempts to remake their lives after 1823 were full of drama.

Galabert was placed under surveillance by the French political police, although he was allowed to return to France.[26] One year after the 1830 Revolution, however, he was elected to the legislature and succeeded in lobbying for a cherished project—the creation of a canal across southwestern France—that would be realized with the opening of the Canal des Pyrénnées. Latapie also staged a dramatic recovery from what appeared to be a hopelessly compromising situation.[27] As deputy commander of the Legion of French Refugees, a formation of anti-Bourbon French volunteers, Latapie expected little mercy from the triumphant armies of Louis XVIII, so he skipped across the border to Portugal when defeat seemed imminent. From his refuge, he somehow managed to convince the government of Ferdinand VII that he had renounced his former political sympathies, that he was now a committed royalist, and that the Spanish government should employ his military services. By the late 1820s he had risen to the rank of brigadier general in the Spanish army and made deputy commander of the Philippine Islands. He was then named inspector of militia to the Canary Islands, where he presumably served out the remainder of his career. Less successful was Colona d'Ornano, who also served as a colonel of foreign volunteers in the constitutionalist army of Spain.[28] Under police surveillance like the others, this former Corsican officer and judge was an object of particular concern because of his family's close ties to the Bonaparte clan. His cousin Simon Colona lived in Rome in the entourage of Laetitia Bonaparte, Napoleon's mother, and was considered to be the "center and agent of all correspondence between Corsica and the members of the imperial family."[29] When the Bourbon French armies rolled across the Pyrénnées into Spain, Colona d'Ornano fled. In October 1823 he appeared before officials in the French Consulate in Tangiers, in the empire of Morocco, protesting that he had not borne arms against his countrymen and asking to be allowed to return to France. His request was refused. He found himself with no choice but to return to the United States, where, he announced, he intended to establish a plantation in the vicinity of Saint-Augustine, Florida, in partnership with Prince Murat, son of the Napoleonic marshal and would-be king of Naples.

In 1830 the start of the French conquest of Algeria opened new possibilities for men of this ilk. One of the Vine and Olive grantees, General Clausel, rose to command this entire endeavor during the 1830s. Another whose star shone almost as brightly in North Africa was Michel Combe.[30] During his American exile Combe had remained on the East Coast, carefully avoiding direct involvement in both the Vine and Olive colony and the Champ d'Asile. In 1823 he married Elisa Walker, daughter of a wealthy family of upstate New York landowners whose father had served as George Washington's aide-de-camp. Combe remained with his wife on her family's estates near Utica until 1830. In that year, the revolution in France made it possible for him to return to his homeland and resume his military career, mainly in Algeria. The resumption of his service in the French army got off to a rocky start. As colonel commanding the 66th Infantry Regiment in 1831–32, he slapped one of his subordinate officers who responded in kind. The general investigating the matter found Combe in the wrong, had him placed under arrest, and then transferred him to the Foreign Legion. Within a year, new scandals had required his transfer to a new unit, the 47th Infantry. In a short time, Combe had managed to alienate all his subordinate officers and become an object of ridicule for his soldiers, who greeted him with jeers and catcalls on parade. Combe went over his immediate superior, and when that only earned him a new spell in prison for ignoring the military hierarchy, he took his case directly to the war ministry. This extraordinary demarche provoked a special meeting of the national Infantry Committee, which reviewed Combe's entire service record. Its conclusion is worth citing at length. The committee found that "the faults for which this officer is blamed today are unfortunately a new chapter in a long story of problems. These derive from his violent and irascible character, simultaneously despotic with his subordinates and independent vis-à-vis his superiors, on the one hand taking advantage of the rigors of discipline to enforce blind submission to his arbitrary desires and, on the other, seeking to elude the regulations in order to free himself from the yoke of authority against which he has always chafed." The committee was forced to recognize, however, that in terms of "capacity, devotion, and bravery, few commanders possess a reputation more brilliant or well-merited than this superior officer."[31] Given that such qualities were immediately necessary for the conquest of Algeria, the committee kept Combe on active service. In 1837 he was killed leading an assault against the heavily defended walls of Constantine and became a national hero.

The Champ d'Asile also furnished its share of adventurers, some of whom must be classified as professional revolutionaries and others as self-seeking scoundrels. The Polish officer Jean Schultz belonged to the former category.[32] After the dissolution of the Texas establishment, where he had commanded the second cohort after the desertion of Charrasin, he returned to New Orleans and from there took passage back to France. Upon his arrival in early 1820, he asked for French citizenship in order to resume his career in the French army. The government refused his request, although it offered to ask the Russian government to grant him special amnesty and allow him to return to Poland. For Schultz, who had been fighting against Russia since the 1780s, this was not an option. He would continue by other means his lifetime struggle against the forces of reaction that had subjugated his homeland. In the fall of 1820 he left France for Constantinople in the company of two other Polish officers, but the group disembarked in Naples where they took part in the abortive invasion led by the secret society of international revolutionaries, the Carbonari. After some time, Schultz left for Spain where he commanded a legion of foreign volunteers in the constitutionalist army. When troops from Bourbon France crossed the Pyrénnées in 1823, Schultz fled to Egypt where he was appointed colonel in the Egyptian expeditionary force occupying Mecca and other points in Arabia on behalf of the Ottoman Empire.

Another Champ d'Asile survivor who was a revolutionary activist in the 1820s was Georges Jeannet. Given his background not merely as a colonial administrator for the French Republic but also as the official charged with effecting slave emancipation in Guyana, it is not surprising to find that Jeannet's hopes centered on the possibility of fomenting slave revolt in the Caribbean.[33] In 1821 and early 1822 he reportedly set in motion a plot to spark a rising of mulattoes and blacks against the white inhabitants of Guadeloupe. The base of the operation was on the nearby island of Saint Barthelemy, in the mercantile house of the brothers Benjamin and Titus Bigard, rich free men of color who had been trusted lieutenants of the French Revolutionary commissar Victor Hugues during the 1790s. Backed by their money and influence, a fleet of corsairs was to disembark eight hundred armed men on Guadeloupe, burn plantations, murder whites, and try to touch off a race war that would destroy the colonial regime. Jeannet was present on the island as late as March 1822, making connections with potential allies on the island, when he was expelled by the governor-general.[34] He returned to New York City via Saint Barthelemy and promptly organized a new expedition, this one against Puerto Rico. In mid-August 1822, accompanied by his son Joseph, two nephews, and two former Napoleonic officers (General Ducoudray-Holstein and Colonel Durutte), Jeannet set sail at the head of a force composed of fifty-two men crammed aboard two small ships.[35] It is unclear how the expedition unfolded, although it certainly did not pose a serious threat to Puerto Rico. Jeannet himself died in 1828 in impoverished circumstances in his hometown, while his son became a small businessman in Peru.

The case of Charles Lallemand, the leader of the Champ d'Asile, is more complex.[36] After his return to New Orleans in 1818, he embarked on a course apparently designed to secure himself respectability and social prominence in the city. By the end of the year, he had become a U.S. citizen and an officer in the Triple Bienfaisance Masonic Lodge of New Orleans. In addition, he had purchased two properties near the city, nine slaves, equipment, and farm animals. Yet rumors continued to circulate that he was planning a new invasion of Texas.[37] Moreover, he had contracted substantial debts—his mortgages alone exceeded twenty-five thousand dollars—and began to ask his former subordinates, like the unfortunate Louis Lauret, to secure his loans.[38] Financially harried, Lallemand may have been tempted to exploit the fund-raising drive organized by the *Minerve Française* to remedy his financial distress. By the end of 1819 the *Minerve* had collected fifteen thousand dollars for the survivors of the Champ d'Asile. Its editors asked the governor of Louisiana to appoint a committee to oversee the distribution of these funds. Chaired by the wealthy Creole planter J. Noël Destrehan, the committee invited Lallemand in March 1819 to furnish it with a list of the men he had commanded in Texas.[39] As the months passed without a response and the meager resources of the Champ d'Asile survivors were consumed by the high cost of living in New Orleans, where at least half had remained in the hope of receiving their share of the *Minerve* funds, suspicions began to grow. At the end of April, the ailing General Rigau, who had only several months left to live, published an open letter in *L'Ami des Lois* asking why his former colleague had not furnished the list. Lallemand shot back with a letter of his own, and soon the pages of all the local newspapers were filled with the salvos of the pro- and anti-Lallemand factions. Finally, on 19 May 1820 Lallemand provided the desired list, although he grandiloquently wrote to the committee that he was relinquishing his own share.[40] It is not clear what Lallemand was hoping to achieve by withholding the list, although his intentions were widely suspected of being self-serving.

With his reputation tarnished, Lallemand did not tarry long in New Orleans. Creditors were hounding him, his IOUs were no longer being accepted, and if he had been hoping for a new chance to intervene in Mexico, the definitive defeat of James Long's filibustering expedition to Texas—the last of its kind—spelled an end to that particular ambition.[41] The constitutionalist movement in Spain, however, offered a new stage for this man of action. By 1823 he had formed the Legion of French Refugees to help defend the Cortes from the invading Bourbon armies. When resistance collapsed, Lallemand retreated over the border to Portugal and then left for England where he became involved in the Greek Committee of London, a nationalist group supporting the struggle for Greek independence from the Ottoman Empire. The committee charged Lallemand with procuring two modern frigates in the United States and gave him £150,000 for that purpose. According to the French foreign minister, "strange malversations" subsequently took place in which all the funds were dissipated, but only one frigate ended up in Greek hands. Lallemand's exact role in these dealings is obscure, but once again suspicions of the gravest kind were raised about his character.[42]

After this affair, Lallemand settled in New York City, where he opened a successful school.[43] But pedagogy held little attraction for him, so when the Revolution of 1830 ushered in a new regime in France, Lallemand petitioned the government to rejoin the French army. His request was granted. Until his death in 1839, he served in a variety of important positions—inspector general of the cavalry, gendarmerie (military police), and military school, member of the Infantry and Cavalry Committee, commander of the military division of Bastia on Corsica—and was named a peer of France.[44] If Lallemand had on more than one occasion covered his more questionable activities with the banner of revolution, the regime that came to power in France in 1830 was more than willing to overlook these indiscretions in its effort to rehabilitate this former Bonapartist stalwart.

As well as leaving an indelible mark on the lives of many of the participants, both the Champ d'Asile and the Vine and Olive colony had a historical impact that went beyond the lives of the individuals who composed these ephemeral settlements. In the case of the Champ d'Asile, the repercussions were truly international. The dissolution of Lallemand's fortified encampment signaled the close of the era of filibustering expeditions in the borderlands and marked a turning point in relations between Spain and the United States. With the exception of Long's ill-fated expedition the following year, never again would incursions of foreign adventurers play a serious role in the Mexican struggle for independence. But in 1818, as the survivors of the Champ d'Asile straggled back to New Orleans, neither the Spanish nor American governments realized this. Instead, Lallemand's foray into the contested borderland zone between the two countries made both acutely aware that their continued failure to agree on a mutually acceptable boundary would perpetuate the power vacuum into which the French general had thrust himself. As long as the frontier remained nebulous, it would exercise a constant attraction on men of his ilk, unpredictable and desperate men whose presence in this sensitive area was sure to generate instability and might even give rise to incidents that could bring the two nations into armed conflict. However much they might covet it, neither the

United States nor Spain was willing to go to war over the Texas borderlands. Their shared interest in peace and stability, moreover, had become mutually evident in the course of Lallemand's adventure. The unauthorized proposals of Onís and Graham aside, neither government had sought to derive advantage from the presence of the French intruders in the neutral zone. Indeed, both had taken steps to remove them from this sensitive area. This created a degree of trust that, when coupled with both governments' keen awareness of the dangers of leaving the Texas border undetermined, played a role in pushing ahead the difficult negotiations then under way between Adams and Onís. Within a year of the dissolution of the Champ d'Asile, these negotiations had produced a document, the Transcontinental Treaty, demarcating the boundary between the two countries.

The Champ d'Asile also became a cause célèbre in France and a rallying point for the anti-Bourbon opposition, whether Bonapartist, liberal, or revolutionary. The French public first became aware of Lallemand's Texas settlement in August 1818, when a prominent opposition journal, the *Minerve Française*, ran a long feature on it. A blatant piece of propaganda, the article offered long excerpts from Lallemand's initial proclamation, as well as instructions on traveling to New Orleans for readers interested in joining the venture.[45] Over the course of the next year, few subsequent editions of the *Minerve* failed to present updates on the remarkable progress of the "colony." Bonapartist bards like Béraud and Béranger used the journal to offer poetic tributes to the Champ d'Asile.[46] Together with a spate of "eyewitness" accounts rushed off the presses in 1819–20, as well as lithographs printed by the thousands for the mass market, these efforts helped forge a lasting (and highly romanticized) image of the Champ d'Asile that persists today. This publicity campaign may even have helped renew French interest in the Americas, a favorite topic of the eighteenth-century Enlightenment that seems to have lost some of its luster as the nineteenth century progressed.[47]

But perhaps even more important at the time was the fund-raising drive organized by the editors of the *Minerve*. Originally the brainchild of Félix Desportes, a former member of the Convention then in exile in Germany, the idea of collecting contributions for the Champ d'Asile was presented in the September 1818 issue of the journal. Money began to pour in, and the *Minerve* started printing increasingly lengthy lists of the donors. This was a brilliant stroke, for it gave those opposed to the Bourbon regime a legal, public forum in which to display their sentiments. As the number of donors grew from the hundreds to the thousands, the *Minerve* began grouping the names by *départe-*

ment and even city, thereby creating the impression that the entire nation was in solidarity with the exiles—and thus opposed to the government that had exiled them. As an anonymous editorialist put it, the lists showed that "France itself is the veritable Champ d'Asile for all the French."[48] Even after it became known in France that Lallemand and his followers had abandoned their encampment and left Texas, contributions for the Champ d'Asile continued to pour into the offices of the *Minerve,* which continued to print lists of donors. By July 1819, when the campaign was ended, it had raised more than ninety-five thousand francs.[49] There was some discussion about using the money to aid the Tombigbee colony, whose praises the *Minerve* also sung, but this idea went nowhere.[50] As everyone—liberal donor and royalist critic alike—understood, the real point of the collection was not to raise money for the exiles, but to send a message to the Bourbon government that "the furors of 1815 have been condemned by public opinion, and that universal sympathy has accompanied the victims of reaction into their exile."[51]

The Vine and Olive colony itself also had important historical consequences. To dismiss it simply as a failure is to overlook the influence its very conspicuous lack of success exerted over future American land policy. Because it gave rise to so much speculation and did not fulfill its original purpose, the Vine and Olive colony discredited this mode of western settlement. No more would the government charter a "colonial" group that proposed to implant a ready-made town in a strategic location on the frontier. Subsequent efforts by such groups to secure federal land grants on which to establish themselves would fail to sway skeptical congressional opinion. In the final months of 1817, for example, a group of Irish immigrants to the United States formed an association to petition Congress for a grant of land in Illinois "on the same or similar terms as those given to the French refugees."[52] Even though "everybody felt satisfied that their design was an honest one," Congress refused their request because of the recent "abuse of the Alabama grant."[53] Similar petitions—like that of the Coffee Land Association, which sought a grant in Florida to establish domestic coffee cultivation and which, moreover, counted six Philadelphian Vine and Olive grantees among its members—were refused.[54] The Vine and Olive colony thus marked the last manifestation of an older approach to western settlement, an approach reminiscent of the seventeenth- and eighteenth-century European efforts to colonize North America and the Caribbean. Henceforth the settlement of the West would be left to the individual and the marketplace.

Appendix: The Grantees and Their Allotments

The appendix is composed of three parts.[1] The first is a list by allotment of the grantees. It is derived from the list of allottees given to the secretary of the treasury by the society at the end of 1818 and an updated list, showing the allocation of the reserves and certain revisions to the initial distribution of principal allotments, furnished in 1825. The list is organized by allotment number and indicates in parentheses the acreage each allotment held. I have given the full names of the grantees, when known, and also an indication of their background. Domingans are identified by **boldface** type. The names of allottees from a military background (militia service excluded) are <u>underlined</u>. Those who joined the Champ d'Asile are *italicized*. And the names of those who set foot on the grant, however briefly, are enclosed in brackets.

The second part of the appendix consists of a reproduction of the allotment map drafted by Vine and Olive member Edouard Paguenaud. With it, the location of an individual's allotment can be easily located.

The third part provides biographical sketches, alphabetically organized, of all the Vine and Olive grantees. The same code used in the list of shareholders—indicating that a given grantee was a Domingan, military veteran, Champ d'Asile participant, or settler—is also employed in these biographical sketches. The information on which they are based comes from a wide range of archival and published sources too numerous to provide in detailed footnotes. The most important archival sources were the land records of the Tombeckbee Association at the National Archives and Records Administration in Washington, D.C., the Kent Gardien Papers at the Alabama Department of Archives and History in Montgomery, the French diplomatic correspondence at the Archive des Affaires Etrangères in Paris, the records of French consulates in the United States at the Centre des Archives Diplomatiques in Nantes, the records of the political police in the Archives Nationales in Paris, and the records of military personnel at the Archives de la Guerre in Vincennes.

List of Shareholders by Allotment

1 (480): [Nicholas-Basile Meslier]
2 (160): [*Louis Lauret*]
3 (120): Honoré Conte
4 (120): [Corneille Roudet (the younger)]
5 (120): Antoine Vial
6 (120): Antoine Bujey
7 (120): **Jean-Baptiste Godemar**
8 (320): *Louis-René Jeannet*
9 (320): **Widow Julie Pastol**
10 (120): [**Henri Allard**]
11 (120): Germain Combes
12 (120): Vincent Combes
13 (240): Sibenthal brothers
14 (240): René Perdreauville
15 (120): Anselme Alma
16 (120): François Salmon
17 (120): [Lintroy]
18 (320): *Jean Schultz*
19 (320): Michel Combe
20 (480): [François Martin]
21 (160): Antoine-Zacharie Pelagot
22 (480): [**Pierre-Edouard-Côme George (father)**]
23 (160): [*François Viole*]
24 (480): **Pierre Lacombe**
25 (160): Paul-Albert Latapie
26 (480): Etienne Richard
27 (160): Etienne Papillot
28 (480): [**Jean-Pierre Frenaye**]
29 (160): Georges Rivet
30 (240): [Jean-Claude-Benoit Boutière]
31 (120): [**Widow Louise-Adèle-Gertrude Davide de Sevré**]
32 (120): [Louis Delaporte]

33 (120): Jean-Ulysse Meynié
34 (240): [*Etienne-Jean-Baptiste Métais*]
35 (120): Lullier Mansuis
36 (120): Louis-Michel Jouny
37 (120): Jean-Vincent Vernhes
38 (480): Louis-Pierre-Joseph Marchand
39 (160): Amédée Martin
40 (240): [Isaac Butaud]
41 (240): Jonas Keller
42 (120): Dieudonné Menou
43 (320): *Ambroise Jourdan*
44 (320): *Emile Vorster*
45 (240): Nicholas-Cadet Bergasse
46 (240): [**Pierre Gallard**]
47 (120): Claude-Joseph Lefeuvre
48 (240): [Edouard Paguenaud]
49 (240): [Jean Transon]
50 (120): Nicholas Gauny
51 (480): Laurent Astolphi
52 (160): Philippe Knappe
53 (320): Alphonse-Frédéric-Emmanuel, marquis de Grouchy
54 (160): [Victor de Grouchy]
55 (160): Pierre Pillero
56 (480): **Pierre Drouet**
57 (120): **Michel Bailly**
58 (480): Pierre-Paul Lemaignen
59 (160): *François Lerouyer*
60 (480): **Jean-Pierre Garesché de la Poterie**
61 (160): *Félix-Marie Formento*
62 (240): **Placide-Laurent Faurès/ Jean-Pierre Garesché de la Poterie**

63 (120): Emmanuel-M. Bürcklé

64 (240): **Coquillon brothers**

65 (240): Samuel Jackson/**Pierre Drouet**

66 (240): Guillaume Montelius/ [Baizeau] (60), [Fagot] (60), [Widow Julie Delpit] (60), *Jean-Baptiste Lapeyre* (60)

67 (120): François-Gaspard Boutière

68 (240): Thomas Robin

69 (240): **Jean-Juste Nartigue**

70 (160): Hyacinthe Gerard

71 (480): [**Auguste-Firmin Follin**]

72 (160): [**Auguste and Firmin Follin (brothers)**]

73 (480): [**Jean-Marie Chapron**]

74 (160): James Weil

75 (480): Nicholas-Alexandre Dupouy

76 (160): [Pierre-Maxime Manoury]

77 (480): **Vital-Marie Garesché Maisonneuve**/[**Catherine-Victoire George**]

78 (160): *Jacques Tournel*

79 (480): L. J. F. Martin Piquet (son)

80 (160): Joseph Martin Piquet (father)/Jacques Moncravie

81 (480): **Joseph Robard**/Henry B. Himley

82 (120): Pierre Martin Piquet

83 (240): Charles and Joseph Auzé (brothers)

84 (240): Jacques Braud/**François-Annet-Charles Bruguière**

85 (160): *Auguste Barraud*

86 (240): François Lecampion

87 (240): Louis Brechemin

88 (160): Jean-Jacques-Etienne Humbert

89 (480): Victor Jamet

90 (160): *Narcisse-Périclès Rigau*

91 (480): [Guillaume Promis]

92 (160): [Alphonse Desmares]

93 (480): *Jean-Baptiste (or François) Durand*

94 (160): Joseph Robaglia

95 (240): Alphonse Garnier (son)

96 (240): *Jean-Baptiste-Emile Pénières (son)*

97 (120): Widow Angélique Audibert

98 (480): **François-Etienne Nidelet**

99 (120): [L. David Cousin]

100 (320): Louis-Jacques Galabert

101 (320): Jean-Baptiste Petitval

102 (480): Mathieu-Bernard Anduze

103 (160): Louis-Auguste Frédéric

104 (480): Joseph-Hilaire Gubert

105 (160): *Joseph-Aristée-Théodore Moynier*

106 (320): *Pierre Douarche*

107 (320): Louis Gruchet

108 (480): [Charles Villars]

109 (160): *J.-Alexandre Pagnière*

110 (480): Louis-Marie Dirat

111 (160): Mondin

112 (480): Pierre Pagaud

113 (160): *Eugène-Hyacinthe Fallot*

114 (480): [**Anne-Gilbert-Marc-Antoine Frenaye**]

115 (120): Clement Laurent

116 (480): Dominique-Joseph-René Vandamme

117 (120): Hyacinthe Angeli

118 (320): [Benoit-M. Poculo]

119 (160): [Prosper Baltard]
120 (160): [Antoine-Marie Moquart]
121 (480): Louis-Antoine Besson
122 (160): J. Joseph Lemeusnier
123 (480): J. Joseph and *Félix-Antoine Lemeusnier* (brothers)/ J. Joseph Lemeusnier (240), not assigned (240)
124 (160): *Henri Germain*
125 (480): *Antoine Rigau*
126 (160): Pompée-M.-A. Mariano
127 (320): Texier de la Pomeraye
128 (160): *Charles Harraneder*
129 (120): Jean-Pierre Métayé
130 (480): **Joseph Martin du Columbier**
131 (160): Jean-Baptiste Campardon
132 (480): [**Frédéric-Guillaume-Marie Ravesies**]
133 (160): Elie Bordas
134 (480): [Charles Debrosse]
135 (160): Etienne Merle
136 (480): M.-François-Auguste Ladurelle
137 (160): *François Canobio*
138 (240): Lawrence A. Davis
139 (240): B. Charles Firmin
140 (160): Hyacinthe Montalegri
141 (480): Jacques-Séraphin Duval
142 (160): Alexandre Baclé (eldest son)
143 (480): Joseph Lakanal
144 (120): [*Léontine Desportes*]
145 (240): **Louis-Etienne and Victor Tulane**
146 (120): Kimbal/Claude Antoine
147 (120): [John Billington]/Claude Antoine

148 (120): [François Boiteau]
149 (480): [Michel Leboutellier]
150 (160): Antoine Plantevigne Jr.
151 (240): Jacques Moncravie
152 (240): F. S. Brown/Paul-Louis Bringier
153 (160): *Charles Monnot*
154 (480): [Jean-Jerome Cluis]
155 (160): Ferdinand Ruffier
156 (480): Jacques Garnier (des Saintes) (father)
157 (160): [Simon]
158 (240): Edward B. Wells and Joseph-P. Leclerc/[Alexandre-René Terrier]
159 (120): Jean-Marie Macré
160 (120): **Antoine Dumas**
161 (120): J. Dalmazeau
162 (480): **Pierre-Frédéric Fontanges**
163 (120): Victorine Godon
164 (480): **Louis-Descoins Belair**
165 (160): Henri-Antoine Sagnier
166 (480): *Charles-François-Antoine Lallemand*
167 (160): Aimée Valcour
168 (480): Bertrand Clausel
169 (160): Blaquerolle
170 (160): Jean-Mathieu-Alexandre Sary
171 (160): Antoine Gatty
172 (160): Benoit Illari
173 (160): Pierre-Solidor Millon
174 (480): **Jean-Thomas Carré**/ Joseph Ducommun
175 (160): [*Charles-François Genin*]
176 (320): *Jean-Philibert Charrasin*
177 (320): *Jean-Emmanuel Vasquez*

178 (320): Jean-François Roland
179 (320): Jean-Claude-Charles Pichon
180 (480): Joseph-Louis Charreton-Raspiller
181 (160): François Grillet
182 (240): [**Jean Texier**]
183 (240): **Pierre-Louis Martinet**
184 (160): *Jean-Baptiste Vitalba*
185 (240): Antoine Jogan
186 (120): Charles Cavoroc
187 (120): John Roster/**François-Annet-Charles Bruguière**
188 (120): Chapon
189 (480): **Jean-Marie Dubarry**
190 (120): **Julien-Léon Salaignac**
191 (240): [Léonard-Alexandre Descourts]
192 (120): Jean-Baptiste Onfroy
193 (120): Augustin-François Pochard
194 (160): *Jean-Louis Fux*
195 (480): [George Noble Stewart]/[Nicholas-Louis Raoul]
196 (160): Gilbert
197 (480): **Joseph Sévelinge**
198 (160): *Honoré Mane*
199 (160): Georges Richard
200 (160): François Nardel
201 (160): Charles Chauvot
202 (160): **François Plaidaut**
203 (240): Charles Bono
204 (120): Jean-Baptiste Tasca
205 (120): Jean Blandin
206 (120): Joseph Azan
207 (480): [Widow Josephine Delaunay née Verrier]
208 (160): Etienne Castan

209 (480): [Jacques and Tougnet Lefrançois (brothers)]
210 (160): *C. Groning*
211 (240): **Simon Pothier**
212 (240): Henry Schubart
213 (160): Jean-Baptiste Néel/**Amand Pfister** (120), Soulas (40)
214 (480): Joseph Beylle
215 (160): *Constantin-Paul Malezewsky*
216 (480): **François-Hyacinthe Teterel**
217 (160): *J.-Alexandre Pagnière*
218 (120): **Guillaume Dubocq**
219 (120): [Edouard George (son)]
220 (120): *Lesueur*
221 (120): Marius Dor
222 (160): *Henri-Pierre-Alexandre-As. Maillet*
223 (480): **Pierre-Ange-Chevalier and [Pierre-François] Stollenwerk (brothers)**
224 (160): *Joseph Vallot*
225 (480): Joseph Mathieu
226 (120): Joseph Allain
227 (240): [**Jean Jeandreau**]
228 (240): Guillaume Caillebaux
229 (120): Nelson/[Isaac Butaud]
230 (320): *François-Louis Taillade*
231 (160): Joseph Olivieri
232 (160): *Pascal Luciani*
233 (480): *Emmanuel, comte de Grouchy*
234 (160): François-Marc DesChamp
235 (160): *César Baumier*
236 (160): Antoine Barbe
237 (160): Charles Stribaud
238 (160): *Charles Desorme*

239 (480): [**Pierre-Edouard Chaudron**]
240 (160): *Antoine Gilbal*
241 (480): **Prosper Martin du Columbier**
242 (160): *Samuel Desplans*
243 (480): François Melizet
244 (160): *François Corso*
245 (480): Victor Hamel
246 (160): Havard
247 (480): [Jean-Augustin Pénières-Delors (father)]
248 (160): *Honoré Fanchon*
249 (480): Lecoq du Marcelay
250 (120): Godat
251 (320): *Fabius Fourni*
252 (320): *Pierre Guillot*
253 (480): Joseph-Thomas Badaraque
254 (160): Marius Conte
255 (160): Charles Desfouch
256 (160): Paul Pascal
257 (160): Pierre Fouasche
258 (160): Henri Bernard
259 (480): Joseph Rapin
260 (160): *Louis Contardi*
261 (480): [Alexandre Saint-Guiron (the younger)]
262 (160): *Dominique-Victor de Mony*
263 (240): **Emile Ravesies**
264 (240): **Honoré-François Fournier**
265 (160): *Abel Farcy Sainte-Marie*
266 (240): Pierre-Jean-Isaac Champenois
267 (240): Alexandre Savary
268 (160): François (father) and Jean-Baptiste (son) Belmère

269 (480): [*Henri-Dominique Lallemand*]
270 (160): Prompt
271 (480): [**Honorè Bayol**]
272 (160): [François-Martin-Marie Durive]
273 (240): Charles Condé
274 (240): [Jonathan Pierce and his brother]/Charles Condé
275 (160): [*Maurice Laurent*]
276 (480): [**Jean-Simon Chaudron**]
277 (120): [Eugénie le Grand de Boislandry]
278 (240): Camille Arnaud
279 (240): René and Zacharie Deprest (brothers)
280 (120): [Charles Batré]
281 (320): Martial-Denis Belangé
282 (320): Benoit Chasserian
283 (480): Pierre-François Réal
284 (160): *Louis Penazi*
285 (240): **Mathieu et Alfred Bujac (brothers)**
286 (240): Alexandre-Ambroise Germond and [**Jean-Amédée Rivière**]
287 (120): **Henri Guibert**
288 (480): **Pierre Ducoing**
289 (160): *Samuel James Stephens*
290 (480): Elie-B. Fourestier
291 (160): *Etienne Grégoire*
292 (160): *Mathieu-Ferdinand Manfredi*
293 (96): Pierre-Charles Dupont
294 (480): [Charles Lefebvre-Desnouettes]
295 (160): Desroures

296 (480): *Georges-Nicholas Jeannet-Oudin (called "Manchot")*

297 (160): *Joseph Jeannet*

298 (240): Antoine Dumenil

299 (120): Joseph Ducommun

300 (120): [F.-Romain Parat]

301 (120): [Jean-Bernard Burgues]

302 (240): **Widow Constance Demerest née Ogé**

303 (240): **Louis-Edmond Bourlon**

304 (160): *Jean-Baptiste Lapeyre*

305 (480): Pierre (father) and Nicholas-Elisée (son) Thouron

306 (120): **Jean-François-Sully Lavau**

307 (480): Léonard Engelbert/ Gaspard Bonno

308 (120): François Landevin

309 (240): Pierre Legris Belleisle

310 (240): [Gilbert Legras]

311 (160): *Etienne Bulliard*

312 (480): **Georges Follin**

313 (160): Francois Fauquier (erroneous entry, should be François Gasquet)

314 (480): Louis Emery and Mathurin Duterte

315 (120): Daniel Vogelsang

316 (480): George Strother Gaines/ [Jean Haez] (120), [**Charles Prudhomme**] (120), **Jean-Marie Morel de Guiramond** (240)

317 (160): Jean-Baptiste Murat

318 (480): [Michel Mestayer]

319 (160): *Gabriel-Valentin-Philippe Riegert*

320 (480): [Nicholas-Simon Parmentier]

321 (160): Joseph Bauzan

322 (480): [Samuel Vorhees]/Charles-Melchior de Villemont (240), [Jean Guilleault] (180), Jean Quésart (60), François Verrier (60)

323 (160): *Fischer*

324 (240): Jean-Jacques Dufourg

325 (120): D. V. Dufourg

326 (120): F. Dufourg

327 (160): *René-François Lacroix*

328 (240): [Pierre-Pascal Saint-Guiron (elder brother)]

329 (120): **André Farrouilh**

330 (120): **Jean-Baptiste-Gilles-Regnaud de Saint-Félix**

331 (120): Marc-Louis Decave

332 (240): **Joseph Barbaroux**

333 (120): Guillaume Cirode

334 (120): Jean-Sebastien Schoen

335 (120): Joseph-Michel Gouiran

336 (480): [Jacques Lajoinie]

337 (160): Joseph Truc

338 (320): Bartolo Colona d'Ornano

339 (160): Toussaint Peraldi

340 (160): Vincent Scasso

341 (240): Alphonse D. Delaroderie

342 (240): Joseph Savournin

343 (160): *Joseph Balbuena de Sotomayor*

344 (480): [**Pierre-Auguste Canonge**]

345 (160): [Lucien Ensfelder]

346 (480): [Guillaume Tabelée]/ **Charles-François Vaugine de**

Nuisemont (240), Joseph Bogy (240)

347 (160): *Jean Torta*

A (40): Colomel

B (40): **Antoine Latapie**

C (40): [**Auguste and César Payen (brothers)**]

D (40): [Barthelemi Bourdichon]

E (40): [M. Bistos]

F (40): [J. Fouquet] and [Sebastien Moulin]

G (40): not assigned

H (40): [*Guillaume Victor de Plenville*]

I (40): [Dupui] and [Ragon]

J (40): [F. Romain Parat]

K (40): [Miot]

L (40): [Pierre Mangon] and [Martial]

M (40): [Mignon]

N (40): [Nicholas Roudel]

O (40): [Dr Delaunay]

P (40): [Fouquet (the elder)]

Q (40): [Jean Perard] and [Amedée Rougier]

R (40): C. Desaifue

S (40): [**Jacques (or Jean) Pueek**]

T (40): Etienne David

U (40): Dominique Blancon and Taverly

V (40): Mahé

W (40): [Mathieu Labrusse]

X (40): Charles Devengen

Y (40): [Mayer]

Z (40): [**F. L. Constantin**] and [Dechoule]

AA (40): [Charles Morin]

BB (40): [Darembert]

CC (40): [Paul Lagay]

DD (40): [**Claude Payen (father)**]

EE (384): [Jean Hurtel]

FF (40): Cuchet

GG (40): Edouard Jenim

HH (40): [Bonneau]

II (40): [Achille Chapotin]

JJ (40): Mathieu Rapin

KK (40): [*Allouard*] and [Victor Achard]

Allotment Maps

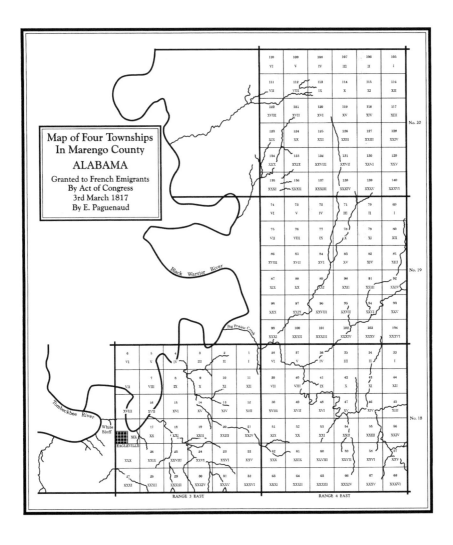

Map of Four Townships
In Marengo County
ALABAMA
Granted to French Emigrants
By Act of Congress
3rd March 1817
By E. Paguenaud

Map of Township 18, Range 3

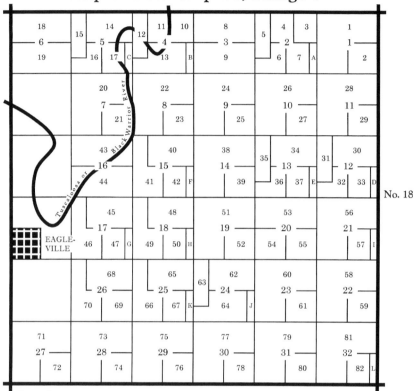

No. 18

Range 3

Map of Township 18, Range 4

95	93	91	89	86	83
38	37	36	35	34	33
96	97	M	94	92	90	87	88	84	85

98	100	102	104	106	108
39	40	41	42	43	44
99	N	101	103	105	107	109

121	118	116	114	112	110
50	49	48	47	46	45
122	119	120	117	P	115	O	113	111

No. 18

123	125	127	130	132	134
51	52	53	54	55	56
124	126	128	129	Q	131	133	135

149	145	143	141	138	136
62	146	61	60	59	58	57
150	147	148	S	144	R	142	139	140	137

151	154	156	158	162	164
63	64	65	159	66	67	68
152	153	155	157	160	161	T	163	U	165

Range 4

Map of Township 19, Range 4

178	176	174	171	170	168	166

178
—74—   —73—   72———71—   70—   69—
179   177   175 | 172 | 173   169   167

180   182   185   189   191   195
7̶5̶   —76—   77—   78—   —79—   80—
181 | 183 | 184   187 | 188 |V   190 |W   193 | 194   196

186

192

211   209   207   203   200 | 199   197
—86—   85—   84—   —83—   —82—   81—
212 | 213   210   208   205 | 206 |X   201 | 202   198

204

No. 19

214   216   219 | 218   223   225   227
87—   88—   89—   90—   91—   92—
215   217   221 | 222   224   226 |Y   228 | 229 |Z

220

243   241   239   236 | 235   233   230
98—   97—   96—   —95—   94—   —93—
244   242   240   237 | 238   234   231 | 232

245   247   249   251   253   256 | 255
99—   100—   101———102—   103———104—
246   248   250 |AA   252   254   257 | 258

Range 4

Map of Township 20, Range 4

271	269	266	263	261	259
110 —	109 —	└ 108 —	└ 107 —	106 —	105 —
272	270	267 | 268	264 | 265	262	260
273	276	278	281	283	285
└ 111 —	112 ┐	└ 113 —	114 —	115 —	└ 116 ┐
274 | 275	277 BB	279 | 280 CC	282	284	286 | 287 DD
299 298	296	294	293| 292	290	288
└ 122 ┐	121 —	120 —	└ 119 —	118 —	117 —
300| 301 FF	297	295	EE	291	289
302	305	307	309	312	314
└ 123 —	124 ┐	125 ┐	└ 126 —	127 —	128 ┐
303 | 304	306 GG	308 HH	310 | 311	313	315 II
329 328	325 324	322	320	318	316
└ 134 ┐	└ 133 —	132 —	131 —	130 —	129 —
330| 331 JJ	326| 327	323	321	319	317
333 332	336	338	341	344	346
└ 135 ┐	136 —	137 —	└ 138 —	139 —	140 —
334| 335 KK	337	339 | 340	342 | 343	345	347

No. 20

Range 4

Biographical Sketches of the Grantees

[Achard, Victor]: In Marengo County in 1822.

Allain, Joseph: In Mobile in 1833.

[**Allard, Henri**]: Possibly from a Domingan family in Philadelphia by 1804. Moved to grant. Was dead by November 1821. Fellow Domingan and Vine and Olive shareholder [**Marc-Antoine Frenaye**] was administrator of his estate.

[*Allouard*]: Former Napoleonic officer. Part of the Champ d'Asile. Briefly on grant.

Alma, Anselme: No information.

Anduze, Mathieu-Bernard: No information.

Angeli, Hyacinthe: In Philadelphia in 1821 when he sold his allotment.

Antoine, Claude: In New Orleans in 1834 when he patented his allotment.

Arnaud, Camille: In New York City in early 1818. Linked to Pierre-François Réal.

Astolphi, Laurent: In Philadelphia from at least 1804. Still there in 1821. A confectioner and innkeeper in partnership with Vine and Olive member Victor Hamel.

Audibert, Angélique Widow (Madame Louis-François Audibert née Thibeau): From western France, Audibert and her husband came to Philadelphia 1793–94 to escape the war in the Vendée. They had a son and a daughter. Unclear when her husband died. In 1817 she was in New Albany, Indiana, working as factotum to fellow Vine and Olive member Garnier des Saintes. She then moved to New Madrid, Missouri, where her daughter Thérèse married fellow Vine and Olive member Alphonse Delaroderie.

Auzé, Charles: Sea captain and merchant. In Philadelphia from at least 1818 until his death on a business trip to Puerto Rico. His widow, Anne-Agnès, then married his brother Joseph (below). His son became a naval officer and his daughter married Henry Raser, a Philadelphian from a family of Vine and Olive patentees.

Auzé, Joseph: Brother of Charles (above). In Philadelphia in 1818, Savannah 1830–35, and Mobile in 1836. A frequent visitor to Philadelphia, he was often the guest of fellow Vine and Olive member **Pierre-Frédéric Fontanges.** On Joseph's death in 1838, his property was divided equally between his own and his brother's children.

Azan, Joseph: From France. In Philadelphia in 1817 if not earlier.

Baclé, Alexandre (eldest son): In Philadelphia in 1817.

Badaraque, Joseph-Thomas: Born in Marseille in 1769. He immigrated to the United States, converted to Protestantism, and became a citizen in 1803. Served briefly as director of the society, but never went to Alabama. He died in Philadelphia in 1834.

Bailly, Michel: From a Domingan family established in Philadelphia in 1790s. A tailor, he made uniforms for the Champ d'Asile expedition.

[Baizeau]: In Aigleville in October 1819.

Balbuena de Sotomayor, Joseph: Napoleonic officer of Spanish ancestry. Reached the rank of captain in the Foreign Colonial Regiment and served as a military administrator in Tours. In early 1817 he sought French citizenship but was refused. He then came to the United States, sold his allotment, and joined the Champ d'Asile.

[Baltard, Prosper]: Among the first settlers to travel to Alabama. In 1818 settled on the grant, but by 1821 he sold out to the Batré brothers and moved to Mobile.

Barbaroux, Joseph: From a Domingan family that fled to Philadelphia. A merchant, he had business relations with Martin Piquet (son), one of his cousins, also of Philadelphia, and in 1821 married Piquet's sister Julia. Soon thereafter, they moved to Jefferson County, Kentucky. Barbaroux became involved in the river shipping business, investing in steamboats traveling between Louisville and New Orleans.

Barbe, Antoine: A Philadelphia merchant in 1817, he immediately sold his allotment. By 1822 had moved to New Orleans.

Barraud, Auguste: From Sainte (Charente-Inférieure). Drafted in 1813, but instead joined the Honor Guards, a unit of young men of good family who wanted to escape conscription. Fought in the campaigns of 1813, 1814, and 1815 when he became a second lieutenant. After Napoleon's final abdication, he left for the United States where he met *Charles Lallemand.* He sold his allotment in late 1817 and accompanied the general to the Champ d'Asile as part of his inner circle.

[Batré, Charles]: A merchant, settled on the grant in 1818. By the mid-1820s in Mobile where he and his brother Adolphe had a store in partnership with fellow Vine and Olive member Joseph Beylle of Philadelphia. Charles often filled in for his brother as agent of the French Consular Agency. The brothers married into Vine and Olive families: Charles to Adèle widow Macré and Adolphe to **Sylvanie Chaudron.**

Baumier, César: Former officer in the Imperial armies. Member of the Champ d'Asile.

Bauzan, Joseph: Possibly the son of Giovanni (Jean) Bauzan, a decorated naval officer in Murat's kingdom of Naples. In New York City in 1818 when he sold his allotment.

[**Bayol, Honoré**]: Former manager of the Bouttes d'Estival plantation in Saint-Domingue. Fled to Philadelphia with his uncle and fellow Vine and Olive member goldsmith [**Pierre Gallard**]. Bayol became a U.S. citizen in Philadelphia in 1808. There he married **Marie-Perrine Bouttes d'Estival née Noël,** the wife of his former employer (who had been killed in the uprising) and relative of fellow Vine and Olive shareholder **Thomas Noël.** Her daughter **Adèle** married Demopolis businessman **Alexandre Fournier** and her other daughter **Josephine** married **Jules Martinière.**

Belair, Louis-Descoins: Born 1758 in Saint-Domingue, the son of a bookseller. After fleeing to Philadelphia, he became a seller of foreign books. His sister **Eulalie-Descoins Belair** married Vine and Olive member [Guillaume Promis] in Philadelphia in 1809, and another sister married another member **Simon Pothier.** Louis-Descoins Belair joined the East Florida Coffee Land Association. He died in Philadelphia in 1833–34.

Belangé, Martial-Denis: Philadelphia merchant. In 1821 traded his allotment to [**Victoire George**] for her house in Normandy. In June 1823 returned to France.

Belmère, François (father): In 1817 in Philadelphia where he asked Stephen Girard to invest in his manufacturing business. In 1822 still in Philadelphia.

Belmère, Jean-Baptiste (son): Married Rebecca Thompson. In 1822 still in Philadelphia.

Bergasse, Nicholas-Cadet: In Philadelphia by 1805, if not earlier, where he was a merchant. In 1820 his wife, Catherine, died. By 1833, he had also died.

Bernard, Henri: Grocer of Swiss nationality, established in Philadelphia by 1817, if not earlier. He became a U.S. citizen in 1866.

Besson, Louis-Antoine: Born in Philadelphia in 1798, the son of an immigrant merchant from France, André-Antoine Besson and his wife, Marie-Louise Verrier. Louis-Antoine became a "fancy storekeeper." He died in 1832 in Mexico City.

Beylle, Joseph: Born at Sassenage (Isère) in 1770. In 1797 in Philadelphia married his first wife, **Marie-Françoise Sévelinge,** sister of a Vine and Olive member. She soon died, and Joseph married **Marie Lemaistre.** Their first daughter was born in 1805. Their second daughter, Josephine-Irma, married **Jean-Baptiste-François Tête,** a Philadelphia merchant who became a Vine and Olive patentee. Their fourth daughter, Louise-Françoise, married **Jean-**

Baptiste A. Herpin, another Philadelphia merchant who acquired Vine and Olive lands. Beylle was a confectioner, distiller, and wine merchant. He also co-owned a store with the Vine and Olive members the Batré brothers. He also lent money to Vine and Olive colonists Henri Sagnier and Antoine Besson, as well as to **Jean-François Hurtel.** Died in Philadelphia in 1832.

[Billington, John]: From a Philadelphia family of lawyers and accountants. In 1818 he went to the grant but had his allotment taken away (probably because he was not French) the following year. He then settled in Mississippi.

[Bistos, M.]: A poor immigrant from France who settled in New Orleans in about 1817. He apprenticed in a candymaker's shop. He lived briefly on the grant.

Blancon, Dominique: No information.

Blandin, Jean: In Philadelphia in 1818 when he sold his allotment.

Blaquerolle: In New York City in 1819 when he sold his allotment.

Bogy, Joseph: Born in French Canada in 1752. Moved to Kaskaskia in the former French Illinois country, where he married Marie-Louise-Dugay Duplassy. Their daughter Catherine married Vine and Olive member Charles-Melchior de Villemont. The family then moved to New Madrid, Missouri. There they knew the Bonos and Delaroderies, as well as the **Nidelets.** Another member of the Bogy family married Vine and Olive member **Charles-François Vaugine de Nuisement.**

[Boislandry, Eugénie le Grand de]: **Victoire George's** niece and ward. She came to Alabama in about 1819. In 1824 she married Lazare Chieusse of Mobile.

[Boiteau, François]: On the grant in 1818–19. Moved to Mobile. Died in about 1832.

[Bonneau]: Resident of Demopolis in 1819. Dead by mid-1821.

[Bonno, Gaspard]: In 1819 moved from Philadelphia to New York City. The following year he relocated to New Orleans and then Demopolis. There he lived with Madame Augustine Figuery. After Bonno's death, she married Jean-Bernard Burgues.

Bono, Charles: From a family established in New Madrid, Missouri, by 1809 if not earlier. He knew Delaroderies and Bogys there. In 1818 he sold his allotment.

Bordas, Elie: A merchant in Veracruz, Mexico, in 1832 when he sold his allotment.

[Bourdichon, Barthelemi]: On the grant in 1818, but sold his allotment and left in 1819.

Bourlon, Louis-Edmond: Born about 1795. Nephew of General Clausel. In about 1815 he settled in Mobile and became a merchant. In 1819 he sold his allotment and died that same year.

Boutière, François-Gaspard: Brother of below. He died in 1827 or 1828.

[Boutière, Jean-Claude-Benoit]: Established on the grant in 1818. Boutière was tutor of Dechoule, his son-in-law and fellow Vine and Olive member, who died in Mobile in 1821. Jean-Claude-Benoit married Vine and Olive member [Josephine Verrier], widow of Pierre-Robert Delaunay. Their daughter, [Floride-Josephine de Boutière], was born in 1819. He died in 1823 and his wife died the following year. After their deaths, Vine and Olive member [Alexandre-Léonard Descourts] became [Floride's] guardian.

Braud, Jacques: Merchant in Philadelphia in 1817. In 1818 became an accountant.

Brechemin, Louis: Jeweler in Philadelphia from 1817 until his death in 1844.

Bringier, Paul-Louis: Son of Marius-Pons Bringier, from a prominent Provençal family that owned plantations in Martinique. They relocated to Louisiana in the mid-1780s. In 1784 their first son, Paul-Louis, was born. The Bringiers owned famous plantations such as Maison Blanche, Bocage, Union, and the Hermitage. Paul-Louis led a wild life. In 1811 he was an Indian trader in New Madrid. In 1812–14 he fought in the war against Great Britain. In 1814 he became a member of the governing junta of the Republic of Mexico. In 1818 he took part in a scheme to acquire silver mines in Mexico (possibly the Champ d'Asile). Following this, he disappeared from sight for a time, but reemerged several years later into respectability, becoming the surveyor general of the state of Louisiana, a post he still held in 1839. He died in 1860.

Brown, F. S: Apparently Samuel Brown of Kentucky, the man credited in Pickett's account with suggesting the site for the Vine and Olive colony.

Bruguière, François-Annet-Charles: Born in 1774 he fled to Philadelphia from Saint-Domingue. In 1803 he became a U.S. citizen and married **Marie-Antoinette Teisseire.** Their son Charles eventually married his cousin, the daughter of **Antoine Teisseire.** In Philadelphia Bruguière was a merchant, both on his own account and as partner of his brother-in-law **Teisseire.** Did business with Victor du Pont. By 1830 Bruguière had moved to New York City, where he died in 1837. His wife died the following year.

Bujac, Alfred: In 1817–18, a Philadelphia merchant who owned a fancy store with his brother. He sold his allotment in December 1817 and moved to New Orleans where he was still living, together with his brother, in 1854.

Bujac, Mathieu-Jules: See above.

Bujey, Antoine: From Grenoble. In 1818–19 letters were sent to him in New Orleans.

Bulliard, Etienne: A surgeon who sold his allotment and joined the Champ d'Asile.

Bürcklé, Emanuel-M.: Merchant from Wurtemburg who immigrated to Philadelphia and became a U.S. citizen in 1818. By 1822 relocated to New York City.

[Burgues, Jean-Bernard]: In about 1822 he married Augustine Figuery, former consort of Gaspard Bono. They lived for a time on the grant and then returned to France.

[Butaud, Isaac]: An engraver from France who immigrated to Philadelphia by 1814, if not earlier. In 1818 he had settled on the grant and served as lieutenant of the local militia company. He married [**Victorie George**] and had two sons, but died in 1820 or 1821.

Caillebaux, Guillaume: A baker living in Philadelphia in 1805. Died there in 1831.

Campardon, Jean-Baptiste: A tailor in Philadelphia 1818–20. He made uniforms for the Champ d'Asile. By 1822 in New Orleans where he was a merchant and tailor.

Canobio, François: A surgeon. Sold his allotment in early December 1817 to join the Champ d'Asile. A partisan of *Charles Lallemand,* he was still in New Orleans in 1820.

[Canonge, Pierre-Auguste]: Nephew of **Jean-François Canonge,** a prominent New Orleans judge, and **Zephir Canonge,** the hotheaded supporter of Mexican independence who caned the Spanish consul Diego Morphy in 1816. The Canonge family fled from Saint-Domingue to Cuba to Philadelphia. Some of the family remained there and others went to New Orleans. Pierre-Auguste was a commission merchant in Philadelphia and also an officer in the Pennsylvania militia. In Demopolis in 1820, he died there in 1821.

Carré, Jean-Thomas: An educator. Ran a school in Philadelphia 1817–20.

Castan, Etienne: Philadelphia watch-case maker, watchmaker, and jeweler.

Cavoroc, Charles: Merchant in Philadelphia. Declared insolvent in 1816.

Champenois, Pierre-Jean-Isaac: A Philadelphia tailor, 1814–17. Became a U.S. citizen in 1816. Relocated to Mobile in 1818.

Chapon: No information.

[Chapotin, Achille]: Son of a lawyer from Auxerre (Yonne). Graduated from the Ecole Polytechnique and sent to the advanced artillery school at Metz in 1813. There he incurred debts that his father would not pay, so he dropped out and enlisted in a Hussar regiment. After 1815 he came to the United States and lived in Demopolis 1819–20.

[**Chapron, Jean-Marie**]: Born in 1787 in Saint-Domingue. Father was an officeholder at Port-de-Paix. The Chaprons fled from the slave uprising and Jean-Marie was sent to boarding school near Philadelphia in 1800. In 1814 he married **Emilie-Catherine Teterel,** daughter of a fellow Vine and Olive member. Chapron was a merchant on his own account and, at various times, in partnership with Vine and Olive members [**Marc-Antoine Frenaye**] and **François-Etienne Nidelet,** his first cousin. Chapron lived in Philadelphia until 1834, when he came to Alabama. He died in 1868 in Hale County.

Charrasin, Jean-Philibert: Born 1786 in Dijon (Côte d'Or). Enlisted in 1806 in the Imperial Guard. By 1815 was a lieutenant in the (Polish) Lancers of the Guard where he may have known _Ambroise Jourdan_ and _Jean Schultz._ Veteran of many Napoleonic campaigns, including the Battle of Eylau, was much wounded and decorated. Rallied to Napoleon in 1815 and was promoted to the rank of captain in the Imperial Guard. He fled to America after Waterloo, where he was sent by Gens. [_Henri Lallemand_] and [Charles Lefebvre-Desnouettes] as an emissary to the Mexican revolutionaries in 1817. Later that year he sold his allotment and joined the Champ d'Asile, where he commanded the second cohort. He soon deserted to the Spanish.

Charreton-Raspiller, Joseph-Louis: No information.

Chasserian, Benoit: Possibly a former paymaster in Napoleon's Egyptian and Haitian campaigns. In 1819 with an English commercial house in Jamaica. In 1823 in Paris.

[**Chaudron, Pierre-Edouard**]: Son of [**Jean-Simon Chaudron**] (below). Born in Philadelphia in 1792. Like his father, he was a merchant, watchmaker, and jeweler. In Demopolis in 1823. By 1831 in Mobile.

[**Chaudron, Jean-Simon**]: Born in Vignery, Champagne, in 1758. Learned watchmaking in Switzerland. Moved to Saint-Domingue where he became a jeweler and silversmith. He married **Melanie Stollenwerk** in 1791 and entered into the import-export business, as well as coffee planting, with his father-in-law, **Pierre-Hubert Stollenwerk.** Chaudron fled to Philadelphia after the slave uprising. There he became active in freemasonry, wrote poetry, and founded _L'Abeille Américaine._ He became a U.S. citizen in 1805. He moved to the grant with his family, but soon relocated to Mobile and died there in 1846.

Chauvot, Charles: In Philadelphia in 1817 when he sold his allotment.

Cirode, Guillaume: Believed to be in New Orleans in 1822.

Clausel, Bertrand: Born Mirepoix (Ariège) in 1772 to a prominent local family. An officer in 1791, he advanced rapidly through the ranks, serving on <u>General</u>

Grouchy's staff in 1798 and becoming a general himself in 1799. He served in Napoleon's ill-fated expedition to Haiti and was shipwrecked on the coast of Florida (probably in company of *Charles Lallemand*) on his return back to France. He continued his military career, mainly in Spain. Named baron in 1810 and count in 1813. Governor of Bordeaux when Napoleon returned from Elba, Clausel declared for his old master and delivered the city to him. For this, Clausel was condemned to death in absentia. He fled to America. In 1817 went to Mobile where he had relatives (Vine and Olive members **Constance Ogé (the widow Demerest), Louis-Edmond Bourlon,** and Madame Desmares née Pitot). Amnestied in 1820, he returned to France, was elected to the legislature in 1829, given command of the Army of Africa in 1830, named marshal of France in 1831, and later governor-general of Algeria. Died in 1842.

[Cluis, Jean-Jerome]: Born 1773 at La Chatre (Indre). Enlisted in 1793 and rose slowly through the ranks. He became a second lieutenant only in 1804. But in 1808 his professional fortunes changed when named aide-de-camp to the Duke of Rovigo (General Savary), then minister of police. Rovigo assigned Cluis to arrest Ferdinand VII, the king of Spain. This earned Cluis inclusion on the proscription list of 24 July 1815. Exiled to the United States, he moved to the grant where he farmed and operated a tavern near Greensboro. He moved to Mobile with his wife, Louise-Emilie de Mazières, with whom he had two children. In 1830 the couple owned just one slave. Cluis died in Mobile in 1834. After his death, it was discovered that he had another family in France, which proceeded to squabble with his American family over his meager fortune.

Colomel: No information.

Colona d'Ornano, Bartolo: Born in Corsica around 1789 to a family with links to the Bonapartes and fanatical devotion to its leading member. In 1807 joined a dragoon regiment commanded by a relative. Seriously wounded in 1809, he left the army, and became a judge in Ajaccio and a colonel in the National Guard. After Napoleon's second abdication, he served in Murat's ill-fated expedition to Naples and had to flee to America. Although he signed over his allotment to *Georges Jeannet,* he did not join the Champ d'Asile. Instead, he went to constitutionalist Spain, where he served as a colonel. When Bourbon France invaded Spain in 1823 to restore absolutism, he fled to Tangiers, where he told French diplomatic officials he would return to the United States to join a new agricultural establishment then being formed in Florida.

Combe, Michel: Born in Feurs (Loire) in 1787. Son of a merchant. Volunteered in 1803 and became an officer in 1809. In 1811 transferred to the Imperial Guard where he became a captain. Served in many campaigns, including the Battle of Jena and retreat from Russia. In 1814 he followed Napoleon to Elba as part of the former emperor's guard. In 1815 he returned to France with Napoleon and was rewarded with the rank of lieutenant colonel. After Waterloo, he went to the United States where he married Elisa Walker, daughter of a wealthy New York colonel who had been Washington's aide-de-camp during the American Revolution. From 1823 to 1830 he lived in Utica, New York, on his wife's family's estate. After the 1830 Revolution, he returned to France and rejoined the army. He served in Algeria and commanded the Foreign Legion. Doubts about his fitness for command were raised, but quickly forgotten when he died storming the breach at the siege of Constantine in 1837. In death he became a national hero.

Combes, Germain: Born in 1748. By 1800 a physician and druggist in Philadelphia. There he became godfather to the son of **Pierre Lacombe,** his brother-in-law. Together with **Lacombe,** he joined the East Florida Coffee Land Association. He died in 1828.

Combes, Vincent: No information.

Condé, Charles: Born in 1778. Hairdresser and perfumer. Died in Philadelphia in 1835.

[**Constantine, F. L.**]: Probably from a Domingan mercantile family that fled to Philadelphia. By 1826 he was in Demopolis. In 1830 he lived in Greene County.

Contardi, Louis: Sold his allotment in early December 1817 to join the Champ d'Asile.

Conte, Honoré: By 1824 he had returned to France and sold his allotment.

Conte, Marius: A self-described Philadelphia gentleman. He sold his allotment in 1819.

Corso, François: An Imperial officer. Sold his allotment and joined the Champ d'Asile.

Coquillon brothers: Possibly related to **Louise Coquillon,** who married Louis-Pierre-Joseph Marchand.

[Cousin, L. David]: In 1818 on the grant with wife, Louise-Sophie Coffinie. By 1823 returned to France.

Cuchet: Dead by mid-1821.

Dalmazeau, J.: No information.

[Darembert]: Briefly on grant.

David, Etienne: Noted in 1814 Philadelphia directory as a shoemaker.

[**Davide de Sevré, Widow Louise-Adèle-Gertrude**]: Widow of general killed in Saint-Domingue, she married Vine and Olive member [**Frédéric Ravesies**] in Philadelphia.

Davis, Lawrence A.: In Philadelphia in 1818 when he sold his allotment.

[Debrosse, Charles]: A Morocco dresser established in Philadelphia. In 1818 settled on the grant, where he petitioned Governor Bibb for a license to practice law in Alabama. Claim supported by Jean-Augustin Pénières who testified that Debrosse had studied at the University of Paris Law School. License granted November 1818.

Decave, Marc-Louis: Born 1787 at Demerary (Dutch Guiana). From a planter family from Cayenne. In 1811 he married Mademoiselle d'Aumont, the daughter of Empress Josephine's personal banker. In 1813 Josephine's recommendation helped him obtain a position in the War Ministry. After Waterloo, he went to Philadelphia and became a partner in the mercantile firm of Decave and Mercier. He sold his allotment in 1818.

[Dechoule]: Son-in-law of Jean-Claude-Benoit de Boutière. Died in 1821 in Mobile.

[Delaporte, Louis]: Became a U.S. citizen in Philadelphia in 1819. From 1820–22 was merchant in Mobile. Visited grant. Lived in San-Luis de Potosi in Mexico 1827–29.

Delaroderie, Alphonse D.: Of New Madrid, Missouri. In 1821 named deputy clerk of New Madrid County circuit court. In 1850 founded a steam sawmill company with son Alfred, with branches in New Madrid and Baton Rouge. By 1852 had moved to Baton Rouge with his wife, Thérèse née Audibert. Alphonse died in 1864; his wife, in 1876.

[Delaunay, Dr]: Briefly settled on grant. Dead by mid-1821.

[Delaunay, Josephine Verrier (widow of Pierre-Robert Delaunay)]: Widowed in Philadelphia in 1813. Her son Peter accompanied her to the grant in 1818. There she married [Jean-Claude-Benoit de Boutière].

[Delpit, Julie]: On the grant in 1819. In 1822 in New Orleans working as a tobacconist.

Demerest, Widow Constance Ogé: Of Mobile. Cousin of <u>Gen. Bertrand Clausel.</u>

Deprest, René: In Philadelphia in 1818 when he sold his allotment.

Deprest, Zacharie: In Philadelphia in 1818 when he sold his allotment.

Desaifue, C.: Dead by mid-1821.

DesChamp, François-Marc: In 1817 a Madame F. DesChamp was noted as a "fancy milliner" in Philadelphia. DesChamp sold his allotment in December 1817.

[Descourts, Léonard-Alexandre]: An officer, in 1817 Descourts and his wife, Emée-Eléonore, ran an inn in New York City that was popular with Bonapartist émigrés. In 1820 settled on the grant where they also ran an inn. In 1825 Descourts became guardian of Floride-Josephine de Boutière. In 1830 census noted as owning ten slaves.

Desfouch, Charles: In Philadelphia in 1817.

[Desmares, Alphonse]: From Normandy. In 1817 a merchant in New Orleans where he married his cousin Odele-Marie Pitot, a relative of General Clausel. Dealt with the *Lallemand* brothers in 1818. Spent some time on the grant.

Desorme, Charles: Sold his allotment to join the Champ d'Asile.

Desplans, Samuel: Sold his allotment to join the Champ d'Asile.

[*Desportes, Léontine*]: Born about 1777. Maid to Madame Lefebvre-Desnouettes and reportedly carried messages for Bonapartist plotters. Described in 1817 as "ugly," "withered," and "with a very high opinion of herself." One of the few women to go to the Champ d'Asile, where she met Vine and Olive member [*François Viole*]. After the Champ d'Asile, they went to the grant and got married in 1818. They soon left for Louisiana and were still living in Saint Martinsville in 1833. She died in 1853.

Desroures: In New York City at the end of 1818 when he sold his allotment.

Devengen, Charles: In Mobile in 1822 when he sold his allotment.

Dirat, Louis-Marie: Former aide-de-camp to his relative Marshal Perignon. Dirat served twelve years in the military and eight in the administration. During the Hundred Days he was financial officer and contributor to the radical journal *Nain Jaune*. For this, he was exiled. He arrived in the United States in 1816. He was vice president and secretary of the society for a time. He was supported by his wife, who was a milliner and mantua maker in Philadelphia. Pardoned in 1819, he returned to France where old political friends spurned him because they feared (correctly) that he had become a police spy.

Dor, Marius: A bandbox maker who immigrated to Philadelphia. By 1816 in financial difficulty. Perhaps for this reason, he sold his allotment as soon as he received it.

Douarche, Pierre: Born in Bessan (Herault) in 1769. Volunteered in 1791 and rose through the ranks. In 1813 colonel commanding a regiment. Many campaigns, wounds, and decorations. Rallied to Napoleon in 1815. In 1816 was caught gambling with regimental funds. Fled to the United States. Joined the Champ d'Asile, commander of first cohort. Died in Jamaica in 1819, leaving in France a widow and two children.

Drouet, Pierre: Wealthy Domingan baker. In 1824 merchant in Williamsburg Virginia. **Marie (Drouet) Teterel,** wife of **François-Hyacinthe Teterel,** was probably a relative.

Dubarry, Jean-Marie: Domingan merchant, he became a U.S. citizen in Philadelphia in 1796. His business contacts included many Vine and Olive members. For a time, he was in formal partnership with Pierre-Robert Delaunay. Was still in Philadelphia in 1823.

Dubocq, Guillaume: Domingan china merchant born in 1770. In the 1790s, he and his wife had a daughter named **Marie-Antoinette.** He became a U.S. citizen in 1804 in Philadelphia, where he was still living in 1817 when he sold his allotment.

Ducoing, Pierre: Domingan merchant and storekeeper. Fled to Philadelphia. Became U.S. citizen in 1797. Business partner with Vine and Olive member **Pierre Lacombe,** Ducoing owned a millinery and fancy store in his own right in 1817. He was godfather of **Pierre-Frédéric Fontanges,** a prominent Vine and Olive member. His wife, Sophie, was the sister of **Joseph Robard,** another member. He died in Philadelphia in 1821.

Ducommun, Joseph: A Philadelphia doctor. In the East Florida Coffee Land Association.

Dufourg, D. V.: No information.

Dufourg, F.: No information.

Dufourg, Jean-Jacques: No information.

Dumas, Antoine: No information.

Dumenil, Antoine: In 1812 established in Lexington, Kentucky, where he owned land. Did business with **Henri Guibert.**

Dupont, Pierre-Charles: In Philadelphia in late 1818.

Dupouy, Nicholas-Alexandre: In Philadelphia in 1804 or even earlier. In 1814 a dancing master. From 1817 to 1820 owned a wine, grocery, and liquor store.

[Dupui]: Present on the grant in 1818. Dead by mid-1821.

Durand, Jean-Baptiste (or François): His identity is unclear. Possibly a former member of the French tax collection administration or a soldier. Witnessed the sale of many Champ d'Asile allotments. Seems to have joined the Champ d'Asile himself. May have taken part in other Mexican adventures.

[Durive, François-Martin-Marie]: On the grant in 1818. Dead by 1834.

Duterte, Mathurin: Barber in Philadelphia from at least 1814 until his death in 1825.

Duval, Jacques-Séraphin: Philadelphia merchant, established in the city from at least 1804. His daughter Sophia married into the Ashe family of Alabama and became one of the principal patentees of grant allotments. Other Duvals marry [**Chaudrons**]. When Duval died in 1842, he owned property in Pennsylvania, Illinois, and Alabama.

Emery, Louis: Hat merchant of Philadelphia, established there from 1804 or earlier. He became a U.S. citizen in 1807. Still in Philadelphia in 1821 when he sold his allotment.

Engelbert, Léonard: Merchant in Philadelphia from at least 1799. Became a U.S. citizen in 1806. In 1811 started a partnership with [**Auguste-Firmin Follin**]. In 1817 opened a store. Lent money to Vine and Olive members Charles Cavoroc and Joseph-Hilaire Gubert. Moved to New Orleans in 1822, but back in Philadelphia by his death in 1844.

[Ensfelder, Lucien]: Napoleonic officer. Present on the grant in 1818. Mismanaged [General Lefebvre-Desnouettes's] store. Left for Mobile at the end of 1818 and sold his allotment. In 1819 established in New Orleans with his wife, Marie-Adelaide Rivière.

[Fagot]: No information; although probably present on the grant in 1819.

Fallot, Eugène-Hyacinthe: Sold his allotment in early December 1817 to join the Champ d'Asile. Was reportedly "devoured by savages."

Fanchon, Honoré: Napoleonic officer. Joined the Champ d'Asile.

Farcy Sainte-Marie, Abel: Young Parisian. Traveled to London where he contracted debts. In 1817 went to Charleston, South Carolina, still in debt. Sold allotment and joined the Champ d'Asile. After it failed, he went to New Orleans where he incurred new debts. Then went to Baton Rouge to recoup his fortune, but failed again. Back in New Orleans, he declared bankruptcy and became a beadle. In 1822 was described as still living there in "the most profound misery."

Farrouilh, André: A Domingan merchant who fled from the slave uprising to Philadelphia via the island of Saint Thomas. Became a U.S. citizen in 1815.

Fauquier, François: Erroneously entered for allotment actually given to François Gasquet.

Faurès, Placide-Laurent: From a Domingan mercantile family established in Philadelphia in 1792. Born there in 1796. Studied at the Collège de Vendôme in Paris. Was classmate of travel writer Edouard de Montulé. In 1822 Faurès returned to Philadelphia as physician. His uncle was Philadelphia merchant André Curcier.

Firmin, B. Charles: No information.

Fischer: Sold his allotment in early December 1817 to join the Champ d'Asile.

[**Follin, Auguste-Firmin**]: A Domingan veterinarian who fled to the United States after the slave uprising. In 1811 started a candle manufactory in Philadelphia with money lent by Leonard Engelbert. In October 1818 was in Charleston, South Carolina, where he was in partnership with his brother **Firmin Follin**. Auguste-Firmin's wife was [**Marie-Jeanne-Mélanie Noël**], relative of the Domingan merchant [**Thomas Noël**]. By 1823 they were established in Marengo County where Auguste-Firmin farmed and practiced veterinary medicine. They were still there in 1831. His wife died in Mobile in 1851.

[**Auguste and Firmin Follin (brothers)**]: Brothers of **Auguste-Firmin** (above). Settled briefly on grant in 1821, then moved to Charleston where they remained into the 1830s.

Follin, Georges: Merchant in Philadelphia in 1817 when he became a U.S. citizen. In 1825 he had moved to Mexico City, where he died in 1849. May be related to the above.

Fontanges, Pierre-Frédéric: Father was a doctor in Saint-Domingue, where Pierre-Frédéric was born in 1790. Godfather was **Pierre Ducoing**. Sister [**Thérèse-Antoinette-Margueritte Fontanges**] married [**Anne-Gilbert-Marc-Antoine Frenaye**]. After the uprising, the Fontanges family fled to Philadelphia. Pierre-Frédéric became a merchant there, both on his own account and in partnership with his brother-in-law [**Frenaye**]. In 1824 was in Mexico City, partner in the business firm of Fontanges, Subervielle, and Company. [**Frenaye**] later joined him there. Fontanges was back in Philadelphia by 1832. He became a prominent member of the Atheneum.

Formento, Félix-Marie: Born in Italy in 1778. Studied medicine at the University of Turin and became a French army doctor. Went to New Orleans (probably after 1815), where he was a doctor. In 1818 became chief doctor at the Champ d'Asile. In 1820 bought a pharmacy in the Vieux Carré. Died in New Orleans.

Fouasche, Pierre: In Philadelphia in 1817 when he sold his allotment.

[Fouquet, J.]: Present on the grant in 1818.

[Fouquet (elder)]: Briefly on grant.

Fourestier, Elie B.: Philadelphia distiller. Became a U.S. citizen in 1809. Sold his allotment in 1825 and remained in Philadelphia until his death in 1851.

Fourni, Fabius: Born in the kingdom of Piedmont in 1776, son of a judge. In 1793 joined the army of Piedmont as an artillery cadet. When Napoleon conquered Italy, Fourni served the satellite kingdoms the emperor set up. By 1815 he had become lieutenant colonel in the artillery of the guard of the king of Naples, Napoleon's brother-in-law Murat. Having participated in Murat's failed attempt to recover his throne, Fourni had to flee to the United States. Sold his Vine and Olive allotment to join the Champ d'Asile. There he commanded the third cohort before deserting to the Spanish.

Fournier, Honoré-François: Philadelphia Domingan merchant who became U.S. citizen in 1805. Remained a merchant in Philadelphia until at least 1823. Related to **Alexandre Fournier Sr.,** Domingan goldsmith and jeweler, and his son, [**Alexandre Jr.**], who became a shopkeeper and merchant in Demopolis.

Frédéric, Louis-Auguste: Philadelphia merchant in 1818. In Jackson, Mississippi, 1832.

[**Frenaye, Jean-Pierre**]: Brother of below. Son of a royal officeholder and member of the Domingan nobility. Jean-Pierre was born on the family coffee plantation in 1786. The family fled to Philadelphia, where Jean-Pierre was a teacher. By 1822 in Marengo County, but soon returned to Philadelphia where his wife, Hetty, ran a dry goods store.

[**Frenaye, Anne-Gilbert-Marc-Antoine**]: Elder brother of above. Born in 1783 on the family coffee plantation. Became a U.S. citizen in 1808. Married [**Thérèse-Antoinette-Margueritte Fontanges**], but marriage annulled in 1829. In Philadelphia, [**Frenaye**] was a merchant, both on his own account and in partnership with various future Vine and Olive shareholders: [**Jean-Marie Chapron**] (1817, 1818, 1820), his brother-in-law **Pierre-Frédéric Fontanges** (1818, 1820), and **François-Hyacinthe Teterel** (1818, 1820). In Marengo County in 1822. In Mexico with **Fontanges** in 1824. In 1828 in New York City, but returned to Philadelphia by 1832. There he served as a confidential agent to the Roman Catholic bishops of the city and helped found the cathedral cemetery.

Fux, Jean-Louis: Sold allotment to join the Champ d'Asile. In 1825–26 in Opelousas, Louisiana. He may have been in business with Vine and Olive member Jonas Keller.

Gaines, George Strother: U.S. Choctaw factor in 1817 and brother of Gen. Edmund Gaines. Urged French to establish their town on White Bluff. In 1819 his allotment was taken from him. He kept close relations with the French settlers, as evidenced in his memoirs.

Galabert, Louis-Jacques: Born in 1773 at Castelnaudary (Aude) to a family linked to the family of Francisco Cabarrus, one-time finance minister of Spain. In 1794 Galabert emigrated from France to England, joined a counter-revolutionary regiment, and participated in the disastrous Quiberon landing, which he blamed on English perfidy. He then began a trip around the world that carried him through India, China, and Mexico (1796–1802). Back in Europe, he entered Napoleon's service, first as a spy (1802–6) and then as a military officer. He served in staff, diplomatic, and espionage roles, especially in the army of Spain. In 1813 became aide-de-camp to Marshal Soult. In 1814 was a lieutenant colonel. Rallied to Napoleon in 1815. After Waterloo, resigned from the army, was placed under surveillance, and left for America. Helped plan the Champ d'Asile. Held secret talks with the Spanish ambassador Onís. Removed from the plot by _Charles Lallemand._ In 1820 served as a colonel in the constitutionalist army of Spain. In 1823 returned to France. Failed to restart his military career, but lobbied for creation of the Canal des Pyrénnées. Elected to the legislature in 1831 and died in 1841.

[**Gallard, Pierre**]: Domingan jeweler in Philadelphia. Became a U.S. citizen in 1808. His nephew was Vine and Olive member [**Honoré Bayol**]. Gallard settled on the grant.

Garesché de la Poterie, Jean-Pierre: Domingan merchant who fled to Philadelphia with his brother (below) in the 1790s. Became a U.S. citizen in 1796. In business both on his own account, as well as in partnership with [**Frédéric Ravesies**] and his brother.

Garesché Maisonneuve, Vital-Marie: Domingan merchant who fled to Philadelphia with his brother (above). Became a U.S. citizen in 1804. In business both on his own account, as well as in partnership with his brother and [**Frédéric Ravesies**].

Garnier (des Saintes), Jacques (father): Born in 1754 in Saintes in western France. A lawyer, elected to the Convention in 1792 where he voted for the death of the king and advocated radical policies. Left the legislature in 1798 and became president of the criminal tribunal in his home town. In 1815 rallied to Napoleon, returned to the legislature, and called for revolutionary measures. Proscribed by the ordinance of 24 July 1815, he fled to Brussels with his son (below) and edited a radical political journal, the _Surveillant._ In 1816 they left for the United States. After a brief stay in Philadelphia, they moved to Kentucky. In 1818 he and his son drowned in a steamboat accident.

Garnier, Alphonse (son): Imperial Guard captain. Drowned with his father in 1818.

Gasquet, Francois: A former officer of the French gunpowder and saltpeter administration. He lived in New York City from 1818 through 1820, if not longer.

Gatty, Antoine: No information.

Gauny, Nicholas: A gunsmith. In Philadelphia in 1818–19, when he sold his allotment.

[Genin, Charles-François]: Former naval gunner taken prisoner by the English. In captivity learned goldsmithing. After 1815 settled in Opelousas, Louisiana. He spent some time on the grant in 1819 where he gained a reputation for raising delicious pears.

[George, Edouard (son)]: Eldest son of the Domingan family (below). Born in 1795 near Philadelphia. Toiled on his family's grant lands, but in 1820 became a supercargo on a Stephen Girard ship. Upon his death in Mobile in 1841, was described as a ship captain.

[George, Pierre-Edouard-Côme (father)]: Born in 1769 near Paris in a prosperous bourgeois family. Married [**Catherine-Victoire Le Grand de Boislandry**] (below) and left in 1791 for Saint-Domingue. Fled to Philadelphia where he worked briefly as a merchant before becoming a supercargo for Stephen Girard. Became a U.S. citizen in 1817. Led a nomadic existence and rarely saw his family. Died in Philadelphia in 1829.

[**George, Catherine-Victoire née le Grand de Boislandry**]: Born in 1770 in L'Aigle (Normandy). Married **Pierre-Edouard-Côme George** in 1791. Went to Saint-Domingue, then fled to Philadelphia. Their first child, [**Victorie**], was born in Saint-Domingue. [**Victorie**] later married [Isaac Butaud] and then Nicholas Thouron. The other children, including [Edouard] (above) were born in Philadelphia. Before 1812 Victoire taught at Madame Rivardi's School for Girls ("Gothic Mansion") in Philadelphia. Moved to grant in 1819. But after several hard years, went to Mobile.

Gerard, Hyacinthe: Born at Neuf-Brisac (Haut-Rhin) in 1789. Enlisted in 1806. In 1814 became second lieutenant, but lost his position in 1815 in Bourbon military downsizing. Went to America. At first intended to sell allotment and join the Champ d'Asile but had second thoughts and threw himself on the mercy of the French ambassador. He secured a pardon and passage back to France by informing on his former colleagues.

Germain, Henri: Born in Savoy in 1791, which was annexed to France during the Revolution. Entered the Saint-Cyr military school in 1811. By 1815 a lieutenant in the Horse Artillery. Sought French citizenship in order to continue his military career but was rebuffed. Went to America and took part in the Champ d'Asile. Returned to New Orleans and married Lakanal's daughter Alexandrine. Became a midranking official in the French consulate there. During the American Civil War, the couple returned to France.

Germond, Alexandre-Ambroise: In New York City in 1818.

Gilbal, Antoine: Born at Moulins (Allier) in 1785. Enlisted in 1804. Second lieutenant in 1814. Fought at the Battles of Friedland and Talavera, among others, and was wounded many times. In 1817 in Philadelphia where he sold his allotment to join the Champ d'Asile. On his return to New Orleans, he publicly denounced *Charles Lallemand.*

Gilbert: No information.

Godat: No information.

Godemar, Jean-Baptiste: No information.

Godon, Victorine: No information.

Gouiran, Joseph-Michel: A Philadelphia jeweler, he became a U.S. citizen in 1822.

Grégoire, Etienne: Joined the Champ d'Asile. Possibly died in New Orleans in 1833.

Grillet, François: In 1834 was living in France.

Groning, C.: Sold his allotment in 1817 to join the Champ d'Asile.

Grouchy, Emmanuel, Comte de: Born in Paris in 1766 to a distinguished noble family. Destined by birth for a brilliant military career. Served in the artillery, cavalry, and royal household guards before the Revolution and was a lieutenant colonel by the age of twenty. Unlike most noble officers, he supported the Revolution and was rewarded with rapid advancement. Became a general in 1792. Shifted his loyalties to Napoleon in 1799 and served in his principal European campaigns. Commanded the "Sacred Battalion" that escorted Napoleon to safety out of Russia. Retained in a command position after Napoleon's first abdication, Grouchy incurred Bourbon wrath by placing his troops at Napoleon's disposition in 1815. The emperor named him marshal and gave him command of an army corps. His failure to reinforce Napoleon may have lost the Battle of Waterloo. In 1816 Grouchy fled to the United States, where he had talks with agents of the Latin American independence movement. His real interest, however, was to obtain a royal pardon and confirmation of his military rank. He got his pardon in 1819, returned to France, but could not get his rank recognized until 1831. He died in 1847.

Grouchy, Alphonse-Frédéric-Emmanuel, Marquis de: Born in 1789, eldest son of above. Graduated Saint-Cyr in 1806. Served as an officer in Napoleon's major campaigns, including Spain and Russia. A colonel in 1815, he was placed on the inactive list by the Bourbons. In 1817 he and his younger brother (below) visited their exiled father in America. They returned to

France a year later. After the 1830 Revolution, Grouchy returned to active service. Became a general the following year and in 1849 was elected to the legislature. Napoleon III appointed him to the Senate in 1852.

[Grouchy, Victor de]: Younger brother of above. Born in 1797. Entered the army in 1813 as an Honor Guard. Lieutenant in 1814, he rallied to Napoleon and served as his father's aide-de-camp in 1815. After Waterloo, placed on the inactive list. In 1817 he and his older brother (above) visited their father in America. Victor briefly visited the grant. He returned to France after one year.

Gruchet, Louis: Born in 1786 in Besançon (Doubs). Enlisted in 1802 and rose through the ranks in the service of Murat, Napoleon's brother-in-law and king of Naples. By 1815 a *chef d'escadron* (major) in the cavalry. Participated in Murat's unsuccessful attempt to recover his throne. Fled to America. In 1817 sold his allotment and tried to go to Cuba. In 1819 he contacted French diplomats, begging for a pardon.

Gubert, Joseph-Hilaire: China merchant in Philadelphia by 1814. In 1818 fell on hard times and had to borrow money from several Vine and Olive members. Became a U.S. citizen in 1835 and died a year later. Daughter Louise Gubert became a famous singer.

Guibert, Henri: In 1818 of Fayette County, Kentucky. May have done business with Antoine Dumenil, also of Kentucky.

[Guilleault, Jean]: Present on the grant in 1818. Sold his allotment in 1832.

Guillot, Pierre: Former artillery lieutenant. Sold allotment to join the Champ d'Asile. On return to New Orleans, taught French, Latin, and mathematics at the Collège d'Orléans. In 1830–31 presented homage of the Louisiana Legion to Louis-Philippe.

[Haez, Jean]: Present on the grant in 1818. Sold his allotment in 1823.

Hamel, Victor: French-born Philadelphia confectioner. Became a U.S. citizen in 1808. Partner of Vine and Olive member Laurent Astolphi. Died in Philadelphia, 1821.

Harraneder, Charles: Young officer, son of a banker. Went to America in 1817 and ran out of money. Sold his allotment and joined the Champ d'Asile.

Havard: No information.

Himley, Henry B.: No information.

Humbert, Jean-Jacques Etienne: In 1818 living in New York City.

[Hurtel, Jean]: Son of **Pierre-Hyacinthe-Baptiste Hurtel,** Domingan merchant and planter who went to New York City after the uprising. Jean's uncle was the Philadelphia printer **Jean-François Hurtel,** a specialist in French and Spanish books. Jean was born in 1797 in New York City. In 1821 in Greensboro, he married his cousin [**Eliza Noël**] (daughter of [**Thomas Noël**] and [**Anne-Déolice Hurtel**]). Eliza died in Mobile in 1868 and Jean the following year. A relative, **Alphonse Hurtel,** became mayor of Mobile.

Illari, Benoit: Possibly related to Camilla Illari, Napoleon's nurse. In Philadelphia in 1818 when he sold his allotment.

Jackson, Samuel: Various Samuel Jacksons listed in Philadelphia directories: a stablekeeper, druggist, professor of penmanship, a doctor, and a painter. Unclear which was the Vine and Olive member. Jackson sold his allotment in 1818.

Jamet, Victor: In 1816 arrived in New York City from France with letters and journals for P. S. du Pont de Nemours. In Pittsburgh at the end of the year.

[**Jeandreau, Jean**]: Present on the grant in 1818. Died in Mobile in 1823.

Jeannet-Oudin, Georges-Nicholas (called "Manchot"): Nephew of Danton. Brother of Gen. Louis-François Jeannet. Born at Arcis-sur-Aube (Aube) in 1762, son of a merchant. Before the Revolution Jeannet was a cotton merchant in his hometown. Elected mayor in its first-ever election in 1790. In 1792 was named by the executive council (on which Danton sat) to represent the civil power at the siege of Thionville. The following year, was sent to French Guyana to effect the emancipation of the slaves. In 1794 went to Philadelphia, taking along the colonial treasury. Returned to France after the demise of Robespierre and was sent back to Guyana. There he became notorious as the jailer of conservative members of the legislature who had been deported there after the coup d'état of 18 fructidor. Later posted to Guadeloupe (along with his brother the general). After Napoleon's seizure of power, Jeannet was recalled to France and given a place in the War Ministry. Founded a sugar beet factory in his home region. Rallied to Napoleon in 1815 and fled to America after Waterloo. Arranged the mass sale of Champ d'Asile allotments. Went to Texas with his wife, son, and another relative. In 1820 his wife died of yellow fever in New Orleans. In 1822 masterminded a plan to foment slave uprisings across the Caribbean. Died in France in 1828 in poverty.

Jeannet, Joseph: Son of the above. Nephew of Gen. Louis-François Jeannet. Born in 1789. Enlisted as an Honor Guard in 1813 and taken prisoner at the Battle of Dresden. Returned to active service in 1814. Rallied to Napoleon the following year and became his uncle's aide-de-camp. After Waterloo, fled with his family to America where he joined the Champ d'Asile. When the 1830 Revolution broke out in France, he was in rural Peru, running a small business. He asked to rejoin the French army but was rebuffed.

Jeannet, Louis-René: A Napoleonic officer and member of the Jeannet clan who joined the Champ d'Asile. In 1822 he took part in *George Jeannet's* scheme to foment slave uprising in the Caribbean. Was probably *George Jeannet's* nephew.

Jenim, Edouard: Still in Philadelphia in 1824.

Jogan, Antoine: No information.

Jouny, Louis-Michel: In Philadelphia in 1818–19. When he sold his allotment in 1825, was a resident of New York City.

Jourdan, Ambroise: Officer in the Polish Light Horse (later Lancers) of the Imperial Guard where he may have known *Charrasin* and *Schultz*. He sold his allotment, joined the Champ d'Asile, and died there.

Keller, Jonas: Possibly a business partner of Jean-Louis Fux of Opelousas.

Kimbal: No information.

Knappe, Philippe: Bottler living in Philadelphia from 1817 until at least 1828, when he became a U.S. citizen. Belonged to the East Florida Coffee Land Association.

[Labrusse, Mathieu]: Merchant in Demopolis from 1818 through at least 1826.

Lacombe, Pierre: Born in Saint-Domingue in 1759. Became a U.S. citizen in Philadelphia in 1798 and married Vine and Olive member Germain Combes's sister. Combes was godfather of their first son. Was a merchant in partnership with **Pierre Ducoing.** In 1808 he owned a ship, the *Lovely Matilda* and in 1819 a dry goods store. Joined the East Florida Coffee Land Association. Died in Philadelphia in 1833.

Lacroix, René-François: Sold allotment to join the Champ d'Asile. Left, returned to the East Coast, and gave eyewitness account to French diplomats under the name Croissac.

Ladurelle, M.-François-Auguste: Of Philadelphia in 1818 when he sold his allotment.

[Lagay, Paul]: In Demopolis at least 1820–23, with his wife, Fanny.

[Lajoinie, Jacques]: Former Napoleonic officer, established on the grant. Captain of the Marengo County militia in 1818. Member of the society's executive council in 1819 at Aigleville. Left the grant by 1830, returned to France, and died in the Invalides in 1832.

Lakanal, Joseph: Born in 1762 at Serres (Ariège). Priest in a teaching order before the Revolution. Elected to the Convention in 1792. Voted death for

Louis XVI, became president of Committee of Public Instruction, and member of the Institute. Removed from office in 1797 during a period of conservative ascendancy. This essentially ended his public life, although he was a government commissioner in 1799 and held a minor administrative post during the Hundred Days. Exiled in 1816 for regicide, he arrived in Philadelphia and soon moved to Vevay, a Franco-Swiss viticultural colony in Kentucky. Accompanied by his wife, Marie-Barbe, and daughter, Alexandrine. Drafted plan to crown Joseph Bonaparte king of Mexico. Became president of the Collège d'Orléans for a time and then settled near Mobile where he died in 1837.

Lallemand, Charles-François-Antoine: Born in Metz (Moselle) in 1774, son of a wigmaker. Enlisted in the first wave of revolutionary enthusiasm and rose through the ranks. Veteran of Napoleon's major campaigns, including the expedition to Saint-Domingue and the Spanish guerilla war. Received title of baron in 1808. In 1811 was made a general. Along with his brother (below) and [Lefebvre-Desnouettes], in 1815 he attempted a military uprising. It failed, but Napoleon rewarded him with high rank in the Light Horse of the Imperial Guard. Wounded at Waterloo. Proscribed by the Bourbons, he tried to join Napoleon in exile on Saint Helena but was held by the British on Malta. Eventually came to America. There he led the Champ d'Asile. After its failure, he became embroiled in a scandal over the funds collected by the *Minerve* for the survivors. This did not prevent him from becoming a prominent officer in the New Orleans masons and an American citizen. In 1823 he went to constitutionalist Spain to raise a Legion of French Refugees. After the defeat of the Cortes, Lallemand went to England where he was given funds by Greek insurgents to purchase modern warships. Another scandal ensued, in which he was accused of taking some of the money. He then returned to the United States and opened a school in New York City. After the 1830 Revolution, he returned to France and resumed his military career. Died in Paris in 1839.

[*Lallemand, Henri-Dominique*]: Brother of above. Born in 1777 in Metz (Moselle). Entered the Ecole Polytechnique in 1797 and became an artillery officer. Served in Napoleon's principal campaigns in the artillery of the Imperial Guard. In 1810 named baron. In 1814 promoted to general. With his brother (above) and [Lefebvre-Desnouettes], he took part in a conspiracy to restore Napoleon to power. Rewarded with command of part of the Guard's Artillery at Waterloo, where he was wounded. Proscribed on 24 July 1815, he fled to the United States. In 1817 married Henriette Girard, niece of Stephen

Girard. Helped lead the Champ d'Asile, but never went to Texas. Returned to the East Coast in 1818 where he died at Joseph Bonaparte's house in Bordentown, New Jersey, in 1823.

Landevin, François: No information.

Lapeyre, Jean-Baptiste: Former officer in the Imperial armies. Sold his allotment in early December 1817, joined the Champ d'Asile, and died there.

Latapie, Antoine: In 1834, living in Louisville, Kentucky.

Latapie, Paul-Albert: From Molières (Tarn). Former Napoleonic officer who commanded a regiment at Waterloo. After collapse of empire, caught forging the war minister's signature. Shot gendarme sent to arrest him. Fled to Belgium, where he worked with Louis-Marie Dirat on the *Nain Jaune,* and then to America. In 1817 he went to Pernambuco in what has been described as an attempt to rescue Napoleon from Saint Helena. Arrested by Portuguese but escaped. Later served constitutionalist Spain, but managed to convince the Spanish royalists after 1823 that he had had a change of heart. By the late 1820s, he was a brigadier in the Spanish army and had served as second-in-command of the Philippines and inspector of militia in the Canary Islands.

Laurent, Clement: No information.

[*Laurent, Maurice*]: Lawyer. Sold allotment to join the Champ d'Asile. Part of the *Lallemands'* inner circle. Served as *commissaire des guerres* of the Champ d'Asile jointly with *Pénières (son).* In late 1818 present on the grant.

[*Lauret, Louis*]: Born in 1797, son of a police commissioner in provincial France. Enlisted as an Honor Guard and became a cavalry officer. After 1815 came to America, sold his allotment, and joined the Champ d'Asile. A member of the *Lallemands'* inner circle and best man at [*Henri Lallemand's*] wedding. After the Champ d'Asile failed, he went to New Orleans where his uncle Paul Lanusse was a prominent merchant. In 1819 he married Josephine Rousseau, daughter of a Louisiana ship captain. In 1820 he lent money to *Charles Lallemand* and *Mathieu-Ferdinand Manfredi,* both of whom defrauded him. Briefly on grant. Farmed near New Orleans for a few years, but by 1826 had given up and returned to Philadelphia. By 1830 he had relocated to the Georgia wilderness, where he lived in a small cabin and caught fish. He planned to travel deep into Florida.

Lavau, Jean-Francois-Sully: In Philadelphia in 1796 or earlier. Sully Lavau and members of his family sponsored baptisms of black and mulatto children of unknown parents. In 1821 he was still in Philadelphia, when he sold his allotment.

[Leboutellier, Michel]: French sea captain born in 1766. Became a U.S. citizen in Philadelphia in 1798. His wife, [Helena Stewart née Counsell] was a store-keeper in the city through 1817. In 1818 the couple moved to the grant with [George N. Stewart], [Helena's] son by her first marriage. Leboutellier petitioned Governor Bibb for a job, but his pleas went unanswered. He died in 1819. [Helena] remarried, this time to Gen. Juan Rico, a Spanish cleric and military man who had fought the French but was equally opposed to Ferdinand VII's absolutism. [Helena] died in Mobile in 1856 at the age of seventy-eight.

Lecampion, François: Born in 1744. A storekeeper established in Philadelphia by 1803 or earlier. Died in Philadelphia in 1825.

Leclerc, Joseph P.: A Philadelphia storekeeper, 1817–19.

Lecoq de Marcelay: Left Nantes for the United States in 1815. In 1826 he was living in Columbia, Tennessee, as a painter and decorator.

[Lefebvre-Desnouettes, Charles]: Born in Paris in 1773, son of a cloth merchant. Ran away to enroll in the army. He rose rapidly and served as Napoleon's aide-de-camp at the critical victory at Marengo. He fought at Austerlitz as a colonel and became a general in 1806. In 1808 given title of count. Implicated in the 1815 military conspiracy with the *Lallemand* brothers, Lefebvre-Desnouettes was rewarded by Napoleon with command of the Light Cavalry of the Guard (at whose head he charged repeatedly at Waterloo) and by the Bourbons with a death sentence. Fled to America in 1816. Largely avoided compromising activities during his exile. The only general to settle on the grant. In 1818 appointed judge of the quorum and opened a store. He sought pardon and permission to return to France. He finally left the United States in 1822, but drowned off the coast of Ireland. His widow was the sister of the banker Lafitte.

Lefeuvre, Claude-Joseph: A French carpenter or turner who came to Baltimore in 1806. Sold his allotment in 1818 and probably settled in New Orleans, where he died in 1822.

[LeFrançois, Jacques]: Present on the grant from 1818 to 1827 with his brother (below).

[LeFrançois, Tougnet]: Present on the grant from 1818 to 1827 with his brother (above).

[Legras, Gilbert]: Present in Aigleville in 1817. Moved to Baton Rouge in 1818.

Legris Belleisle, Pierre: Former president of the commercial court of Falaise (Calvados). In 1817 was resident of Gallipolis, Ohio. In 1818 was living in Philadelphia.

Lemaignien, Pierre-Paul: In Philadelphia in 1818 when he sold his grant.

Lemeusnier, J. Joseph: Born in 1790 and died in Mobile in 1835. His brother (below) joined the Champ d'Asile.

Lemeusnier, Félix-Antoine: Joined the Champ d'Asile, where he drowned.

Lerouyer, François: Joined the Champ d'Asile, where he drowned.

Lesueur: Probably the artist Charles-Alexandre Lesueur. Born at Le Havre in 1778. Was a naval officer during the 1790s. In 1799 sent by Bonaparte to Australia and Tasmania as part of a voyage of exploration. Was one of the expedition's few survivors. In 1815, when the Bourbons cut funding for publication of the expedition's findings, Lesueur went to the United States. Undertook several voyages of exploration around America but was based in Philadelphia where he taught drawing and painting to young ladies. After 1825 he lived for a time in New Harmony, Indiana. In 1837 he returned to France.

[Lintroy]: In 1817 taught writing at **Jean-Thomas Carré's** Philadelphia school. Briefly on grant. In 1820 in New Orleans. In 1831 Mary Lintroy of Mobile sold his allotment.

Luciani, Pascal: Born in Corsica in 1786. Related to the Bonaparte family. Decorated Napoleonic officer. Became a U.S. citizen in Philadelphia in 1817. In 1818–19 worked there as a confectioner. By 1828 had married Rosana Wentling of Pennsylvania. In 1849 they moved to Montgomery where they both died in 1853. Their daughter Victoria reportedly suggested "Dixie" as the national anthem of the Confederacy.

Macré, Jean-Marie: Died in Philadelphia in November 1817. Left a widow and two minor children: Adolphe (who died in Mobile a minor) and Eugénie (who married Charles H. Austin of Mobile). His widow [Adèle] married [Charles Batré].

Mahé: no information.

Maillet, Henri-Pierre-Alexandre-As.: Became a U.S. citizen in 1804. Sold his allotment in 1817 to join the Champ d'Asile.

Malezewsky, Constantin-Paul: Polish officer in Napoleonic service. In 1810 on staff of the Prince de Wagram and Neuchâtel. After 1815 went to America, sold allotment, and joined the Champ d'Asile. Served constitutionalists in Spain, 1820–23.

Mane, Honoré: Surgeon. Sold his allotment in 1817 and joined the Champ d'Asile.

Manfredi, Mathieu-Ferdinand: Sold his allotment in 1817 and joined the Champ d'Asile. Returned to New Orleans where he defrauded *Louis Lauret.* Fled to Havana where he died in the hospital soon thereafter.

[Mangon, Pierre]: A wheelwright, present on grant in 1818. Still there in 1860.

[Manoury, Pierre-Maxime]: Present on grant in 1819. In 1820 in New Orleans. Described in 1822 New Orleans directory as a dry goods merchant. Still there in 1824.

Mansuis, Lullier: Musician. In Philadelphia in 1818 when he sold his allotment.

Marchand, Louis-Pierre-Joseph: In 1818 in Philadelphia. In 1819 a merchant in Blakely, Alabama. Married to **Louise Coquillon,** possibly related to the **Coquillon** brothers.

Mariano, Pompée-M.-A.: Also known as Count de l'Estadas. Before 1815 finance minister of the duchy of Parma. After 1815 came to Philadelphia where he gave music lessons. He sold his allotment in 1818 and went to Canada and Kentucky. In 1819 unsuccessfully sought appointment as secretary to the commission to draw the boundary between Spanish and United States territories in America. Died suddenly in 1821.

[Martial]: Briefly on grant. One of his children died in Mobile in 1839.

Martin, Amédée: In Philadelphia in 1819 when he sold his allotment.

[Martin, François]: Son of Joseph Martin-Piquet. Became a U.S. citizen in 1808. A shopkeeper in Philadelphia where he lived until at least 1817. By 1823 he had settled on the grant and remained there until at least 1834.

Martin du Columbier, Joseph: Medical doctor, born in 1761. Father of below. Before the slave uprising, owned a coffee plantation in Saint-Domingue. In Philadelphia he practiced medicine and served briefly as treasurer of the society.

Martin du Columbier, Prosper: Engineer, son of above. Owner of an iron foundry. Died in Philadelphia in 1851.

Martin-Piquet, Joseph (father): Merchant, born in 1736. Died in Philadelphia in 1822.

Martin-Piquet, L. J. F (son): Merchant, son of above. In Philadelphia 1821, Ohio 1832, and Kentucky 1834. His daughter Julia married his nephew **Joseph Barbaroux.**

Martin-Piquet, Pierre: Probably the brother of Joseph Martin-Piquet.

Martinet, Pierre-Louis: Of Philadelphia until 1818, of New York 1818–26. Belonged to the East Florida Coffee Land Association.

Mathieu, Joseph: Medical doctor, born in 1756. In Philadelphia from 1802, if not earlier. Became a U.S. citizen in 1805. Died in Philadelphia in 1831.

[Mayer]: Briefly on grant. Dead by mid-1821.

Melizet, François: A storekeeper and merchant who sometimes kept Stephen Girard's books and also worked for the firm of Curcier and [**Ravesies**]. Married Lydie-Sophie Roudet, sister of [Corneille Roudet]. Remained in Philadelphia until his death in 1823.

Menou, Dieudonné: No information.

Merle, Etienne: Possibly a sergeant-major in Napoleon's Elban guard.

[Meslier, Nicholas-Basile]: Jeweler and watchmaker, born in 1779. Married to [**Augustine-Elizabeth**], sister of **Amand Pfister.** Meslier was one of the society's commissioner-explorers. Established on the grant in 1818 and became Marengo County's first justice of the peace. Moved to Mobile around 1825. Died there in 1849.

[Mestayer, Michel]: Businessman in Philadelphia. Became a U.S. citizen in 1808. On the grant from 1818. On the society's executive council in Aigleville. Was the society's archivist 1820–24. Then moved to Saint Charles Parish, Louisiana.

[*Métais, Etienne-Jean-Baptiste*]: Joined the Champ d'Asile. After it failed, he went briefly to the grant in 1819, but then returned to New Orleans the following year.

Métayé, Jean-Pierre: No information.

Meynié, Jean-Ulysse: Merchant of Philadelphia. Became a U.S. citizen in 1817. Close to **Honoré-François Fournier** and [**Frédéric Ravesies**]. Died in 1832 in Philadelphia.

[Mignon]: Present on the grant in 1818.

Millon, Pierre-Solidor: In Norfolk, Virginia, in 1819 when he sold his allotment.

[Miot]: In New York City in 1818. Briefly on grant. Dead by mid-1821.

Moncravie, Jacques: Philadelphia baker. Sold allotment in 1818.

Mondin: No information.

Monnot, Charles: Surgeon, born in Vaufrey in eastern France. Sold allotment to join the Champ d'Asile. After it failed, went to Louisiana and founded Napoleonville plantation. Marched in New Orleans in Napoleon's funeral procession. Died on eve of American Civil War.

Montalegri, Hyacinthe: In Philadelphia in 1818 when he sold his allotment.

Montelius, Guillaume: From a family of merchants and tobacconists in Philadelphia. In 1819 allotment taken from him and divided into four parts. He remained in Philadelphia.

Mony, Dominique-Victor de: Named cavalry lieutenant in the royal household guards in 1814, during the First Restoration. After Waterloo, went to America, sold allotment, and joined the Champ d'Asile.

[Moquart, Antoine-Marie]: In Philadelphia in 1817. One of the first arrivals on the grant. Present between 1818 and 1837, if not longer.

Morel de Guiramond, Jean-Marie: Possibly a notary in Saint-Domingue before the uprising or, alternatively, a young royalist lawyer in the *parlement* at Port-au-Prince. Established in New Orleans in 1821. In 1827 was parish judge and notary public for Saint Charles Parish, Louisiana. Still in New Orleans in 1831.

[Morin, Charles]: Present on the grant at least 1821–34.

[Moulin, Sebastien]: In 1824 described as resident of Demopolis.

Moynier, Joseph-Aristée-Théodore: Veterinarian. Joined the Champ d'Asile.

Murat, Jean-Baptiste: Noted as a tailor in the 1819–20 Philadelphia directories.

Nardel, François: In Philadelphia in December 1817 when he sold his allotment.

Nartigue, Jean-Juste: Born in 1786 in Saint-Domingue to a family with a small coffee plantation. In Philadelphia from 1803, if not earlier. Became a U.S. citizen there in 1806. A merchant by trade, he moved with his wife to New Orleans in 1819.

Néel, Jean-Baptiste: Naval aspirant from Saint Malo. Caught distributing patriotic pamphlets after Waterloo, fled to America. Revealed to French diplomats there that *Charles Lallemand* had held talks with the Spanish ambassador. For these revelations, he was pardoned and returned to France. His allotment was taken from him in 1819.

Nelson: In October 1819 his allotment was transferred to Isaac Butaud.

Nidelet, François-Etienne: Born in Saint-Domingue in 1789. Soon after his birth, his family fled to Philadelphia. His father had been a militia artillery captain with a coffee plantation and property in Port-au-Prince. His mother, **Countess Elisabeth de la Forge de Nidelet,** did not go to Philadelphia, but remained in Saint-Domingue for a time and then fled to Cuba. She arrived in New Orleans in 1809. Nidelet's uncle **François Chapron** (father of his cousin **[Jean-Marie Chapron]**) was his godfather. In Philadelphia, Nidelet went into the silk business, both on his own account and in partnership with his cousin. Other business associates were the **Gareschés,** Cadet Bergasse, Jacques Duval, André Curcier, **Jean-Marie Dubarry,** the **Fourniers,** the **[Georges]**, and **[Frédéric Ravesies]**. In 1826 Nidelet married Celeste Pratte of Saint Louis and thus became connected to the Chouteau and Laclède families of the city. In 1827 Nidelet became a U.S. citizen and moved to Saint Louis. He died there in 1856.

[**Noël, Thomas**]: Merchant, born in 1770 in Saint-Domingue of French Canadian parents. Noël fled Saint-Domingue around 1800 and went to Virginia with members of his family. The Noël marriages put them at the center of one of the Vine and Olive colony's largest family groupings. Thomas married

[**Anne-Déolice Hurtel**], his sister [**Eliza**] married [Jean Hurtel], and his sister [**Déolice**] married [**Syriac-Firmin Hurtel**]. Thomas was related to the Noël sisters. One, [**Marie-Perrine**], married the Domingan planter **Bouttes d'Estival** in her first marriage and then her former estate manager [**Honoré Bayol**] in her second marriage. Another, [**Marie-Jeanne-Mélanie**], married [**Auguste-Firmin Follin**]). The third Noël sister was the widow **Sophie Willemin.** The **Bouttes d'Estival** sisters (daughters of [**Marie-Perrine**]) married Demopolis residents **Alexandre Fournier** and **Jules A. Chasseloup de la Martinière.**

Olivieri, Joseph: In Italy in 1830 when he authorized <u>Pascal Luciani</u> to sell his allotment.

Onfroy, Jean-Baptiste: No information.

Pagaud, Pierre: Peddler from Bordeaux, close to <u>Louis-Marie Dirat.</u> Ostensibly employed by *L'Abeille Américaine* in 1817 but suspected by French authorities of carrying messages between Bonapartists in France and America. Resident of Bordeaux in 1834 when he patented his allotment.

Pagnière, J.-Alexandre: Sold his allotment to join the Champ d'Asile.

[Paguenaud, Edouard]: Engineer who drafted allotment map for the General Land Office (reproduced above). Resident of Demopolis in 1823. Died in about 1833.

<u>Papillot, Etienne</u>: Captain in the Imperial armies. Went to America in 1816 on the same ship as Lakanal. In Philadelphia in 1818 when he sold his allotment.

[Parat, F. Romain]: Merchant in Philadelphia until 1818. In 1819 went to the grant. Member of society's executive council at Aigleville. In 1824 moved to Mobile.

[Parmentier, Nicholas-Simon]: Left France for Philadelphia in 1808. Involved in several business, notably a distillery. A U.S. citizen by 1812, became a militia colonel in the war against England. In 1816 became secretary of the society. Led the first party of settlers to the grant in mid-1817. In 1818 became chief justice of Marengo County. Also served as notary public. In 1821 he left the grant for Pensacola, where he got a minor post, probably in the customs service. He was still there at the end of 1826.

Pascal, Paul: In Philadelphia at the end of 1817 when he sold his allotment.

Pastol, Widow Julie: In Havana, Cuba, in 1820 when she sold her allotment.

[**Payen, Auguste (younger brother)**]: Present on the grant in 1820. In 1831 in Mobile. Died in 1840, leaving four or five children.

[**Payen, César (older brother)**]: Present on the grant in 1820. In 1831 in Mobile.

[**Payen, Claude (father)**]: Present on the grant 1819–25. In Mobile 1831–34.

Pelagot, Antoine-Zacharie: No information.

Penazi, Louis: Born in Parma in 1790. Joined the Imperial Guard in 1806. Transferred to the light infantry as second lieutenant in 1809. Served in Napoleon's principal campaigns (Poland, Prussia, Spain, Austria, and Russia). Taken prisoner in the retreat from Russia. Claimed rank of captain in 1815. Went to the United States after the collapse of Napoleon's empire and joined the Champ d'Asile.

Pénières, Jean-Baptiste-Emile (son): Son of below. Co-*commissaire des guerres* (with *Maurice Laurent*) of the Champ d'Asile. In *Charles Lallemand's* inner circle. Still in New Orleans in 1821.

[Pénières-Delors, Jean-Augustin (father):] Born in the Corrèze in 1762 to a family of landed lawyers. Became a lawyer himself. Elected to legislatures 1792–1815. As a deputy in the Convention, voted to spare Louis XVI's life. He remained moderate in spite of the Convention's growing radicalism. During the Hundred Days, he accepted a place in the legislature. This, together with his membership in the Convention, led to his exile in 1816. Went to America in 1816. Was an exploring commissioner of the society. Present on the grant in 1818. Became a U.S. citizen, moved to Florida, and became a government agent for the Seminoles. He died there of yellow fever in 1821.

Peraldi, Toussaint: Probably from one of the numerous Corsican Bonapartist families of that name. In Philadelphia in 1818 when he sold his grant.

[Perard, Jean]: In 1819 François Melizet and [Corneille Roudet] paid for his passage from France to Alabama. He died soon after arriving on the grant.

Perdreauville, René de: Norman nobleman who had been mentor of Marie-Antoinette's pages before the Revolution and had resumed a similar function in the Imperial court. In about 1818 he and his wife opened the Lancastrean Academy for Young Ladies in New Orleans and remained there as its director-owner until at least 1822.

Petitval, Jean-Baptiste: Architect, engineer, and inventor whose creations included a tree-stump remover and a fireproof steering apparatus for steamboats. City engineer of Charleston, South Carolina, 1821–27. By the mid-1830s had moved to New York City, where he wrote about reorganizing the U.S. Corps of Military Engineers.

Pfister, Amand: Fled Saint-Domingue in the early 1790s to Philadelphia where he became a storekeeper. Received part of Jean-Baptiste Néel's allotment and moved to Mobile. His sister [**Augustine-Elizabeth**] married [Nicholas-Basile Meslier]. His daughter **Amanda** married William Raser, a patentee. His son **Amand Jr.** was an important Alabama freemason.

Pichon, Jean-Claude-Charles: Went into exile with Pierre-François Réal. By 1827 had returned to Paris where he did chemistry experiments with Réal. Still in Paris in 1832.

[Pierce brothers]: Jonathan Pierce present on grant in 1818. No information about the other brothers.

Pillero, Pierre: No information.

Plaidaut, François: In Philadelphia in December 1817 when he sold his allotment. Married **Marie-Angélique Ravesies,** the sister of [**Frédéric Ravesies**].

Plantevigne, Antoine, Jr.: Probably a merchant in New Orleans from 1816 to 1822. Back in France by 1834 when he patented his allotment. Probably from Bordeaux.

[*Plenville, Guillaume-Victor de*]: Of Champ d'Asile. Briefly on grant. Dead mid-1821.

Pochard, Augustin-François: Close to Réal. In 1817 a visitor to <u>Descourts's</u> Bonapartist tavern in New York City. Sold his allotment in 1818.

[Poculo, Benoit-M].: Settled on the grant in mid-1817. Dead by November 1821.

Pothier, Simon: Members of the Pothier family were established in Philadelphia by 1803, if not earlier. Married sister of **Louis-Descoins Belair.**

[Promis, Guillaume]: Jeweler in Philadelphia from at least 1809, the year he married [**Eulalie-Descoins Belair**], the daughter of **Louis-Descoins Belair.** Settled on grant. In 1850 [**Eulalie**] was still alive in Marengo County.

Prompt: No information.

[**Prudhomme, Charles**]: Tinman, established in Philadelphia in 1817. Present on the grant in 1818. By 1824 had moved to Mobile where he was still living in 1832.

[**Pueek, Jacques (or Jean)**]: Merchant (or son of a merchant) from Saint-Domingue. Present on the grant in 1819 and 1820. In 1821 he relocated to New Orleans where he became a hardware merchant. He died a few months later.

Quésart, Jean: Became a U.S. citizen in Philadelphia in 1805. By 1822 established in New Orleans as a tobacco and chocolate manufacturer.

[Ragon]: Briefly on grant.

[<u>Raoul, Nicholas-Louis</u>]: Born in 1788 in the Vosges, son of a general. Graduate of the Ecole Polytechnique, joined the artillery of the Imperial Guard. Captain by 1814. Married [Thérèse-Albora de Sinabaldi], maid of honor to Napoleon's sister, Queen Caroline of Naples. Raoul followed Napoleon to Elba, where he was given command of the Guard's artillery. Was in the vanguard of the troops who led Napoleon back to France in 1815. Rewarded with promotion to the rank of major and command of a portion of the artillery of the Imperial Guard. In this capacity, he fought at Waterloo, was wounded, and taken prisoner. Discharged in December 1815 as a captain, he left for Rome where he was entrusted with educating one of Napoleon's nephews. He then left for America, where he served briefly as general in the army of the insurgent republic of Buenos Aires before coming to the United States. By 1822 on the grant, where he ran a ferry and, with his wife, an inn. In 1824 they left for Central America, where the couple was divorced. Raoul married a local woman but that marriage also ended. By 1832 he was major-general of the Guatemalan artillery but still sought reinstatement in the French army. He was welcomed back and given the rank of lieutenant colonel. In 1833 his use of cannon against the revolutionary workers of Lyon helped crush their uprising. The regime promoted him to colonel and gave him a regiment. Soon after, he married his third wife, Josephine-Françoise-Octavie Pavans de Ceccaty, who came from a prominent Besançon family and brought with her a substantial dowry. In 1845 Raoul became a general and was placed in charge of the artillery school at Besançon. He died in 1850.

[Rapin, Mathieu]: Nephew of below. Passed through grant on way to Pointe Coupée, Louisiana, where he resided 1822–27.

Rapin, Joseph: In 1822 described himself as a gentleman of Philadelphia.

Ravesies, Emile: Brother of below. Of Philadelphia in 1820 when he sold his allotment.

[**Ravesies, Frédéric-Guillaume-Marie**]: From a Domingan family that had owned coffee plantations but sold them before 1789. Some of his family were killed in the revolt. He fled to Philadelphia and became a U.S. citizen in 1803. His first wife, **Marie Roan,** was also a Domingan refugee. She died in 1815. He married [**Adèle-Gertrude de Sevré**], widow of General David who had been killed in the troubles of Saint-Domingue. Ravesies was a prominent Philadelphia businessman, both in his own right and in partnership with the **Garesché de la Poterie** brothers and André Curcier. Ravesies also employed two other grantees, **Julien-Lèon Salaignac** and François Melizet. He came to the grant after 1820. Became the society's agent, founder of Arcola, and most influential Frenchman in Marengo County. In Demopolis, he entered a business partnership with **Jules Martinière** in 1828. In 1830 he owned forty-five slaves and in 1850 more than eighty, a measure of his success. He eventually moved to Mobile where he died in 1856. Daughter, [**Josephine**], married [John McRae], an important Vine and Olive patentee. Son, [**Frédéric Jr.**], married [Isabella Strudwick], daughter of another family of Vine and Olive patentees. Sister **Marie-Angélique** married grantee **François Plaidaut**. Stepdaughter [**Marie-Pauline**] married [George N. Stewart], and stepdaughter [**Cecilia-Agnès**] married Col. John Foy, another Vine and Olive patentee.

Réal, Pierre-François: Born near Paris in 1757, son of a gamekeeper. Skilled orator and criminal lawyer who made a name for himself during the Revolution as a prosecutor. Helped draft the Napoleonic Code. During the empire, was one of four councilors of state under Fouché in charge of the national police. Was responsible for Paris. Napoleon named him count in 1808. During the Hundred Days was chief commissioner of police. Exiled on 24 July 1815, he went to the United States. Bought land in upstate New York and began a business with Edmund Genet. He sought royal pardon, which arrived in 1819. He remained in the United States, however, until 1827 when, in failing health, he was brought back to France by his daughter. He stayed out of public life and died in Paris in 1834.

Richard, Etienne: A self-described gentleman. In Philadelphia in 1819 but had relocated to New York City by 1831.

Richard, Georges: In Philadelphia at the end of 1817 when he sold his allotment.

Riegert, Gabriel-Valentin-Philippe: Born at Tallien (Isère) in 1794. Graduated Saint-Cyr in 1811. Lieutenant in 1815. Went to America and joined the Champ d'Asile. Dismissed from the army in 1822. Reintegrated in 1825 as a lieutenant, he achieved the rank of captain six years later. On the inactive list in 1834 and retired in 1849.

Rigau, Antoine: Born in 1758 at Agen (Lot-et-Garonnne), son of a postmaster. Married Anne-Joseph Loyers in 1788 and in 1805 Marie-Margueritte Probst. Soldier in the royal army before 1789. Captain in 1792 and rose through the ranks. General in 1807, named baron in 1808. Much decorated and wounded, kept on active service by the Bourbons in 1814. He rallied to Napoleon in 1815 and sheltered the fugitive [Lefebvre-Desnouettes] in his house. Named in the proscription ordinance of 24 July 1815, he fled the country and was sentenced to death in absentia. In 1817 went to the United States with his son, *Narcisse-Périclès,* and daughter, *Antonia*. They accompanied him to the Champ d'Asile. After returning to New Orleans, Rigau denounced *Charles Lallemand.* He died in 1820 in Louisiana in the company of his daughter, who had become a teacher in Opelousas.

Rigau, Narcisse-Périclès: Son of above. Born at Lille in 1794. Graduated Saint-Cyr in 1812 and became a captain two years later. As his father's aide-de-camp, fought at the Battle of Dresden, where he was wounded twice. Went with his father and sister to America and sold his allotment to join the Champ d'Asile. After it failed, he stayed in Louisiana until 1821. By 1831 had rejoined the French army as lieutenant colonel.

Rivet, Georges: Died in New York City in 1820.

[**Rivière, Jean-Amédée**]: Surgeon. Present on the grant from 1818 to 1822. Then moved to Point Coupée, near New Orleans, where he practiced medicine. Then moved to Tennessee where he scraped by giving French and Spanish lessons.

Robaglia, Joseph: Probably a former Napoleonic officer from Ajaccio (Corsica) who, by the late 1820s, had become the personal secretary of Napoleon's mother, in exile in Rome. He enjoyed the trust and confidence of Joseph Bonaparte.

Robard, Joseph: Philadelphia merchant from 1808. U.S. citizen by 1808. Brother-in-law of **Pierre Ducoing,** married to his sister Sophie. Died in Philadelphia in 1824.

Robin, Thomas: Resident of New York City in 1818.

Roland, Jean-François: Born in 1770, probably at Lons le Saunier (Jura) where he owned land. Nephew of Pierre-François Réal. A commissioner-general of police under his uncle during the empire. Accompanied Réal to the United States in 1816.

Roster, John: No information.

[Roudel, Nicholas]: A farmer on the grant from 1821–23, if not longer.

[Roudet, Corneille (the younger)]: Brother-in-law of François Melizet, who married his sister. Roudet himself married Melizet's sister, [Marie-Thérèse]. Their elder son, Jean-Baptiste, became a grocer in Mobile, and their younger son, [Pierre-Corneille], became a planter on the grant and became the second husband of [Marie-Anne-Ursule Thouron]. Corneille Roudet was on the grant in 1818 when named ensign of the county militia company. In 1819 a member of the executive council at Aigleville. In 1831 published an article on vine cultivation. Roudet and his wife moved to Mobile in 1837. When he died, [Marie-Thérèse] went back to Philadelphia where she died in 1852 or 1853.

[Rougier, Amédée]: Latecomer to grant, who shared a forty-acre reserve with [Jean Perard].

Ruffier, Ferdinand: No information.

Saignier, Henri-Antoine: Riding master, offering stabling services and riding lessons in Philadelphia in 1818–20. Sold his allotment in December 1817.

Saint-Félix, Jean-Baptiste-Gilles Regnaud de: Born in 1790 in Saint-Domingue to a coffee planter family. Became a U.S. citizen in Philadelphia in 1812. A merchant, Saint-Félix married the daughter of Charles Maltby, also a Philadelphia merchant, in 1818.

[Saint-Guiron, Alexandre]: Younger brother of below. In Philadelphia until 1818 when he moved to the grant. By 1825 he had returned to Roquefort (Landes) in France.

[Saint-Guiron, Pierre-Pascal]: Elder brother of above. Present on grant in 1823, but by 1830 in Mobile where he died in 1849.

Salaignac, Julien-Léon: Son of a refugee Domingan coffee planter who fled to the United States. When his father died, the will was witnessed by Vine and Olive members Germain Combes and **Pierre Lacombe.** On his death, he owed money to Vine and Olive members [Nicholas Parmentier] and **Louis Tulane,** among others. Julien-Léon was born in New York City in 1796. His elder brother **Auguste-Casimir** worked for the firm of Curcier and [**Ravesies**].

Salmon, François: Possibly an accountant. In Philadelphia in 1817.

Sary, Jean-Mathieu-Alexandre.: Born in 1792 in Corsica to a family related to the Bonapartes. Graduated Saint-Cyr in 1807 and joined the navy. In 1814 joined Napoleon in exile on Elba where he was commander-in-second of the *Inconstant,* the principal vessel in the Elban fleet. Sary helped convey Napoleon back to France in 1815, for which he was pursued by the Bourbons. Fled to Corsica, Italy, and then the United States where he served Joseph Bonaparte until 1835. Sary sold his allotment in 1817, planning to join the Champ d'Asile. But he did not. Instead, he married **Emma Saint-Georges,** a refugee Domingan in Philadelphia. In 1835 they moved to Paris where Sary founded a pottery factory. In the late 1840s, became president of the Philanthropic Society of the Old Imperial Army. A true Bonapartist, he named his son Napoleon. He died in 1862.

[Savary, Alexandre (or Joseph)]: Became a U.S. citizen in Philadelphia in 1816. In 1818 he moved to Mobile where he lived from 1820 to 1825. In 1825 he went to the grant.

Savournin, Joseph: Sold his allotment in early December 1817.

Scasso, Vincent: No information.

Schoen, Jean-Sebastien: In Philadelphia in 1818 when he sold his grant. Several months later he wrote to Stephen Girard, describing his financial straits and asking for a job.

Schubart, Henry: In Philadelphia in 1818 when he sold his grant. Stayed until the 1830s.

Schultz, Jean: Born in Warsaw in 1768. Joined the Polish army as a cavalry officer in 1783. Served Poland until it disappeared in the Third Partition in 1795. Then joined a Polish legion in the French army. By 1806 a captain. In 1808 joined the Lancers of the Vistula, but taken prisoner in Spain. Spent 1809–13 in English jails. In 1814 released and joined Napoleon's guard on Elba. Returned to France with the former emperor in 1815, was promoted to captain with the rank of lieutenant colonel in the (Polish) Lancers of the Imperial Guard in which *Charrasin* and *Jourdan* had served. After Waterloo, imprisoned by the British on Malta with *Charles Lallemand.* Released in 1816, fled to America where he joined the Champ d'Asile. In 1820 returned to France (with *Malezewsky*) and tried to rejoin the French army. Rebuffed, he went to Italy where he joined the Carbonari's ill-fated attempt to conquer Naples. Then went to constitutionalist Spain where he commanded a body of foreign volunteers. When the constitutionalist cause collapsed, became a colonel in the Egyptian army occupying Mecca in the 1820s.

Sévelinge, Joseph: Cordial distiller, son of a Domingan family that owned coffee plantations. Became a U.S. citizen in 1813. His sister **Marie-Françoise** married Joseph Beylle. Beylle was godfather to one of Joseph's sons. He died in Philadelphia in 1836.

Sibenthal brothers: No information.

[Simon]: Possibly Mathurin Simon, Bordeaux beltmaker born in 1782. Went to New Orleans in 1811. On the grant in 1818–19. In 1825 was a farmer in western Georgia.

Soulas: No information.

Stephens, Samuel James: Born in Dublin, Ireland, 1790. Joined Napoleon's Irish Regiment in 1807, but captured by the English in 1809. Escaped in 1811 and rejoined the French army. Second lieutenant in 1812. Promoted to lieutenant during the Hundred Days. Went to America after Waterloo, sold his allotment, and joined the Champ d'Asile. On return to New Orleans, married a widow. Lived in Saint Tammany Parish.

[Stewart, George Noble]: Born in 1799 to Catholic parents. His father, a former naval officer and merchant, died in 1804. His mother [Helena Stewart née Counsell] married Vine and Olive member [Michel Leboutellier]. Stewart was raised and educated in Philadelphia. Became a clerk in a drug concern. In 1818 went to the grant, with his mother and Leboutellier, who died there in 1810. On the grant, his widowed mother married Gen. Juan Rico. In Alabama, George Stewart studied law. Admitted to the bar in 1821. This began a career in law and politics that took him to the state senate in 1847. Stewart married [**Marie-Pauline Davide**], stepdaughter of [**Frédéric Ravesies**]. In

1827 Stewart moved to Tuscaloosa and became mayor. Then moved to Mobile.

Stollenwerk, Pierre-Ange-Chevalier: Born about 1777, second son of Domingan watchmaker, coffee planter, and merchant **Pierre-Hubert Stollenwerk.** Family fled to Philadelphia in 1793, but then moved to New York City. Pierre-Ange-Chevalier apprenticed as a watchmaker and jeweler, probably with his uncle **Pierre-Martin Stollenwerk.** He died in September 1817 in Saint Stephens, Alabama, en route to the grant.

[**Stollenwerk, Pierre-François**]: Born in Saint-Domingue in 1775. Eldest son of **Pierre-Hubert Stollenwerk.** Like his brother (above), he apprenticed as a watchmaker and jeweler in the family shop in New York. Married another Domingan refugee, [**Geneviève-Antoinette Dagneaux**], widow of **Antoine Coupery.** They moved to the grant and had a large family that was the core (with the [**Chaudrons**]) of the Vine and Olive colony's largest family grouping.

Stribaud, Charles: No information.

[Tabelée, Guillaume]: In 1817 Philadelphia lottery and exchange broker. On grant at end of 1817 when appointed postmaster of Aigleville. Appointment revoked a few weeks later.

Taillade, François-Louis: Born 1775 at Lorient (Morbihan). In 1787 became a cabin boy in the royal navy. Served the Revolution and empire. In 1802 embarked for Saint-Domingue where he served in the ill-fated campaign to reconquer the island. After, he continued his service in the navy. In 1814 joined Napoleon on Elba, where he was captain of the *Inconstant,* the Elban navy's main ship. Relieved of his post when he ran the ship aground. Given command of the marines of the Imperial Guard. Returned with Napoleon to France. Discharged from the navy by the Bourbons in 1815. Went to America where he became General Vandamme's supporter. Died in Baltimore in 1819.

Tasca, Jean-Baptiste: Italian confectioner. Went to Philadelphia and became a U.S. citizen in 1817. Stayed in Philadelphia until 1820. In 1824 died in Alvarado, Mexico.

Taverly: No information.

Teisseire, Antoine: Philadelphia merchant from at least 1803 when became a U.S. citizen. In 1817 formed a partnership with **Charles Bruguière.** Teisseire's daughter **Hester-Héloise** married **Charles Bruguière Jr.** Died in Paris in 1834.

[Terrier, Alexandre-René]: In Philadelphia from 1794. Became a U.S. citizen in 1818. Lived on the grant from 1819 to 1821.

Teterel, François-Hyacinthe: Born in 1752 near Havre de Grace, France. In 1782 merchant in Saint-Domingue with a large bakery that employed sixteen slaves. His daughter [**Emilie-Catherine**] married [**Jean-Marie Chapron**] in Philadelphia. In Philadelphia, Teterel was a merchant on his own account and in partnership with [**Marc-Antoine Frenaye**]. His wife, **Marie née Drouet,** was probably related to **Pierre Drouet**. Teterel died in Philadelphia in 1824.

[**Texier, Jean**]: Present on grant in 1818. Resident of Greensboro, 1827–30.

Texier de la Pommeraye: In Philadelphia 1818–22. Sold allotment in 1818 and tried to sell a politically sensitive document on the Pichegru conspiracy to French diplomats. Styled himself "former chief of the general staff of the French army." French authorities called him a lieutenant colonel. In 1822 he wrote a book of grammar.

Thouron, Pierre (father): Born 1757 in La Rochelle, son of a Protestant landlord. Naval officer and merchant before 1789. Fought against the English at Pondichery in 1778. In the early 1780s resigned from the navy and became a merchant. At the outbreak of the Revolution, joined the local National Guard, beginning a decadelong military career spent fighting the rebels of the Vendée. In the early 1800s he and his family left France. In 1802 arrived in Philadelphia, where he was a teacher and accountant. His granddaughter [Marie-Anne-Ursule Thouron] married [Pierre-Corneille Roudet]. Letters to Grouchy were addressed to him care of Thouron, as were the Lakanal conspiracy papers. Thouron died in Philadelphia in 1824.

Thouron, Nicolas-Elisée (son): Born in La Rochelle in 1788. Arrived in Philadelphia with his father in 1802. Became a U.S. citizen in 1814. Was a merchant. In 1826 he married [**Victorie Butaud née George**] in her second marriage. In 1827 she died in Philadelphia. Nicholas-Elisée remained in Philadelphia where he died in 1868.vb

Torta, Jean: Sold his allotment to join the Champ d'Asile.

Tournel, Jacques: Spanish officer. Sold his allotment to join the Champ d'Asile.

[Transon, Jean]: Present on the grant in 1818. Died 1821, leaving a widow, [Anne-Clement Transon], who remained in Demopolis.

Truc, Joseph: Left Marseille in 1816 for New Orleans and opened a store. He left in France large debts and angry creditors. His store failed; he was incarcerated for fraud and died in prison in 1819, two hundred thousand francs in debt.

Tulane, Louis-Etienne: Son of **Louis Tulane,** a bourgeois of Tours. **Louis** went to Saint-Domingue with his brother-in-law. They ran a lumber business employing two thousand slaves. With the uprising, the Tulanes went to

Philadelphia in 1791 and then Princeton, New Jersey, in 1792. They had several children there including the future Vine and Olive members **Louis-Etienne** and **Victor,** as well as **Paul,** founder of Tulane University. **Louis-Etienne** and his brother **Victor** went to New Orleans as very young men.

Tulane, Victor: See above.

Valcour, Aimée: Founded Austerlitz plantation in Point Coupée, Louisiana. Was so successful that he was known as the Prince of the Planters. Specialized in sugar cane and in the 1850s went to Cuba to learn new techniques. Had Bonapartist sympathies.

Vallot, Joseph: Born in 1794 in Dijon (Côte d'Or) to a wealthy family. Graduated Saint-Cyr in 1812–13 and became a second lieutenant in the Imperial Guard. Noted for his outspoken Bonapartist sentiments, was dismissed from the army in 1815. Went to America, sold his allotment, and joined the Champ d'Asile. Back in France by 1822, working as a teacher. Had died by 1861, if not earlier.

Vandamme, Dominique-Joseph-René: Born in Cassel (Flandre) in 1770. Joined the colonial troops before the Revolution. Posted to Martinique. In 1790 deserted and returned to France. Raised a company and became its captain. A born warrior, he rose rapidly. Became a general in 1793. A pillager, lined his own pockets by levying contributions on French and foreign civilians. His depredations were so egregious that he was suspended. But his battlefield prowess saved his career, and in 1808 Napoleon named him count. In 1815 Vandamme was exiled. He came to the United States in 1817. Sought Bourbon clemency. During his exile, he was notorious for verbal attacks on Grouchy, blaming him for losing the Battle of Waterloo. Vandamme returned to France in 1819 and was pardoned. Recovered his rank, but retired in 1825. Died in 1830.

Vasquez, Jean-Emmanuel: Spanish colonel who sold his allotment and joined the Champ d'Asile. His wife sought to join him there, but got sick and had to remain in New Orleans. Vasquez's son was in the French army from 1807 until at least 1820.

Vaugine de Nuisement, Charles-François: His mother owned property in Saint-Domingue. He himself lived in Arkansas Post, where he married Mademoiselle Bogy.

Vernhes, Jean-Vincent: In the textile business in Philadelphia, where he still lived in 1830.

Verrier, François: In 1833 in New Orleans. Married [Floride-Josephine née Boutière].

Vial, Antoine: In Philadelphia in 1819 when he sold his allotment.

[Villars, Charles]: Philadelphia china dealer. Became U.S. citizen in 1806. One-time vice president of the society. Went to the grant in 1817. By 1820 a merchant in New Orleans.

Villemont, Charles Melchior de: Commander of Arkansas Post under the Spanish. In 1802 he left to take up a new post under the Spanish in Pensacola. He married Catherine Bogy, daughter of Joseph and Marie-Louis-Dugay Bogy. He returned to Arkansas around 1810–11 to claim his extensive Spanish land grants. He died in 1823.

[*Viole, François*]: Joined the Champ d'Asile, where he met his future wife, [*Léontine Desportes*]. In 1818 they went to the grant where they were married. Viole was described by [Corneille Roudet] as "an intimate friend of [General Lefebvre's]" and was responsible for bringing Madeira vines from New Orleans to the colony. By 1833 Viole and his wife had gone to Saint Martinsville in Louisiana. He was dead by 1846.

Vitalba, Jean-Baptiste: Napoleonic officer. Sold allotment to join the Champ d'Asile.

Vogelsang, Daniel: Cabinetmaker, described as Swedish in some documents, French in others. Became U.S. citizen in Philadelphia in 1818, the same year he sold his allotment.

[Vorhees, Samuel]: Present on the grant in 1818. In 1819 his allotment was taken away.

Vorster, Emile: Born at Schweln (Grand Duchy of Berg) in 1788. Became a second lieutenant in the army of Berg in 1808 and rose through the ranks. In 1814 transferred to the French army with the rank of major. In 1815 he rallied to Napoleon. Went to America, sold his allotment, and joined the Champ d'Asile, where he drowned.

Weil, James: No information.

Wells, Edward B.: In 1818 described as an emigrant from France living in Philadelphia.

[**Willemin, Sophie (née Noël)**]: Widow, related to [**Thomas Noël**] and sister-in-law to [**Honoré Bayol**]. She was still living in Marengo County in the 1830s.

Notes

Abbreviations used in notes:

AAE	Archives des Affaires Etrangères
ADAH	Alabama Department of Archives and History
Adams papers	Microfilmed Presidential Papers, John Quincy Adams
AG	Archives de la Guerre
AHN	Archivo Histórico Nacional
AN	Archives Nationales
Apodaca correspondence	Huntington Library
APS	American Philosophical Society
CAD	Centre des Archives Diplomatiques
CP	Correspondence Politique (in AAE)
FO	Foreign Office (in PRO)
NARA	National Archives and Records Administration
PRO	Public Records Office
RG	Record Group

Introduction

1. "Demopolis, Alabama: Worth an extra day . . . ," promotional brochure from the Demopolis Area Chamber of Commerce.

2. There is unfortunately no cultural history of the creation of southern planter identity. There are, however, many works that address aspects of the question. See, for example, Thomas Perkins Abernathy, *The Formative Period in Alabama, 1815–1828* (Tuscaloosa and London: University of Alabama Press, 1990); W. J. Cash, *The Mind of the South* (1941), reprint (New York: Vintage Books, 1969); Charles Shepard Davis, *The Cotton Kingdom in Alabama* (Montgomery: Alabama State Department of Archives and History, 1939); Daniel S. Dupre, *Transforming the Cotton Frontier: Madison County, Alabama, 1800–1840* (Baton Rouge: Louisiana State University Press, 1997); Virginia Van der Veer Hamilton, *Alabama: A History* (New York and London: W. W. Norton, 1984); Harvey H. Jackson, "Time, Frontier, and the Alabama Black Belt: Searching for W. J. Cash's Planter," *Alabama Review* 44, no. 4

(October 1991): 243–68; Florence King, *Southern Ladies and Gentlemen* (New York: Stein and Day, 1975); James Oakes, *The Ruling Race: A History of American Slaveholders* (New York: Knopf, 1982); and Bertram Wyatt-Brown, *Yankee Saints and Southern Sinners* (Baton Rouge: Louisiana State University Press, 1985), 131–54.

3. Albert James Pickett, *History of Alabama and Incidentally of Georgia and Mississippi from the Earliest Period* (1851), reprint (Birmingham, Ala.: Birmingham Book and Magazine), 2:386–99. For an example of a romanticized account see, Anne Bozeman Lyon, "Bonapartists in Alabama," a piece originally published in the *Southern Home Journal* in 1900 and then reprinted in the *Gulf States Historical Magazine* in 1903, and finally in the *Alabama Historical Quarterly* 25, nos. 3–4 (fall–winter 1963): 227–41.

4. Gaius Whitfield Jr., "The French Grants in Alabama: A History of the Founding of Demopolis," *Transactions of the Alabama Historical Society* 4 (1899–1903): 321–55.

5. For example, Judge S. G. Woolf and Col. F. G. Jonah, "Demopolis Founded in 1818 by Exiled French Royalists," *Selma Times-Journal* (2 March 1927); Frank Willis Barnett, "Demopolis, Site of Early French Settlement, among the Most Romantic Spots in Alabama: Venture in Growing Olives and Grapes Turned Out to Be Failure," *Birmingham News* (May 21, 1932); and James Saxon Childers, "A Tale of Old France in New Alabama," *Birmingham News* (January 23, 1938).

6. Winston Smith, *Days of Exile: The Story of the Vine and Olive Colony* (Tuscaloosa: University of Alabama Press, 1967), 69.

7. Kent Gardien, "The Splendid Fools: Philadelphia Origins of Alabama's Vine and Olive Colony," *Pennsylvania Magazine of History and Biography* 104, no. 4 (October 1980): 491–507; Gardien, "The Domingan Kettle: Philadelphia-Émigré Planters in Alabama," *National Genealogical Society Quarterly* 76, no. 3 (September 1988): 173–87; and Gardien, "Take Pity on Our Glory: Men of the Champ d'Asile," *Southwestern Historical Quarterly* 87, no. 3 (January 1984): 241–68. Gardien's research notes, on deposit at the Alabama Department of Archives and History, are an invaluable source on not only the inhabitants of the Vine and Olive colony but also the Domingan diaspora in America more generally.

8. For example, Jose Maria Miquel I Vergès, *Diccionario de Insurgentes* (Mexico: Porrúa, 1969) does not mention important non-Hispanic actors in the Mexican Revolution, such as Louis-Michel Aury who founded the insurgent privateer base on Galveston Island and held from the Mexican Congress the office of military and civil governor of Texas.

9. A notable exception is Julius Scott, "The Common Wind: Currents of Afro-American Communication in the Era of the Haitian Revolution," Ph.D. diss., Duke University, 1986.

10. Dorothy Burne Goebel, "British Trade to the Spanish Colonies, 1796–1823," *American Historical Review* 43, no. 2 (January 1938): 288–320; R. A. Humphreys, "British Merchants and South American Independence," in Humphreys, *Tradition and Revolt in Latin America and Other Essays* (London: Weidenfeld and Nicolson, 1969), 106–29; William W. Kaufman, *British Policy and the Independence of Latin America, 1804–1828* (New Haven: Yale University Press, 1951); W. Alison Philips, "Great Britain and the Continental Alliance, 1816–1822," in A. W. Ward and G. P. Gooch, eds., *The Cambridge History of British Foreign Policy, 1783–1919* (New York: Cambridge University press, 1923), 2:3–50; Charles Kingsley Webster,

The Foreign Policy of Castlereagh, 1812–1815: Britain and the Reconstruction of Europe (London: G. Bell and Sons, 1931); and Webster, *Britain and the Foreign Policy of Castlereagh, 1815–1822: Britain and the European Alliance* (London: G. Bell and Sons, 1925).

11. Samuel Flagg Bemis, *John Quincy Adams and the Foundations of American Foreign Policy* (New York: Alfred A. Knopf, 1965); Isaac Joslin Cox, *The West Florida Controversy, 1798–1813: A Study in American Diplomacy* (Baltimore: Johns Hopkins University Press, 1918); Worthington Chauncey Ford, "John Quincy Adams and the Monroe Doctrine," *American Historical Review* 7, no. 4 (July 1902): 676–96; Hubert Bruce Fuller, *The Purchase of Florida: Its History and Diplomacy* (Cleveland: Burrows Brothers, 1906); Charles Carroll Griffin, *The United States and the Disruption of the Spanish Empire, 1810–1822: A Study of the Relations of the United States with Spain and with the Rebel Spanish Colonies* (New York: Columbia University Press, 1937); Dexter Perkins, *The Monroe Doctrine, 1823–1826* (Cambridge: Harvard University Press, 1927); and Arthur Preston Whitaker, *The United States and the Independence of Latin America, 1800–1830* (Baltimore: Johns Hopkins University Press, 1941).

12. J. Fred Rippy, *Rivalry of the United States and Great Britain over Latin America (1808–1830)* (Baltimore: Johns Hopkins University Press, 1929); Humphreys, "Anglo-American Rivalries and Spanish American Emancipation," in Humphreys, *Tradition and Revolt*, 130–53; Bradford Perkins, *Castlereagh and Adams: England and the United States, 1812–1823* (Berkeley: University of California Press, 1964); and Edward Howland Tatum Jr., *The United States and Europe, 1815–1823: A Study in the Background of the Monroe Doctrine* (Berkeley: University of California Press, 1936);.

13. Timothy E. Anna, *Spain and the Loss of America* (Lincoln: University of Nebraska Press, 1983); Russell H. Bartley, *Imperial Russia and the Struggle for Latin American Independence, 1808–1828* (Austin: University of Texas Press, 1978); Michael P. Costeloe, "Spain and the Latin American Wars of Independence: The Free Trade Controversy, 1810–1820," *Hispanic American Historical Review* 61, no. 2 (1981): 209–34; and William Spence Robertson, *France and Latin American Independence* (Baltimore: Johns Hopkins University Press, 1939).

Chapter 1

1. The title of this chapter is a quote from Jean-Guillaume Hyde de Neuville. See n. 9 below for the source of the quote.

2. The following paragraph is based on a variety of accounts: R. F. Delderfield, *The Golden Millstones: Napoleon's Brothers and Sisters* (London: Weidenfeld and Nicolson, 1964), 210–35; Gilbert Martineau, *Lucien Bonaparte, prince de Canino* (Paris: Editions France-Empire, 1989), 284–302; Bernardine Melchior-Bonnet, *Jerome Bonaparte ou l'envers de l'épopée* (Paris: Librairie Académique Perrin, 1979), 300–321; Desmond Seward, *Napoleon's Family* (London: Weidenfeld and Nicolson, 1986), 179–92; and David Stacton, *The Bonapartes* (New York: Simon and Schuster, 1966), 161–76.

3. Accounts of Napoleon's odyssey abound. Among the better ones are Jean Duhamel, *The Fifty Days: Napoleon in England,* trans. R. A. Hall (London: Hunt-Davis, 1969), and

Gilbert Martineau, *Napoleon Surrenders,* trans. Frances Partridge (London: John Murray, 1971).

4. Having left France as a young man in 1774, Girard had, after a two-year sojourn in Saint-Domingue, come to the United States and grown wealthy by establishing new trade routes between Philadelphia and Canton. A serviceable biography of Girard is John Bach McMaster, *The Life and Times of Stephen Girard: Mariner and Merchant,* 2 vols. (Philadelphia: J. B. Lippincott, 1918). On the development of the China trade, see Jonathan Goldstein, *Philadelphia and the China Trade, 1682–1846: Commercial, Cultural, and Attitudinal Effects* (University Park: Pennsylvania State University Press, 1978).

5. It was known as Point Breeze. Girard not only managed Joseph's finances, but also supervised the construction of Joseph's estate. APS, Stephen Girard papers, reel 61, Joseph, Count de Survilliers to Stephen Girard (Philadelphia, 11/25 and 12/4/1815, 1/6, 1/7, and 1/11/1816).

6. CAD, postes, Philadelphia, subseries B, 18, Consul at New York to Consul at Philadelphia (New York, 3/30/1816).

7. Owen Connelly, *The Gentle Bonaparte: The Story of Napoleon's Elder Brother* (New York: Macmillan, 1968). Much of the preceding information on Joseph in America is drawn from this work.

8. For a general overview of the French exiles in America after 1815, see Ronald Creagh, *Nos cousins d'Amérique: Histoire des français aux Etats-Unis* (Paris: Payot, 1988), 228–36; Marcel Doher, *Proscrits et exilés après Waterloo* (Paris: J. Peyronnet, 1965); Edith Philips, "Les refugiés Bonapartistes en Amérique (1815–1830)," Ph.D. diss., Université de Paris, 1923; Jesse S. Reeves, *The Napoleonic Exiles in America: A Study in American Diplomatic History* (Baltimore: Johns Hopkins University Press, 1905); Joseph George Rosengarten, *French Colonists and Exiles in the United States* (Philadelphia: J. B. Lippincott, 1907); and Simone de la Souchère Deléry, *Napoleon's Soldiers in America* (Gretna, La.: Pelican, 1972). On French refugees in America in an earlier period, see Frances Sergeant Childs, *French Refugee Life in the United States, 1790–1800* (Baltimore: Johns Hopkins University Press, 1940).

9. AAE, CP, U.S., 74, Hyde de Neuville to the Duke de Richelieu (New Brunswick, 10/17/1817). On Hyde, see Françoise Watel, *Jean-Guillaume Hyde de Neuville (1776–1857): Conspirateur et diplomate* (Paris: Direction des Archives et de la Documentation, Ministère des Affaires Etrangères, 1987).

10. Guillaume de Bertier de Sauvigny, *The Bourbon Restoration,* trans. Lynn M. Case (Philadelphia: University of Pennsylvania Press, 1966), 117; Daniel Resnick, *The White Terror and the Political Reaction after Waterloo* (Cambridge: Harvard University Press, 1966), 67–70; and Jean Tulard, *Joseph Fouché* (Paris: Fayard, 1998), 347–48.

11. The text of the ordinance of July 24, 1815 can be found in J. Madival and E. Laurent, eds., *Archives parlementaires de 1787 à 1860* (Paris: Librairie Administrative de Paul Dupont, 1867–1913, 1985), ser. 2, 15:25–26. The text of the law of January 12, 1816 can be found in ser. 2, 16:6.

12. The debate on these measures extended from November 10, 1815 through January 12, 1816. The text of the speeches and interventions can be found in Madival and Laurent, eds., *Archives parlementaires,* ser. 2, vols.15 and 16.

13. Cited in Bertier de Sauvigny, *Bourbon Restoration,* 132.

14. Resnick, *White Terror,* 5–19.

15. For a discussion of the White Terror in the Gard and its roots in the revolutionary past, see Gwynne Lewis, *The Second Vendee: The Continuity of Counterrevolution in the Department of the Gard, 1789–1815* (Oxford: Clarendon Press, 1978), 187–218.

16. A colorful description of these episodes may be found in Henry Houssaye, *1815: La seconde abdication—La Terreur blanche* (Paris: Perrin, 1918), 438–80.

17. Bertier de Sauvigny, *Bourbon Restoration,* 119. For an interpretation which stresses the Bourbon government's attempts at "forgetting" and reconciliation, see Sheryl Kroen, *Politics and Theater: The Crisis of Legitimacy in Restoration France, 1815–1830* (Berkeley: University of California Press, 2000), 39–75.

18. On the formulation and implementation of this repressive legislation, see Resnick, *White Terror,* 63–115. A more detailed overview of the period is found in Achille de Vaulabelle, *Histoire des deux Restaurations* (Paris: Garnier frères, 1874), 5:1–425. On the Bourbon secret police, see Ernest Daudet, *La police politique: Chronique des temps de la restauration* (Paris: Plon, 1912).

19. Resnick, *White Terror,* 114. For a more detailed breakdown of this figure, see Resnick, *White Terror,* 126–39.

20. Bertier de Sauvigny, *Bourbon Restoration,* 134–35.

21. Alan B. Spitzer, *Old Hatreds and Young Hopes: The French Carbonari against the Bourbon Restoration* (Cambridge: Harvard University Press, 1971), 20. For a typical contemporary statement of this view, see CAD, postes, Philadelphia, subseries B, 18, Consul at New York to Consul at Philadelphia (New York, 2/6/1816).

22. There is no in-depth study of the plot, perhaps because the relevant documents were destroyed after Waterloo to make it more difficult for the returning Bourbons to secure convictions. On the destruction of the documents, see AG, personal dossier of Gen. Charles Lallemand, GD 2, Decaze to Reporter of the 2nd Permanent War Council at Paris (Paris, 12/23/1815). For brief descriptions of the plot, see Arthur Chuquet, *Les Cent Jours: Le départ de l'île d'Elbe* (Paris: E. Leroux, 1920), 91–98; Edouard Guillon, *Les complots militaires sous la Restauration* (Paris: Plon, 1895), 7–10; and Henry Houssaye, *1815: La première Restauration, le retour de l'île d'Elbe, Les Cent Jours* (Paris: Perrin, 1894), 283–88.

23. There are many accounts of Napoleon's second return to power. One good overview is Norman Mackenzie, *The Escape from Elba: The Fall and Flight of Napoleon, 1814–1815* (New York: Oxford University Press, 1982).

24. On these operations, see Jean Vidalenc, *Les demi-solde: Étude d'une catégorie sociale* (Paris: Rivière, 1955), 17–32. The statistics on half-pay officers are from p.24. On the military establishment of the Restoration more generally, see Pierre Chalmin, *L'officier français de 1815 à 1870* (Paris: Rivière, 1957), and Raoul Girardet, *La société militaire et la France contemporaine* (Paris: Plon, 1953).

25. Alfred de Vigny, *Servitude and Grandeur of Arms,* trans. Roger Gard (London: Penguin, 1996), 4.

26. The following paragraph is based on Vidalenc, *Demi-solde,* 115–20.

27. On the role of French volunteers in the cause of Latin American independence, see

Jean Descola, *Les messagers de l'indépendance: Les français en Amérique latine de Bolivar à Castro* (Paris: R. Laffont, 1973), 137–210. Although it concentrates on the role of British adventurers, another useful work on the involvement of foreigners in the wars of Latin American independence is Alfred Hasbrouck, *Foreign Legionaries in the Liberation of Spanish South America* (New York: [n.p.], 1928).

28. The role of French adventurers in the struggle for the borderlands is poorly known. A notable exception is Harris Gaylord Warren, *The Sword Was Their Passport: A History of American Filibustering in the Mexican Revolution* (Baton Rouge: Louisiana State University Press, 1943). The term "Great Game" was coined in the mid-nineteenth century to describe the game of cat-and-mouse played between British and Russian agents as they sought to extend the influence of their respective empires into Central Asia.

29. This section heading is taken from a poem published in the journal *L'Abeille Américaine* 2, no. 26 (4/6/1816): 419. In the following issue of April 13, 1816, one irate reader objected to the comparison on the grounds that unlike Coriolanus, who returned to his homeland "sword and torch in hand," the military exiles in America were waiting peacefully for "less stormy days and more equitable resolutions," *L'Abeille* 2, no. 27 (4/13/1816) 43–45.

30. On the exiled regicides, see Albert Tournier, *Les conventionnels en exil* (Paris: Flammarion, 1910), and Eugène Welvert, *Lendemains révolutionnaires: Les régicides* (Paris: Calmann-Lévy, 1907). These works offer only biographical sketches. There is no analytical study of the exiled regicides, let alone the post-1815 Bonapartist diaspora.

31. Madival and Laurent, eds., *Archives parlementaires,* ser. 2, 15:25.

32. On the meritocratic transformation of the French army during this period, see Rafe Blaufarb, *The French Army, 1750–1820: Careers, Talent, Merit* (Manchester, UK: University of Manchester Press, 2002).

33. Unless otherwise noted, the information in this paragraph is taken from AG, Grouchy's personal dossier, MF 26; Emmanuel, comte de Grouchy, *Mémoires du maréchal de Grouchy* (Paris: E. Dentu, 1874), 5 vols.; Dr. Hoefer, *Nouvelle biographie générale depuis les temps les plus reculés jusqu'à nos jours* (Paris: Firmin-Didot frères, 1863), 22:221–29; and Georges Six, *Dictionnaire biographique des généraux et amiraux français de la Révolution et de l'Empire (1792–1814)* (Paris: G. Saffroy, 1934), 1:531–33.

34. APS, Stephen Girard papers, reel 58, Grouchy to Stephen Girard (Baltimore, 1/27/1816).

35. This famous controversy—turning on the question of whether Grouchy did or did not fail to march to the sound of the guns as he should have—is reported as having poisoned relations between himself and the other exiles, especially General Vandamme.

36. Unless otherwise noted, the information in this paragraph is drawn from AG, Henri Lallemand's personal dossier, 8 YD 1650; Hoefer, *Nouvelle biographie,* 29:7–8; and Six, *Dictionnaire biographique,* 2:40.

37. *L'Abeille* 3, no. 6 (5/23/1816): 89.

38. Unless otherwise noted, the information in this paragraph is drawn from the biographical notices on Lefebvre-Desnouettes provided in Hoefer, *Nouvelle biographie,* 30:320–22, and Six, *Dictionnaire biographique,* 2:92–94.

39. Of all of the officers treated in this work, only Lefebvre-Desnouettes and Grouchy

were deemed worthy of inclusion in General Thoumas's work, *Les grands cavaliers du premier empire* (Paris: Berger-Levrault, 1909), 3 vols. The entry on Lefebvre-Desnouettes is found in 3:153–202.

40. AN, F⁷ 6682, "245ème rapport" (4/4/1816), and "Note secret" (Lille, 3/5/1818). His wife was the daughter of the banker Lafitte.

41. Unless otherwise noted, the information in this paragraph is drawn from AG, Clausel's personal dossier 6 YD; Hoefer, *Nouvelle biographie*, 10:707–10; and Six, *Dictionnaire biographique*, 1:243–44.

42. On the murky circumstances of Clausel's escape, see CAD, correspondance interministérielle, police générale, 520, Minister of General Police to Minister of Foreign Affairs (Paris, 2/12/1816); AN, F⁷ 6679, dossier Clausel; and AN, F⁷ 6678, "Etat des individus qui, d'après l'ordonance du 24 juillet 1815, doivent être arretés et conduits devant les conseils de guerre de leurs divisions respectives."

42. Unless otherwise noted, the information in this paragraph is from AG, Vandamme's personal dossier, 7 YD 303; AN F⁷ 6678, "Situation des personnes comprises dans l'ordonnance du 24 juillet 1815"; AN F⁷ 6683, dossier Vandamme; Albert du Casse, *Le général Vandamme et sa correspondance* (Paris: Didier, 1870), 2 vols.; Hoefer, *Nouvelle biographie*, 45:907–11; and Six, *Dictionnaire biographique*, 2:528–29.

44. Unless otherwise noted, the information in this paragraph is drawn from AN, F⁷ 6683, dossier Réal; Tulard, *Joseph Fouché*, 414–19; and Hoefer, *Nouvelle biographie*, 41:790–94.

45. CAD, postes, Philadelphia, subseries B, 18, Consul at New York to Consul at Philadelphia (New York, 8/15/1816).

46. Unless otherwise indicated, the information in this paragraph is drawn from AN, F⁷ 6712, dossier Garnier des Saintes; AN, F⁷ 6678, "Etat des differentes personnes comprises dans l'ordonnance du 24 juillet 1815"; "Situation des individus compris dans l'article 2 de l'ordonnance du 24 juillet 1815"; and Hoefer, *Nouvelle biographie*, 19:517–19.

47. Unless otherwise noted, the information in this paragraph is drawn from AN, F⁷ 6713 dossier Lakanal; John Charles Dawson, *Lakanal the Regicide: A Biographical and Historical Study of the Career of Joseph Lakanal* (Tuscaloosa: University of Alabama Press, 1948); Hoefer, *Nouvelle biographie*, 28:931–35; Tournier, *Conventionnels en exil*, 268–74; and Eugène Welvert, "Lakanal en Amérique," *Feuilles d'histoire du XVIIe au XXe siécle* 4, no. 9 (September 1910): 252–371.

48. The French consul in New York described him as "ultra-pedantic." CAD, postes, Philadelphia, subseries B, 18, Consul at New York to Consul at Philadelphia (New York, 3/30/1816). This seems to have been just one manifestation of the fragility of his ego. Lakanal relished his presidency of the Committee of Public Instruction not just because of the prestige it conferred, but also because the leading intellectuals of France—members of the Academy, scientists, and philosophers—came begging for favors, protection, and sometimes even their lives. He never parted with their fawning letters, but took them with him into exile. Examples of these—from Daubenton, Jussieu, Lavoisier, and Voleny, to name a few— can be found at Tulane University, Joseph Lakanal collection, and at Louisiana State University, Joseph Lakanal papers.

49. Unless otherwise noted, the information in this paragraph is from AN, F⁷ 6714,

dossier Jean-Augustin Pénières-Delors; Victor Faure, *De la Corrèze à la Floride: Jean-Augustin Pénières, conventionnel et député d'Ussel* (Ussel: Musée du pays d'Ussel, 1989); and Hoefer, *Nouvelle biographie,* 39:524–25.

50. Information on Dirat is drawn from AN, F[7] 6680, dossier Louis-Marie Dirat, and periodic police reports in AN, F[7] 6678.

51. AN, F[7] 6680, Minister of General Police to the Prefect of the Haute-Garonne (Paris, 10/24/1815), and Prefect of the Haute-Garonne to the Minister of General Police (Montauban, 10/30/1815).

52. Unless otherwise noted, information on Cluis is drawn from CAD, postes, New Orleans, personal files, subseries D, 199, dossier J. Jerome Cluis, and periodic police reports in AN, F[7] 6678.

53. ADAH, Pickett papers, "Notes Taken from the Lips of the Honorable George N. Stewart."

54. This section heading is taken from *L'Abeille* 3, no. 19 (8/22/1816): 292.

55. Unless otherwise indicated, information on Raoul is from AG, Raoul's personal dossier, 8, YD 3040, and ADAH, LPR 46, "Colonel Raoul," extracted from the *Mobile Commercial Register* (2/10/1831).

56. Mackenzie, *Escape from Elba,* 245.

57. CAD, postes, New York, subseries C, 2*, Consul-General Petry to the Duke de Richelieu (New York, 4/28/1818).

58. AG, 8 YD 3040, Raoul to Minister of War (Rome, 11/24/1818).

59. Unless otherwise indicated, information on Combe is drawn from AG, Combe's pension file, 3 YF 53221,and Doher, *Proscrits et exilés,* 191–208.

60. AN., F[7] 6702, Prefect of the Loire to Minister of General Police (Montbrison, 3/17/21).

61. Georges Blond, *Les Cent-Jours* (Paris: Julliard, 1983), 42; Mackenzie, *Escape from Elba,* 90; Chuquet, *Cent Jours,* 16; and Bernard and Danielle Quintin, *Dictionnaire des colonels de Napoléon* (Paris: SPM, 1996), 930.

62. AG, X[ab] 65, "Contrôle nominatif des sous-officiers, caporals, tambours, et grenadiers composant la première compagnie de la Garde de Napoléon," and "Etat nominatif et classement des sous-officiers de la première compagnie du bataillon sacré" (Paris, 4/29/1815).

63. Information on Fourni is from the Apodaca correspondence, reel 4, dispatch 78, and Kent Gardien, "Take Pity on Our Glory: Men of Champ d'Asile," *Southwestern Historical Quarterly* 87, no. 3 (January 1984): 253. On Murat's botched attempt to recover the kingdom of Naples, see Frédéric Masson, *Revue d'ombres* (Paris: Ollendorff, n.d.), 115–212.

64. On Gruchet, see CAD, postes, New York, subseries C, 2*, Consul-General to Duke de Richelieu (New York, 5/5/1819). Gruchet was the protégé of General Belliard, one of Murat's staunchest supporters, who had also participated in his patron's attempt to recover the throne of Naples. See Six, *Dictionnaire biographique,* 1:77–78. On Lavaudray, see CAD, postes, New York, subseries B, 122, Consul at Baltimore to Consul at New York (Baltimore, 5/24/1817). Although described in this report as one of the "exiles or refugees planning on making an establishment . . . on the Tombigbee," he ultimately declined to take part in the enterprise.

65. Information on Schultz is in AG, his personal dossier, and AN, F⁷ 6758, "Officiers polonais."

66. Information on Malezewski is from AN, F⁷ 6758, "Officiers polonais," and Quintin, *Colonels*, 919. Information on Jourdan is from the New Orleans newspaper *L'Ami des Lois* (8/16/1817).

67. Unless otherwise noted, information on Galabert is from his personal dossier (misleadingly labeled "Jacques Galabert"); his pension file, 10 YF "Louis-Jacques Galabert"; and administrative papers in Xʰ 8, "Premier régiment étranger: La Tour d'Auvergne," all in AG.

68. AG, 1 K 45, Fichier Pinasseau, 40, "Etat du corps d'infanterie commandé par le major comte de Williamson" (Jersey, 1795), from the Puisaye papers at the British Museum, vol. 66, "Rassemblement des émigrés à Jersey."

69. On the role of Anglophobia in the origins of French nationalism, see David A. Bell, *The Cult of the Nation in France: Inventing Nationalism, 1680–1800* (Cambridge: Harvard University Press, 2001), 78–106. See also, Norman Hampson, *The Perfidy of Albion: French Perceptions of England during the French Revolution* (London: Macmillan, 1998).

70. AG, Xʰ 8, "Déclaration des officiers du 3ème bataillon du régiment de la Tour d'Auvergne, Galabert" (Phalsbourg, 5/25/1806). The Galabert family was noted as being "linked to the first families of Spain." AG, personal dossier of Marc-Antoine-Fulcran-Alfred Galabert, untitled note (Paris, 9/1/25). His uncle, Francisco Cabbarrus, was the Spanish minister of finances in the 1790s.

71. Examples can be found in *L'Abeille* in November and December 1817. See vol. 5, nos.17–21.

72. AG, Xʰ 8, "Mutations survenues parmi MM. les officiers depuis le 1ᵉʳ avril jusqu'au 1ᵉʳ septembre 1808."

73. Unless otherwise indicated, the information in this paragraph is drawn from AG, Douarche's personal dossier, and the brief notice in Quintin, *Colonels*, 287–88.

74. AG, Douarche's personal dossier, "Note du ministre" (n.d.).

75. A detailed account dated 1 October 1816, showing how Douarche had embezzled over the years is in his personal dossier at the AG.

76. Unless otherwise noted, this paragraph is based on documents in AG, Charrasin's personal dossier.

77. Citation from AG, Charrasin's personal dossier, "Rapport fait au ministre de la guerre" (Paris, 1/17/1815).

78. Information on the elusive Latapie is from AN, F⁷ 6913, dossier Le comte Doulcet de Pontecoulant, Adolphe Doulcet de Pontecoulant, le colonel Latapie, Pierre-Remi Raulet.

79. Honoré de Balzac, *A Bachelor's Establishment*, in *The Works of Honore de Balzac* trans. George Saintsbury, 4:36 (New York: Charles C. Bigelow, 1900).

80. For example, Dieudonné Rigau—son of an exiled general who joined the Vine and Olive venture in late 1817—claimed at the end of 1824 that "the only obstacle" to his return to active service and promotion to colonel had been "the circumstances of my father." AG, 3 Y F 55864, pension file of Dieudonné Rigau, Rigau to the Minister of War (Paris, 12/21/1824). His brother Narcisse-Périclès was dismissed from the service on the grounds that he was "the son of a man who contributed with all his means to the return of the usurper." AG,

Narcisse-Périclès Rigau's personal dossier, "Rapport au Roi" (Paris, 7/19/1816). Even Victor de Grouchy's illustrious lineage did not save him from being removed from active duty, in part for being "the son of a general who played a prominent role in the Hundred Days." AG, Victor de Grouchy's personal dossier, "Rapport particulier" (Caen, 2/1/1817).

81. Jack Dabbs, "Additional Notes on Champ d'Asile," *Southwestern Historical Quarterly* 54, no. 3 (1950–51): 347–58, and Hartmann and Millard, *Le Texas, ou notice historique sur le champ d'asile, comprenant tout ce qui s'est passé depuis la formation jusqu'à la disolution de cette colonie* (Paris: Béguin, 1819).

82. Just Girard [Just-Jean-Etienne Roy], *The Adventures of a Captain, at Present a Planter in Texas, formerly a Refugee of Camp Asylum,* trans. Lady Blanche Murphy (Cincinnati [etc.]: Benziger Brothers, 1878), 18.

83. Ibid., 20.

84. Ibid., 24–25.

85. Ibid., 26–27.

86. APS, Stephen Girard papers, reel 64, Charles Haraneeder to Stephen Girard (Philadelphia, 12/12/1817).

87. CAD, postes, Philadelphia, subseries B, 45*, minutes of correspondence (4/23/1818).

88. CAD, postes, New York, subseries C, 2*, Consul-General at New York to Duke de Richelieu (New York, 12/10/1817).

89. Since the United States did not begin collecting statistics on immigration until 1818, it is impossible to provide exact figures. On the problem of measuring pre-1818 French immigration, see Imre Ferenczi, *International Migrations,* vol. 1, *Statistics* (New York: National Bureau of Economic Research, 1929), 106.

90. Nicole Fouché, *Emigration alsacienne aux Etats-Unis, 1815–1870* (Paris: Publications de la Sorbonne, 1992), and Camile Maire, *L'émigration des lorrains en Amérique, 1815–1870* (Metz: Centre de Recherches Relations Internationales de l'Université de Metz, 1980). The famine of 1817 effected the entire Rhine valley, provoking the emigration of thousands of Swiss and Germans as well.

91. AN, F^7 6138^8, "Note pour son excellence, le ministre de police générale" (Paris, 4/5/1817).

92. William Lee to James Monroe (Bordeaux, 10/20/1815) and William Lee to James Madison (New York, 11/8/1816), in Lee, *A Yankee Jeffersonian: Selections from the Diary and Letters of William Lee of Massachusetts, Written from 1796 to 1840,* ed. Mary Lee Mann (Cambridge: Belknap Press of Harvard University Press, 1958), 175–77 and 183–84.

93. A good statistical analysis, however, is found in Fouché, *Emigration alsacienne,* 44–50. A description of the typical sea voyage of the emigrants is found in Camille Maire, *En route pour l'Amérique: L'odyssée des émigrants en France au 19ème siécle* (Nancy: Presses Universitaires de Nancy, 1993).

94. CAD, postes, New York, subseries C, 2*, Consul-General at New York to Duke de Richelieu (New York, 8/4/1817).

95. AN, F^7 6716, Declaration of Captain Bonnefoi (10/17/1816).

96. It is estimated that between 60 and 80 percent of the white population of New Orleans was French speaking *before* the massive influx of refugees from Saint-Domingue in

1809, which doubled the population of the city. Paul F. Lachance, "The 1809 Immigration of Saint-Domingue Refugees to New Orleans: Reception, Integration, and Impact," *Louisiana History* 29, no. 2 (spring 1988): 127.

97. AAE, CP, U.S., 73, Hyde de Neuville to Duke de Richelieu (Washington, 1/10/1817). Hyde's impression was shared by worried Anglo-Americans in Louisiana, one of whom commented in 1810 that "we are at this moment a French province." Lachance, "The 1809 Immigration," 117.

98. Jo Ann Carrigan, *The Saffron Scourge: A History of Yellow Fever in Louisiana, 1796–1905* (Lafayette: Center for Louisiana Studies, University of Southwestern Louisiana, 1994), 55.

99. CAD, postes, New Orleans, unclassified personal files, subseries D, dossier Truc.

100. CAD, postes, New Orleans, unclassified personal dossiers, subseries D, dossier Bistos.

101. Donald Greer, *The Incidence of Emigration during the French Revolution* (Cambridge: Harvard University Press, 1951), 20.

102. David Patrick Geggus, *Slavery, War, and Revolution: The British Occupation of Saint-Domingue, 1793–1798* (Oxford: Clarendon Press, 1982), 6. The following discussion of Domingan colonial society is based on Geggus's excellent introductory chapter, "Saint-Domingue on the Eve of the Revolution," 6–32.

103. Robert Louis Stein, *The French Slave Trade in the Eighteenth Century: An Old Regime Business* (Madison: University of Wisconsin Press, 1979), 38.

104. This paragraph is based on Carolyn E. Fick, *The Making of Haiti: The Saint-Domingue Revolution from Below* (Knoxville: University of Tennessee Press, 1990), 15–45; Geggus, *British Occupation*, 23–30; Sidney W. Mintz, *Sweetness and Power: The Place of Sugar in Modern History* (New York: Elisabeth Sifton Books, 1985), 19–73; Arthur L. Stinchcombe, *Sugar Island Slavery in the Age of Enlightenment: The Political Economy of the Caribbean World* (Princeton: Princeton University Press, 1995), 3–171; and Dale W. Tomich, *Slavery in the Circuit of Sugar: Martinique and the World Economy, 1830–1848* (Baltimore: Johns Hopkins University Press, 1990), 139–258.

105. Joseph C. Miller, *Way of Death: Merchant Capitalism and the Angolan Slave Trade, 1730–1830* (Madison: University of Wisconsin Press, 1988), 657–92.

106. Childs, *French Refugee Life* 15.

107. On the movement of Domingan refugees into the United States, see John E. Baur, "International Repercussions of the Haitian Revolution," *Americas* 26, no. 4 (April 1970): 394–418.

108. One scholar has recently estimated the number of Domingan refugees in Cuba at 25,000. Thomas Fiehrer, "Saint-Domingue/Haiti: Louisiana's Caribbean Connection," *Louisiana History* 30, no. 4 (fall 1988): 430. A contemporary observer suggested the figure of 15,000 families. AAE, consulates, Havana, reel 5, "Mémoire sur le Cuba soumis au Baron de Rayneval, conseiller d'état" (n.d.).

109. The group which came to New Orleans via Cuba has received more scholarly attention than any other contingent of Domingan refugees thanks largely to the pioneering work of Gabriel Debien. See his article "The Saint-Domingue Refugees in Cuba, 1793–1815," trans. David Cheramie, in Carl A. Brasseaux and Glenn R. Conrad, *The Road to Louisiana: The Saint-Domingue Refugees, 1792–1809* (Lafayette: Center for Louisiana Studies, University of

Southwestern Louisiana, 1992), 31–112. The figure is from p. 93. See also, Debien and René le Gardeur, "Les colons de Saint-Domingue refugiés à la Louisiane (1792–1804)" *Notes d'histoire coloniale* 10, no. 211. The definitive study of marriage patterns of the Domingan refugees in Louisiana is Paul Lachance, "Intermarriage and French Cultural Persistence in Late Spanish and Early American New Orleans," *Histoire sociale/Social History* 15, no. 29 (mai-May 1982): 47–81.

110. Lachance, "The 1809 Immigration," 110–111 and 128.

111. Although it ends abruptly in 1800, an exception to this is the good chapter on the expatriate French community in Philadelphia in Childs, *French Refugee Life,* 103–21. Another useful work, which unfortunately limits its scope to the Domingan exodus in the cities of the American South, is Winston C. Babb, "French Refugees from Saint Domingue to the Southern United States: 1791–1810," Ph.D. diss., University of Virginia, 1954.

112. Fiehrer, "Saint-Domingue/Haiti," 434.

113. Lachance, "The 1809 Immigration," 111. On slaveholding by free persons of color in Saint-Domingue, see Michel-Rolph Trouillot, "Coffee, Color, and Slavery in Eighteenth-Century Saint-Domingue," Review 5 (1980): 331–388. There do not appear to have been any mulattoes or free people of color among the Vine and Olive colonists. However, one of their number, Jean-François-Sully Lavau, became the godfather of several black Domingan children in Philadelphia during the 1790s. See ADAH, Gardien papers, entry for Lavau.

114. Lachance, "The 1809 Immigration," 133.

115. The New Orleans figures may overrepresent the mercantile, artisanal, and professional sectors at the expense of the agricultural categories one would find in similar records from the rural areas into which some of the refugees eventually dispersed. A recent study of the professions of rural refugees in Louisiana in 1850 has found that 27 percent were farmers, 7 percent fishermen, and 7 percent laborers. See the introduction in Brasseaux and Conrad, eds., *The Road to Louisiana,* xvi–xvii.

116. Unless otherwise noted, the biographical information in the remainder of this section is based on the alphabetically organized entries in ADAH, Gardien papers.

117. AAE, affaires diverses politiques, U.S., 2, dossier Auguste Follin.

118. There were also five non-Domingan jewelers among the Vine and Olive colonists: Louis Brechemin, Etienne Castan, Joseph-Michel Gouiran, Nicholas-Basile Meslier, and Guillaume Promis.

119. This information on Chaprons, Nidelets, Teterels, and Frenayes is from Kent Gardien, "The Domingan Kettle: Philadelphia-Emigré Planters in Alabama," *National Genealogical Society Quarterly* 76 (September 1988): 178–81.

120. Naturally, many Domingan refugees formed business partnerships with one another without also contracting marriage alliances between their families. See for example, the lengthy partnership of Pierre Lacombe and Pierre Ducoing, Léonard Engelbert and Auguste-Firmin Follin, and Frédéric Ravesies and the Garesché de la Poterie brothers.

121. Filson Historical Society, Barbaroux family papers, Barbaroux to Martin Piquet [father] (Louisville, 7/7 and 8/15/1820).

122. Filson Historical Society, Barbaroux family papers, Alexandre Fournier to Martin Piquet [father] (Demopolis, 7/13/1841).

123. Filson Historical Society, Barbaroux family papers, Alexandre Fournier to Martin Piquet [father] (Demopolis, 1/29/1841).

124. Filson Historical Society, Barbaroux family papers, Alexandre Fournier to Martin Piquet [father] (Demopolis 6/10/1845). In a lighter vein, although no less revealing of the cultural differences between the French and Anglo-Americans, Fournier noted that the legs of Sylphide—a French dancer then touring the United States and whose show he had seen in New Orleans—were shapely, but in no way deserved the fuss outraged Americans ("prudish republicans" in Fournier's words) were making.

125. Filson Historical Society, Barbaroux family papers, Alexandre Fournier to Martin Piquet [father] (Demopolis, 1/11/1845).

126. Frank Stollenwerck and Dixie Orum Stollenwerck, *The Stollenwerck, Chaudron, and Billon Families in America* (Baltimore: [n.p.], 1948).

Chapter 2

1. NARA, M34, reel 20, Albert Gallatin to James Monroe (Paris, 7/12/1816).

2. On American Anglophobia, see Edward Howland Tatum Jr., *The United States and Europe, 1815–1823: A Study in the Background of the Monroe Doctrine* (Berkeley: University of California Press, 1936), 57–85 and 141–82.

3. James Monroe papers, reel 6, Richard Rush to James Monroe (Washington, 4/24/1817). The administration rejected the offer for a number of reasons, not least of which was the fear that it would antagonize England.

4. Andrew Jackson papers, reel 21, Edward Livingston to Andrew Jackson (New Orleans, 11/7/1816). The Duke de Richelieu, warned Hyde at about this time to avoid exacerbating American paranoia. "The federal government might have the idea [that there is] some secret coalition of European powers arrayed against it. This opinion might push it to take some extreme action or make it follow the wrong course." AAE, CP, U.S., 73, "Exposé faisant suite à la dépêche no. 14."

5. The celebration was described in *L'Abeille* 3, no. 5 (5/16/1816): 78–80.

6. CAD, postes, New York, subseries B, 114, Consul at Boston to Consul at New York (5/5/1817); and CAD, postes, Philadelphia, subseries B, 45*, Consul-General to Duke de Richelieu (5/16/1817).

7. For a general discussion of the diplomatic tensions generated by the American welcome of the French exiles, see Watel, *Jean-Guillaume Hyde de Neuville*, 125–28.

8. NARA, M53, reel 3, Hyde de Neuville to James Monroe (New Brunswick, 7/11/1816).

9. James Madison to James Monroe (Montpellier, 8/28/1816), in, Madison, *The Writings of James Madison*, ed. Gaillard Hunt (New York: G. P. Putnam's Sons, 1908), 362.

10. NARA, M 77, James Monroe to Albert Gallatin (Washington, 9/10/1816).

11. Perhaps the most visible manifestation of Bonapartist sentiment in antebellum New Orleans was the funeral ceremony held for Napoleon in December 1821. See A. E. Fossier, "The Funeral Ceremony of Napoleon in New Orleans, December 19, 1821," *Louisiana Historical Quarterly* 13, no. 2 (April 1930): 246–52.

12. PRO, FO/115, 27, Consul at New Orleans to Consul-General (New Orleans, 5/15/1817).

13. CAD, postes, New Orleans, subseries A, 144, Consul at New Orleans to Hyde de Neuville (New Orleans, 3/19/1817).

14. NARA, M 179, reel 40, John Dick to John Quincy Adams (New Orleans, 1/10/1818). The attack on Morphy is described in Stanley Faye, "Consuls of Spain in New Orleans, 1804–1821," *Louisiana Historical Quarterly* 21, no. 3 (July 1938): 682.

15. AAE, CP, U.S., 74, Hyde de Neuville to Duke de Richelieu (Washington, 5/22/1817).

16. *L'Ami des Lois* (14 mai 1817). On Leclerc's revolutionary past in France, see David Nicholls and Peter Marsh, eds., *A Biographical Dictionary of Modern European Radicals and Socialists* (Sussex, UK: Harvester Press, 1988), 1:163–5. The following description of the incident is from NARA, M 53, reel 3, "Précis de ce qui s'est passé à la Nouvelle Orléans le 4 mai 1817."

17. AAE, CP, U.S., 73, Hyde de Neuville to Duke de Richelieu (Washington, 7/12/1816).

18. To arguments of this kind, Hyde invariably responded that he must therefore bypass the federal government entirely and address the complaints of his government directly to the state in question. Hyde noted with glee "how much the administration is frightened by this reasoning; it can imagine the consequences," especially if it implied a direct political relationship between France and the state of Louisiana. AAE, CP, U.S., 74, Hyde de Neuville to Duke de Richelieu (Washington, 6/5/1817).

19. APS, Stephen Girard papers, reel 58, Marshal Grouchy to Stephen Girard (Baltimore, 1/27/1816), and reel 60, Joseph Bonaparte to Stephen Girard (Point Breeze, 9/16/1816).

20. Examples may be found in the Jefferson papers (Grouchy and Clausel letters, for example) and published Henry Clay papers. See Marquis de Lafayette to Henry Clay (La Grance, 12/26/1815) in Clay, *The papers of Henry Clay,* ed. James F. Hopkins (Lexington: University of Kentucky Press, 1959), 2:112–15.

21. Faure, *De la Corrèze,* 187–88.

22. Dawson, *Lakanal the Regicide,* 98.

23. Six, *Dictionnaire biographique,* 1:83–84.

24. AN, F^7 6716, "Bulletin" (Marseille, 10/17/1816) and "Bulletin" (Marseille, 8/22/1816). Postwar demobilization of American naval forces also adversely affected the exiles' chances of gaining employment with the privateers commissioned by the Spanish American patriots and fitted out in the ports of the United States (especially Baltimore) after 1815. See Peggy K. Liss, *Atlantic Empires: The Network of Trade and Revolution, 1713–1826* (Baltimore: Johns Hopkins University Press, 1983), 202.

25. CAD, postes, New York, subseries C, 2*, Consul-General to Duke de Richelieu (New York, 8/4/1817).

26. AN, F^7 6717, "Bulletin" (Marseille, 3/19/1817) and "Bulletin" (Marseille, 4/23/1817).

27. AAE, CP, U.S., 74, Consul-General to Duke de Richelieu (Philadelphia, 5/24/1817).

28. APS, Stephen Girard papers, reel 81, F. M. Durant to Stephen Girard (Hôpital de la Pennsylvanie, 5/20/1822). On Durand's participation in Mina's expedition, see Pablo Chacon to Don Alexandro Ramirez (Baltimore, 10/15/1816) in Jose L. Franco, ed., *Documentos para*

la Historia de Mexico Existentes en el Archivo Nacional de Cuba (La Habana: Publicaciones del Archivo Nacional de Cuba, 1961), 70.

29. Adams papers, reel 442, Pierre-Paul-François Degrand to John Quincy Adams (Boston, 1/15/1818).

30. AG, MF 26, Marshal Grouchy's personal dossier, Jorge Ochoa Romani, president of the Jose Miguel Carera Commission, to the Invalides (Santiago, 8/23/1989).

31. CAD, postes, Philadelphia, subseries B, 45*, dispatch of 10/10/1816.

32. PRO, FO/115, 26, Ambassador to Foreign Minister (Washington, 7/4/1816).

33. CAD, postes, New Orleans, subseries A, 2, Consul to Duke de Richelieu (New Orleans, 4/10/1817); and AAE, CP USA, 74, Hyde de Neuville to Duke de Richelieu (Washington, 5/14/1817 and 5/20/1817).

34. Edouard de Montulé, *Travels in America, 1816–1817,* trans. Edward D. Seeber (Bloomington: Indiana University Press, 1950), 75–6.

35. Information on Humbert is drawn from Edouard Guillon, *La France et l'Irlande pendant la Révolution: Hoche et Humbert* (Paris: Armand Colin, 1888); Henry Poulet, *Un soldat lorrain méconnu: Le général Humbert (1767–1823)* (Nancy: Ancienne Imprimerie Vagner, 1928); and Six, *Dictionnaire biographique,* 1:584–85.

36. "Junta del Goberniemente" (New Orleans, 4/12/14) in Franco, ed., *Documentos para la Historia de Mexico,* 36–37.

37. AAE, CP, U.S., 76, Consul at New Orleans to Duke de Richelieu (New Orleans, 12/12/1818).

38. Montulé, *Travels in America,* 87.

39. AAE, CP, U.S., 73, "Note de Lefebvre sur le Mexique," and CAD, correspondance interministérielle, police générale 520, Duke de Richelieu to Minister of General Police (Paris, 5/9/1817).

40. Stanley Faye, "The Great Stroke of Pierre Lafitte," *Louisiana Historical Quarterly* 23, no. 3 (July 1940): 774. The Spanish diplomatic corps in the United States suspected that the French exiles had established contact with Mina earlier, when the insurgent general was fitting out his expedition on the east coast. Rumors circulated, moreover, that Mina was expecting reinforcements of five hundred to one thousand troops led by Lefebvre-Desnouettes once he had made a lodgement on the Mexican mainland. Pablo Chacon to Don Alexandro Ramirez (Baltimore, 10/15/1816) and dispatch of Tomas Gener (Matanzas, 1/9/1817), in Franco, ed., *Documentos para la Historia de Mexico,* 73 and 87.

41. Pierre to Jean Lafitte (Galveston, 7/23/1817), in Franco, ed., *Documentos para la Historia de Mexico,* 134–35.

42. Adams papers, reel 442, Pierre-Paul-François Degrand to John Quincy Adams (Boston, 1/15/1815).

43. CAD, postes, NYC, subseries C, 2*, Consul-General to Duke de Richelieu (New York, 7/19/1817). Officers with specialist skills (engineers, artillerists, and navigators) received more favorable treatment in the top-heavy—but technically weak—armies of the Latin American insurgents. See NARA, M 84, "Robert Atkinson to John Graham" (Baltimore, 12/6/1816).

44. CAD, correspondance interministérielle, 520, Minister of General Police to Duke de Richelieu (Paris, 9/11/1817).

45. The abortive adventures of Dreyer and Dubois in America are detailed in CAD, postes, Philadelphia, subseries B, 45*, dispatch of 4/25/1817.

46. AAE, CP, U.S., 74, Duke de Richelieu to Ambassador to Great Britain (Paris, 9/4/1817). For a more detailed discussion of Latapie's involvement in the Pernambuco revolution, see Mario de Lima-Barbosa, *Les français dans l'histoire du Brésil* (Rio di Janeiro: F. Briguiet, 1923), 240–54, and J. A. da Costa, "Napoléon Ier au Brésil," *Revue du monde latin* 8 (janvier–avril 1886): 205–16 and 339–49.

47. CAD, postes, New York, subseries C, 2*, dispatch of 10/10/1817.

48. A good description of foreign involvement in privateering, as well as how it could degenerate into outright piracy is contained in Governor Villeré's message of 5 March 1818 to the Louisiana State Legislature reprinted in *Le Courrier de la Louisiane* (3/6/1818).

49. PRO, FO/115, 26, Ambassador to the United States to Foreign Minister (Washington, 7/4/1816).

50. la Souchère Deléry, *Napoleon's Soldiers,* 42–43.

51. *L'Abeille* 5, no. 21 (12/4/1817): 338; and APS, Stephen Girard papers, reel 82, Henri Saignier to Stephen Girard (Philadelphia, 12/26/1822).

52. Durand Echeverria, *Mirage in the West: A History of the French Image of American Society to 1815* (Princeton: Princeton University Press, 1957), 197–200. Citation from p.199.

53. APS, Stephen Girard papers, reel 81, Texier de la Pommeraye to Stephen Girard (Philadelphia, 7/23/1822). Texier was also involved in the potentially more lucrative business of selling a politically sensitive manuscript in his possession (on the Pichegru conspiracy) to the French government. CAD, postes, Philadelphia, subseries B, 45*, dispatches of 11/4 and 11/17/1818; and CAD, postes, New York, subseries B, 106, Hyde de Neuville to Consul-General (Washington, 11/21/1818). CAD, postes, Philadelphia, subseries B, 45*, dispatch of 11/4/1818 described Texier as a lieutenant colonel.

54. *L'Abeille* 5, no. 26 (1/8/1818): 405–6.

55. Montulé, *Travels in America,* 122–23.

56. CAD, postes, New York, subseries C, 2* (7/3/1817); and CAD, postes, Philadelphia, subseries B, 45*, dispatch of 7/11/1817.

57. AAE, CP, U.S., 74, Hyde de Neuville to Duke de Richelieu (Washington, 5/20/1817).

58. On the propensity of the Napoleonic exiles for careers in education, see Simone de la Souchère Deléry, "Some French Soldiers Who Became Louisiana Educators," *Louisiana Historical Quarterly* 31, no. 4 (October 1948): 849–55.

59. Thomas Wood Clarke, *Emigrés in the Wilderness* (New York: Macmillan, 1941), 140–44.

60. AAE, CP, U.S., 73, Hyde de Neuville to Duke de Richelieu (Washington, 1/10/1817). One of the more enterprising exiles, Réal also went into business with Jean Genet, the rabble-rousing former ambassador to the United States from revolutionary France. AAE, CP, U.S., 75, "Copie d'un rapport à Hyde de Neuville, par un de ses agents secrets" (8/25/1817).

61. CAD, postes, Philadelphia, subseries B, 18, Consul at New York to Consul at Philadelphia (New York, 3/30/1816).

62. *L'Abeille* 2, no. 25 (3/30/1816): 399.

63. Madison papers, reel 17, Joseph Lakanal to James Madison (Gallatin County, near Vevay, 6/1/1816), and Dawson, *Lakanal the Regicide,* 101–3.

64. CAD, postes, New Orleans, personal files, subseries D, dossier Lecoq; and Montulé, *Travels in America,* 121–22.

65. APS, Stephen Girard papers, reel 61, Lecoq de Marcelay to Stephen Girard (Louisville, 1/6/1817).

66. *L'Abeille* 3, no. 19 (8/22/1816): 292–4. All citations in this paragraph are from this article, as is the section title.

67. A good survey of these ideas is Echeverria. There is also a vast literature on the related concept of the "noble savage," examples of which include the classic work by Hoxie Neale Fairchild, *The Noble Savage: A Study in Romantic Naturalism* (New York: Columbia University Press, 1928), or the more recent book by Ter Ellingson, *The Myth of the Noble Savage* (Berkeley: University of California Press, 2001).

68. For an overview of these efforts, see Rosengarten, *French Colonists,* 125–50.

69. Theodore Thomas Belote, *The Scioto Speculation and the French Settlement at Gallipolis* (Cincinnati: University of Cincinnati Press, 1907); Hélène Foure-Selter, *Gallipolis, Ohio: Histoire de l'établissement de cinq cents français dans la vallée de l'Ohio à la fin du XVIIIé siécle* (Paris: Jouve, 1939); Jean Houpert, *Les lorrains en Amérique du Nord* (Sherbrooke, Quebec: Namaan, 1985), 87–88; Jocelyne Moreau-Zanelli, *Gallipolis: Histoire d'un mirage américain au XVIIIé siécle* (Paris: L'Harmattan, 2000); and William G. Sibley, *The French Five Hundred* (Gallipolis, Ind.: Gallia County Historical Society, 1933).

70. The standard works on Asylum are Rev. David Craft, *The French Settlement at Asylum, Bradford County, Pa., 1793* (Wilkes-Barre, Pa.: E. B. Yordy, 1900); Louise Welles Murray, *The Story of Some French Refugees and Their "Azilum," 1793–1800* (Athens, Pa.: N.p., 1903); and Elsie Murray, *Azilum: French Refugee Colony of 1793* (Athens, Pa.: Tioga Point Museum, 1940).

71. Dawson, *Lakanal the Regicide,* 101.

72. *Le Courrier de la Louisiane* (11/27/1818).

73. *L'Abeille* 4, no. 5 (11/14/1816): 70.

74. Ibid., no. 15 (1/23/1817): 239–40.

75. AN, F^7 6716, "Bulletin" (Marseille, 11/1818).

76. *L'Abeille* 4, no. 13 (1/9/1817): 203–5.

77. Pickett, *History of Alabama,* 623.

78. *L'Abeille* 4, no. 13 (1/9/1817): 205–7.

79. Inès Murat, *Napoleon and the American Dream,* trans. Frances Frenaye (Baton Rouge: Louisiana State University Press, 1981), 110–15.

80. Jefferson papers, reel 49, Thomas Jefferson to William Lee (Monticello, 1/16/1817).

81. Kent Gardien has previously made this point in his excellent article, "The Splendid Fools," 502.

82. James Madison papers, reel 18, William Lee to James Madison (New York, 11/8/1816); Andrew Jackson papers, reel 21, Andrew Hynes to Andrew Jackson (Philadelphia, 6/19/1816); Massachusetts Historical Society, Pickering papers, reel 31, William Lee to Pickering (Washington, 2/25/1817); and Henry Clay to Joseph Lakanal (Washington 3/20/1817) in Clay, *Papers of Henry Clay,* 2:328–29.

83. Jean-Simon Chaudron to Joseph Lakanal (Philadelphia, 1/6/1817), in Toussaint Nigoul, *Lakanal* (Paris: C. Marpon and E. Flammarion, 1879), 149.

84. *The Debates and Proceedings in the Congress of the United States, 14th Congress, 2nd Session* (Washington, D.,C.: Gales and Seaton, 1854), 108.

85. Ibid., 114, 136–37, 139, and 1019. Those voting in favor were Ashmun, Barbour, Brown, Campbell, Chace, Condit, Dana, Fromentin, Gaillard, Goldsborough, Horsey, Howell, Hunter, King, Lacock, Macon, Morrow, Noble, Roberts, Sanford, Stokes, Tait, Talbot, Taylor, Tichenor, Troup, Varnum, Wells, and Wilson. Those opposed were Daggett, Hardin, Mason of New Hampshire, Ruggles, and Smith. No roll call vote survived for the House.

86. Ibid., 1039–40. This account was originally published in the February 28, 1817 issue of the *National Intelligencer.*

87. *Aurora* (11/19/1816).

88. *Columbian Centinel* (1/11/1817).

89. *Huntsville Republican* 11, no. 9 (10/28/1817).

90. *Alabama Republican* 11, no. 29 (4/4/1818).

91. *Niles' Weekly Register* 24, no. 362 (8/8/1818).

92. James Monroe to John Quincy Adams (Washington, 12/10/1815), in William R. Manning, ed., *Diplomatic Correspondence of the United States Concerning the Independence of the Latin-American Nations* (New York: Oxford University Press, 1925), 1:17. Recognizing the dangers of a British takeover of Florida, Congress passed a secret resolution, the so-called "No Transfer Resolution," in 1811 authorizing the president to respond with military force to such a contingency. Samuel Flagg Bemis, *The Latin American Policy of the United States: An Historical Interpretation* (New York: Harcourt, Brace, 1943), 27–30.

93. On the challenges that territorial expansion—mainly at the expense of Spain's crumbling empire—posed to the ideal of "union," see James E. Lewis, *The American Union and the Problem of Neighborhood: The United States and the Collapse of the Spanish Empire, 1783–1829* (Chapel Hill, NC: University of North Carolina Press, 1998). Lengthier explanations of Florida's strategic importance may be found in numerous works. One of the best discussions is in Samuel Flagg Bemis, *John Quincy Adams and the Foundations of American Foreign Policy* (New York: Alfred A. Knopf, 1965), 302–5.

94. The following discussion of the Gulf campaign of 1814–15 is based on Frank Lawrence Owsley Jr., *Struggle for the Gulf Borderlands: The Creek War and the Battle of New Orleans, 1812–1815* (Gainesville, Fl: University Presses of Florida, 1981).

95. This was Louis Bringier whose younger brother, Michel-Doradou, served as Jackson's aid-de-camp at the battle. See Tulane University, Bringier papers.

96. Jackson papers, reel 20, Mauricio de Zuniga to Andrew Jackson (Pensacola, 5/26/1816).

97. On the history of the Negro Fort, see Jane Landers, *Black Society in Spanish Florida*

(Urbana: University of Illinois Press, 1999), 229–35; Frank Lawrence Owsley Jr. and Gene A. Smith, *Filibusters and Expansionists: Jeffersonian Manifest Destiny, 1800–1821* (Tuscaloosa and London: University of Alabama Press, 1997), 103–17; and Claudio Saunt, *A New Order of Things: Property, Power, and the Transformation of the Creek Indians, 1733–1816* (Cambridge: Cambridge University Press, 1999), 273–90.

98. Owsley and Smith, *Filibusters and Expansionists*, 141–63.

99. ADAH, SG 24709, Message of Governor Bibb to the Gentlemen of the Legislative Council and of the House of Representatives (Saint Stephens, 11/3/1818).

100. ADAH, SG 24709, Marengo County Militia Roll.

101. ADAH, Pickett papers, "Notes Taken from the Lips of the Honorable George N. Stewart."

102. Jackson papers, reel 21, Andrew Jackson to James Monroe (Nashville, 11/12/1816).

103. On the American occupation of Mobile and the British attempts to capture it, see Owsley, *Struggle for the Gulf Borderlands,* 21–23, 95–112, and 169–77.

104. Although eager to keep an eye on movements to and from the French grant, Hyde de Neuville refused to station an accredited agent at Mobile on the grounds that such a move would imply French acceptance of the American claim. The consul-general suggested the alternative of stationing an unofficial agent there. This measure seems to have been accepted, for in mid-1820s, the brothers and Vine and Olive landowners Adolphe and Charles Batré were serving in this capacity. CAD, postes, New York City, subseries C, 2*, Consul-General to Duke de Richelieu (New York, 1/12/1818).

105. AAE, CP, Spain, 701, Spanish Ambassador to France to Duke de Richelieu (Paris, 3/2/1818). Don Luis de Onís was convinced that the Vine and Olive colony was intended to serve as a base from which an expedition against Spanish Florida could be secretly organized. In a panic, he urged the viceroy of New Spain to destroy it with a surprise attack. AHN, estado, legajo 5642, dispatch of 10/9/1817; and Apodaca correspondence, reel 3, dispatch 43 (3/31/1818).

106. Garcia de Leon y Pizarro, Jose, "Exposición Hecha al Rey Nuestro Señor sobre Nuestras Relaciones Politicas y Diferencias Actuales con el Gobierno de los Estados Unidos de America" (Madrid, 6/4/1817) in Alvaro Alonso-Castrillo, *Memorias* (Madrid: Revista de Occidente, n.d.), 2:189.

107. The projected canal would link Lake Michigan with the Mississippi and the Tennessee with the Tombigbee, upriver from the French Grant. Rufus King to Charles Gore (Washington, 12/14/1817) in King, *The Life and Correspondence of Rufus King, Comprising His Letters, Private and Official, His Public Documents, and His Speeches,* ed. Charles R. King. (New York: Da Capo Press, 1971), 6:85.

108. William H. Stewart Jr., *The Tennessee-Tombigbee Waterway: A Case Study in the Politics of Water Transportation* (Tuscaloosa: Bureau of Public Administration, University of Alabama, 1971).

109. Adams papers, reel 143, John Quincy Adams to William Eustis (Ealing, 3/29/1816).

110. Rufus King to Charles Gore (Washington, 2/23/1817) in King, *The Life and Correspondence of Rufus King,* 64.

111. The quotation is from Bemis, *John Quincy,* 307.

112. Jackson papers, reel 22, James Monroe to Andrew Jackson (Washington, 12/14/1816).

113. Andrew Jackson to James Monroe (Nashville, 3/4/1817) in Jackson, *Correspondence of Andrew Jackson,* ed. John Spencer Bassett (1927), reprint (New York, Kraus, 1969), 2:277.

114. In the midst of the publicity campaign he mounted in the pages of *L'Abeille,* Chaudron predicted that thousands of "persecuted" French Canadians would flee English domination to settle in the Vine and Olive colony. This massive migration would not only rapidly increase the size of the settlement, but also have the added benefit of draining the population of British Canada. *L'Abeille* 4, no. 7 (11/28/1816): 107.

115. Andrew Jackson papers, reel 22, Andrew Jackson to James Monroe (Nashville, 1/6/1817).

116. *L'Abeille* 4, no. 25 (4/3/1817): 398.

117. The following description of the group's journey to the Tombigbee is based on Smith, *Days of Exile,* 31–38. Parmentier is known to have been accompanied by Prosper Baltard, Jacques Lefrançois, Antoine-Marie Moquart, Benoit-M. Poculo, and George N. Stewart. ADAH, Pickett papers, "Notes from the Lips of the Honorable George N. Stewart."

118. Demopolis Public Library, Winston Smith papers, Nicholas Parmentier and Benoit Poculo to Major F. Freeman, Surveyor General of the Mississippi Territory (White Bluff, 8/8/817).

119. *L'Abeille* 5, no. 7 (8/28/1817): 114. Other observers concurred with Parmentier's assessment. One, Israel Pickens, governor of Alabama in the early 1820s, described the land at the confluence of the Tombigbee and Black Warrior Rivers as "the richest body of land in the state" and himself purchased many acres in the area. ADAH, LPR 46, letter of 7/10/19.

120. CAD, postes, Philadelphia, subseries B, 45*, dispatch of 10/21/1817.

121. *Niles' Weekly Register* 30 (9/6/1817), reprint of an article that first appeared in the *National Intelligencer.*

122. *L'Abeille* 5, no. 7 (8/28/1817): 112–14. This article was translated into English and printed in important national papers like the *National Intelligencer.*

123. CAD, postes, New York, subseries B, 123, Consul at New York to Consul at New Orleans (New York, 9/2/1817). On Clausel's kinship with Madame Desmares, see AAE, CP, U.S., 74, Consul-General to Duke de Richelieu (Philadelphia, 8/19/1817).

124. Jean-Guillaume Hyde de Neuville, *Mémoires et souvenirs du baron Hyde de Neuville* (Paris: Plon, 1888–92), 2:207.

125. AAE, CP, U.S., 73, Hyde de Neuville to Duke de Richelieu (Washington, 1/10/1817).

126. CAD, postes, New Orleans, subseries A, 144, Hyde de Neuville to Consul at New Orleans (Washington, 3/27/1817).

127. Hyde, *Mémoires et souvenirs,* 209–11.

128. AAE, CP, U.S., 73, Hyde de Neuville to Duke de Richelieu (Washington, 1/10/1817).

129. AAE, CP, U.S., 73, Duke de Richelieu to Hyde de Neuville (Paris, 4/18/1817).

Chapter 3

1. The chapter title is taken from a phrase in Adams papers, reel 146, John Quincy Adams to Pierre-Paul-François Degrand (Washington, 1/21/1818).

2. AAE, CP, U.S., 73, Hyde de Neuville to French chargé d'affaires in the United States (n.p., 5/8/1816).

3. AAE, CP, U.S., 74, Hyde de Neuville to Duke de Richelieu (Washington, 5/14/1817).

4. "Nota Pasada a las Potencias sobre la Necesidad de una Intervención en América," in Garcia de Leon y Pizarro, *Memorias,* 2:185.

5. The ambassador of Portugal, José Corrêa da Serra, described Baltimore, a city that rivaled New Orleans as an American haven of insurgent privateers, as the "new Algiers." José Corrêa da Serra, *José Corrêa da Serra: Ambassadeur du Royaume-Uni de Portugal et Brésil à Washington, 1816–1820,* ed. Léon Bourdon (Paris: Fundaçao Calouste Gulbenkian Centro Cultural Português , 1975), 106.

6. CAD, postes, New York, subseries B, 122, Consul at Baltimore to Consul-General (Baltimore, 3/24/1817).

7. AAE, CP, U.S., 73, Hyde de Neuville to Duke de Richelieu (Washington, 1/10/1817).

8. AAE, CP, U.S., 73, French chargé d'affaires to Hyde de Neuville (Washington, 4/5/1817).

9. To be sure, French nationalism was not the invention of the Revolution. On its roots in the Old Regime, see Bell, *Cult of the Nation.*

10. Don Louis de Onís, *Memoir upon the Negotiations between Spain and the United States of America, which led to the Treaty of 1819,* trans. Tobias Watkins (Philadelphia: E. de Krafft, 1821), 14–15.

11. Dispatch of Jose Cienfuegos (La Habana, 12/4/1817), in Franco, ed., *Documentos para la Historia de Mexico,* 155–56.

12. Descola, *Messagers de l'independance;* Lillian Estelle Fisher, *The Background of the Revolution for Mexican Independence* (Boston: Christopher, 1934); Luis Alberto de Herrera, *La Revolución Francesa y Sud América* (Paris: Dupont, 1910); Bernard Moses, *The Intellectual Background of the Revolution in South America, 1810–1824* (New York: Columbia University Press, 1926); and Charles Kingsley Webster, "British, French, and American Influences," in R. A. Humphreys and John Lynch, eds., *The Origins of the Latin American Revolutions, 1808–1826* (New York: Alfred A. Knopf, 1966), 75–83.

13. The fundamental work on the Lafittes as Spanish agents is Stanley Faye, "Great Stroke," 733–826. Some additional material may be found in Harris Gaylord Warren, "Documents Relating to Pierre Lafitte's Entrance into the Service of Spain," *Southwestern Historical Quarterly* 44, no. 1 (July 1940): 76–87.

14. Adams papers, reel 146, John Quincy Adams to Pierre-Paul-François Degrand (Washington, 1/21/1818).

15. Charles Carroll Griffin discusses this point at length in *The United States and the Disruption of the Spanish Empire, 1810–1822* (New York: Columbia University Press, 1937), 121–287.

16. An overview can be found in Owsley and Smith, *Filibusters and Expansionists,* 118–40 and 173–75.

17. The most comprehensive work on Mina's expedition remains William Davis Robinson, *Memoirs of the Mexican Revolution* (Philadelphia: Lydia R. Bailley, Printer, 1820). More compact descriptions may be found in Owsley and Smith, *Filibusters and Expansionists,* 173–5; J. M. Miquel I. Vergés, *Mina, el Español Frente a España* (Mexico: Xochitl, 1945); and

Harris Gaylord Warren, "The Origin of General Mina's Invasion of Mexico," *Southwestern Historical Quarterly* 42, no. 1 (July 1938): 1–20.

18. Guadalupe Jiménez Codinach, "La Confédération Napoléonnie. El Desempeño de los Conspiradores Militares y las Sociedades Secretas en la Independencia de México," *Historia Mexicana* 38, no. 1 (julio–septiembre 1988): 53.

19. The following discussion of Aury at Galveston is based on Lancaster E. Dabney, "Louis Aury: The First Governor of Texas under the Mexican Republic," *Southwestern Historical Quarterly* 42, no. 2 (October 1938): 108–16; Stanley Faye, "Commodore Aury," manuscript at the University of Texas at Austin, Center for American History, Aury papers, 85–183; Harris Gaylord Warren, "Documents Relating to the Establishment of Privateers at Galveston, 1816–1817," *Louisiana Historical Quarterly* 21, no. 4 (October 1938): 1086–1109; and A. Curtis Wilgus, "Spanish Patriot Activity along the Gulf Coast of the United States, 1811–1822," *Louisiana Historical Quarterly* 8, no. 2 (April 1925): 193–215.

20. On Aury's break with Bolivar, considered at the time to be a serious blow to the "Liberator's" prospects of success, see Simon Bolivar, *Memoirs of Simon Bolivar*, ed. H. L. V. Ducoudray Holstein (Boston: S. G. Goodrich, 1829), 123–26.

21. Unless otherwise noted, the following discussion of the Amelia Island affair is based on T. Frederick Davis, "MacGregor's Invasion of Florida, 1817," *Quarterly Periodical of the Florida Historical Society* 7, no. 1 (July 1928): 3–71; Stanley Faye, "Commodore Aury," 184–219; and Owsley and Smith, *Filibusters and Expansionists,* 118–40.

22. Adams papers, reel 442, John Stuart Skinner to John Mason (n.p., 2/19/1818); Madison papers, reel 18, James Madison to James Monroe (Montpellier, 7/18/1818).

23. PRO, FO/115, 30, Ambassador to Foreign Minister (Washington, 4/25/1817).

24. Adams papers, reel 440, "Lallemand aux députés espagnols" (Schuykill Falls, 7/5/1817).

25. AAE, CP, U.S., 75, Duke de Richelieu to Hyde de Neuville (Paris, 1/17/1818); and NARA, M 179, reel 38, Joel R. Poinsett to the Secretary of State (Charleston, 8/10/1817).

26. Adams papers, reel 441, Charles Collins to John Quincy Adams (Bristol, 12/24/1817); NARA, M 179, reel 40, Charles Collins to John Quincy Adams (Bristol, 1/13/1818) and Charles Collins to John Quincy Adams (Bristol, 1/19/1818); PRO, FO/115, 32, Ambassador to Foreign Minister (Washington, 5/6/1818); John Quincy Adams, *The Memoirs of John Quincy Adams,* ed. Charles Francis Adams (Philadelphia: J. B. Lippincott, 1874–77), vol. 4, entry for 1/14/1818; and *Niles' Weekly Register* (9/12/1818): 42.

27. Although the general accounts of Amelia Island treat the power struggle, particularly cogent descriptions can be found in NARA, M 179, reel 38, John H. McIntosh to the Secretary of State (the Refuge near Jefferson, Camden County, 10/30/1817); and *Narrative of a Voyage to the Spanish Main in the Ship Two Friends, the Occupation of Amelia Island, etc.* (London: J. Miller, 1819), 95–100.

28. For typical complaints about Amelia Island, see NARA, M 179, reel 37, Charles Harris to John Quincy Adams (Savannah, 6/8/1817) and William Johnson Jr. to John Quincy Adams (Charleston, 6/12/1817); reel 38, John H. McIntosh to John Quincy Adams (the Refuge Near Jefferson, Camden County, 10/30/1817) and Joel R. Poinsett to John Quincy Adams (Charleston, 8/10/1817).

29. NARA, M 179, reel 91, Belton A. Copp to John Quincy Adams (Saint Mary's, 4/1818).

30. AAE, CP, U.S., 74, Hyde de Neuville to Duke de Richelieu (Washington, 5/14/1817).

31. Onís's protests against the privateers and filibusters allowed to conduct their preparations on American soil may be found in Manning, ed., *Diplomatic Correspondence*, vol. 3. While there is unfortunately no comprehensive study of Onís's covert activities, nor even a biography of this important figure in Spain's struggle against the colonial independence movement, there are a few articles treating particular aspects of the Spanish counterespionage effort in America. Especially illuminating are Faye, "Great Stroke," 733–826; Warren, *Sword Was Their Passport;* and Warren, "José Alvarez de Toledo's Reconciliation with Spain and Projects for Suppressing Rebellion in the Spanish Colonies," *Louisiana Historical Quarterly* 23, no. 3 (July 1940): 827–63.

32. It was rumored at the time that Spain was so desperate to acquire a navy that it had offered the island of Minorca to the czar of Russia for warships. Eventually, Spain purchased an entire Russian fleet with money paid to it by Great Britain in exchange a promise to abolish the slave trade. When they arrived in Cadiz in February 1818, all but two were discovered to be unseaworthy. Within five years, only one still remained—the others had been sold for firewood. On this transaction, see Russell Bartley, *Imperial Russia and the Struggle for Latin American Independence, 1808–1828* (Austin: Institute of Latin American Studies, University of Texas at Austin, 1978), 121–27.

33. Corrêa da Serra, *José Corrêa da Serra,* 104.

34. The Spanish Cabinet's search for and eventual rejection of a moderate policy toward the rebellious colonies is discussed with great clarity by Timothy E. Anna, *Spain and the Loss of America* (Lincoln and London: University of Nebraska Press, 1983), 148–220. An earlier treatment of Spain's approach to the independence movement is A. F. Zimmerman, "Spain and Its Colonies, 1808–1820," *Hispanic American Historical Review* 11, no. 4 (November 1931): 439–63.

35. Pizarro's most important position papers and recommendations to the Cabinet may be found in Garcia de Leon y Pizarro, *Memorias,* 2:180–299.

36. Archivo General de Indias, estado, América en General, legajo 3, "Ideas del Señor D. Luis de Onís" (n.d.).

37. Garcia de Leon y Pizarro, "Exposicion Hecha al Rey Nuestro Señor y a su Consejo de estado sobre Nuestras Relaciones Politicas y Diferencias Actuales con el Gobierno de los estados Unidos de America" (Madrid, junio 4, 1817), *Memorias,* 2:217. On the aims of Wilkinson and Burr toward Mexico, see Isaac Joslin Cox, "Hispanic-American Phases of the 'Burr Conspiracy'," *Hispanic American Historical Review* 12, no. 2 (May 1932): 145–75.

38. Garcia de Leon y Pizarro, "Memoria Dirigada al Consejo de estado sobre la Pacificación de América" (Palacio, junio 9, 1818), *Memorias,* 2:270.

39. Anna, *Spain and the Loss of America,* 148. An illuminating discussion of a specific instance of the moderates' inability to overcome the opposition of hard-liners and entrenched mercantile interests may be found in Michael P. Costeloe, "Spain and the Latin American Wars of Independence: The Free Trade Controversy, 1810–1820," *Hispanic American Historical Review* 61, no. 2 (1981): 209–34.

40. Spain's ultimately unsuccessful effort to secure European intervention is treated in all accounts of the diplomacy of Latin American independence. Especially useful treatments may be found in Bartley, *Imperial Russia,* 103–30; Antonin Debidour, *Histoire diplomatique de l'Europe* (Paris: Félix Alcan, 1891), 105–10; Dexter Perkins, "Russia and the Spanish Colonies, 1817–1818," *American Historical Review* 28, no. 4 (July 1923): 656–72; J. Fred Rippy, *Latin America in World Politics* (New York: Alfred A. Knopf, 1928), 24–53; and William Spence Robertson, "Russia and the Emancipation of Spanish America, 1816–1826," *Hispanic American Historical Review* 21, no. 2 (May 1941): 196–221. Some of the best studies of European intervention examine the issue from the perspective of Britain's tireless efforts to prevent it. See n. 56 this chapter for a list of these works.

41. The possibilities and perils of Spain's delaying policy were laid out by Garcia de Leon y Pizarro in his "Exposicion hecha al Rey," *Memorias,* 2:217.

42. Hyde de Neuville, *Mémoires et souvenirs,* 2:333.

43. There are many excellent discussions of American foreign policy and the question of Latin American independence. Some of the most useful are Bemis, *Latin American Policy;* Bemis, *John Quincy Adams;* Worthington Chauncey Ford, "John Quincy Adams and the Monroe Doctrine," *American Historical Review* 7, no. 4 (July 1902): 676–96; Fuller, *Purchase of Florida;* Griffin, *United States and the Disruption of the Spanish Empire;* Lewis, *American Union;* Perkins, *Monroe Doctrine, 1823–1826;* Tatum, *United States and Europe,* 56–85; William Earl Weeks, *John Quincy Adams and American Global Empire* (Lexington: University Press of Kentucky, 1992); and Arthur Preston Whitaker, *United States and the Independence of Latin America.*

44. Garcia de Leon y Pizarro, "Exposicion hecha al Rey," *Memorias,* 2:221. Should the American government not acknowledge the "justice" of the Spanish cause and the "impropriety" of their own "pretensions," Pizarro suggested, the Spanish ambassador should suggest submitting their territorial differences to "the decision of one or two friendly, mediating powers." The prospect that European monarchies would weigh the respective claims of Spain and the United States to Florida, for which the Americans clearly had no legal title, was alone sufficient threat to keep the American government at the bargaining table.

45. Madison papers, reel 18, William H. Crawford to James Madison (Washington, 9/27/1816).

46. Whitaker, *United States and the Independence of Latin America,* 115–40.

47. Hyde de Neuville, *Mémoires et souvenirs,* 2:317.

48. Toledo, "Posicion de la España con respecto a la Inglaterra y los estados Unidos del Norte de América," in Garcia de Leon y Pizarro, *Memorias,* 2:186.

49. Lewis, *American Union.*

50. On these expeditions, see Cox, *West Florida Controversy;* Owsley and Smith, *Filibusters and Expansionists;* and Julius W. Pratt, *Expansionists of 1812* (New York: Macmillan, 1925).

51. "Presidential Proclamation Prohibitory of Illegal Expeditions in the United States" (September 1, 1815), *American State papers,* Class I Foreign Relations, vol. 4 (Washington, D.C., 1834), 1.

52. As reported by John Quincy Adams in his memoirs, cited by Bemis, *John Quincy Adams,* 304.

53. AAE, CP, U.S., 73, Hyde de Neuville to Duke de Richelieu (n.p., 7/12/1816).

54. NARA, M 78, reel 1, Secretary of State to Thomas L. Halsey (Washington, 4/21/1817) and (Washington, 1/22/1818); and NARA, M 179, reel 40, Thomas L. Halsey to James de Wolf (Buenos Aires, 8/9/1817).

55. For Jessup's inflammatory letters, see Jackson papers, reel 21, Colonel Jessup to General Jackson (New Orleans, 8/18, 8/21, 9/5, 9/11, and 9/23/1816). For the administration's response, see Madison papers, reel 17, James Madison to James Monroe (Montpellier, 9/22/1816), James Madison to William H. Crawford (Montpellier, 9/23/1816), William H. Crawford to Secretary of the Navy Crowinshield (Washington, 9/27/1816); reel 18, William H. Crawford to Andrew Jackson (Washington, 9/27/1816), and William H. Crawford to James Madison (Washington, 9/27/1816).

56. There are a number of excellent studies of British Latin American diplomacy during this period. Perkins, *Castlereagh and Adams;* Humphreys, "Anglo-American Rivalries," 130–53; Kaufman, *British Policy and the Independence of Latin America;* Philips, "Great Britain and the Continental Alliance," 3–50; Rippy, *Rivalry of the United States and Great Britain;* Tatum, *United States and Europe,* 141–82; Sir Charles Kingsely Webster, "Castlereagh and the Spanish Colonies, 1815–1818," *English Historical Review* 27, no. 105 (January 1912): 78–95; Webster, "Castlereagh and the Spanish Colonies, 1818–1822," *English Historical Review* 30 (1915): 631–45; and Webster, *Foreign Policy of Castlereagh.*

57. Goebel, "British Trade to the Spanish Colonies," 288–320, and Humphreys, "British Merchants and South American Independence," 106–129.

58. Armand-Emmanuel du Plessis, duc de Richelieu, *Lettres du duc de Richelieu au marquis d'Osmond, 1816–1818,* ed. Sébastien Charlety (Paris: Gallimard, 1939), 188.

59. Jefferson's embargo (1807–9) only served to increase the economic dependence of Great Britain on trade with South America, thereby ensuring that country's future involvement in the affairs of the Western hemisphere.

60. Toledo, "Extracto de la Segunda Memoria que, en Ampliación o Explicación de la Primera, Pidió al Señor Don José Alvarez de Toledo el Ministro de estado" (septiembre 1, 1817), in Garcia de Leon y Pizarro, *Memorias,* 234.

61. On the success of the pacification in Mexico in 1817–18, see Hubert Howe Bancroft, *History of Mexico* (San Francisco: History Company, 1886), 12:645–85 (within vol. 4). A more comprehensive overview of the pacification may be found in Jaime Delgado, "La 'Pacificación de América' en 1818," *Revista de Indias,* 10, núm. 39 (enero–marzo 1950): 7–67, and núm.40 (abril–junio 1950): 263–310.

62. There is no satisfactory overview of British covert involvement in the Latin American rebellion. There are, however, several works on the volunteers, as well as a number of personal memoirs. See Hasbrouck, *Foreign Legionaries;* and W. H. Koebel, *British Exploits in South America: A History of British Activities in Exploration, Military Adventure, Diplomacy, Science and Trade in Latin America* (New York: Century Co., 1917).

63. AAE, CP, U.S., 74, Hyde de Neuville to Duke de Richelieu (Washington, 5/14/1817).

64. Toledo, "Posicion de la España," in Garcia de Leon y Pizarro, *Memorias,* 2:186.

65. Garcia de Leon y Pizarro, "Exposicion Hecha al Rey," in Garcia de Leon y Pizarro, *Memorias,* 2:213.

66. For a good example of this strategy, see Pizarro to the Spanish Ambassador to Great Britain (Palacio, 6/22/1817), Garcia de Leon y Pizarro, *Memorias*, 2:223–28.

67. Garcia de Leon y Pizarro, "Exposicion Hecha al Rey," Garcia de Leon y Pizarro, *Memorias*, 2:212.

68. The following paragraphs on French policy toward Latin American independence are based on my own analysis of the correspondence of the Duke de Richelieu, Hyde de Neuville, and the various consular officials. The only existing survey of the subject is badly in need of an update and, in any event, particularly weak on the period of the 1810s. Robertson, *France and Latin American Independence*. Another discussion of French policy may be found in Tatum, *United States and Europe*, 87–111.

69. "Pozzo di Borgo to Nesselrode" (Paris, 7/15/1816) in Carlo Andrea Pozzo di Borgo, comte de, *Correspondance diplomatique du comte Pozzo di Borgo, ambassadeur de Russie en France et du comte de Nesselrode depuis la Restauration des Bourbons jusqu'au Congrès d'Aix-la-Chapelle, 1814–1818* (Paris: Calmann-Lévy, 1890), 1:390.

70. "Instructions to Hyde de Neuville, French minister to the United States" (1/26/1816), reprinted in Watel, *Jean-Guillaume Hyde de Neuville*, 223–29.

71. Monroe papers, reel 6, Richard Rush to James Monroe (Washington, 4/24/1817).

72. AAE, CP, U.S., 74, Hyde de Neuville to Duke de Richelieu (Washington, 5/14/1817).

73. AAE, CP, U.S., 75, Hyde de Neuville to Duke de Richelieu (Washington, 6/4/1818).

74. Adams, *Memoirs,* entry for 12/25/1818.

75. Perkins, *Castlereagh and Adams,* 294.

76. So convinced was the French government of the importance of these markets that it instructed Hyde to avoid alienating the representatives of the insurgent colonies—whose eventual independence it took for granted—and investigate the commercial possibilities open to French trade in the liberated areas. "Instructions," reprinted in Watel, *Jean-Guillaume Hyde de Neuville,* 226.

77. On the idea of creating Latin American kingdoms under Bourbon princes, see Harold Temperley, "French Designs on Spanish America in 1820–5," *English Historical Review* 40 (1925): 34–53.

78. Richelieu, *Lettres du duc de Richelieu,* 154. The British government naturally rejected this proposal. Anything that would end the rebellion on terms other than those dictated by Britain—and obviously a solution that involved installing French princes on Latin American thrones—was anathema to his policy. AAE, CP, England, 610, Marquis d'Osmond to Duke de Richelieu (London, 2/13/1818).

79. AAE, CP, U.S., 75, Hyde de Neuville to Duke de Richelieu (Washington, 6/4/1818).

80. Richelieu, *Lettres du duc de Richelieu,* 232–3. Cousins to the ruling branch of the Bourbon family, the Orléans family had compromised itself with political machinations throughout the eighteenth century and had even welcomed the French Revolution. In 1793 the head of the family, who had renamed himself Philippe Egalité (Equality) and been elected to the National Convention, had voted for the death of Louis XVI.

81. AAE, CP, England, 610, Marquis d'Osmond to Duke de Richelieu (London, 5/2/1818).

82. AAE, CP, England, 610, Marquis d'Osmond to Duke de Richelieu (London, 5/16/1818).

83. AAE, CP, England, 610, Marquis d'Osmond to Duke de Richelieu (London, 6/2/1818).

84. Richelieu, *Lettres du duc de Richelieu*, 198.

85. Ibid.,196–97.

86. AAE, CP, Spain, 701, Duke de Fernan Nuñez et de Montellano to Duke de Richelieu (Paris, 3/2/1818).

87. AAE, CP, U.S., 74, Hyde de Neuville to Duke de Richelieu (New Brunswick, 8/4/1817). For an example of the specifically American fear that a resurgent Napoleon in the New World would conquer Louisiana, see NARA, M 179, reel 40, Joshua Childs to John Quincy Adams (Pinckneyville, 3/20/1818).

88. AAE, CP, U.S., 73 Hyde de Neuville to Duke de Richelieu (Washington, 1/10/1817) and (New Brunswick, 7/12/1816).

89. Descriptions of the many rescue attempts, real and imagined, may be found in the following works: Ulane Bonnel, "Espoirs de délivrance," in *Sainte-Hélène, terre d'exil,* ed. Marcel Dunan (Paris: Hachette, 1971), 229–57; Raoul Brice, *Les espoirs de Napoléon à Sainte-Hélène* (Paris: Payot, 1938); J. Lucas-Dubreton, *Le culte de Napoléon: 1815–1848* (Paris: Albin-Michel, 1960), 91–108; Paul Pierre Ebeyer, *Revelations Concerning Napoleon's Escape from St. Helena* (New Orleans: Windmill Publishing, 1947; and Clarence Edward Macartney and Gordon Dorrance, *The Bonapartes in America* (Philadelphia: Dorrance, 1939), 241–72.

90. AN, F^7 6717, "Bulletin particulier" (n.d.).

91. AN, F^7 6716, "Bulletin" (Marseille, 3/25/1817).

92. AN, F^7 6866, "Report of the Royal Gendarmerie of Loiret" (Orléans, 11/19/1818).

93. Bonnel, "Espoirs," 274. A complete description of the Latapie's mission to Pernambuco may be found in Da Costa, "Napoléon Ier au Brésil," 205–16 and 339–49.

94. *New York Evening Post* (2/25/1818), cited in Warren, *Sword Was Their Passport,* 195.

95. Richelieu, *Lettres de Richelieu,* 62.

96. "Instructions" reprinted in Watel, 227–28.

97. CAD, postes, New York, subseries B, 110, Hyde de Neuville to Consul at New York (Washington, 5/26/1818).

98. CAD, postes, New Orleans, subseries A, 487, "Registre servant à inscrire le nom des passagers arrivants de France, commencé le 1er janvier 1817."

99. PRO, FO/5, 122, Hyde de Neuville to the British ambassador to the United States (New Brunswick, 7/19/1817).

100. AAE, CP, U.S., 74, Hyde de Neuville to Duke de Richelieu (New Brunswick, 8/4/1817).

101. AAE, CP, U.S., 74, Consult-General to Hyde de Neuville (Philadelphia, 7/24/1817) and "Suite des declarations de Raoul faites devant M. le consul-général et adressés par ce dernier au ministre du Roi aux Etats-Unis" (Philadelphia, 7/25/1817).

102. AAE, CP, U.S., 74, Hyde de Neuville to Duke de Richelieu (New Brunswick, 7/26/1817), Consul-General to Hyde de Neuville (Philadelphia, 7/29/1817), and Hyde de Neuville to Duke de Richelieu (New Brunswick, 8/11/1817).

103. CAD, postes, Baltimore, subseries A, 37, Consul-General to Consul at Baltimore (Philadelphia, 7/26/1817).

104. AAE, CP, U.S., 74, Hyde de Neuville to Duke de Richelieu (Philadelphia, 7/29/1817).

105. AAE, CP, U.S., 74, Hyde de Neuville to Duke de Richelieu (New Brunswick, 8/4/1817).

106. AAE, CP, U.S., 74, Hyde de Neuville to Duke de Richelieu (New Brunswick, 8/4/1817).

107. The following description of Lakanal's plan is based on copies of the documents transmitted by Hyde de Neuville to the British government. PRO FO/5, 123, "Rapport adressé à Sa Majesté le Roi des Espagnes et des Indes, par ses fideles sujets les citoyens composant la Confederation Napoléonienne," "Tableau des nations indiennes qui demeurent dans la Louisiane septroniale depuis le cours de Missouri et à l'Ouest de ce fleuve, jusqu'aux montagnes qui bornent à l'est le Nouveau Mexique," "Vocabulaire Enigmatique," "Ultimatum," and "Petition." Copies of the translations made by the American government in 1817 are available at the National Archives in Washington, D.C. They can be consulted more conveniently in Reeves, *Napoleonic Exiles,* 52–60. The translations in this paragraph are my own. On Lee's confirmation of Lakanal's authorship, see AAE, CP, U.S., 74, Hyde de Neuville to Duke de Richelieu (Washington, 9/14/1817).

108. AAE, CP, U.S., 74, Hyde de Neuville to Duke de Richelieu (New Brunswick, 8/31/1817).

109. AAE, CP, U.S., 74, Hyde de Neuville to Richard Rush (Philadelphia, 8/30/1817).

110. Adams papers, reel 439, Richard Rush to John Quincy Adams (Washington, 9/2/1817).

111. Adams papers, reel 146, John Quincy Adams to James Monroe (Washington, 9/25/1817).

112. Adams papers, reel 439, John Quincy Adams to Hyde de Neuville (Washington, 9/24/1817).

113. AAE, CP, U.S., 74, Hyde de Neuville to John Quincy Adams (Washington, 9/25/1817).

114. Adams papers, reel 146, John Quincy Adams to James Monroe (Washington, 10/4/1817).

115. Adams papers, reel 440, James Monroe to John Quincy Adams (Albermarle, 10/11/1817).

116. Monroe papers, reel 6, "Monroe's Notes for Cabinet Meeting" (10/1817). They are also found in Adams papers, reel 440, "Notes" (10/25/1817), but Adams's agenda does not include the publication question. Hyde was finally informed of the government's decision not to publish on November 10, 1817. NARA, M 38, reel 2, John Quincy Adams to Hyde de Neuville (Washington, 11/10/1817).

117. Adams papers, reel 146, John Quincy Adams to James Monroe (Washington, 9/27/1817).

118. Adams papers, reel 146, John Quincy Adams to James Monroe (Washington, 9/29/1817).

119. Adams papers, reel 146, John Quincy Adams to James Monroe (Washington, 10/8/1817).

120. AAE, CP, U.S., 74, Hyde de Neuville to Duke de Richelieu (New Brunswick, 9/29/1817).

121. AAE, CP, U.S., 74, Hyde de Neuville to Duke de Richelieu (New Brunswick, 10/5/1817).

122. AAE, CP, U.S., 74, Hyde de Neuville to Duke de Richelieu (New Brunswick, 10/11/1817).

123. NARA, M 38, reel 2, John Quincy Adams to Hyde de Neuville (Washington, 12/5/1817); and Adams, *Memoirs,* entry for 9/29/1817.

124. See for example the report of John Dick, United States attorney general for the district of Louisiana, on the enforcement of the Neutrality Act in the port of New Orleans. NARA, M 179, reel 40, John Dick to John Quincy Adams (New Orleans, 2/2/1818).

125. On the stronger neutrality law of 1818, see Robertson, *Hispanic-American Relations with the United States,* 28–29.

126. NARA, M 179, reel 39, Judge Harry Toulmin to John Quincy Adams (Tensaw, 12/10/1817). In a meeting with Onís on January 14, 1818, Adams did not scruple to use this plan of conquest, as well as MacGregor's projected landing at Tampa Bay, to pressure the Spanish ambassador to give way in the ongoing boundary negotiations. "If we should not come to an early conclusion of the Florida negotiation," Adams threatened, "Spain would not have possession of Florida to give us." Adams, *Memoirs,* entry for 1/14/1818. It is possible that the movements against Pensacola at the end of 1817 had originated a year earlier as a subsidiary operation connected with Mina's invasion of Mexico. On this possibility, see Harris Gaylord Warren, "Pensacola and the Filibusters, 1816–1817," *Louisiana Historical Quarterly* 21, no. 3 (July 1938): 806–22. For a list of French nationals—including several Vine and Olive members—involved in the machinations against Pensacola, see AHN, estado, legajo 194, dispatch 43.

127. Adams papers, reel 440, Secretary of the Navy to Captain John Henley (Washington, 11/14/1817).

128. Adams, *Memoirs,* entry for 1/9/1818.

129. AAE, CP, U.S., 74, Hyde de Neuville to Duke de Richelieu (New Brunswick, 8/31/1817).

130. AAE, CP, U.S., 75, Louis de Mun to Hyde de Neuville (Washington, 4/20/1818) and Lavaud to Hyde de Neuville (Washington, 4/28/1818).

131. AAE, CP, U.S., 74, Hyde de Neuville to Duke de Richelieu (New Brunswick, 9/29/1817).

Chapter 4

1. The term "ultra-quixotism" was coined by John Quincy Adams to describe the machinations of the French expatriates. Adams papers, reel 146, John Quincy Adams to James Monroe (Washington, 10/4/1817).

2. The phrase "the Bonaparte of the New World," is from AAE, CP, U.S., 76, Consul at New Orleans to Hyde de Neuville (3/23/1819).

3. Unless otherwise noted, the information in this and the following paragraph is taken from AG, Lallemand's personal dossier, GD 2; Hoefer, 29:3–7; and Six, 2:39–40.

4. Jules Silvestre, *De Waterloo à Sainte-Hélène (20 juin-16 octobre 1816)* (Paris: F(lix Alcan, 1904), 177. For an overview of Lallemand's role at this critical juncture, see his "Extrait du journal du général Charles-Frédéric-Antoine Lallemand, juillet-août 1816," *The French American Review* 2, no. 2 (April–June 1949): 63–80.

5. A good description of Lallemand's peregrinations can be found in the memoirs of his traveling companion, General Savary. Anne-Jean-Marie-René Savary, *Memoirs of the Duke of Rovigo* (London: H. Colburn, 1828), 4:187–203.

6. PRO, FO/115, 25, Lord Bathurst to Lord Castlereagh (London, 5/16/1816), and Lord Castlereagh to the British Ambassador to the United States (London, 7/2/1816).

7. CAD, correspondance interministérielle, police générale, 520, Duke de Richelieu to the Minister of General Police (Paris, 6/23/1816).

8. CAD, correspondance interministérielle, police générale, 520, Minister of General Police to Duke de Richelieu (Paris, 7/4/1817); CAD, postes, Philadelphia, subseries B, 45*, Consul-General to Hyde de Neuville (Philadelphia, 5/16/1817); and CAD, postes, New York City, subseries B, 126, Consul at New York to Consul at Philadelphia (New York, 5/10/1817). The quote is from *L'Abeille* 3, no. 14 (7/18/1816), 224.

9. Unless otherwise noted, the information in this paragraph is drawn from AG, Rigau's personal file, 8 YD 1099; Hoefer, *Nouvelle biographie,* 42:287–88; and Six, *Dictionnaire biographique,* 2:370–71.

10. AG, 8 YD 1099, Juge de paix of Dax to Minister of War (Dax, 2/8/1808).

11. Information on Jeannet is from documents in ADAH, Gardien papers, and a variety of published works: Yves Benot, *La Guyanne sous la Révolution, où l'impasse de la Révolution pacifique* (Kourou, Guyane: Ibis Rouge, 1997), 57–161; Michel L. Martin and Alain Yacou, eds., *De la Révolution française aux révolutions créole et nègres* (Paris: Editions Caribéennes, 1989), 102; Laurent Dubois, "The Promise of Revolution: Saint-Domingue and the Struggle for Autonomy in Guadeloupe, 1797–1802," in *The Impact of the Haitian Revolution in the Atlantic World,* ed. David P. Geggus (Columbia: University of South Carolina Press, 2001), 121; Arthur Henry, *La Guyane française: Son histoire, 1604–1946* (1950), reprint (Cayenne, Guyane: Le Mayouri, 1981), 128–40; and Auguste Lacour, *Histoire de la Guadeloupe* (1857), reprint (Paris: Maisonneuve, 1960), 3:49–110.

12. AAE, CP, U.S., 75, Consul at New Orleans to Duke de Richelieu (New Orleans, 3/14/1818).

13. Dabbs, "Additional Notes," 350.

14. Adams papers, reel 442, William Lee to John Quincy Adams (n.p., 1/20/1818); and AAE, CP, U.S., 76, Consul at New Orleans to Duke de Richelieu (New Orleans, 3/23/1819. On desertions from French regiments stationed in the Caribbean, see CAD, postes, New York, subseries C, 2*, Consul-General to Duke de Richelieu (New York, 8/6/1817).

15. CAD, postes, New York, subseries C, 2*, Consul-General to Duke de Richelieu (New York, 12/31/1817).

16. Adams, *Memoirs,* entry for 11/9/1817. The Anglophobic Colonel Galabert later boasted that he had single-handedly convinced more than four hundred French officers to steer clear

of MacGregor's enterprise—on the grounds that it would be dishonorable to serve under an Englishman in a project widely suspected of secretly furthering the aims of Great Britain. AHN, estado, legajo 5642, dispatch 175 (Philadelphia, 10/9/1817).

17. Adams papers, reel 442, Pierre-Paul-François Degrand to John Quincy Adams (Boston, 1/28/1818).

18. Unless otherwise noted, the following description of the meeting is based on CAD, postes, New York, subseries C, 2*, Consul-General to Duke de Richelieu (New York, 9/25/1817). For a translation of the Consul-General's report, see Rafe Blaufarb, "Notes and Documents: French Consular Reports on the Association of French Emigrants: The Organization of the Vine and Olive Colony," *Alabama Review* 56, no. 2 (April 2003): 104–24.

19. *L'Abeille* 5, no. 17, 267–70.

20. Adams papers, reel 439, William Lee to John Quincy Adams (n.p., 9/27/1817).

21. APS, Girard family papers, Lallemand file, Henri to Henriette Lallemand (Philadelphia, 10/23/1817).

22. *Niles' Weekly Register* (11/8/1817): 166.

23. CAD, postes, New York, subseries C, 2*, Consul-General to Duke de Richelieu (New York, 11/10/1817).

24. AAE, CP, U.S., 74, Hyde de Neuville to Duke de Richelieu (New Brunswick, 10/17/1817).

25. For a semiofficial description of the October 26 meeting at which the allotments were final distributed, see *L'Abeille* 5, no. 16 (10/30/1817): 245–48, and 5, no. 18 (11/13/1817): 277–84. For a more critical view, see the translations of the French consular reports in Blaufarb, "Notes and Documents."

26. Gardien, "Take Pity on Our Glory," 254.

27. NARA, RG 49, 234–38.

28. These figures represent the Champ d'Asile allotments for which deeds of sale exist in the NARA, as well as those allotments for which no documents exist, but whose owners granted power-of-attorney to Georges Jeannet. If these probable, but unconfirmed sales, are excluded, the figures fall to eight thousand acres sold for a bit more than eight thousand dollars. These calculations are based on NARA, RG 49, 234–38.

29. NARA, M 179, reel no. 3, Pierre Palmerani to John Quincy Adams (Philadelphia 12/18/1817).

30. CAD, postes, Philadelphia, subseries B, 45*, Consul-General to Hyde de Neuville (New York, 4/23/1818).

31. CAD, postes, New York, C 2*, Consul-General to Duke de Richelieu (New York, 12/10 and 12/28/1817).

32. "Germans" was the code word used by Pierre-Paul-François Degrand and John Quincy Adams to designate the Lallemand brothers. The "Don" was the Spanish ambassador Don Luis de Onís.

33. Adams papers, reel 439, William Lee to John Quincy Adams (n.p., 9/27/1817).

34. Adams papers, reel 440, Lallemand brothers to William Lee (Philadelphia, 10/3/1817).

35. AHN, estado, legajo 5642, dispatch 175 (Philadelphia, 10/9/1817). On Latour, see

Edwin H. Carpenter, ed., "Latour's Report on Spanish-American Relations in the Southwest," *Louisiana Historical Quarterly* 30, no. 3 (July 1947): 715–17.

36. Adams papers, reel 442, Pierre-Paul-François Degrand to John Quincy Adams (Boston, 1/15/1818).

37. Unless otherwise noted, the following description of the Onís-Galabert discussions is based on AHN, estado, legajo 5642, dispatch 175 (Philadelphia, 10/9/1817).

38. Galabert's ideas are summarized in AHN, estado, legajo 5642, dispatch 180 (Philadelphia, 10/26/1817).

39. AHN, estado, legajo 5642, dispatch 175 (Philadelphia, 10/9/1817).

40. Many observers questioned the ambassador's judgment. The viceroy of Mexico categorically disapproved of Onís's dealings with the French exiles. And even Degrand believed that the ambassador had lost his sense of reality, probably because he was panicked by the thought of so many former Napoleonic officers gathered in Alabama near the frontier with Spanish Florida. "There can be no doubt that the great fears excited in the breast of the Spanish minister by the assemblage of so many military men on the Tombigbee have made him lose, in some measure, the benefit of cool reflection and made him adopt this desperate expedient." Adams papers, reel 442, Pierre-Paul-François Degrand to John Quincy Adams (Boston, 1/15/1818).

41. Unless otherwise noted, citations in the following paragraph are taken from Adams, *Memoirs*, 18–20.

42. This request appears to have been turned down on the grounds that the president ought not meet with someone who had been "outlawed and under sentence of death in France" for high treason without provoking unnecessary tension with that country. Adams, *Memoirs*, 20.

43. Adams papers, reel 146, John Quincy Adams to Pierre-Paul-François Degrand (Washington, 11/13/1817).

44. On December 8, the repentant Néel met with the French consul-general and, in exchange for amnesty and passage back to France, revealed the substance of Lallemand's negotiations with Onís. The consul-general, who had been directed by the Duke de Richelieu to correspond directly with him, did not inform his chief, the ambassador Hyde de Neuville. When Hyde found out that the consul-general had long known about this surprising development, he became outraged. The resulting conflict between the two men—a conflict, one suspects, that was fostered by Richelieu whose encouragement of parallel correspondence was largely responsible for it—dragged on throughout the spring and summer of 1818.

45. CAD, postes, New York, subseries C, 2*, Consul-General to Duke de Richelieu (New York, 12/31/1817).

46. AHN, estado, legajo 5642, dispatch 198 (Washington, 11/29/1817).

47. AAE, CP, U.S., 74, Hyde de Neuville to Duke de Richelieu (Washington, 12/28/1817).

48. Apodaca correspondence, reel 3, dispatch 43 (Mexico, 3/31/1818).

49. This paragraph is based on Apodaca correspondence, reel 3, especially Don Luis de

Onís to Viceroy Apodaca (Washington, 12/28/1817); and CAD, postes, New York, subseries C, 2*, Consul-General to Duke de Richelieu (New York, 12/10, 12/28, and 12/31/1817).

50. "Croissac," a code name for René-François Lacroix, estimated the number at 80. AAE, CP, U.S., 75, "Résumé de la deposition du Sieur Croissac." Two Spanish officers, who had been captured by privateers and taken to Galveston, agreed on this number. AHN, estado, legajo 5643, dispatch 56 (Washington, 4/6/1818). Another eyewitness put the number at 90, of whom there were one general (Rigau), 15 colonels or majors, 3 battalion adjutants, ten captains, 30 lieutenants, three non-commissioned officers, seven doctors, 13 staff officers, and eight laborers. Dabbs, "Additional Notes," 351.

51. Gardien, "Take Pity on Our Glory," 254.

52. The best published accounts are Hartmann and Millard, *Le Texas;* Dabbs, "Additional Notes"; and Girard, *The Adventures of a Captain.* The following paragraphs describing the journey to the Champ d'Asile are based on these, as well as AAE, CP, U.S., 75, "Résumé de la deposition du Sieur Croissac"; AAE, CP, U.S., 76, Consul-General to Duke de Richelieu (Philadelphia, 11/30/1818); and AAE, CP, U.S., 76, Consul-General to Richelieu (Philadelphia, 12/21/1818).

53. AAE, CP, U.S., 76, Consul-General to Duke de Richelieu (Philadelphia, 12/21/1818); Dabbs, "Additional Notes," 351; Hartmann and Millard, *Le Texas,* 23.

54. AAE, CP, U.S., 75, "Résumé du Sieur Croissac"; and Dabbs, "Additional Notes," 350.

55. This sum was never paid by Lallemand—a fate experienced by many of those who had financial dealings with the former general. See AAE, CP, U.S., 76, Consul-General to Duke de Richelieu (Philadelphia, 11/30/1818); and APS, Stephen Girard papers, Henri Lallemand to Stephen Girard (Philadelphia, 5/28/1818).

56. AAE, CP, U.S., 76, Consul-General to Duke de Richelieu (Philadelphia, 11/30/1818); and Dabbs, 352.

57. In addition to drawing on the sources noted in footnote 52, this description of Galveston is also based on AHN, estado, legajo 5643, dispatch 56 (Washington, 4/6/1818).

58. Dabbs, "Additional Notes," 353.

59. Apodaca correspondence, reel 3, dispatch 61 (Mexico, 9/30/1818).

60. APS, Stephen Girard papers, Henri Lallemand to Stephen Girard (Philadelphia, 5/28/1818). Given Aury's activities on Amelia, as well as a revealing hint dropped in another letter from Henri Lallemand to Stephen Girard, it seems more likely that the "captured negroes" would have been smuggled into Louisiana and sold to the eager planters of that state.

61. *L'Ami des Lois* (2/5/1818).

62. APS, Stephen Girard papers, Henri Lallemand to Stephen Girard (New Orleans, 2/7/1818). It is not inconceivable that this letter served another purpose—to give rise to the idea that the Lallemands and their enterprise were being supported by Girard. Henri Lallemand had already written to Henriette, while aboard the *Actress* in New York harbor, to inform her (dishonestly) of his imminent departure for the Tombigbee settlement. APS, Girard family papers, Henri to Henriette Lallemand (New York, 12/27/1817).

63. AAE, CP, U.S., 75, Consul at New Orleans to Duke de Richelieu (New Orleans,

2/16 and 3/14/1818); and AAE, CP, U.S., 76, Consul-General to Duke de Richelieu (Philadelphia, 12/21/1818).

64. APS, Stephen Girard papers, Henri Lallemand to Stephen Girard (New Orleans, 2/14/1818, and Philadelphia, 5/28/1818).

65. AAE, CP, U.S., 76, Consul-General to Duke de Richelieu (Philadelphia, 12/21/1818).

66. APS, Stephen Girard papers, Henri Lallemand to Stephen Girard (Philadelphia, 5/28/1818).

67. CAD, postes, Philadelphia, subseries B, 45*, Consul-General to Hyde de Neuville (Philadelphia, 6/22/1818).

68. APS, Stephen Girard papers, Henri Lallemand to Stephen Girard (New Orleans, 2/20 and 4/10/1818). Spanish documents detailing a plan of the Lafitte brothers to capture Lallemand and his traveling companions (including General Humbert) suggest that they went to Galveston by sea in the brig *New Enterprise*. This, the first of three plots hatched by the Lafittes against Lallemand, failed because the brig was detained by Beverly Chew, the chief custom's inspector of New Orleans and the Lafittes' personal enemy. See Faye, "Great Stroke", pp.782–87.

69. Dabbs, "Additional Notes," 353; and Hartmann and Millard, *Le Texas,* 28. He arrived in early March, probably 7 March.

70. On archaeological efforts to locate the site, see Betje Black Klier, "Champ D'Asile, Texas," in *The French in Texas: History, Migration, Culture,* ed. François Lagarde (Austin: University of Texas Press, 2003), 79.

71. This and the following paragraph are based on the sources cited in note 51, but especially on the accounts of Dabbs and Hartmann and Millard. All citations are from Dabbs, "Additional Notes," 354.

72. AAE, CP, U.S., 76, Consul-General to Duke de Richelieu (Philadelphia, 11/30/1818).

73. This paragraph is based on AAE, CP, U.S., 76, Consul-General to Duke de Richelieu (Philadelphia, 11/30/1818) and (Philadelphia, 12/21/1818); and Gardien, "Take Pity on Our Glory," 252–53.

74. The original text is in CAD, microfilm, 2 MI, 245, Mémoire du général Lallemand. Translated excerpts appeared under various titles in all the major U.S. newspapers.

75. Picked up in metropolitan France by journalists, writers, and poets opposed to the Bourbon regime, the term "Champ d'Asile" was used not only to refer to Lallemand's Texas establishment, but also to the spatial and existential world of the Bonapartist exiles in America. In an especially deft formulation, one journalist turned the concept of exile on its head to declare that, under the tyrannical rule of the Bourbons, "France is the veritable *Champ d'Asile* of all the French." J. P. P. "Lettre sur Paris," in *La Minerve Française* 4 (Paris:1818), 572.

76. It was true that small groups of Indians hunted in the land, the proclamation acknowledged, but they had forfeited any claim to ownership by "leaving uncultivated these vast and fertile tracts." The Consul-General Petry was astounded at these lines: "They recall the olden times when Europeans descended upon these same lands and simply took them." CAD, postes, New York, subseries C, 2*, Consul-General to Duke de Richelieu (New York, 7/25/1818).

77. AAE, CP, U.S., 76, Consul-General to Duke de Richelieu (Philadelphia, 11/30/1818).

78. AAE, CP, U.S., 75, Consul at New Orleans to Duke de Richelieu (New Orleans, 4/2/1818).

79. AAE, CP, U.S., 75, Consul at New Orleans to Duke de Richelieu (New Orleans, 2/16, 3/14, and 3/26/1818); AAE, CP, U.S., 76, Consul-General to Duke de Richelieu (Philadelphia, 12/21/1818); Apodaca correspondence, reel 3, dispatch 48 (Mexico, 4/30/1818); Archivo General Nacional, historia, legajo 152, Felipe de Fatio to Viceroy Apodaca (New Orleans, 3/25/1818); and Andrew Jackson papers, reel 24, Lieutenant-Colonel Trimble to Andrew Jackson (New Orleans, 3/24/1818).

80. AAE, CP, U.S., 75, Hyde de Neuville to Luis de Onís (Washington, 5/8/1818).

81. L'Abeille 6, no. 23 (6/18/1818): 367.

82. L'Ami des Lois (7/23 and 9/12/1818).

83. Niles' Weekly Register (8/8, 9/26, and 11/7/1818).

84. For an example, see the National Intelligencer (4/24/1818).

85. See the numerous articles and poems, as well as the subscription lists, in La Minerve Française (Paris, 1818–19), esp. vols. 2–6. The Minerve's campaign for the Champ d'Asile is treated in the conclusion.

86. AAE, CP, U.S., 75, Luis de Onís to Hyde de Neuville (Washington, 5/1/1818).

87. NARA, M 179, reel 40, Joshua Childs to John Quincy Adams (Pinckneyville, 3/20/1818); and AAE, CP, U.S., 75, Hyde de Neuville to Duke de Richelieu (Washington, 5/9/1818).

88. AHN, estado, legajo 5643, dispatch 43 (Washington, 3/13/1818).

89. AAE, CP, U.S., 75, Hyde de Neuville to Luis de Onís (Washington, 5/8/1818).

90. AAE, CP, U.S., 76, Consul at New Orleans to Duke de Richelieu (New Orleans, 3/23/1818).

91. AAE, CP, U.S., 75, Consul at New Orleans to Duke de Richelieu (New Orleans, 5/25/1818); Apodaca correspondence, reel 3, dispatch 61 (Mexico, 9/30/1818).

92. CAD, postes, Philadelphia, subseries B, 45*, Consul-General to Hyde de Neuville (New York, 8/15/1818).

93. AAE, CP, U.S., 76, Consul at New Orleans to Duke de Richelieu (New Orleans, 3/23/1819).

94. AAE, CP, U.S., 76, Consul-General to Duke de Richelieu (Philadelphia, 11/30/1818). Building such extensive fortifications not only kept the men occupied, but also supported Lallemand's claim that thousands of reinforcements were on the way.

95. AAE, CP, U.S., 76, M. Dumouy, Vice-consul at New Orleans to M. d'Hauterive (New Orleans, 8/28/1818).

96. AAE, CP, U.S., 75, "Résumé de la deposition du Sieur Croissac"; Apodaca correspondence, reel 3, dispatch 61 (Mexico, 9/30/1818).

97. AAE, CP, U.S., 76, Consul-General to Duke de Richelieu (Philadelphia, 10/11/1818).

98. AAE, CP, U.S., 76, Consul-General to Duke de Richelieu (Philadelphia, 11/30/1818).

99. They were Tournelle, Molina, Izquierdo, Francois Roffiac, Fourni, Charrasin, Holzer, and three unnamed orderlies. All but Roffiac and the orderlies have been identified as non-French.

100. AAE, CP, U.S. 75, "Résumé du Sieur Croissac"; Apodaca correspondence, reel 3, dispatch 61, "Declarations of Molina and Tournelle" (New Orleans, 5/21 and 5/22/1818). Molina and Tournelle claimed that only sixty-five were left.

101. This was noted with glee by French diplomatic officials. AAE, CP, U.S., 76, Consul-General to Duke de Richelieu (Philadelphia, 8/29/1818).

102. Adams papers, reel 443, Pierre-Paul-François Degrand to John Quincy Adams (Boston, 4/27/1818).

103. *Niles' Weekly Register* (8/8/1818).

104. Ibid. (7/28/1818).

105. Document 287, "Lands Allotted to Encourage the Cultivation of the Vine and Olive" (12/14/1818) in Walter Lowrie et. al, eds., *Documents Legislative and Executive of the Congress of the United States* (Washington, D.C.: Gales and Seaton, 1834–60), 3:396. The investigation found that "many of the persons inscribed upon the list [of Vine and Olive shareholders] have transferred their shares and followed the banners of the French generals who have made or attempted to make an establishment on the river Trinity, or engaged in other pursuits which exclude the idea, that any other object was contemplated by their joining in the association than sheer speculation."

106. Monroe first revealed his decision to break up the establishment at Galveston by force in his Message to the Congress of December 2, 1817. That was followed by a detailed report by the Committee on Foreign Relations, from which the citation is taken. See these in Lowrie et al., eds., *Documents Legislative and Executive,* 4:129–44. In addition to Hyde and Onís, the Portuguese Ambassador, José Corrêa da Serra, considered it likely that "Lallemand is a repetition of MacGregor, and this expedition is a stratagem of this government [the United States] to avoid the opprobrium of taking possession of Texas without a greater provocation." Corrêa da Serra to Portuguese Foreign Minister (Washington, 5/5/1818) in *José Corrêa da Serra,* 393.

107. AAE, CP, U.S., 75, Hyde de Neuville to Duke de Richelieu (Washington, 6/4/1818).

108. AAE, CP, U.S., 75, Hyde de Neuville to Duke de Richelieu (Washington, 7/2/1818). Other important letters for understanding Hyde's thinking about the broader strategic import of Lallemand's expedition are AAE, CP, U.S., 75, Hyde de Neuville to Duke de Richelieu (Washington, 6/29/1818); and AAE, CP, U.S., 76, Hyde de Neuville to Duke de Richelieu (Washington, 11/8/1818).

109. AAE, CP, U.S., 76, Consul at New Orleans to Duke de Richelieu (New Orleans, 3/23/1819).

110. Adams papers, reel 146, John Quincy Adams to Pierre-Paul-François Degrand (Washington, 11/13/1817).

111. Adams, *Memoirs,* entries for 3/18 and 4/30/1818 (Hyde de Neuville), 3/30/1818 (British ambassador Charles Bagot), and 5/25/1818 (Onís). See also, AHN, estado, legajo 5642, dispatch 84, "Copia de una nota que he pasado el Excelentisimo Señor Don Luis de Onís al Señor de Adams, Secretario de estado" (Washington, 5/6/1818).

112. Adams, *Memoirs,* entries for 5/13, 5/16, and 5/18/1818. The Graham mission is described in Walter Prichard, "George Graham's Mission to Galveston in 1818: Two Important Documents Bearing upon Louisiana History," *Louisiana Historical Quarterly* 20, no. 3 (July

1937): 619–50. See also the original letters between Graham and Jean Lafitte, Louisiana State University, Graham papers.

113. NARA, M 40, John Quincy Adams to George Graham (Washington, 6/2/1818). A copy of the instructions can be found in Prichard, "George Graham's Mission," 640–2.

114. The date is from Apodaca correspondence, reel 4, dispatch 78, deposition of Charesti, Fourni, and Holzer (Bexar, 11/24/1818).

115. The troops whose approach had given Lallemand such a fright were nothing more than a small scouting party. See "Great Stroke," 792–3. See also letters 54 (6/7/1818), 55 (6/10/1818), and 57 (6/17/1818) from Antonio Martinez, governor of Texas, to Viceroy Apodaca in Antonio Martinez, *Letters from Gov. Antonio Martinez to the Viceroy Juan Ruiz de Apodaca,* trans. Virginia H. Taylor (San Antonio: Texas: Research Center for the Arts and Humanities, 1983), 20–1.

116. Unless otherwise noted, the following account of these discussions is based on George Graham's official report to John Quincy Adams, reprinted in Prichard, "George Graham's Mission," 642–50.

117. Stanley Faye advanced this hypothesis in "Great Stroke," 797. Details of Graham's proposal are found in a dispatch of Onís to the Captain-General of Cuba (11/25/1818) translated and published in Harris Gaylord Warren, "Documents Relating to George Graham's Proposal to Jean Laffite for the Occupation of the Texas Coast," *Louisiana Historical Quarterly* 21, no. 1 (January 1938): 215; dispatch of Viceroy of Mexico to the Spanish Foreign Minister (10/30/1818), reprinted in "Great Stroke", 798; Apodaca correspondence, reel 3, dispatch 70 (Mexico, 10/31/1818), and reel 4, dispatch 78, deposition of Charesti, Fourni, and Holzer (Bexar, 11/24/1818); and AHN, estado, legajo 5643, dispatch 201 (Washington, 11/25/1818).

118. As reported by Viceroy Apodaca, cited in Faye, "Great Stroke," 798.

119. AAE, CP, U.S., 75, Hyde de Neuville to Duke de Richelieu (Washington, 7/2/1818), quoting a dispatch from the French consul at New Orleans.

120. Adams, *Memoirs,* entry for 11/20/1818. It has also been suggested that the growing sectional conflict over the issue of slavery may have led to Monroe's change of heart. See Faye, "Great Stroke," 797.

121. The subtitle for this section is from CAD, postes, New York, subseries B, 123, Consul at New Orleans to Consul at New York (New Orleans, 11/10/1818).

122. Apodaca correspondence, reel 3, dispatch 43 (Mexico, 3/31/1818).

123. Apodaca correspondence, reel 3, dispatch 43 (Mexico, 3/31/1818), and Archivo General Nacional, historia, legajo 152, Viceroy Apodaca to Minister of War (Mexico, 4/30/1818). This diversionary scheme had already been recommended by Colonel Galabert. Adams papers, reel 443, Louis Galabert to William Lee (Philadelphia 5/14/1818).

124. Apodaca correspondence, reel 3, dispatch 43, Orders to the Commanders of Tampico, Veracruz, the Eastern Internal Provinces, and Texas (Mexico, 4/8/1818).

125. The meeting and plan are recounted in great detail in Apodaca correspondence, reel 3, dispatch 61 (Mexico, 9/30/1818). A translation of another account of the same meeting is provided in Faye, "Great Stroke," 789–92. This was the Laffite brothers' second attempt to betray Lallemand to the Spanish.

126. Apodaca correspondence, reel 3, dispatch 61 (Mexico, 9/30/1818).

127. Apodaca correspondence, reel 3, dispatch 50 (Mexico, 5/27/1818).

128. Apodaca correspondence, reel 3, dispatch 59 (Mexico, 6/25/1818).

129. Apodaca correspondence, reel 3, dispatch 61 (Mexico, 9/22/1818).

130. This description of the march to the Trinity and subsequent negotiations with Rigau are based on Apodaca correspondence, reel 4, dispatch 78 (Mexico, n.d.), and especially the diary of Don Juan Castaneda.

131. Apodaca correspondence, reel 4, dispatch 78 (Mexico, n.d.). Apodaca approved of Castaneda's actions and protected him from court martial.

132. Apodaca correspondence, reel 4, dispatch 78 (Mexico, n.d.).

133. Two men who tried to desert by land were reportedly devoured by cannibalistic Indians, the Carancahuas. Of those who left by sea, presumably in small boats, fifteen reportedly drowned. Apodaca correspondence, reel 4, dispatch 78 (Mexico, n.d.); and AAE, CP, U.S., 76, Consul at New Orleans to Duke de Richelieu (New Orleans, 12/12/1818).

134. Dabbs, "Additional Notes," 355–6.

135. AHN, estado, legajo 5644, "Rapport des evenements survenus à Galveston depuis le 12 octobre 1818." This document provides nominative lists of the various factions.

136. AAE, CP, U.S., 76, Consul at New Orleans to Duke de Richelieu (New Orleans, 11/12/1818).

137. CAD, postes, New York, subseries B, 123, Consul at New Orleans to Consul at New York (New Orleans, 11/10/1818).

138. AAE, CP, U.S., 76, extract of the last letters of the Consul at New Orleans to Hyde de Neuville (New Orleans, 9/25/1818).

139. AAE, CP, U.S., 76, Consul-General to Duke de Richelieu (Philadelphia, 12/21/1818). Other sources speculating that this was Lallemand's motive are AAE, CP, U.S., 75, Hyde de Neuville to Duke de Richelieu (Philadelphia, 4/18/1818) and Consul-General to Duke de Richelieu (Philadelphia, 6/26/1818).

140. AAE, CP, U.S., 76, Consul at New Orleans to Duke de Richelieu (New Orleans, 3/23/1819).

Chapter 5

1. Document 287, "Lands Allotted to Encourage the Cultivation of the Vine and Olive" (Treasury Department, 12/14/1818) in Lowrie et al., eds., *Documents Legislative and Executive,* 3:396–99.

2. For example, Winston Smith describes them as "Bonapartists all," *Days of Exile,* 24.

3. University of North Carolina, Lefebvre-Desnouettes papers, Lefebvre-Desnouettes to Clausel (Aigleville, 6/20/1818) and (Demopolis, 8/1/1819).

4. APS, miscellaneous manuscripts, Lefebvre-Desnouettes and Raoul to Henri Lallemand (Demopolis, 6/22/1821).

5. Nearly every letter Lefebvre-Desnouettes wrote to Clausel during the period 1818–21 contained such a plea. Numerous examples may be found in University of North Carolina, Lefebvre-Desnouettes papers.

6. Eric Saugera, who is editing the correspondence of Jacques Lajoinie, one of the few soldiers to settle on the grant, will shed new light on both civilian and military settlers when his book is published.

7. NARA, RG 49, 237, Certificate 205 (no. 51, Astolphi), and 236, Certificate 167 (no. 245, Hamel).

8. Newman may have owned up to four more allotments (1,160 acres), but gaps in the chain of deeds for those parcels makes it impossible to verify his ownership. Information on Newman's holdings was gleaned from a variety of certificate folders in NARA, RG 49, 234–38.

9. NARA, RG 49, 236, Certificate 156 (no. 233, Grouchy).

10. Document 357, "Lands Allotted to the Cultivation of the Vine and Olive" (3/18/1822) in Lowrie et al., eds., *Documents Legislative and Executive*, 537.

11. APS, Stephen Girard papers, Victoire George to Stephen Girard (George Villa, 9/7/1820).

12. APS, Stephen Girard papers, reel 82, Edouard George to Roberjot (George Villa, 9/28/1822).

13. Smith, *Days of Exile*, 60; and ADAH, Gardien papers, entry for Lintroy.

14. NARA, RG 49, 235, Certificate 72 (no. 78).

15. NARA, RG 49, 235, Certificate 92 (no. 320); University of North Carolina, Lefebvre-Desnouettes papers, Lefebvre-Desnouettes to Clausel (Demopolis, 10/18/1819).

16. *L'Abeille* (4/23/1818): 6, no. 15, 228–330.

17. APS, Stephen Girard papers, reel 73, Victoire George to Stephen Girard (Demopolis, 3/9/1820).

18. APS, Stephen Girard papers, reel 72 (Mobile, 12/24/1819).

19. APS, Stephen Girard papers, reel 72 (Demopolis, 2/2/1820).

20. APS, Stephen Girard papers, reel 72 (Demopolis, 2/9/1820).

21. APS, Stephen Girard papers, reel 73 (Demopolis, 3/2/1820).

22. APS, Stephen Girard papers, reel 74 (George Villa, 12/14/1820).

23. APS, Stephen Girard papers, reel 76 (George Villa, 2/29/1821).

24. APS, Stephen Girard papers, reel 82, Edouard George to Roberjot (George Villa, 10/15/1822).

25. APS, Girard family papers, Henri to Henriette Lallemand (Cap Vincent, 11/13/1821); and APS, Stephen Girard papers, reel 78, Henri Lallemand to Stephen Girard (Tombigbee, 9/20/1821).

26. Citation from APS, Stephen Girard papers, reel 78, Henri Lallemand to Stephen Girard (Tombigbee, 9/20/1821). On Lallemand's projected trip to Virginia, see APS, Stephen Girard papers, reel 72, Victoire George to Stephen Girard (Demopolis, 2/9/1820).

27. APS, miscellaneous manuscripts, Lefebvre-Desnouettes and Raoul to Henri Lallemand (Demopolis, 6/22/1821); and APS, Stephen Girard papers, reel 78, Henri Lallemand to Stephen Girard (Tombigbee, 9/20/1821).

28. *L'Abeille* 6, no. 15 (4/23/1818): 228.

29. Document 592, "Grants Made to French Emigrants to Cultivate the Vine and Olive" (Treasury Department, 12/21/1827) in Lowrie et al., eds., *Documents Legislative and Executive*, 5:14–15.

30. Most, if not all, of the grantees planted corn as their first crop. In the early days of

the settlement, it was, according to Victoire George, "the most important article, being the principal type of food." APS, Stephen Girard papers, reel 72, Victoire George to Stephen Girard (Demopolis, 2/9/1820).

31. APS, Stephen Girard papers, reel 86, Victoire George to Stephen Girard (2/11/1824). Not a single house built by the original settlers on the grant still stands.

32. Document 592, "Report of William L. Adams" (Spring Grove, Tuscaloosa, 2/1827), in Lowrie et al., eds., *Documents Legislative and Executive*, 5:22.

33. The other principal store on the grant, no more successful than Lefebvre-Desnouette's, was run by Victoire George. "We can meet our expenses here by keeping a store," she wrote optimistically within days of arriving on the grant. APS, Stephen Girard papers, reel 72, Victoire George to Stephen Girard (2/2/1820). Others seem to have imported goods and sold them on a much smaller scale. For example, Jacques Lefrançois earned extra money by selling sells raisins and looking glasses to the grantees. ADAH, Gardien papers, entry for Jacques Lefrançois.

34. University of North Carolina, Lefebvre-Desnouettes papers, Lefebvre-Desnouettes to Clausel (Aigleville, 1/28/1819).

35. University of North Carolina, Lefebvre-Desnouettes papers, Lefebvre-Desnouettes to Clausel (Aigleville, 2/24/1819). It was at this point that the two generals considered re-locating to Cuba. These plans came to nothing.

36. University of North Carolina, Lefebvre-Desnouettes papers, Lefebvre-Desnouettes to Clausel (Aigleville, 7/15 and 8/25/1819).

37. Smith, *Days of Exile*, 72.

38. ADAH, SG 24709, Parmentier to Governor Bibb (Aigleville, 4/14/1817).

39. University of North Carolina, Lefebvre-Desnouettes papers, Lefebvre-Desnouettes to Clausel (Aigleville, 4/19/1819).

40. Smith, *Days of Exile*, 72.

41. ADAH, Mabel Morris Scrapbook, Dr. J. W. Beeson, "Vine and Olive Colony History," *Demopolis Times* (3/22/1962), reprinted from 1885.

42. ADAH, Gardien papers, entry for Pierre Mangon.

43. Michel LeBoutellier to Governor Bibb (White Bluff, 11/10/1818), in Clarence Edwin Carter, ed., *Territorial Papers of the United States, Territory of Alabama (1817–1819)* (Washington, D.C.: Government Printing Office, 1952), 457.

44. University of North Carolina, Lefebvre-Desnouettes papers, Lefebvre-Desnouettes to Clausel (Aigleville, 3/21/1819).

45. APS, Stephen Girard papers, reel 73, Victoire George to Stephen Girard (Demopolis, 3/9/1820); and Document 357, "Lands Allotted to the Cultivation of the Vine and Olive" (Treasury Department, 3/18/1822) in Lowrie et al., eds., *Documents Legislative and Executive*, 3:537.

46. APS, Stephen Girard papers, reel 81, Edouard George to Stephen Girard (Demopolis, 7/3/1822).

47. APS, Stephen Girard papers, reel 85, Victoire George to Stephen Girard (George Villa, 9/6/1823).

48. Document 592, "Grants Made to French Emigrants to Cultivate the Vine and Olive"

(Treasury Department, 12/21/1827), in Lowrie et al., eds., *Documents Legislative and Executive*, 5:15; and Smith, *Days of Exile*, 123.

49. APS, Stephen Girard papers, reel 82, Edouard George to Roberjot (George Villa, 10/15/1822).

50. Descending the river was much quicker, taking only six or seven days. ADAH, Gardien papers, entry for Lintroy; APS, Stephen Girard papers, reel 72, Victoire George to Stephen George (Mobile, 1/7/1820); and University of North Carolina, Lefebvre-Desnouettes papers, Lefebvre-Desnouettes to Clausel (Aigleville, 10/18/1819).

51. Document 592, "Grants Made to French Emigrants to Cultivate the Vine and Olive" (Treasury Department, 12/21/1827), in Lowrie et al., eds., *Documents Legislative and Executive*, 5:15.

52. APS, Stephen Girard papers, reel 82, Edouard George to Stephen Girard (Mobile, 12/12/1822).

53. ADAH, Gardien papers, entry for Victor Grouchy.

54. AAE, CP, U.S., 76, Consul-General to Duke de Richelieu (Philadelphia, 8/29/1818).

55. APS, Stephen Girard papers, reel 72, Victoire George to Stephen Girard (Mobile, 1/7/1820), and reel 124, Stephen Girard to Victoire George (Philadelphia, 1/29/1820).

56. APS, Girard family papers, Henri to Henriette Lallemand (Demopolis, 9/13/1820).

57. Smith, *Days of Exile,* 69.

58. *L'Abeille* (10/23/1817): 5, no. 15, 242.

59. Sickness in the George family during 1822–23 is chronicled in APS, Stephen Girard papers, reels 82 and 83.

60. APS, Stephen Girard papers, reel 85, Victoire George to Stephen Girard (George Villa, 10/8/1823).

61. Thomas Freeman to Josiah Meigs (Saint Stephens, 2/18/1818), 258–60; Freeman to Meigs (Washington, Mississippi Territory, 8/3/1818 and 1/12/1819) all in Carter, ed., *Territorial papers,* 390–92, 525. See also, Smith, *Days of Exile,* 47–49.

62. *L'Abeille* reported that the town featured two transversal streets, the Rue de France and the Rue de la République, names which also gestured simultaneously toward the settlers' past and present homeland. *L'Abeille* 6, no. 15 (4/23/1818): 228.

63. Smith, *Days of Exile,* 77–81.

64. NARA, RG 49, 238, Certificate 270.

65. NARA, RG 49, 234–8.

66. NARA, RG 49, 238, Certificate 275.

67. NARA, RG 49, Certificate 267.

68. NARA, RG 49, 234, Certificate 39. This curious incident was first brought to my attention by Nick Cobbs, Esq., of Greensboro.

69. APS, Stephen Girard papers, reel, 89, Françoise Rivière to Stephen Girard (Philadelphia, 12/10/1824).

70. APS, Stephen Girard papers, reel 89, Victoire George to Stephen Girard (George Villa, 12/2/1824).

71. APS, Stephen Girard papers, reel 85 (George Villa, 9/6/1823).

72. This paragraph is based on Document 320, "Lands Allotted to the Cultivation of the

Vine and Olive" (Treasury Department, 4/18/1820), in Lowrie et al., eds., *Documents Legislative and Executive,* 3:435–36.

73. *Niles' Weekly Register* 18 (4/29/1820): 163.

74. This paragraph is based on Document 357, "Lands Allotted to the Cultivation of the Vine and Olive" (Treasury Department, 3/18/1822), in Lowrie et al., eds., *Documents Legislative and Executive,* 3:536–37.

75. Basil Meslier, one of the important founding members of the Vine and Olive Society, predicted that a personal visit by the general to the secretary of the treasury would have "a good effect." APS, miscellaneous manuscripts, Basile Meslier to General Lefebvre-Desnouettes (Demopolis, 4/13/1822).

76. Document 357, "Lands Allotted to the Cultivation of the Vine and Olive" (Treasury Department, 3/18/1822), in Lowrie et al., eds., *Documents Legislative and Executive,* 3:536.

77. *Niles' Weekly Register* 22 (4/27/1822): 142.

78. Richard Peters, ed., *Public Statutes of the United States of America* (Boston: Charles C. Little and James Brown, 1850–55), 3:667, chap 33. "An Act supplementary to an act entitled 'An act to set apart and dispose of certain public lands for the encouragement of the cultivation of the vine and olive.'".

79. Unless otherwise noted, the remainder of this paragraph is based on Document 592, "Grants Made to French Emigrants to Cultivate the Vine and Olive," (Treasury Department, 12/21/1827), in Lowrie et al., eds., *Documents Legislative and Executive,* 5:14–16.

80. Document 649, "Grants Made to French Emigrants for the Cultivation of the Vine and the Olive" (Treasury Department, 2/14/1828), in Lowrie et al., eds., *Documents Legislative and Executive,* 5:466–70. The remainder of the paragraph is based on this source.

81. Ibid.

82. Document 592, "Grants Made to French Emigrants to Cultivate the Vine and Olive" (Treasury Department, 12/21/1827), in Lowrie et al., eds., *Documents Legislative and Executive,* 5:14–15.

83. ADAH, Gardien papers, entry for François-Etienne Nidelet.

84. APS, Stephen Girard papers, reel 72, Victoire George to Stephen Girard (Demopolis, 2/21820).

85. APS, Stephen Girard papers, reel 78 (George Villa, 11/8/1821).

86. APS, Stephen Girard papers, reel 89 (George Villa, 10/7/1824).

87. Corneille Roudet, "The Grape Vine," *Southern Advocate* (9/10/1831 and 10/22/1831).

88. Chapron's interest in silkworm cultivation is detailed in ADAH, Gardien papers, Chapron letter book.

89. Document 592, "Grants Made to French Emigrants to Cultivate the Vine and Olive" (Treasury Department, 12/21/1827), in Lowrie et al., eds., *Documents Legislative and Executive,* 5:15; and Document 649, "Grants Made to French Emigrants for the Cultivation of the Vine and the Olive" (Treasury Department, 2/14/1828), in Lowrie et al., eds., *Documents Legislative and Executive,* 5:467.

90. *Niles' Weekly Register* 33 (2/23/1828): 449.

91. Document 758, "Condition of the Tombeckbee Association for the Cultivation of the

Vine and Olive" (Aigleville, 11/18/1829), in Lowrie et al., eds., *Documents Legislative and Executive*, 6:19–21.

92. "An Act to alter and amend 'An act to set apart and dispose of certain public lands for the encouragement of the cultivation of the vine and olive'" in Peters, ed., *Public Statutes*, 4:444.

93. "An Act to amend an act, entitled 'An act to alter and amend an act to set apart and dispose of certain public lands for the encouragement of the cultivation of the vine and olive;' approved nineteenth February, one thousand eight hundred and thirty-one," in Peters, ed., *Public Statutes*, 4:611–12.

94. NARA, RG 49, 241, Felix Grundy to the Secretary of the Treasury (Washington, 4/18/1839).

95. These findings are based on exhaustive analysis of the deeds in NARA, RG 49, 234–38. I am assuming that the eleven men who signed away their allotments to Jeannet in November 1817, but for whom no records exist at NARA, sold their allotments in early December, along with the other members of the Champ d'Asile (see table 5.3).

96. I have identified the buyers by analyzing all the deeds in NARA, RG 49, 234–38. Information on their familial and business connections is from ADAH, Gardien papers.

97. A second non-French merchant, the Jewish-Austrian émigré Hyman Gratz, joined the consortium in 1818. Another Domingan merchant, Honoré Fournier, acted as an intermediary, buying parcels of land from Jeannet, but reselling them at cost only days later to the principal buyers. Fournier did not retain any of the allotments he purchased. The reasons for this curious arrangement are unknown.

98. By way of comparison, Daniel Feller has found in his broader national survey that the average price of land in 1817 was $2.35; in 1818, $2.95; and in 1819, $3.37. Daniel Feller, *The Public Lands in Jacksonian Politics* (Madison: University of Wisconsin Press, 1984), 18, 20, and 22.

99. NARA, RG 49, Tombeckbee Association, 234–38.

100. These were allotments 200, 201, 202, 255, 256, 257, and 258. The similarity of this transaction and that orchestrated by Jeannet—the collective sale through a joint power-of-attorney, the predominance of 160-acre allotments, the participation of the same Philadelphia merchants, and the simultaneity of the sales—suggest that some of the seventy-four early sellers might in fact have been involved in the Champ d'Asile though there is no record of their participation in the Lallemands' adventure.

101. Document 287, "Lands Allotted to Encourage the Cultivation of the Vine and Olive" (Treasury Department, 12/14/1818), in Lowrie et al., eds., *Documents Legislative and Executive*, 3:396.

102. Feller, *Public Lands*, 30.

103. NARA, RG 49, 234–38.

104. For Curcier's sellout to Ravesies, see NARA, RG 49, 236, Certificate 162. For that of Villars to Badaraque, see NARA, RG 49, 234, Certificate 29.

105. To address these likely distortions, I have compared annual price averages, ranges in price, and median prices in table 5.6.

106. ADAH, SG 4352, "French Field Notes."

107. Document 592, "Grants Made to French Emigrants to Cultivate the Vine and Olive" (Treasury Department, 12/21/1827), in Lowrie et al., eds., *Documents Legislative and Executive,* 5:22.

108. Smith, *Days of Exile,* 123.

109. The figures in this paragraph are based on analysis of the deeds in NARA, RG 49, 234–38.

110. For example, In 1827 James Childress sold an allotment (no. 10, 120 acres) to Ravesies. NARA, RG 49, 234, Certificate 1.

111. Document 758, "Condition of the Tombeckbee Association for the Cultivation of the Vine and Olive" (Aigleville, 11/18/1829), in Lowrie et al., eds., *Documents Legislative and Executive,* vol. 6.

112. Document 998, "On Application for Right of Pre-Emption to Lands Granted for the Encouragement of the Cultivation of the Vine and Olive" (Aigleville, 12/12/1831), in Lowrie et al., eds., *Documents Legislative and Executive,* 7:374.

113. These figures are based on the Adams report and the supplemental information provided by Ravesies the following year. Document 592, "Grants Made to French Emigrants to Cultivate the Vine and Olive" (Treasury Department, 12/21/1827) and Document 649, "Grants Made to French Emigrants for the Cultivation of the Vine and the Olive" (Treasury Department, 2/14/1828), in Lowrie et al., eds., *Documents Legislative and Executive,* 5:14–28 and 466–70.

114. The figures in this paragraph are based on analysis of the deeds in NARA, RG 49, 234–38.

115. Document 758, "Condition of the Tombeckbee Association for the Cultivation of the Vine and Olive" (Aigleville, 11/18/1829), in Lowrie et al., eds., *Documents Legislative and Executive,* vol. 6.

116. Figures on patents issued in this paragraph and the following paragraph are derived from NARA, RG 49, 234–38; and ADAH, SG 4580.

Conclusion

1. AAE, CP, U.S., 76, Hyde de Neuville to Duke de Richelieu (Washington, 12/12/1818).

2. The remainder of this paragraph is based on Six, *Dictionnaire biographique,* 1:243–4.

3. Bertrand Clausel, *Nouvelles observations de M. le maréchal Clauzel sur la colonisation d'Alger: Adressées à M. le maréchal, ministre de la guerre, président du conseil.* Paris: Selligue, 1833. Napoleon had considered founding similar veterans' colonies in the Rhineland and Northern Italy as a way of securing the French hold over these territories.

4. On the circumstances of Garnier's death, see AN, F^7 6680, dossier Garnier des Saintes. On Pénière's death, see AAE, CP, U.S., 78, Hyde de Neuville to Baron de Pasquier (Washington, 10/23/1821).

5. Tulane University, Joseph Lakanal papers, Dr. Yves R. Lemonnier to Grace King (New Orleans, 4/2/1919).

6. Tulane University, Fortier papers, "Notes on the Old Collège d'Orléans, written by Tante Louise in the year 1841."

7. Unless otherwise noted, the information in this paragraph is from Gardien, *The Chatelaine of George Villa;* and Frank Stollenwerck and Dixie Orum Stollenwerck, *The Stollenwerck, Chaudron, and Billon Families.*

8. Charles himself was married to Adèle Macré, widow of Jean-Marie Macré, a grantee who had died in Philadelphia in 1817.

9. Thomas McAdory Owen, *History of Alabama and Dictionary of Alabama Biography* (Chicago: S. J. Clarke, 1921), 4:1355.

10. Unless otherwise noted, biographical information in this paragraph is from the relevant entries in ADAH, Gardien papers.

11. NARA, RG 49, 237, Certificate 217.

12. NARA, RG 49, 238, Certificate 260.

13. Information on Cluis is from CAD, postes, New Orleans, subseries D, 199, dossier Jean-Jerome Cluis.

14. Information on Parmentier is from CAD, postes, New Orleans, subseries D, 197, dossier Nicholas S. Parmentier.

15. On the Canonge family, see Stanley Clisby Arthur, *Old Families of Louisiana* (New Orleans: Harmanson, 1931), 137–40; and Grace King, *Creole Families of New Orleans* (New York: Macmillan, 1921), 392–96.

16. Information on the Tulanes is from John Smith Kendall, "Paul Tulane," *Louisiana Historical Quarterly* 20, no. 4 (October 1937): 1020–25.

17. la Souchère Deléry, *Napoleon's Soldiers,* 118.

18. On the Bringiers, see Arthur, *Old Families,* 426–30; King, *Creole Families,* 413–18; Historic New Orleans Collection, Robert Juddice collection; Louisiana State University, Bringier papers; and Tulane University, Bringier papers.

19. CAD, postes, New Orleans, subseries D, 197, dossier Joseph Truc.

20. CAD, postes, New Orleans, subseries D, 194, dossier Farcy.

21. CAD, postes, New Orleans, subseries D, "French Consul at New Orleans to Foreign Ministry in Paris" (New Orleans, 1/18/1822).

22. APS, Stephen Girard papers, reel 87, Louis Lauret to Stephen Girard (New Orleans, 3/10/1824).

23. Information in the following paragraph is from APS, Stephen Girard papers, reel 87, Louis Lauret to Stephen Girard (New Orleans, 3/10/1824) as well as APS, Girard family papers, Louis Lauret to Madame Lallemand (Bethel, Georgia, 11/14/1830).

24. This and the following two paragraphs are based primarily on the relevant biographical entries in ADAH, Gardien papers, as well as information gleaned from CAD, postes, New Orleans, subseries D. Supplementary information is from various New Orleans city directories and NARA, RG 49, Tombeckbee Association.

25. The following paragraph is based on AG, Raoul's personal dossier.

26. AN, F^7 6665, "Etat des transfuges français en Espagne;" and AG, Galabert's personal dossier.

27. Information on Latapie is from AN, F^7 6913, dossier Le comte Doulcet de Pontecoulant, Adolphe Doulcet de Pontecoulant, le colonel Latapie, Pierre-Remi Raulet.

28. Information on Colona d'Ornano is from AN, F^7 6663, dossier Colona, Bartolo, né en Corse, ex-colonel, se disant comte d'Ornano.

29. AN, F^7 6663, "Extract of a letter from the Minister of the Interior to the Minister of General Police." (n.d.).

30. Information on Michel Combe is from AG, his personal dossier.

31. AG, Michel Combe personal dossier, "Extract from the register of deliberations of the Infantry and Cavalry Committee" (4/7/1834).

32. The following paragraph is based on documents at AG, in Schultz's personal dossier, as well as AN, F^7 6758, dossier Jean Schultz.

33. The following paragraph is based primarily on AAE, affaires diverses politiques, U.S., 2, dossier Le Sieur Jeannet et Ducoudray-Holstein: Tentatives d'expedition d'armée contres les Antilles (Guadeloupe, Saint Barthelemy, La Margueritte, et Porto Rico, 1822–23).

34. Information on this first plot is from correspondence in CAD, postes, New Orleans, 186.

35. AAE, CP, U.S., 79, Hyde de Neuville to Viscount de Montmorency (New York, 8/18/1822).

36. Unless otherwise indicated, the following paragraphs on Lallemand are based on AG, his personal dossier.

37. AAE, CP, U.S., 76, Consul at New Orleans to Duke de Richelieu (New Orleans, 12/12/1818).

38. Gardien, "Take Pity on Our Glory," 259.

39. In 1819 the editorial board of the *Minerve* had seriously considered sending the money to "the Tombigbee colony" because the subscription had been opened on behalf of "the establishment of a colony," not "some individuals." After "profound discussion," however, the decision was made to direct the money to the individual survivors of the Texas endeavor. "Souscription pour le Champ d'Asile," in *La Minerve Française* 8 (Paris, 11/1819): 318.

40. Ibid., 258–60. Transcriptions of the relevant newspaper articles can be found in ADAH, Gardien papers.

41. Owsley and Smith, *Filibusters and Expansionists,* 178–80.

42. On the affair of the Greek frigates, see AN, F^7 6681, Foreign Minister to Minister of the Interior (Paris, 10/31/1826).

43. la Souchère Deléry, *Napoleon's Soldiers,* 95.

44. Six, *Dictionnaire biographique,* 2:40.

45. *La Minerve Française,* 3:256–63.

46. See for example, Béraud's poem, "Le Champ d'Asile," with its refrain "Noble debris of the field of honor, fertilize the *Champ d'Asile*." *La Minerve Française,* 3:577–79.

47. Suggestive in this regard is the name "A. Tocqueville" that appears on the sixteenth subscription list under the heading "Bolbec (Seine-Inférieure)." *La Minerve Française,* 5:416.

Did the publicity given the Champ d'Asile—and to a lesser extent the Vine and Olive colony—in the pages of the *Minerve* play a role in sparking Tocqueville's interest in America?

48. Ibid., 5:572.

49. Ibid., 6:447.

50. Ibid., 6:292.

51. Ibid., 8:320.

52. CAD, postes, New York, subseries C, 2*, Consul-General to Duke de Richelieu (New York, 12/5/1817).

53. *Niles' Weekly Register,* 14 (8/8/1818): 393.

54. Document 353, "Application of the 'Coffee Land Association' for a Grant of Twenty-four Thousand Acres in Florida, at Minimum Price," in Lowrie et al., eds., *Documents Legislative and Executive,* 3:518–30.

Appendix

1. The first list is reproduced in Document 287, "Lands Allotted to Encourage the Cultivation of the Vine and Olive" (Treasury Department 12/14/1818), and the second in Document 450, "Encouragement of the Cultivation of the Vine and Olive with the Allotment of Land for the Purpose" (Treasury Department, 2/15/1825), both in Lowrie et al., eds., *Documents Legislative and Executive,* 3:397–99 and 4:150–52. Changes to the original list and the allocation of the reserves are indicated after slashes.

Bibliography

Archival and Manuscript Sources

ALABAMA DEPARTMENT OF ARCHIVES AND HISTORY, MONTGOMERY, ALA.

Blue, Matthew. Papers. PB/range H/section 7/shelf b.
Gardien, Kent. Research Papers.
LPR 35, Tait Papers.
LPR 46, Israel Pickens Papers.
LPR 88, B. E. Brown Papers.
Morris, Mabel Simpson. Scrapbook. 7N/box 4/range A/section 1/shelf a.
Pickett, Albert. Papers. PB/range J/section 3/shelf d.
SG 3114, Correspondence of the Governor of the Mississippi Territory.
SG 4352, Saint Stephens Survey.
SG 4580, Receiver's Journal of Public Land Sales.
SG 5216, Demopolis Land Office—Register of Lands Sold, 1834–37.
SG 6886, Demopolis.
SG 24709 (reel 22), Correspondence of Gov. William Bibb.
SG 24838 (reel 23), Correspondence of Gov. Israel Pickens.
SPR 22, John Woodson Henley Private Papers.

AMERICAN PHILOSOPHICAL SOCIETY, PHILADELPHIA, PA.

Girard, Stephen. Papers.
Girard Family. Papers.
Miscellaneous Manuscripts.

ARCHIVES DE LA GUERRE, PARIS

Series:
C^{16} 40, Commission d'examen (1815–17).
X^{ab} 65, Bataillon Napoléon.
X^{em} 43, Ordonnance du 24 juillet 1815.
X^h 8, Régiment de la Tour d'Auvergne.
X^s 156, Commision de 1830.

Various personal dossiers, generals' dossiers, and pension files.

ARCHIVES DES AFFAIRES ÉTRANGÈRES, VINCENNES

Series:
　Affaires Diverses Politiques.
　　United States, 2.
　　Spain, 17.
　Consulates.
　　Havana, reel 5.
　Correspondance Politique.
　　England, 610–11.
　　Spain, 700–703.
　　United States, 73–80.
　Mémoires et Documents.
　　America, 34–35.
　　United States, 18–20, 27.

ARCHIVES NATIONALES, PARIS

Series:
　Police: F^7 6138^8–10, 6663, $6664^{a,}$ 6665, 6678–83, 6702, 6703, 6712–14, 6716, 6717, 6758, 6866, 6898, 6911, 6913, 6924, 6959, 6978, 12039.

ARCHIVO GENERAL DE INDIAS, SEVILLA.

Series:
　Estado, America en General.
　　Legajo 3.

ARCHIVO GENERAL NACIONAL, MEXICO CITY

Series:
　Historia.
　　Legajo 152.
　Provincias Interioras.
　　Legajo 239, 244.

ARCHIVO HISTÓRICO NACIONAL, MADRID

Series:
　Estado.
　　Legajo 5614, 5641–45, 5660.

BIRMINGHAM PUBLIC LIBRARY, DEPARTMENT OF ARCHIVES AND MANUSCRIPTS, BIRMINGHAM, ALA.

　Scruggs, J. Hubert. Manuscript Collection.

CENTRES DES ARCHIVES DIPLOMATIQUES, NANTES

Series:
Correspondance avec le Corps Diplomatique.
  United States, 627.
Correspondance Interministérielle.
  Guerre, 298.
  Intérieur, 338.
  Police générale, 520.
Microfilm.
  2 MI, 245.
Postes, Baltimore.
  Subseries A, Correspondance, 37, 43.
Postes, New York.
  Subseries B, Correspondance, 106, 110, 113–15, 122, 123, 126.
  Subseries C, Correspondance avec la Direction Politique, 2*.
Postes, New Orleans.
  Subseries A, Correspondance, 2, 143–45, 183–86, 487.
  Subseries D, Personal Files, 194–99, 203, and Unclassified Files.
Postes, Philadelphia.
  Subseries B, Correspondance, 18, 45*.

DEMOPOLIS PUBLIC LIBRARY, DEMOPOLIS, ALA.

Smith, Winston. Papers.

FILSON HISTORICAL SOCIETY, LOUISVILLE, KY.

Barbaroux Family. Papers.

HISTORIC NEW ORLEANS COLLECTION, WILLIAMS RESEARCH CENTER, ARCHIVES
AND MANUSCRIPTS, NEW ORLEANS

Bringier Family. Papers.
Juddice, Robert. Collection.

HUNTINGTON LIBRARY, SAN MARINO, CALIF.

HM 226, Official Manuscript Letter Books of the Secret Correspondence of Don Juan
Ruiz de Apodaca.

LIBRARY OF CONGRESS, WASHINGTON, D.C.

Lee-Palfrey Family. Papers.

LOUISIANA STATE UNIVERSITY, HILL MEMORIAL LIBRARY, SPECIAL COLLECTIONS,
BATON ROUGE, LA.

Bringier, Louis-Amédée. Papers.

Graham, George. Papers.
Lakanal, Joseph. Papers.

MASSACHUSETTS HISTORICAL SOCIETY, BOSTON, MASS.

Pickering Papers.

MICROFILMED PRESIDENTIAL PAPERS

Adams, John Quincy.
Jackson, Andrew.
Jefferson, Thomas.
Madison, James.
Monroe, James.

MISSOURI HISTORICAL SOCIETY, SAINT LOUIS, MO.

Nidelet Collection.

NATIONAL ARCHIVES AND RECORDS ADMINISTRATION, WASHINGTON, D.C.

M 7, Confidential Letters from the Secretary of War.
M 22, Register of Letters Received by the War Department.
M 25, Miscellaneous Correspondence of the General Land Office.
M 31, Correspondence of the U.S. Ambassador to Spain.
M 34, Correspondence of the U.S. Ambassador to France.
M 37, Special Agents.
M 38, Communications from the Secretary of State to Foreign Ministers.
M 40, Domestic Letters of the Secretary of State.
M 47, Notes from the Argentinean Ambassador to the Secretary of State.
M 50, Notes from the Ambassador of Great Britain to the Secretary of State.
M 53, Notes from the French Ambassador to the Secretary of State.
M 70, Dispatches from the U.S. Consulate in Buenos Aires.
M 73, Notes from the Chilean Ambassador to the Secretary of State.
M 77, Diplomatic Instructions from the Secretary of State to U.S. Ambassadors.
M 78, Instructions from the Secretary of State to U.S. Consuls.
M 84, Dispatches from the U.S. Consulate in La Guaira.
M 127, Letters from the Secretary of War to the President.
M 179, Miscellaneous Letters to the Secretary of State.
M 455, Dispatches from the U.S. Consulate in Manilla.
M 664, Notes from Foreign Consuls to the State Department.
M 1251, Legislative Journal of the U.S. Senate.
T 164, Dispatches from the U.S. Consulate in Bordeaux.
T 217, Dispatches from the U.S. Consulate in Malaga.
T 286, Correspondence Relative to Filibustering Expeditions.
T 344, Dispatches from the U.S. Consulate in Pernambuco.

Record Group 49, Alabama Land Entry Files, Demopolis Land Office, 1833–61, Tombeckbee Association Patent Certificate Files, 234–38, 241.

PUBLIC RECORDS OFFICE, LONDON

Series:
Foreign Office/5: Correspondence of Ambassador to the United States to the Foreign Minister, 120, 122, 123, 128, 129, 132, 133.
Foreign Office/115: Correspondence of Foreign Minister to Ambassador to the United States, 24–27, 30, 31–41.

TULANE UNIVERSITY, HOWARD-TILTON MEMORIAL LIBRARY, MANUSCRIPT DEPARTMENT, NEW ORLEANS, LA.

Bringier Papers.
Fortier, Louis-Augustin. Papers.
Lakanal, Joseph. Collection.
Lakanal, Joseph. Papers.
New Orleans Municipal Papers.
Tulane Papers.

UNIVERSITY OF NORTH CAROLINA, SOUTHERN HISTORICAL COLLECTION, CHAPEL HILL, N.C.

Lefebvre-Desnouettes, Charles. Papers.
Chapron, John M. Papers.

UNIVERSITY OF TEXAS AT AUSTIN, CENTER FOR AMERICAN HISTORY, AUSTIN, TEX.

Aury, Louis. Papers.

VIRGINIA HISTORICAL SOCIETY, RICHMOND, VA.

Bayol Family. Papers.

Newspapers and Periodicals

Alabama Republican.
Aurora.
Birmingham News.
Columbia Centinel.
Demopolis Times.
Greensboro Watchman.
Huntsville Republican.
L'Abeille Américaine: Journal Historique, Politique, et Literaire.
L'Ami des Lois.
La Minerve Française.

Le Courrier de la Louisiane.
Louisiana Gazette and Mercantile Advertiser.
National Intelligencer.
Niles' Weekly Register.
Selma Times-Journal.

Published Sources

Abernathy, Thomas Perkins. *The Formative Period in Alabama, 1815–1828.* Tuscaloosa and London: University of Alabama Press, 1990.

Adams, John Quincy. *John Quincy Adams and American Continental Empire: Letters, Papers, and Speeches.* Ed. Walter LaFeber. Chicago: Quadrangle, 1965.

———. *Memoirs of John Quincy Adams, Comprising Portions of His Diary from 1795 to 1848.* Ed. Charles Francis Adams. Vol. 4. Philadelphia: J. B. Lippincott, 1874–77.

———. *The Writings of John Quincy Adams.* Ed. Worthington Chauncey Ford. Vol.6. New York: Macmillan, 1916.

American State Papers: Documents Legislative and Executive of the Congress of the United States, Class I, Foreign Relations. Vol.4. Washington, D.C.: [n.p.], 1832–61.

Anna, Timothy E. *Spain and the Loss of America.* Lincoln, Nebraska and London: University of Nebraska Press, 1983.

Archer, Christon I., ed. *The Wars of Independence in Spanish America.* Wilmington, Del.: Scholarly Resources, 2000.

Aronson, Theo. *Les Bonaparte: Histoire d'une famille.* Trans. Rose Celli .Paris: Fayard, 1967.

Arthur, Stanley Clisby. *Old Families of Louisiana.* New Orleans: Harmanson, 1931.

Babb, Winston C. "French Refugees from Saint Domingue to the Southern United States: 1791–1810." Ph.D. diss., University of Virginia, 1954.

Balzac, Honoré de. *A Bachelor's Establishment. Works of Honoré de Balzac.* Vol.4. Trans. George Saintsbury. New York: Charles C. Bigelow, 1900.

Bancroft, Hubert Howe. *The Works of Hubert Howe Bancroft.* Vol.12, *History of Mexico, 1804–1824,* within vol. 4. San Francisco: History Company, 1886.

———. *The Works of Hubert Howe Bancroft.* Vol.16, *History of the North Mexican States and Texas, 1801–1888,* within vol. 2. San Francisco: History Company, 1889.

Barefield, Marilyn Davis. *Old Demopolis Land Office Records & Military Warrants, 1818–1860, and Records of the Vine and Olive Colony.* Birmingham, Ala.:Marilyn Davis Barefield, 1988.

Bartley, Russell H. *Imperial Russia and the Struggle for Latin American Independence, 1808–1828.* Austin: Institute of Latin American Studies, University of Texas at Austin, 1978.

Baur, John E. "International Repercussions of the Haitian Revolution." *The Americas* 26, no. 4 (April 1970): 394–418.

Baxter, Maurice G. *Henry Clay and the American System.* Lexington: University of Kentucky Press, 1995.

Beaucour, Fernand, "Un fidèle de l'Empéreur en son époque: Jean-Mathieu Sari (1792–1862)." Ph.D. diss., Université de Lille, 1972.

Bell, David A. *The Cult of the Nation in France: Inventing Nationalism, 1680–1800*. Cambridge: Harvard University Press, 2001.

Belote, Theodore Thomas. *The Scioto Speculation and the French Settlement at Gallipolis*. Cincinnati: University of Cincinnati Press, 1907.

Bemis, Samuel Flagg. *John Quincy Adams and the Foundations of American Foreign Policy*. New York: Knopf, 1965.

———. *The Latin American Policy of the United States: An Historical Interpretation*. New York: Harcourt, Brace, 1943).

———, ed. *The American Secretaries of States and Their Diplomacy*. Vols. 3 and 4. New York: Knopf, 1927–28.

Benot, Yves. *La Guyane sous la Révolution, ou l'impasse de la Révolution pacifique*. Kourou, Guyane: Ibis Rouge, 1997.

——— *La Révolution française et la fin des colonies*. Paris: Decouverte, 1988.

Bertier de Sauvigny, Guillaume de. *The Bourbon Restoration*. Trans. Lynn M. Case. Philadelphia: University of Pennsylvania Press, 1966.

Blaufarb, Rafe. *The French Army, 1750–1820: Careers, Talent, Merit*. Manchester: University of Manchester Press, 2002.

———. "Notes and Documents: French Consular Reports on the Association of French Emigrants: The Organization of the Vine and Olive Colony." *Alabama Review* 56, no. 2 (April 2003): 104–24.

Blond, Georges. *Histoire de la flibuste*. Paris: Stock, 1969.

———. *Les Cent-Jours*. Paris: Julliard, 1983.

Bodinier, Gilbert. *Dictionnaire des officiers de l'armée royale qui ont combattu aux Etats-Unis pendant la guerre d'Indépendance*. Vincennes: Ministère de la Guerre, 1982.

Bolivar, Simon. *Memoir of Simon Bolivar, President Liberator of the Republic of Columbia and of His Principal Generals*. Ed. H. L. V. Ducoudray Holstein. Boston: S. G. Goodrich, 1829.

Bonnel, Ulane. "Espoirs de délivrance." In *Sainte-Hélène, terre d'exil*, ed. Marcel Dunan, 229–57. Paris: Hachette, 1971.

———. *La France, les Etats-Unis, et la guerre de course (1797–1815)*. Paris: Nouvelle Editions Latines, 1961.

Bradley, Jared W. "W. C. C. Claiborne and Spain: Foreign Affairs under Jefferson and Madison, 1801–1811." *Louisiana History* 12, no. 4 (fall 1971): 297–314, and 13, no. 1 (winter 1972): 5–26.

Brasseaux, Carl A., and Glenn R. Conrad, eds. *The Road to Louisiana: The Saint-Domingue Refugees, 1792–1809*. Lafayette: Center for Louisiana Studies, University of Southwestern Louisiana, 1992.

Brice, Raoul. *Les espoirs de Napoléon à Saint-Hélène*. Paris: Payot, 1938.

Bruley, Georges. *Les Antilles pendant la Révolution française*. Paris: Editions Caribéennes, 1989.

Calvet, Louis-Jean. *Barataria: L'etrange histoire de Jean Lafitte, pirate*. Paris: Plon, 1998.

Carmer, Carl. *Stars Fell on Alabama*. New York: Farrar and Rinehart, 1934.

Carpenter, Edwin H., ed. "Latour's Report on Spanish-American Relations in the Southwest." *Louisiana Historical Quarterly* 30, no. 3 (July 1947): 715–37.

Carrigan, Jo Ann. *The Saffron Scourge: A History of Yellow Fever in Louisiana, 1796–1905.* Lafayette: Center for Louisiana Studies, University of Southwestern Louisiana, 1994.

Carter, Clarence Edwin, ed. *Territorial Papers of the United States, Territory of Alabama (1817–1819).* Washington, D.C.: Government Printing Office, 1952.

Cash, W. J. *The Mind of the South.* 1941. Reprint. New York: Vintage Books, 1969.

Casse, Albert du. *Le général Vandamme et sa correspondance.* 2 vols. Paris: Didier, 1870.

Castlereagh, Robert Stewart. *Correspondence, Despatches, and Other Papers of Viscount Castlereagh, Second Marquess of Londonderry, Edited by his Brother, Charles William Vane, Marquess of Londonderry.* 4 vols. London: William Shoberl, 1851.

Chalmin, Pierre. *L'officier français de 1815 à 1870.* Paris: Rivière, 1957.

Childs, Frances Sergeant. *French Refugee Life in the United States, 1790–1800.* Baltimore: Johns Hopkins University Press, 1940.

Chuquet, Arthur. *Les Cent Jours: Le départ de l'île d'Elbe.* Paris: E. Leroux, 1920.

Clarke, Thomas Wood. *Emigrés in the Wilderness.* New York: Macmillan, 1941.

Clausel, Bertrand. *Nouvelles observations de M. le maréchal Clauzel sur la colonisation d'Alger: adressées à M. le maréchal, ministre de la guerre, président du conseil.* Paris: Selligue, 1833.

Clay, Henry. *The Papers of Henry Clay.* Ed. James F. Hopkins. Vol.2. Lexington: University of Kentucky Press, 1959.

Cobbs, Hamner. "Geography of the Vine and Olive Colony." *Alabama Review* 14, no. 2 (April 1961): 83–97.

Codinach, Guadalupe Jiménez. "La Confédération Napoléonnie: El Desempeño de los Conspiradores Militares y las Sociedades Secretas en la Independencia de México." *Historia Mexicana* 38, no. 1 (julio–septiembre 1988): 43–68.

Connelly, Owen. *The Gentle Bonaparte: The Story of Napoleon's Elder Brother.* New York: Macmillan, 1968.

Contamine, Henry. *Diplomatie et diplomates sous la Restauration, 1814–1830.* Paris: Hachette, 1970.

Corrêa da Serra, José. *José Corrêa da Serra: Ambassadeur du royaume-uni de Portugal et Brésil à Washington, 1816–1820.* Ed. Léon Bourdon. Paris: Fundaçao Calouste Gulbenkian Centro Cultural Português, 1975.

Costeloe, Michael P. *Response to Revolution: Imperial Spain and the Spanish American revolutions, 1810–1840.* Cambridge: Cambridge University Press, 1986.

———. "Spain and the Latin American Wars of Independence: The Free Trade Controversy, 1810–1820." *Hispanic American Historical Review* 61, no. 2 (1981): 209–34.

Cox, Cynthia. *Talleyrand's Successor: Armand-Emmanuel du Plessis, duc de Richelieu, 1766–1822.* New York: Vanguard Press, 1959.

Cox, Isaac Joslin. "Hispanic-American Phases of the 'Burr Conspiracy'." *Hispanic American Historical Review* 12, no. 2 (May 1932): 145–75.

———. *The West Florida Controversy, 1798–1813: A Study in American Diplomacy.* Baltimore: Johns Hopkins University Press, 1918.

Craft, David. *The French Settlement at Asylum, Bradford County, Pa, 1793.* Wilkes-Barre, Pa.: E. B. Yordy, 1900.

Creagh, Ronald. *Nos cousins d'Amérique: Histoire des français aux Etats-Unis.* Paris: Payot, 1988.

Cusachs, Gaspar. "Lafitte, the Louisiana Pirate and Patriot." *Louisiana Historical Quarterly* 2, no. 4 (October 1919): 418–38.

Dabbs, Jack Autrey. "Additional Notes on the Champ-d'Asile." *Southwestern Historical Quarterly* 54, no. 3 (January 1951): 347–58.

Dabney, Lancaster E. "Louis Aury: The First Governor of Texas under the Mexican Republic." *Southwestern Historical Quarterly* 42, no. 2 (October 1938): 108–16.

Da Costa, J. A. "Napoléon Iᵉʳ au Brésil." *Revue du monde latin* 8 (janvier–avril 1886): 205–16 and 339–49.

Daudet, Ernest. *La police politique: Chronique des temps de la restauration.* Paris: Plon, 1912.

Davis, Charles Shepard *The Cotton Kingdom in Alabama.* Montgomery: Alabama State Department of Archives and History, 1939.

Davis, T. Frederick. "MacGregor's Invasion of Florida, 1817." *Quarterly Periodical of the Florida Historical Society* 7, no. 1 (July 1928): 3–71.

Dawson, John Charles. *Lakanal the Regicide: A Biographical and Historical Study of the Career of Joseph Lakanal.* Tuscaloosa: University of Alabama Press, 1948.

The Debates and Proceedings in the Congress of the United States, 14th Congress, 2nd Session. Washington, D.C.: Gales and Seaton, 1854.

Debidour, Antonin. *Histoire diplomatique de l'Europe depuis l'ouverture du Congrès de Vienne jusqu'à la fermeture du Congrès de Berlin (1814–1878).* Paris: Félix Alcan, 1891.

Debien, Gabriel. "The Saint-Domingue Refugees in Cuba, 1793–1815." Trans. David Cheramie. In *The Road to Louisiana: The Saint-Domingue Refugees, 1792–1809,* ed. Carl A. Brasseaux and Glenn R. Conrad , 31–112. Lafayette: Center for Louisiana Studies, University of Southwestern Louisiana, 1992.

Debien, Gabriel, and René Le Gardeur. "Les colons de Saint-Domingue refugiés à la Louisiane (1792–1804)." *Notes d'histoire coloniale* 10, no. 211.

Delderfield, R. F. *The Golden Millstones: Napoleon's Brothers and Sisters.* London: Weidenfeld and Nicolson, 1964.

Delgado, Jaime. "La 'Pacificació de América' en 1818." *Revista de Indias* 10, núm. 39 (enero–marzo 1950): 7–67, and núm. 40 (abril–junio): 263–310.

Descola, Jean. *Les messagers de l'indépendance: Les français en Amérique latine de Bolivar à Castro.* Paris: R. Laffont, 1973.

Dismukes, Camillus J. "The French Colony in Marengo County, Alabama." *Alabama Historical Quarterly* 32, nos.1 and 2 (spring and summer 1970): 81–113.

Doher, Marcel. *Proscrits et exilés après Waterloo.* Paris: J. Peyronnet, 1965.

Dubois, Laurent. *Les esclaves de la République: L'Histoire oubliée de la première émancipation, 1789–1794.* Paris: Calmann-Lévy, 1998.

———. "The Promise of Revolution: Saint-Domingue and the Struggle for Autonomy in Guadeloupe, 1797–1802." In *The Impact of the Haitian Revolution in the Atlantic World,* ed. David P. Geggus. Columbia: University of South Carolina Press, 2001.

Duhamel, Jean. *The Fifty Days: Napoleon in England.* Trans. R. A. Hall. London: Hunt-Davis, 1969.

Dupre, Daniel S. *Transforming the Cotton Frontier: Madison County, Alabama, 1800–1840.* Baton Rouge and London: Louisiana State University Press, 1997.

Dyer, John Percy. *Tulane: The Biography of a University, 1834–1965.* New York: Harper & Row, 1966.

Ebeyer, Paul Pierre. *Revelations Concerning Napoleon's Escape from St. Helena.* New Orleans: Windmill Publishing, 1947.

Echeverria, Durand. *Mirage in the West: A History of the French Image of American Society to 1815.* Princeton: Princeton University Press, 1957.

Ellingson, Ter. *The Myth of the Noble Savage.* Berkeley: University of California Press, 2001.

Emerson, O. B. "The Bonapartist Exiles in Alabama." *Alabama Review* 11, no. 2 (April 1958): 135–43.

Espitalier, Albert. *Deux artisans du retour de l'île d'Elbe: Le chirugien Emery et le gantier Dumoulin.* Grenoble: B. Arthaud, 1934.

Fairchild, Hoxie Neale. *The Noble Savage: A Study in Romantic Naturalism.* New York: Columbia University Press, 1928.

Faure, Victor. *De la Corrèze à la Floride: Jean-Augustin Pénières: Conventionnel et député d'Ussel.* Ussel: Musée du pays d'Ussel, 1989.

Faye, Stanley. "Consuls of Spain in New Orleans, 1804–1821." *Louisiana Historical Quarterly* 21, no. 3 (July 1938): 677–84.

———. "The Great Stroke of Pierre Lafitte" *Louisiana Historical Quarterly* 23, no. 3 (July 1940): 733–826.

———. "Privateersmen of the Gulf and Their Prizes." *Louisiana Historical Quarterly* 22, no. 4 (October 1939): 1012–94.

———. "Privateers of Guadeloupe and Their Establishment in Barataria." *Louisiana Historical Quarterly* 23, no. 2 (April 1940): 428–44.

———. "Types of Privateer Vessels, Their Armament and Flags, in the Gulf of Mexico." *Louisiana Historical Quarterly* 23, no. 1 (January 1940): 118–30.

Feller, Daniel. *The Public Lands in Jacksonian Politics.* Madison: University of Wisconsin Press, 1984.

Ferenczi, Imre. *International Migrations.* Vol. 1, *Statistics.* New York: National Bureau of Economic Research, 1929.

Fick, Carolyn E. *The Making of Haiti: The Saint Domingue Revolution from Below.* Knoxville: University of Tennessee Press, 1990.

Fiehrer, Thomas. "Saint-Domingue/Haiti: Louisiana's Caribbean Connection." *Louisiana History* 30, no. 4 (fall 1986): 419–37.

Fisher, Lillian Estelle. *The Background of the Revolution for Mexican Independence.* Boston: Christopher, 1934.

Flores Caballero, Romeo. *Counterrevolution: The Role of the Spaniards in the Independence of Mexico, 1804–38.* Trans. Jaime E. Rodriguez O. Lincoln: University of Nebraska Press, 1969.

Ford, Worthington Chauncey. "John Quincy Adams and the Monroe Doctrine." *American Historical Review* 7, no. 4 (July 1902): 676–96.

Fossier, A. E. "The Funeral Ceremony of Napoleon in New Orleans, December 19, 1821." *Louisiana Historical Quarterly* 13, no. 2 (April 1930): 246–52.

Fouché, Nicole. *Emigration alsacienne aux Etats-Unis, 1815–1870.* Paris: Publications de la Sorbonne, 1992.

Foure-Selter, Hélène. *Gallipolis, Ohio: Histoire de l'établissement de cinq cents français dans la vallée de l'Ohio à la fin du XVIIIè siècle.* Paris: Jouve, 1939.

Franco, Jose L., ed. *Documentos para la Historia de Mexico Existentes en el Archivo Nacional de Cuba.* La Habana: Publicaciones del Archivo Nacional de Cuba, 1961.

Fuller, Hubert Bruce. *The Purchase of Florida: Its History and Diplomacy.* Cleveland: Burrows Brothers, 1906.

Gaines, George Strother. *The Reminiscences of George Strother Gaines, Pioneer and Statesman of Early Alabama and Mississippi, 1805–1843.* Ed. James P. Pate. Tuscaloosa and London: University of Alabama Press, 1998.

Garcia de Leon y Pizarro, Jose. *Memorias.* Ed. Alvaro Alonso-Castrillo. 2 vols. Madrid: Revista de Occidente, 1964.

Gardien, Kent. *The Chatelaine of George Villa.* Demopolis, Ala.: Marengo County Historical Society, 1979.

———. "The Domingan Kettle: Philadelphian-Émigré Planters in Alabama." *National Genealogical Society Quarterly* 76, no. 3 (September 1988): 173–87.

———. "The Splendid Fools: Philadelphia Origins of Alabama's Vine and Olive Colony." *Pennsylvania Magazine of History and Biography* 104, no. 4 (October 1980): 491–507.

———. "Take Pity on Our Glory: Men of Champ d'Asile." *Southwestern Historical Quarterly* 87, no. 3 (January 1984): 241–68.

Gaspar, David Barry, and David Patrick Geggus, eds. *A Turbulent Time: The French Revolution and the Greater Caribbean.* Bloomington and Indianapolis: Indiana University Press, 1997.

Geggus, David Patrick. *Haitian Revolutionary Studies.* Bloomington and Indianapolis: Indiana University Press, 2002.

———. *Slavery, War, and Revolution: The British Occupation of Saint Domingue, 1793–1798.* Oxford: Clarendon Press, 1982.

———, ed. *The Impact of the Haitian Revolution in the Atlantic World.* Columbia: University of South Carolina Press, 2001.

Girard, Just [Just-Jean-Etienne Roy]. *The Adventures of a French Captain, at Present a Planter in Texas, Formerly a Refugee of Camp Asylum.* Trans. Lady Blanche Murphy. New York, Cincinnati [etc.]: Benziger Brothers, 1878.

Girardet, Raoul. *La société militaire et la France contemporaine.* Paris: Plon, 1953.

Goebel, Dorothy Burne. "British Trade to the Spanish Colonies, 1796–1823." *American Historical Review* 43, no. 2 (January 1938): 288–320.

Goldstein, Jonathan. *Philadelphia and the China trade, 1682–1846: Commercial, Cultural, and Attitudinal Effects.* University Park: Pennsylvania State University Press, 1978.

Greer, Donald. *The Incidence of the Emigration During the French Revolution.* Cambridge: Harvard University Press, 1951.

Griffin, Charles Carroll. "Economic and Social Aspects of the Era of Spanish-American Independence." *Hispanic American Historical Review* 29, no. 2 (May 1949): 170–87.

———. *The United States and the Disruption of the Spanish Empire, 1810–1822: A Study of the*

Relations of the United States with Spain and with the Rebel Spanish Colonies. New York: Columbia University Press, 1937.

Grouchy, Emmanuel, comte de. *Mémoires du maréchal de Grouchy.* 5 vols. Paris: E. Dentu, 1873–74.

Guillon, Edouard. *Les complots militaires sous la restauration, d'après les documents d'Archives.* Paris: Plon, 1895.

———. *La France et l'Irlande pendant la Révolution: Hoche et Humbert.* Paris: Armand Colin, 1888.

Hamilton, Virginia Van der Verr. *Alabama: A History.* New York and London: W. W. Norton, 1984.

Hamnett, Brian R. "Mexico's Royalist Coalition: The Response to Revolution, 1808–1821." *Journal of Latin American Studies* 12, no. 1 (May 1980): 55–86.

———. "Process and Pattern: A Re-examination of the Ibero-American Independence Movements, 1808–1826." *Journal of Latin American Studies* 29 (1997): 279–328.

Hampson, Norman. *The Perfidy of Albion: French Perceptions of England during the French Revolution.* London: Macmillan, 1998.

Hartmann, L., and Millard. *Le Texas, ou notice historique sur le Champ d'Asile, comprenant tout ce qui s'est passé depuis la formation jusqu'à la dissolution de cette colonie.* Paris: Béguin, 1819.

Hasbrouck, Alfred. *Foreign Legionaries in the Liberation of Spanish South America.* New York: [n.p.], 1928.

Henry, Arthur. *La Guyane française: Son histoire, 1604–1946.* 1950. Reprint. Cayenne, Guyana: Mayouri, 1981.

Heredia, Edumndo A. *Planes Españoles para Reonquistar Hispanoamérica (1810–1818).* Buenos Aires: Editorial Universitaria de Buenos Aires, 1974.

Herrera, Luis Alberto de. *La Revolución Francesa y Sud América.* Paris: Dupont, 1910.

Hoefer, Ferd. *Nouvelle biographie générale depuis les temps les plus reculés jusqu'à nos jours.* 46 vols. Paris: Firmin Didot frères, 1863.

Hoffman, Paul E. *Florida's Frontiers.* Bloomington: Indiana University Press, 2002.

Houpert, Jean. *Les lorrains en Amérique du Nord.* Sherbrooke, Quebec: Namaan, 1985.

Houssaye, Henry. *1815: La première Restauration, le retour de l'île d'Elbe, les Cent Jours.* Paris: Perrin, 1894.

———. *1815: La seconde abdication—La Terreur blanche.* Paris: Perrin, 1918.

Humphreys, R. A. *Tradition and Revolt in Latin America and Other Essays.* London: Weidenfeld and Nicolson, 1969.

Humphreys, R. A., and John Lynch, eds. *The Origins of the Latin American Revolutions, 1808–1826.* New York: Knopf, 1966.

Hutchinson, C. A. "Mexican Federalists in New Orleans and the Texas Revolution." *Louisiana Historical Quarterly* 39, no. 1 (January 1956): 1–47.

Hyde de Neuville, Jean-Guillaume, baron. *Mémoires et souvenirs du baron Hyde de Neuville.* 3 vols. Paris: Plon, 1888–92.

Jackson, Andrew. *Correspondence of Andrew Jackson.* Ed. John Spencer Bassett. Vol. 2. 1927. Reprint. New York: Kraus, 1969.

Jackson, Harvey H. "Time, Frontier, and the Alabama Black Belt: Searching for J. W. Cash's Planter." *Alabama Review* 44, no. 4 (October 1991): 243–68.

Jefferson, Thomas. *The Writings of Thomas Jefferson.* Ed. Paul Leicester Ford. Vol.10. New York and London: G. P. Putnam's Sons, 1899.

Jefferson, Thomas, and Pierre-Samuel Dupont de Nemours. *The Correspondence of Jefferson and Du Pont de Nemours, with an Introduction on Jefferson and the Physiocrats.* Ed. Gilbert Chinard. New York: Arno Press, 1979.

Jordan, Weymouth T. *Ante-Bellum Alabama: Town and Country.* 1957. Reprint. Tuscaloosa and London: University of Alabama Press, 1987.

Kaufman, William W. *British Policy and the Independence of Latin America.* New Haven: Yale University Press, 1951.

Keen, Benjamin. *David Curtis DeForrest and the Revolution of Buenos Aires.* New Haven: Yale University Press, 1947.

Kendall, John S. "Paul Tulane." *Louisiana Historical Quarterly* 20, no. 4 (October 1937).

———. "Piracy in the Gulf of Mexico, 1816–1823." *Louisiana Historical Quarterly* 8, no. 3 (July 1925): 341–68.

———. "The Successors of Lafitte." *Louisiana Historical Quarterly* 24, no. 2 (April 1941): 360–77.

King, Florence. *Southern Ladies and Gentlemen.* New York: Stein and Day, 1975.

King, Grace. *Creole Families of New Orleans.* New York: Macmillan, 1921.

King, Rufus. *The Life and Correspondence of Rufus King, Comprising His Letters, Private and Official, His Public Documents, and His Speeches.* Ed. Charles R. King. Vol.6. New York: Da Capo Press, 1971.

Kinsbruner, Jay. *Independence in Spanish America: Civil Wars, Revolutions, and Underdevelopment.* Albuquerque: University of New Mexico Press, 2000.

Klier, Betje Black. "Champ D'Asile, Texas." In *The French in Texas: History, Migration, Culture,* ed. François Lagarde. Austin: University of Texas Press, 2003.

Koebel, W. H. *British Exploits in South America: A History of British Activities in Exploration, Military Adventure, Diplomacy, Science, and Trade, in Latin America.* New York: The Century Co., 1917.

Kroen, Sheryl. *Politics and Theater: The Crisis of Legitimacy in Restoration France, 1815–1830.* Berkeley: University of California Press, 2000.

Lachance, Paul F. "The 1809 Immigration of Saint-Domingue Refugees to New Orleans: Reception, Integration, and Impact." *Louisiana History* 29, no. 2 (spring 1988): 109–41.

———. "Intermarriage and French Cultural Persistence in Late Spanish and Early American New Orleans." *Histoire sociale/Social History* 15, no. 29 (mai/May 1982), 47–81.

Lacour, Auguste. *Histoire de la Guadeloupe.* 1857. Vols.2 and 3. Reprint. Paris: Maisonneuve, 1960.

Lagarde, François, ed. *The French in Texas: History, Migration, Culture.* Austin: University of Texas Press, 2003.

Lallemand, Charles-Frédéric-Antoine. "Napoléon refuse de passer en Amérique: Extrait du journal du général Charles-Frédéric-Antoine Lallemand, juillet-août 1816." *French American Review* 2, no. 2 (April–June 1949): 63–80.

Landers, Jane. *Black Society in Spanish Florida.* Urbana: University of Illinois Press, 1999.

Langley, Lester D. *The Americas in the Age of Revolution, 1750–1850.* New Haven: Yale University Press, 1996.

———. *Struggle for the American Mediterranean: United States-European Rivalry in the Gulf-Caribbean, 1776–1904.* Athens, GA: University of Georgia Press, 1976.

La Souchère Délery, Simone de. *Napoleon's Soldiers in America.* Gretna, La.: Pelican, 1972.

———. "Some French Soldiers Who Became Louisiana Educators." *Louisiana Historical Quarterly* 31, no. 4 (October 1948): 849–55.

Lee, William. *Les Etats-Unis et l'Angleterre, ou souvenirs et reflexions d'un citoyen american.* Bordeaux: P. Coudert, 1814.

———. *A Yankee Jeffersonian: Selections from the Diary and Letters of William Lee of Massachusetts, Written from 1796 to 1840.* Ed. Mary Lee Mann. Cambridge: Belknap Press of Harvard University Press, 1958.

"Letters Relating to MacGregor's Attempted Conquest of East Florida, 1817." *Quarterly Periodical of the Florida Historical Society* 5, no. 1 (July 1926): 54–7.

Lewis, Gwynne. *The Second Vendée: The Continuity of Counterrevolution in the Department of the Gard, 1789–1815.* Oxford: Clarendon Press, 1978.

Lewis, James E., Jr. *The American Union and the Problem of Neighborhood: The United States and the Collapse of the Spanish Empire, 1783–1829.* Chapel Hill, NC: University of North Carolina Press, 1998.

Lima-Barbosa, Mario de. *Les français dans l'histoire du Brésil.* Rio de Janeiro: F. Briguiet, 1923.

Liss, Peggy K. *Atlantic Empires: The Network of Trade and Revolution, 1713–1826.* Baltimore: Johns Hopkins University Press, 1983.

Lowrie, Walter, et al., eds. *Documents Legislative and Executive of the Congress of the United States.* Vols.3–6. Washington, D.C.: Gales and Seaton, 1834–60.

Lucas-Dubreton, J. *Le culte de Napoléon, 1815–1848.* Paris: Albin Michel, 1960.

Lyon, Anne Bozeman. "The Bonapartists in Alabama." *Alabama Historical Quarterly* 25, nos.3 and 4 (fall and winter, 1963): 227–41.

Macartney, Clarence Edward, and Gordon Dorrance. *The Bonapartes in America.* Philadelphia: Dorrance, 1939.

Mackenzie, Norman. *The Escape from Elba: The Fall and Flight of Napoleon, 1814–1815.* New York: Oxford University Press, 1982.

Madison, James. *The Writings of James Madison, Comprising His Public Papers and His Private Correspondence, Including Numerous Letters and Documents Now for the First Time Printed.* Ed. Gaillard Hunt. Vol.8. New York and London: G. P. Putnam's Sons, 1908.

Madival, J., and E. Laurent, eds. *Archives parlementaires de 1787 à 1860.* Ser. 2, 127 vols. Paris: Librairie Administrative de Paul Dupont, 1867–1913, 1985.

Maire, Camille. *En route pour l'Amérique: L'odyssée des émigrants en France au XIXe siècle.* Nancy: Presses Universitaires de Nancy, 1993.

———. *L'émigration des Lorrains en Amérique, 1815–1870.* Metz: Centre de Recherches Relations Internationales de l'Université de Metz, 1980.

Manning, William R., ed. *Diplomatic Correspondence of the United States Concerning the Independence of the Latin-American Nations.* 3 vols. New York: Oxford University Press, 1925.

Marino, Samuel J. "Early French-Language Newspapers in New Orleans." *Louisiana History* 7, no. 4 (fall 1966): 309–21.

Martin, Michel L., and Alain Yacou, eds. *De la Révolution française aux révolutions créoles et negres.* Paris: Editions Caribéennes, 1989.

Martin, Thomas W. *French Military Adventurers in Alabama, 1818–1828.* Birmingham, Ala.: Birmingham Publishing, 1937.

Martineau, Gilbert. *Lucien Bonaparte: Prince de Canino.* Paris: Editions France-Empire, 1989.

——. *Napoleon Surrenders.* Trans. Frances Partridge. London: John Murray, 1971.

Martinez, Antonio. *Letters from Gov. Antonio Martinez to the Viceroy Juan Ruiz de Apodaca.* Trans. Virginia H. Taylor. San Antonio, Tex.: Research Center for the Arts and Humanities, 1983.

——. *The Letters of Antonio Martinez, Last Spanish Governor of Texas, 1817–1822.* Trans. Virginia H. Taylor. Austin: Texas State Library, 1957.

Masson, Frédéric. *Revue d'ombres.* Paris: Ollendorff, n.d.

May, Robert E. *The Southern Dream of a Caribbean Empire, 1854–1861.* Baton Rouge: Louisiana State University Press, 1973.

McConnell, Roland C. *Negro Troops of Antebellum Louisiana: A History of the Battalion of Free Men of Color.* Baton Rouge: Louisiana State University Press, 1968.

McFarlane, Anthony, and Eduardo Posada-Carbó, eds. *Independence and Revolution in Spanish America: Perspectives and Problems.* London: Institute of Latin American Studies, 1999.

McMaster, John Bach. *The Life and Times of Stephen Girard: Mariner and Merchant.* 2 vols. Philadelphia and London: J. B. Lippincott, 1918.

Melchior-Bonnet, Bernardine. *Jerome Bonaparte ou l'envers de l'epopée.* Paris: Librairie Académique Perrin, 1979.

Miller, Joseph C. *Way of Death: Merchant Capitalism and the Angolan Slave Trade, 1730–1830.* Madison: University of Wisconsin Press, 1988.

Mintz, Sidney W. *Sweetness and Power: The Place of Sugar in Modern History.* New York: Elisabeth Sifton Books, 1985.

Miquel I Vergès, J. M. *Diccionario de Insurgentes.* Mexico: Porrúa, 1969.

——. *Mina: El Español Frente a España.* Mexico: Xochitl, 1945.

Monroe, James. *The Writings of James Monroe, Including a Collection of His Public and Private Papers and Correspondence Now for the First Time Printed.* Ed. Stanislaus Murray Hamilton. Vol.6. New York and London: G. P. Putnam's Sons, 1898–1903.

Montulé, Edouard de. *Travels in America, 1816–1817.* Trans. Edward D. Seeber. Bloomington: Indiana University Press, 1950.

Mora, Isidro A. Beluche. "Privateers of Cartagena." *Louisiana Historical Quarterly* 39, no. 1 (January 1956): 74–91.

Moreau-Zanelli, Jocelyne. *Gallipolis: Histoire d'un mirage américain au XVIIIè siècle.* Paris: L'Harmattan, 2000.

Moses, Bernard. *The Intellectual Background of the Revolution in South America, 1810–1824.* New York: Columbia University Press, 1926.

Murat, Inès. *Napoleon and the American Dream.* Trans. Frances Frenaye. Baton Rouge: Louisiana State University Press, 1981.

Murray, Elsie. *Azilum: French Refugee Colony of 1793.* Athens, Pa.: Tioga Point Museum, 1940.

Murray, Louise Welles. *The Story of Some French Refugees and Their 'Azilum', 1793–1800.* Athens, Pa.: N.p., 1903.

Narrative of a Voyage to the Spanish Main in the Ship Two Friends, *the Occupation of Amelia by McGregor, etc.* London: J. Miller, 1819.

Nicholls, David, and Peter Marsh, eds. *A Biographical Dictionary of Modern European Radicals and Socialists, 1780–1815.* Sussex, UK: Harvester Press, 1988.

Nigoul, Toussaint. *Lakanal.* Paris: C. Marpon and E. Flammarion, 1879.

Oakes, James. *The Ruling Race: A History of American Slaveholders.* New York: Knopf, 1982.

Onís, Luis de. *Memoir upon the Negotiations between Spain and the United States of America Which Led to the Treaty of 1819.* Trans. Tobias Watkins. Philadelphia: E. de Krafft, 1821.

———. *Observations on the Existing Differences between the Government of Spain and the United States.* Philadelphia: [n.p.], 1817.

Owen, Thomas McAdory. *History of Alabama and Dictionary of Alabama Biography.* Chicago: S. J. Clarke, 1921.

Owsley, Frank Lawrence, Jr. *Struggle for the Gulf Borderlands: The Creek War and the Battle of New Orleans, 1812–1815.* Gainesville: University Presses of Florida, 1981.

Owsley, Frank Lawrence, Jr. and Gene A. Smith. *Filibusters and Expansionists: Jeffersonian Manifest Destiny, 1800–1821.* Tuscaloosa and London: University of Alabama Press, 1997.

Perkins, Bradford. *The Cambridge History of American Foreign Relations, volume I: The Creation of a Republican Empire, 1776–1865.* Cambridge: Cambridge University Press, 1993.

———. *Castlereagh and Adams: England and the United States, 1812–1823.* Berkeley: University of California Press, 1964.

Perkins, Dexter. "Europe, Spanish America, and the Monroe Doctrine." *American Historical Review* 27, no. 2 (January 1922): 207–18.

———. "John Quincy Adams." In *The American Secretaries of State and Their Diplomacy,* ed. Samuel Flagg Bemis, 4:3–11. New York: Knopf, 1928.

———. *The Monroe Doctrine, 1823–1826.* Cambridge: Harvard University Press, 1927.

———. "Russia and the Spanish Colonies, 1817–1818." *American Historical Review* 28, no. 4 (July 1923): 656–72.

———. *The United States and Latin America.* Baton Rouge: Louisiana State University Press, 1961.

Peters, Richard, ed. *Public Statutes of the United States of America.* Vols.3 and 4. Boston: Charles C. Little and James Brown, 1850–55.

Philips, Edith. "Les refugiés Bonapartistes en Amérique (1815–1830)." Ph.D. diss, Université de Paris, 1923.

Philips, W. Alison. "Great Britain and the Continental Alliance, 1816–1822." In *The Cambridge History of British Foreign Policy, 1783–1919,* ed. A. W. Ward and G. P. Gooch, 2:3–50. New York: Cambridge University Press, 1923.

Pickett, Albert James. *History of Alabama and Incidentally of Georgia and Mississippi from the Earliest Period.* 1851. Reprint. Birmingham, Ala.: Birmingham Book and Magazine, 1962.

Poulet, Henry. *Un soldat lorrain méconnu: Le général Humbert (1767–1823).* Nancy: Ancienne Imprimerie Vagner, 1928.

Pozzo di Borgo, Carlo Andrea. *Correspondance diplomatique du comte Pozzo di Borgo, ambassadeur de Russie en France, et du comte de Nesselrode, depuis la Restauration des Bourbons jusqu'au Congrès d'Aix-la-Chapelle.* 2 vols. Paris: Calmann-Lévy, 1890–97.

Pratt, Julius W. *Expansionists of 1812.* New York: Macmillan, 1925.

Prichard, Walter, ed. "George Graham's Mission to Galveston in 1818: Two Important Documents Bearing upon Louisiana History." *Louisiana Historical Quarterly* 20, no. 3 (July 1937): 619–50.

Quintin, Bernard and Danielle. *Dictionnaire des colonels de Napoléon.* Paris: SPM, 1996.

Ramsdell, Charles, Jr. "Why Jean Lafitte Became a Pirate." *Southwestern Historical Quarterly* 43, no. 4 (April 1940): 465–71.

Reeves, Jesse S. *The Napoleonic Exiles in America: A Study in American Diplomatic History, 1815–1819.* Baltimore: Johns Hopkins University Press, 1905.

Rémond, Réné. *Les Etats-Unis devant l'opinion française, 1815–1852.* 2 vols. Paris: Armand Colin, 1962.

Resnick, Daniel. *The White Terror and the Political Reaction after Waterloo.* Cambridge: Harvard University Press, 1966.

Richelieu, Armand-Emmanuel du Plessis, duc de. *Lettres du duc de Richelieu au marquis d'Osmond, 1816–1818.* Ed. Sébastien Charlety. Paris: Gallimard, 1939.

Rippy, J. Fred. *Latin America in World Politics: An Outline Survey.* New York: Knopf, 1928.

———. *Rivalry of the United States and Great Britain over Latin America (1808–1830).* Baltimore: Johns Hopkins University Press, 1929.

Robertson, William Spence. *France and Latin-American Independence.* Baltimore: Johns Hopkins University Press, 1939.

———. *Hispanic-American Relations with the United States.* Ed. David Kinley. New York: Oxford University Press, 1923.

———. "Metternich's Attitude toward Revolutions in Latin America." *Hispanic American Historical Review* 21, no. 4 (November 1941): 538–58.

———. *Rise of the Spanish-American Republics as Told in the Lives of Their Liberators.* New York and London: D. Appleton, 1918.

———. "Russia and the Emancipation of Spanish America, 1816–1826." *Hispanic American Historical Review* 21, no. 2 (May 1941): 196–221.

Robinson, William Davis. *Memoirs of the Mexican Revolution Including a Narrative of the Expedition of General Xavier Mina.* Philadelphia: Lydia R. Bailley, Printer, 1820.

Rosengarten, Joseph George. *French Colonists and Exiles in the United States.* Philadelphia: J. B. Lippincott, 1907.

Rouen, Bussiere, "L'Abeille de la Nouvelle-Orleans." *Louisiana Historical Quarterly* 8, no. 4 (October 1925): 585–88.

Saunt, Claudio. *A New Order of Things: Property, Power, and the Transformation of the Creek Indians, 1733–1816.* Cambridge: Cambridge University Press, 1999.

Savary, Anne-Jean-Marie-René, duc de Rovigo. *Memoirs of the Duke of Rovigo.* 4 vols. London: H. Colburn, 1828.

Scott, Julius. "The Common Wind: Currents of Afro-American Communication in the Era of the Haitian Revolution." Ph.D. diss., Duke University, 1986.

Seward, Desmond. *Napoleon's Family*. London: Weidenfeld and Nicolson, 1986.

Sibley, William G. *The French Five Hundred*. Gallipolis, Ind.: Gallia County Historical Society, 1933.

Silvestre, Jules. *De Waterloo à Sainte-Hélène (20 juin-16 octobre 1816)*. Paris: Félix Alcan, 1904.

Six, Georges. *Dictionnaire biographique des généraux et amiraux français de la Révolution et de l'Empire (1792–1814)*. 2 vols. Paris: G. Saffroy, 1934.

Socard, Emile. *Biographie des personnages de Troyes et du département de l'Aube*. Troyes: L. Lacroix, 1882.

Smith, Winston. *Days of Exile: The Story of the Vine and Olive Colony in Alabama*. Tuscaloosa: University of Alabama Press, 1967.

Soublin, Jean. *Le champ d'asile*. Paris: Seuil, 1985.

Spitzer, Alan B. *Old Hatreds and Young Hopes: The French Carbonari against the Bourbon Restoration*. Cambridge: Harvard University Press, 1971.

Stacton, David. *The Bonapartes*. New York: Simon and Schuster, 1966.

Stein, Robert Louis. *The French Slave Trade in the Eighteenth Century: An Old Regime Business*. Madison: University of Wisconsin Press, 1979.

Sterne, Emma Gelders. *Some Plant Olive Trees*. New York: Dodd Mead, 1937.

Stewart, William H., Jr. *The Tennessee-Tombigbee Waterway: A Case Study in the Politics of Water Transportation*. Tuscaloosa, Ala.: Bureau of Public Administration, University of Alabama, 1971.

Stinchcombe, Arthur L. *Sugar Island Slavery in the Age of Enlightenment: The Political Economy of the Caribbean World*. Princeton, NJ: Princeton University Press, 1995.

Stollenwerck, Frank, and Dixie Orum Stollenwerck. *The Stollenwerck, Chaudron, and Billon Families in America*. Baltimore: [n.p.], 1948.

Strong, Russell W. "General Count Bertrand Clauzel and the Vine and Olive Colony." In *The Consortium on Revolutionary Europe, 1750–1850: Proceedings, 1992*, ed. Gordon C. Bond and John W. Rooney Jr., 395–402. Tallahassee: Institute on Napoleon and the French Revolution, Florida State University, 1993.

Tatum, Edward Howland, Jr. *The United States and Europe, 1815–1823: A Study in the Background of the Monroe Doctrine*. Berkeley: University of California Press, 1936.

Temperley, Harold. "French Designs on Spanish America in 1820-5." *English Historical Review* 40 (1925): 34–53.

Thornton, J. Mills, III. *Politics and Power in a Slave Society: Alabama, 1800–1860*. Baton Rouge: Louisiana State University Press, 1978.

Thoumas, Ch. *Les grands cavaliers du premier empire: Notices biographiques*. 3 vols. Paris and Nancy: Berger-Levrault, 1909.

Tomich, Dale W. *Slavery in the Circuit of Sugar: Martinique and the World Economy, 1830–1848*. Baltimore and London: Johns Hopkins University Press, 1990.

Tournier, Albert. *Les conventionnels en exil*. Paris: Flammarion, 1910.

Trouillot, Michel-Rolph. "Coffee, Color, and Slavery in Eighteenth-Century Saint-Domingue." *Review* 5 (1980): 331–88.

Tulard, Jean. *Joseph Fouché*. Paris: Fayard, 1998.

Vaulabelle, Achille de. *Histoire des deux Restaurations.* Vol.5. Paris; Garnier frères, 1874

Vidalenc, Jean. *Les demi-solde: Étude d'une catégorie sociale.* Paris: Rivière, 1955.

Vigny, Afred de. *Servitude and Grandeur of Arms.* Trans. Roger Gard. London: Penguin, 1996.

Warren, Harris Gaylord. "Documents Relating to the Establishment of Privateers at Galveston, 1816–1817." *Louisiana Historical Quarterly* 21, no. 4 (October 1938): 1086–1109.

———. "The Firebrand Affair: A Forgotten Incident of the Mexican Revolution." *Louisiana Historical Quarterly* 21, no. 1 (January 1938): 203–12.

———. "José Alvarez de Toledo's Reconciliation with Spain and Projects for Suppressing Rebellion in the Spanish Colonies." *Louisiana Historical Quarterly* 23, no. 3 (July 1940): 827–63.

———. "The Origin of General Mina's Invasion of Mexico." *Southwestern Historical Quarterly* 42, no. 1 (July 1938): 1–20.

———. "Pensacola and the Filibusters, 1816–1817." *Louisiana Historical Quarterly* 21, no. 3 (July 1938): 806–22.

———. *The Sword Was Their Passport: A History of American Filibustering in the Mexican Revolution.* Baton Rouge: Louisiana State University Press, 1943.

———, ed. "Documents Relating to Pierre Lafitte's Entrance into the Service of Spain." *Southwestern Historical Quarterly* 44, no. 1 (July 1940): 76–87.

Watel, Françoise. *Jean-Guillaume Hyde de Neuville (1776–1857): Conspirateur et diplomate.* Paris: Direction des Archives et de la Documentation, Ministère des Affaires Etrangères, 1987.

Weber, David J. *The Spanish Frontier in North America.* New Haven: Yale University Press, 1992.

Webster, Charles Kingsley, "Castlereagh and the Spanish Colonies, 1815–1818." *English Historical Review* 27 (January 1912): 78–95.

———. "Castlereagh and the Spanish Colonies, 1818–1822." *English Historical Review* 30 (1915), 631–45.

———. *The Foreign Policy of Castlereagh, 1812–1815: Britain and the Reconstruction of Europe.* London: G. Bell and Sons, 1931.

———. *The Foreign Policy of Castlereagh, 1815–1822: Britain and the European Alliance.* London: G. Bell and Sons, 1925.

———, ed. *Britain and the Independence of Latin America, 1812–1830: Select Documents from the Foreign Office Archives.* New York: Octagon, 1970.

Weeks, William Earl. *John Quincy Adams and the American Global Empire.* Lexington: University Press of Kentucky, 1992.

Wellborn, Alfred Toledano. "The Relations between New Orleans and Latin America, 1810–1824." *Louisiana Historical Quarterly* 22, no. 3 (July 1939): 710–94.

Welvert, Eugène. "Lakanal en Amérique." *Feuilles d'histoire du XVIIe au XXe siècle* 4, no. 9 (1 septembre 1910): 252–371.

———. *Lendemains révolutionaires: Les régicides.* Paris: Calmann-Lévy, 1907.

Whitaker, Arthur Preston. *The United States and the Independence of Latin America, 1800–1830.* Baltimore: Johns Hopkins University Press, 1941.

White, Patrick C. T., ed. *The Critical Years: American Foreign Policy, 1793–1823.* New York: John Wiley and Sons, 1970.

Whitfield, Gaius, Jr. "The French Grant in Alabama: A History of the Founding of Demopolis." *Transactions of the Alabama Historical Society* 4, 321–55.

Wilgus, A. Curtis. "Some Activities of United States Citizens in the South American Wars of Independence, 1808–1824." *Louisiana Historical Quarterly* 14, no. 2 (April 1931): 182–203.

———. "Spanish American Patriot Activity along the Gulf Coast of the United States, 1811–1822." *Louisiana Historical Quarterly* 8, no. 2 (April 1925): 193–215.

Winston, James E. "A Faithful Picture of the Political Situation in New Orleans at the Close of the Last and the Beginning of the Present Year, 1807." *Louisiana Historical Quarterly* 11, no. 3 (July 1928): 359–433.

———. "New Orleans and the Texas Revolution." *Louisiana Historical Quarterly* 10, no. 3 (July 1927): 317–54.

Woodward, Margaret L. "The Spanish Army and the Loss of America, 1810–1824." *Hispanic American Historical Review* 48, no. 4 (November 1968): 586–607.

Wyatt-Brown, Bertram. *Yankee Saints and Southern Sinners.* Baton Rouge: Louisiana State University Press, 1985.

Zimmerman, A. F. "Spain and Its Colonies, 1808–1820." *Hispanic American Historical Review* 11, no. 4 (November 1931): 439–63.

Index